yright First Edition 1987
ond Edition Part 1 1997
seo de Historia del Mormonismo en Mexico A. C.
vo, Utah, 84604
rights reserved

rary of Congress Cataloging-in-Publication Data

, F. LaMond, 1935-
ons in Mexico

iography: p.
des index.
ch of Jesus Christ of Latter-Day Saints -
- Mexico - History. 2. Mormon Church -
-Mexico - History. 3. Sociology Christian
. 4. Mormons - Mexico. 5. Mexico - church
Title.
T85   1987   289.3'72   87-14782
21-130-1

ven in 1996 to El Museo de Historia del Mormonismo en
. to translate the first part of the book into Spanish.

B. Kelley Nielsen;
R. P. Bissland

Richard Firmage

courtesy of *The Church of Jesus Christ of Latter-*
, Historical Division.

of Mormon church members, Cholula,

tion of LDS chapel at San Gabriel,
1930.

MORMONS
IN
MEXICO

The Dynamics of Faith and

F. LaMond Tu

LOS
MORM
MÉ

La Dinámic

TRADUCI

El Museo de

Tulli
Morm

Bib
Inclu
1. Chur
Missions
Missions
(Mormon)
history. I
BV2835.2.
ISBN 0-874

Permission gi
Mexico, A. C

Cartography by
map design by

Cover design by

Cover photograph
day Saints Archive

Front cover: Group
Puebla, 1923.

Back cover: Inaugura
Ometoxtla, Puebla, ca

For Jason and Lesley

Table of Contents

COMENTARIO

"...Adán y Eva, nuestros primeros padres,..." (1 Nefi 5:11) "... tuvieron hijos, sí la familia de toda la tierra." (2 Nefi 2:20). La escritura nos indica que había una sola familia, la familia de Dios, la raza de Dios, y por lo tanto una nación. Poco después, y por desobediencia, se inició una segunda raza que fue desterrada del lugar donde vivía el resto de la familia de Adán y "habitó en tierra de Nod, al oriente del Eden" (Génesis 4:16). Tal vez las naciones se han formado a razón de la desobediencia, como en el caso de Caín, y/o por necesidades y diferencias que resultan por el uso del libre albedrío al ejercer sus necesidades, circunstancias, y/o talentos. "...y fue Abel pastor de ovejas, y Caín fue labrador de la tierra". (Génesis 4:2) "....Jabal, el cual fue padre de los que habitan en tiendas, y crían ganados"; "....el nombre de su hermano Jubal, el cual fue padre de todos los que manejan arpa y órgano", "...Tubal-Caín, acicalador de toda obra de metal y hierro" (Génesis 4:20-22). Cual sea el caso, sabemos que se han formado.

"La raza y nación en la cual el hombre nace en este mundo es un resultado de su vida en la preexistencia. Todos los espíritus del cielo que se encontraron dignos de recibir un cuerpo mortal fueron preordenados para pasar su probación terrenal dentro de una raza y nación de acuerdo a sus necesidades, circunstancias y talentos. (Doctrina Mormona p. 616 Tema: Raza del Hombre versión en ingles).

Que teníamos nuestro libre albedrío en la preexistencia, no cabe duda. Que había obediencia y desobediencia también es evidente. Ahora continuamos en esta vida terrenal usando nuestro libre albedrío y diariamente escogiendo obedecer o desobedecer.

El propósito de traducir el libro "Los Mormones en México" al español tiene el único fin de que los miembros mexicanos conozcan mejor sus raíces espirituales y que les ayude a apreciar el sacrificio que muchos otros, cual haya sido su origen, han hecho para que nosotros gocemos de las bendiciones del verdadero Evangelio. Sin raíces verdaderas y bien fundadas el árbol no crece.

El libro debe ser leído con un entendimiento de que somos, todos, hijos de Dios pero aun mas importante de que por haber sido bendecidos con el conocimiento del verdadero Evangelio ya no somos "...extranjeros ni advenedizos, sino juntamente ciudadanos con los santos, y de la casa de Dios" (Efesios 2:19). Tenemos que aceptar que es mas importante ser ciudadanos del Reino de Dios. La escritura dice: "Mas nuestra ciudadanía está en los cielos, de donde también esperamos al Salvador, al Señor Jesucristo" (Filipenses 2:20). Y todas las injusticias, si es que las hay, Dios las cobrará en su debido tiempo.

PRESENTACIÓN

EL LIBRO

La llegada a México de los primeros misioneros de la 'Iglesia Mormona', en la segunda mitad del siglo XIX, marcó el comienzo de una etapa nueva en la historia reciente de un país que actualmente se beneficia con el mensaje del evangelio restaurado.

El glorioso futuro de esta nación de casi 100 millones de habitantes --prefigurado en las bendiciones del *Libro de Mormón*-- fue una de las razones principales para que aquellos dedicados pioneros se internaran en territorio mexicano, recorriendo inicialmente los estados de Chihuahua y Sonora para más tarde llegar a la ciudad de México y sus poblados colindantes.

Fascinante por el amplio rescate de fuentes históricas para su realización, el libro de F. LaMond Tullis *Mormons in México* es producto de un arduo trabajo de investigación --que estaría incompleto si el público de habla española no tuviera acceso a él. Es por ello que nos complace el poder presentar por vez primera la traducción de esta obra clave al lector hispanohablante, sabiendo que será de gran ayuda para la comprensión cabal de la historia del mormonismo en México.

ADVERTENCIA

La Iglesia de Jesucristo de Los Santos de los Últimos Días es el nombre oficial de la comúnmente llamada 'Iglesia Mormona'. Entre sus miembros existe la costumbre --no muy generalizada-- de referirse a sí mismos como 'santos', mas no en el sentido adjetival del término sino en el que se aplica a los miembros de la Iglesia de Jesucristo en la *Biblia,* es decir como sustantivo.

Estos son algunos de los nombramientos más comunes en la Iglesia: profeta, apóstol, setenta, presidente (de la Iglesia, de Misión, Estaca, Distrito, Rama), obispo, sumo sacerdote, misionero o élder, consejero, etcétera. Entre la membresía se acostumbra referirse unos a otros como 'hermanos' y 'hermanas'.

EL MUSEO DE HISTORIA DEL MORMONISMO EN MEXICO A. C.

With the desire to search out, compile the history of Mormonism in Mexico, and make it available for local exhibition, three members of the Church of Jesus Christ of Latter Day Saints acted on a dream. Inspired by the legacy of Sister Consuelo Gomez Gonzalez's collection of documents and photographs were motivated to create a Museum in which the past, present, and future of Mormonism in Mexico could be exhibited. "La Tia Consuelo" as she was known to them, one of the first converts, a teacher, poet, and pioneer in the Educational System of the Church in Mexico, was the inspiration in making a beautiful dream become a reality.

More than fifty thousand have visited EL MUSEO since it opened it's doors in October of 1994. Among it's collection is the original translation of selected passages of the Book of Mormon - **TROZOS SELECTOS DEL LIBRO DE MORMON** - whose only edition was made in 1875, a collection of eight books personally signed by Apostle Moses Thatcher on December 10, 1880 while he served as the first mission president among the Mexican People. Three beautiful paintings created exclusively for the Museo by Sister **Irene Becerril**, an international renown artist, and the figurine **LEHI'S FAMILY** created by **J Del Morris** of Salt Lake City, Utah. A collection which includes more than 1,500 photographs and historical documents.

Grateful to my wife for the support she has given me in my desire to make this dream a reality. I also thank my cousin Raymundo, and his wife Yolanda for their dedication and care they have given the MUSEO.

Fernando R. Gómez Páez
Presidente

MEXICO:
Av. 510 no. 79
Unidad Aragon, Sec. 1
Telephone: 52-5-771-0072

USA:
945 E. North Temple Dr.
Provo, Utah, 84604
Telephone: 801-377-3953

E-MAIL: museo@writeme.com
WEBB PAGE:http:members.aol.com/~Museo1

EL MUSEO DE HISTORIA DEL MORMONISMO EN MEXICO A. C.

Con el deseo de rescatar la historia del Mormonismo en México y poder preservarla y exhibirla localmente, tres miembros de la Iglesia de Jesucristo de Los Santos de los Ultimos Días iniciaron un sueño, inspirados todos ellos en la hermana Consuelo Gómez González que con su herencia documental y fotográfica los motivó a la creación de un espacio en el que se presentará el pasado, presente y futuro del Mormonismo en México. "La Tía Consuelo", como era conocida por ellos, miembro pionero y de las primeras maestras del Sistema Educativo de la Iglesia en México, fue la base para hacer de un lindo sueño toda una realidad.

El Museo abrió sus puertas en Octubre de 1994 y ha sido visitado por mas de 50,000 personas. Cuenta con una colección que incluye selecciones de la primera y única traducción del Libro de Mormón del año 1875 titulada **TROZOS SELECTOS DEL LIBRO DE MORMON,** una colección de ocho libros firmados por el primer presidente de misión, Apóstol Moisés Thatcher el 10 de Diciembre de 1880. Pinturas originales pintadas por la hermana **Irene Becerril,** reconocida internacionalmente y la escultura titulada **LA FAMILIA DE LEHI,** donada por el artista **J. Dell Morris.** Un acervo extenso que incluye más de 1500 fotografías y documentos históricos.

Agradezco a mi esposa, Enriqueta por el apoyo que me ha prestado en mi deseo de hacer de este sueño toda una realidad. En igual manera a mi primo Raymundo, y su esposa Yolanda por su dedicación y cuidado del Museo.

Fernando R. Gómez Páez
Presidente

DIRECCION:

México: Av. 510 No. 79
Unidad Aragón, Sec. 1
Teléfono: 52-5-771-0072

USA: 945 E. North Temple Dr.
Provo, Utah, 84604
Teléfono: 801-377-3953

E-MAIL: museo@writeme.com
WEBB PAGE: http://members.aol.com/`Museo1

Ilustraciones:

The Index in the book refer only to Part 1 in English. References starting with page 171 are irrelevant as they belong to Part 2, which is not included in this book,

El Indice en el libro es irrelevante para la Primera Parte en Español. Unicamente es para usarse en la porción en Ingles.

Preface

The last quarter century of my life has been a period of academic and practical reflection on Latin America, principally on matters of modernization, development, and domestic and international political economy. In all these categories institutional religion and religiously based cultural beliefs have affected political, economic, and social events, especially in Mexico. They have therefore interested me, and over the years I have reflected upon their general importance in trying to understand contemporary Latin American issues. In an ancillary way, several of the works I have offered for public review have implicitly reflected upon these themes of culture and religion.*

However, except for an occasional article and an edited volume (listed in the Bibliography), until 1972 I had not explicitly focused upon Mormonism in Latin America. While I have always had a commitment to and an intrinsic interest in the Mormon experience, a sustained academic one fell outside my research agenda.

The circumstance that changed all this was my appointment in 1972 to join fifteen other scholars in what was then called the Mormon church's Sesquicentennial History Project, an individually authored sixteen-volume historical update and current scholarly analysis in celebration of the 150th anniversary of the church's founding. I was assigned the volume on Latin America.

---

*Particularly, *Lord and Peasant in Peru, Politics and Social Change in Third World Countries*, "The Current View on Rural Development: Fad or Breakthrough in Latin America," and "Food Aid and Political Instability."

Following three summers' research in the church's archives and five months' interviewing in Latin America in 1975 and 1976—principally in Mexico, Guatemala, Brazil, Uruguay, Argentina, Bolivia, and Chile—I concentrated on bringing the almost unbelievably complex materials together. By 1978 I had a draft of multiple chapters on Mexico, Argentina, and Brazil.

In the meantime the Sesquicentennial Project ran into trouble and was canceled. One Utah publisher of books aimed at the Latter-day Saint market was nevertheless interested in a volume on Mexico, which I submitted in 1979. I had written it for an LDS audience but was told that the necessary inclusion of ethnic conflict and leadership struggles in Mexico was a sensitive matter cross culturally for some Mormons and therefore the firm could not publish it.

For several years the manuscript lay moribund in my files, read occasionally by colleagues or friends, all of whom chastised me for not bringing it out. Eventually the Keter Foundation, under the direction of Dennis Packard and James Faulconer, took an interest in the work. They, Maxine Hanks, and especially Sibyl Johnson helped me editorially and in other matters with a version intended for a general audience. My thanks to the Foundation for supporting the editing and preparation of this manuscript for publication.

Redrafting a volume originally intended for an LDS audience has been more difficult than I had supposed. Aside from statistical updating required in any event because of the long lapse between drafts, I have had to drop or alter most of the internally understood imagery and vocabulary and many of my own reflections. Additional explanations have also been required. I offer the volume now for a general audience because I believe it is intrinsically interesting and because it offers a scholarly and experiential message that otherwise would be unavailable for public review.

Intellectual debts both stated and unrecognized are many in a volume such as this, as are debts for support. I greatly profited from critiques of various chapter drafts and other insights given by Linda Hunter Adams, James B. Allen, Leonard J. Arrington, Dale Beecher, David Earle Bohn, Eliot Butler, Howard Christy, Carlos Colorado, Ronald D. Dennis, Wilson Duffles, Mark Grover, John P. Hawkins, Elizabeth Hernandez, Thomas K. Hinckley,

W. Ladd Hollist, Gordon Irving, Reba L. Keele, Edward L. Kimball, Arthur Henry King, Peggy Lee, Louis C. Midgley, Noel Owen, Mario Salazar, Don Sorensen, Marta Morrill Tullis, Michael Tullis, Olivia Villalobos, L. Robert Webb, Andrew Wilson, and several unnamed reviewers. Marta Tullis, in particular, spent over a decade intermittently reflecting on this project. Marilyn Webb, Evelyn Schiess, and their staffs efficiently prepared several drafts of the manuscript, as likewise did the staff of Brigham Young University's Philosophy Department and the College of Humanities Publications Center. B. Kelly Nielsen prepared the maps. Karl Batdorff set the type.

I am grateful to Brigham Young University, and especially to Dean Martin B. Hickman, for providing funding and time for archival research and fieldwork in Latin America.

I am very much indebted to the Mexicans and Anglo-Americans who shared their lives, confidences and trust with me in many hours of interviews. I have listed most of their names in the interview section of resources I have consulted.

Consistent with contemporary practice, when quoting from relatively old personal journals, manuscripts, and diaries, I have used modern spelling.

Though it may seem trite to say so, those who have written will understand: I am responsible for the errors and shortcomings in this book; I recognize that many of its strengths, such as they may be, are in large part the property of both my colleagues and my critics.

Scholars of modernization and social change, political economy, and development will readily detect the book's indebtedness to the literature in those fields. Others will recognize that I have also reflected on history as one vitally interested in a segment of my own Mormon faith and heritage.

Covered Bridge Canyon, Utah
June 1987

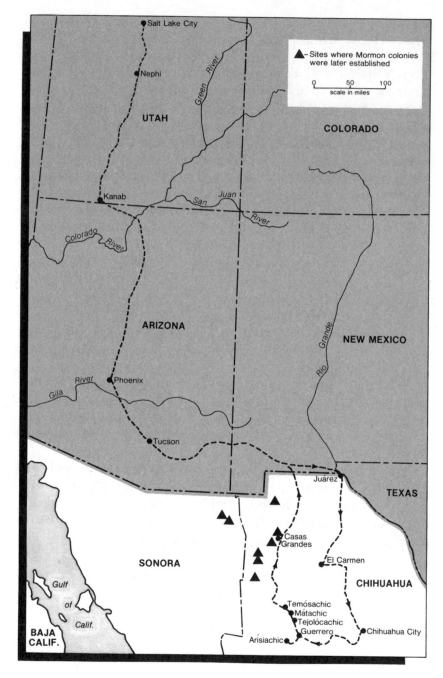

Figure 1.   First exploration and proselyting journey to Mexico, 1875–76.
Cartography by B. Kelley Nielsen.

Part I

Historical Foundations of the Mormon Experience in Mexico

ADDITIONAL DATA - DATOS ADICIONALES

This information is the research of EL MUSEO and presented here to help the reader better understand the history of Mormonism in Mexico. The text is in English and Spanish so as not to alter the intent of the writer. Reference page numbers and chapters are from the English section.

Esta información es parte de la investigación hecha por EL MUSEO y se presenta para ayudar al lector entender mejor la historia del Mormonismo en México. Se ha presentado en ambos idiomas para así no alterar el intento de la fuente. Las referencias a paginas y capítulos son de la sección en ingles.

A. PAGE 19 OF CHAPTER 1: DESERET NEWS OCT., 13, 1875 PAGE 585: "....ELDER GEO. Q. CANNON - read the following names of persons called to be missionaries, the appointments being unanimously sustained by the conference: .....Daniel W. Jones - A W Ivins - Ammon M Tenny - Wiley C Jones -James L Stewart - Helaman Pratt - Robert H Smith"....

Whether Daniel W. Jones suggested, requested, or convinced the brethren to have his son join the group, we don't know. Wiley Jones name was presented and his appointment sustained by the conference as a missionary.

B. PAGE 22 OF CHAPTER 1: THE BLESSING GIVEN TO HELAMAN PRATT BY ORSON PRATT, PRIOR TO HIS DEPARTURE SAYS: "I also feel at this time to ordain thee to be one of the seventies to go forth & administer in that office & calling & to baptize those who repent ....."

DANIEL W. JONES IN HIS BOOK *FORTY YEARS AMONG THE INDIANS* INDICATES ON PAGE 258 THE FOLLOWING: ".... I should be satisfied even if we did not baptize a single person; that our mission was more as prospectors going through to prepare the way, and that President Young so understood it. We were to be governed by circumstances and not to feel disappointed if we could get to distribute our books and learn about the country and make friendly acquaintance with the people. This was all that would be expected of us on the trip. This was our calling. We were not sent to baptize and organize branches, neither were we forbidden to do so. That was an open question to be decided upon according to the openings made."

C. PAGE 25 OF CHAPTER 1: THE PRESS RELEASE IN SPANISH SAYS THAT THE MEETING WAS HELD THE LAST DAY OF THE WEEK OR SATURDAY. THE ARTICLE WAS ON THE EDITION PUBLISHED ON THE 12, A WEDNESDAY. "El último día de la semana pasada......" meaning the last day of the week or Saturday.

THE DOCUMENT "HISTORY OF THE MEXICAN MISSION READS: "On Friday, April 7th, the brethren received permission from Governor Luis Terrazas to hold meetings in the city of Chihuahua. Consequently on Saturday evening, April 8th, 1876, they held their first and only meeting in a "cock pit" or large hall and preached to about five hundred people."

D. PAGE 25 OF CHAPTER 1: THE "HISTORY OF THE MEXICAN MISSION" SAYS : "On Wednesday, April 5, 1876, the brethren mailed about 500 copies of "Trozos Selectos" to prominent men in the principal cities of Mexico."

E. PAGE 33 OF CHAPTER 1: HISTORY OF THE MEXICAN MISSION DATED FEBRUARY TO JUNE 1877 INDICATES THE FOLLOWING:
"On the 19th of February, 1877, the missionaries arrived at Tubac, near the Mexican line. At this place the brethren held a council on the 20th of that month, and after engaging in earnest prayer to the Almighty, they decided to cross the national boundary line into Sonora, two and two, and at different points. Elders Pratt and Terry went into Mexico by way of Altar, and the two Stewart's and Garff and Trejo by way of Magdalena. The two Stewart's returned soon afterwards into Arizona, and thence made their way to El Paso, Texas; but Elders Louis Garff and Trejo continued their operations further into the country and finally reached Hermosillo, the capital of Sonora. Elder Trejo and Garff spent several days in Hermosillo and visited two or three other settlements. They were kindly received and listened to with interest, with but one exception, ..." - "Quite a number of meetings were held in Sonora, four of the missionaries being constantly engaged in traveling and preaching in the cities and towns of that State for three months." "Elders Militon G. Trejo and Louis Garff baptized five persons at Hermosillo, ... Elder Trejo returned to his home in October, 1877, about two months ahead of his missionary companions." - "Elders Helaman Pratt and George Terry also went to Hermosillo, arriving there on the 16th of April, 1877. They remained there for some time, assisting the other brethren in holding meetings, etc. On Monday, May 28, 1877, Elders Pratt and Terry left Hermosillo and traveled by stage coach to Guaymas on the Gulf of California. There they visited the American Consul on the 29th, and on the same day they embarked on a little steamboat for the mouth of the Yaqui River where they arrived in the evening. On the morning of the 30th they walked a distance of about four miles to the house of one of the Indian governors. On the 1st of June they returned to Guaymas; thence they traveled by way of Hermosillo and up the Sonora River and via Arispe; Thence they traveled to Santa Cruz in Arizona, and arrived in Tucson July 4, 1877." - "....we thought best for us to go over into Sonora and try to open up a field in that State. It was decided that Elders Pratt and Terry should go by way of Saric and that the other Elders, Stewart, Trejo, Stewart, and Garff should go to Magdalena. This was decided upon at a meeting held on March

21st , at which all the Elders were present and concurred in, and Elders Pratt and Terry started the same afternoon to Saric." - "...on the 29th of March we started for Magdalena, Sonora......." - "On Sunday, April 8th , we all decided that it would be best for two of us, Elders Trejo and Garff to travel around in Sonora visiting different settlements as they felt directed by the Spirit, and that Elders J. Z. and Isaac J. Stewart return to Arizona, visiting the settlements along the Santa Cruz River and hold meetings wherever opportunity were offered, and on Monday, April 9th , 1877, we separated leaving Elders Trejo and Garff in Sonora and the Elders Stewart started toward Arizona. At this time Elders Helaman Pratt and George Terry were somewhere in Sonora on their way to visit the Yaqui Indians in the Southern part of the State." - "Elder Trejo and Garff, after leaving the other Elders at Magdalena, visited and labored in other settlements as far South as Hermosillo, where they were joined by Elders Pratt and Terry, and they all labored there from April 16th to May 28th, when Elders Pratt and Terry left for Guaymas by stage and upon their arrival there, they visited the American Consul, as it was their intention to visit the Yaqui Indians. They explained to the American Consul their desires to visit the Yaqui country, and he told them that that was a very risky undertaking as the Yaqui seldom, if ever, allowed any on who went into their country to return, and he told them that he could not offer them any protection and advised them to not go: but on April 29th , the day of their visit to the Consul they took steamer for the mouth of the Yaqui River where they arrived the same evening." - "The next morning they walked four miles to the home of one of the Yaqui Governors, and were at once taken into custody and placed among their instruments of torture and a council of eight judges considered what they should do with them. These formed a circle around the Elders, each sticking his cane into the ground and, after a discussion lasting only a few minutes, the judges trembling like leaves, informed the Elders that they should not go any farther, neither should they remain there, but they would allow them to return from whence they came, and, of course, the Elders decided to return and the Yaqui sent a guard with them to see that they did return the same way they came. The Elders were perfectly calm while before the judges, while the judges trembled like leaves, but after the Elders had crossed the river and were perfectly safe, fear came upon them and they saw the danger in which they were placed and they both trembled as badly as the judges had done while standing in judgment upon them." - "The Elders left Guaymas on July 1st, and visited a number of the settlements along the way passing by Hermosillo, traveling up the Sonora River by Arispe and Santa Cruz, arriving at Tucson July 4th, 1877, where they joined Elders Trejo and Garff." - "While laboring in Hermosillo, Sonora, Elders Trejo and Garff baptized five persons and quite a number more desired baptism, and several were healed through administration, by the power of God." - "Upon reaching Tucson, Elder Trejo desired to return home as it was his wish to move his family to some part of Arizona or Old Mexico, and he left the other elders for that purpose, and reached home in

October, 1877." - "On August 7th, Elders Pratt, Garff, and Terry left Tucson for San Elizario, Texas, to join the Elders Stewart who were then laboring in El Paso County, Texas where they arrived on August 28th, 1877, where, on a former mission, Elders J. Z. Stewart and Helaman Pratt had labored and made some converts who contemplate moving to Utah."

FROM THE JOURNAL OF LOUIS GARFF WE READ: "On Sunday, May 20th, 1877, I baptized José Apifaro Jesús. May 24th, thur. I baptized José Severo Rodriguez, María Ta Cruz Parra, José Visente Parrra at a village a few leagues from the City of Hermosillo, in the State of Sonora. These five being the first ever baptized in Old Mexico into the Church of Jesús Christ of Latter-day Saints. At Hermosillo we (myself and Milton Trejo) met with Elder Helaman Pratt and George Terry, who had come down through the country in a different direction. Here we enjoyed the Holy Spirit greatly, not withstanding the persecution we endured at this place. We were stoned some 17 times, while walking about on the street or wherever we would appear. Our meeting with the two Elders were so unexpected, we were all very pleasantly surprised, having traveled some 1200 miles."

HISTORY OF THE MEXICAN MISSION DATED FEBRUARY TO JUNE 1877 INDICATES THE FOLLOWING: "On the 28 day of August, we were joined by Elders Pratt, Garff, and Terry, who had come pursuant to the suggestion of President Young in his letter to Elder James Z. Stewart regarding the colonizing matter."

DIARY OF HELAMAN PRATT INDICATES THE FOLLOWING WITH RESPECT TO THE SECOND MISSIONARY JOURNEY TO SONORA, MEXICO. - "May 29 Visited the American Consul Mr. Wileret, & was kindly received & at 11 o'clock we started in a sail boat across a neck of the Gulf for the Yaqui river a distance of 30 or 40 miles. Slept in the Boat all night, & in the (May 30) morning went up the river about 4 miles to the house of one of the Governors of the Yaquis, he sent immediately in search of the head chief José María by name......The head chief sent for our book of Mormon & after reading it returned it to us but the Governor would not tell us where the Chief was but said if we would go up the river about 15 miles to a village where the Indians were having a fiesta we might be able to find him , & he volunteered to go with us, we accordingly started on foot after partaking of a meal of beans & water - melons, & when we came to the village we found the Priest from Guimas [Guaymas] was there, & the Indians were gathered by the thousands & holding a big fiesta....They also have instruments of torture of various kinds for punishing the human body we were marched in the center of these & invited to take a seat & a council of the leading men was called & we were asked to state our business, we said we wished to talk with their head Chief as we had some books for him & c & c we were then told that he was some 40 miles farther up

4

the river & that we would not be permitted to go any farther nor to remain there but if we wished to return we could do so, we were then furnished with an escort to conduct us out of the country we returned to the house of the Governor after a walk or rather a run of 90 miles." - "June 1 Returned to Guaymas, reported ourselves to the American Consul who was quite astonished when he learned we had been to the river Yaqui & returned in safety, he said that those Indians are now in a state of rebellion, & it is not considered safe for any one to go among them, & we certainly acknowledge the hand of the Lord in our preservation as we were completely in their hands & they were very much excited at our being among them & nothing but the power of God could have delivered us but thanks to him we were permitted to return in safety." - "Remained two days at Guimas [Guaymas] conversing with the people." - "June 4 returned to Hermosillo, stayed over night at the house of Mr. Barnett who was very kind to us." - "Jun 5 visited our friends in that vicinity & bade them farewell, & in the evening started on foot for Urace [Ures] where we arrived on the 9 of June, stopping with an American by the name of Favorite until the evening of the 10 when we again started for Arispe."

F. PAGE 35 OF CHAPTER 1: "We've found the gospel," he said, "and we want you to give us the Aaronic priesthood so we can begin proselyting in Mexico." Apparently this words are attributed to Plotino C. Rhodakanaty. His two letter we have read as follows:

Orson Pratt Esqre   City of Mexico México,
Elder of Mormon Church   November 15th 1878
     My dear Sir.

     Having read a Spanish translation of the Mormon Bible, which has found its way down here, I have become convinced of the truth and purity of the Mormon faith, and am anxious to become a member of your Church, but as there are no Mormon missionaries here, I would request that one be sent here, with ample authority to preach and convert.
     I think this would prove a very profitable field of missionary labor, as there are many that I am sure would become converts, as there is a manifest indifference among a large class of people to the numerous and unmeaning ceremonies of the Roman Catholic Church, and as there is here, perfect religious toleration, I do not think tha [that] a missionary enterprise would be attended with many difficulties.
     If you would answer this as soon as possible, and if you think proper, send a good and devote preacher to this country, I and many others will be for ever indebted to you.

               I have the honor to be
                  Sir, yours very respectfully
                  Dr. Plotino C. Rhodakanaty.

A SECOND LETTER READS:

Ssmos. Y RRvds. Presidente y Apóstoles de "la Iglesia Cristiana de los Santos de los Ultimos Días."
Respetasilisimos Hermanos en Nuestro Señor Jesu - Cristo.

Los que suscribimos vecinos de la capital de México ante el dignísimo Gobierno Teocrático de esa Santa Iglesia con el mas profundo respeto exponemos:

Que habiendo sido convocados a una junta privada en la propia casa del Sr. Dr. Dn. Plotino Constantino Rhodakanaty, Promotor Gerente de la misma Iglesia, con el objeto de organizar un pequeño circulo o congregación de propaganda religiosa y social en esta capital, dicho Señor nos leyó al efecto una obra intitulada "Trozos Selectos del Libro de Mormón, traducido al español por los RR. Elder Meliton G. Trejo y Daniel W. Jones" cuyo sentido místico y altamente trascendental nos fue después dilucidado por el mismo Doctor, quien nos probo y convenció plenamente hasta la evidencia del origen divino de tan precioso Libro y de la alta misión que su doctrina tiene que desempeñar en el mundo obrando por su influencia toda providencial y divina una completa palingenesia o transformación humanitaria tanto en el orden religioso, como también en el moral, social y político.

Tan bella perspectiva de una reforma radical en nuestra querida patria (a quien esa Santa Iglesia hace una invitación directamente para que adopte la verdadera creencia que ella profesa), como la que tiene que obrar su influencia moral, no ha podido menos de cautivar nuestras mentes y enternecer nuestros corazones a nosotros los que soñamos con el bello ideal de la vida patriarcal, a nosotros los que nos hallamos sedientos de caridad y justicia a la vez que da esa felicidad que a no dudarlo solamente reside hoy en el seno de esa santa y misteriosa institución depositaria absoluta y continuadora legitima de aquella primitiva Iglesia de Jerusalén que es el mas hermoso y sublime paradigma de la caridad, del amor, y de la fraternidad universal.

Así pues, estas y otras varias consideraciones que hemos meditado profundamente en nuestras almas, nos han impulsado por una misión divina, no solo a abrazar esa Doctrina teóricamente, sino también a practicarla y lo que es mas aun a constituirnos, a pesar de nuestra humilde posición social de honrados y laboriosos obreros, en digno ministros o Pastores de su Santo Culto, para lo cual hoy nos dirigimos respetuosamente a ese santo y sabio Apostolado de la Iglesia en solicitud urgente de nuestra ordenación al Sacerdocio Menor , que no dudamos nos será conferido sino por sabiduría o instrucción de mundana erudición de que carecemos de por nuestra fe de que nos hallamos poseídos y vehementes deseos de desempeñar nuestra misión como instrumentos providenciales de la voluntad divina para la salvación de tantas pobres almas como hoy yacen en este país, víctimas del error y de las impostura de las falsas y pretendidas Iglesias que se dicen Cristianas, y que desgraciadamente pululan entre nosotros extraviando las conciencias, fraccionando la unidad social y lacerando los corazones sensibles con su egoísmo y continuos ultrajes que hacen a la caridad, negando así al Espíritu Santo, que es el Espíritu de toda verdad y la base mas sólida de toda solidaridad en el cielo y en la tierra.

Perseverante en nuestro buen propósito de constituirnos en campeones de la verdad religiosa con el único fin de atacar el error hasta sus últimos atrincheramientos y de castigar a las rebeldes por su iniquidad perfidia y egoísmo con que extorsionan y matan a los pobres y escogidos del Señor, hoy nos acercamos sumisamente ante el dignísimo Apostolado de esa Santa Iglesia solicitando oficialmente por órgano del eminente e infatigable propagador de la fe, nuestro respetable y amado Hermano Meliton G. Trejo Elder de la Iglesia, se nos confiera pronta y eficazmente con dispensa de tramite el Sacerdocio menor al cual nos creemos con derecho sino de nacimiento como ha sido declarado felizmente nuestro maestro e iniciador en la nueva fe, el Dr. Rhodakanaty, si por vocación para el desempeño y practica de tan sagrado Ministerio para obtener la competente autorización de predicar en nuestra nación la plenitud del evangelio y la continuación de la divina revelación para alcanzar la reforma radical y la salvación no solo de nuestro, sino del mundo entero nuestra patria porque somos cosmopolitas conforme al espíritu de Cristo nuestro Señor y nuestro Dios.

Sírvanse UU dignísimos Hermanos acceder a nuestra justa y humilde petición en lo que recibirá el universo entero una prueba mas de que nuestra Santa Religión es la verdadera por que no desecha las suplicas de sus fervientes prosélitos impartiendo así la caridad en la gracia que concede a sus siervos en la fe.

Ciudad de México, Diciembre 15 de 1878.

Como propagador Gerente de la Iglesia

Dr. Plotino C. Rhodakanaty

Domingo Mejia	Dario F. Fernández
Miguel Enríquez	José Cleofaz G. y Sánchez
Felix Rodríguez y Luis	Luis J. Rabia

G. PAGE 36 CHAPTER 1: "The party took a steamer, crossed the Gulf of Mexico, and reached Veracruz on 14 November 1879. Two days later they arrived in Mexico City and lodged in the principal hotel, the Iturbide."

Moses Thatcher's diary states: "On Friday morning the 14th November we entered the harbor of Vera Cruz.......Arrived at the City of Mexico Saturday evening Nov. 15th 1879 - 7 o'clock..."

H. PAGE 36 CHAPTER 1: BY THE END OF 1879 THEY HAD BAPTIZED SIXTEEN PERSONS.

Moses Thatcher's recording of the baptisms performed in Mexico indicate 14.

I. PAGE 41 CHAPTER 1: "In April 1881, four months after Thatcher's return to Mexico he took his missionaries and a handful of Saints (some of whom had remained from the original Rhodakanaty group)
........and two other Mexican members whose names are unknown."

Of the four local members who participated in the conference held in the Volcano Popocatepetl, only Silviano Artiaga was baptized in 1879. Fernando A. Lara was baptized February 20, 1880 and Ventura Paez on May 23, 1880. Lino Zarate was not baptized until January 30th 1881.

The other two were non-members, Marciano Perez, Lino Zarate's brother in-law and Florentino Paez a nephew of Ventura Paez.

J. PAGE 42 CHAPTER 1: "Among the missionaries were Lino Zarate, Julían Rojas, and an Elder Candanosa. ...."

Moses Thatcher's list of baptisms indicate Elder Candanosa's first name as Marciano.

K. PAGE 42 CHAPTER 1: "Isaac J. Stewart, who had accompanied his brother to the Yaquis several years before, soon joined the group."

James Z. Stewart and Isaac J. Stewart went to Sonora in 1876 and 1877. They visited the town of Magdalena but did not get to Yaqui territory as did Helaman Pratt and George Terry. See note 5 above.

L. PAGE 56 CHAPTER 2: "By 1912 the Mormons had settled over four thousand people in nine Mexican colonies-seven in the Mexican state of Chihuahua and two in the state of Sonora.

There were the plateau colonies of Juárez........ , Dublán, aNd Díaz ......; the mountain colonies of Cave Valley, Pacheco...., Garcia ......, and Chuichupa, all in the state of Chihuahua; and in Sonora there were the semi-tropical colonies of Oaxaca and Morelos."

The Mormons established a total of 9 colonies in northern Mexico, 6 in the state of Chihuahua and 3 in the state of Sonora. They were: Juárez, Dublán, Chuichupa, Díaz, Pacheco and Garcia in Chihuahua and Morelos, Oaxaca and San José in Sonora.

M. PAGE 70 CHAPTER 2: "The 241 native Mormons in central Mexico and the more than forty northern Mexican Indians were left to take care of themselves as best they could."

The record shows a total of 63 baptized during 1888 in Sonora.

N. PAGE 70 CHAPTER 2: "But many remained loyal to the church during its thirteen year absence (elders did not return until 1901)."

The Mexican Mission was closed on June 3, 1889 and reopened on June 8, 1901 for an absence of 12 years.

O. PAGE 78-79 CHAPTER 3: Milton H. Pratt in his writings refers to Aclantla. The correct name is Atlautla.

P. PAGE 79-80 CHAPTER 3: In these two pages reference is made to a "Mormon man named Camacho".

Baptismal records show that his first name was Senobio and that he was baptized by H. Cummings on May 1st, 1887.

Q. PAGE 123 CHAPTER 5: "Bautista's book rapidly gained wide circulation among Mexican Mormons and became a sort of mini-best seller.......One missionary of the time remembers that many Saints preferred to quote from Bautista's work than from the Book of Mormon."

The Museo feels that the description "rapidly gained wide circulation among Mexican Mormons and became a sort of mini-best seller" is too generous to Bautista, his book and the capacity of the members of that time. The book, as Tullis explains "is lengthy and haphazardly organized. ...trying to handle such a huge chunk of material made the manuscript longer and longer and had a crippling effect on its organization." The membership of the Church in Mexico in the early 30's was between 2,000 and 3,000, mostly children and women and few who had an education that would allow them to read such a complex book. Our aunt, Consuelo Gómez, who was baptized in 1925 a school teacher and spoke French and English, was the source of gospel information for the congregation in Pachuca, Hidalgo during that period even teaching the Priesthood class because of the lack of ability of the brethren to read.

R. PAGE 123 CHAPTER 5: "...., Bernabe Parra, a counselor in the Mexican district presidency, had contributed heavily (his picture was printed in the book with an acknowledgment), ..."

The picture of Bernabe Parra nor and acknowledgment by him appear in the book.

S. PAGE 128 CHAPTER 5 NOTE # 5: The name Pilar is used in Mexico for both sexes. Pilar Paez was a man. His activity in the Church indicates he received the priesthood. He was one of those excommunicated for his activity in the Third Convention.
1. Continues: "Sunday, March 25. (1923) A Genealogical Society was organized in San Marcos, Tula, Hidalgo, Mexico, with the following officers: President: Bernabe Parra;....."
2. The Manuscript History of the Mexican Mission shows on the date of February 1, 1928 the following: "Wednesday, Feb. 1. A circular letter was sent to branch presidents in Mexico stating that a committee consisting of Isaías Juárez, Pilar Paez and Abel Paez had been appointed to hold conferences in

9

San Pedro Martir, Feb. 25 and 26, Tecalco, March 3 and 4, and San Marcos, Mexico, March 10 and 11."

3. It also shows that on "Monday, July 23, (1928) Elder Bernabe Parra was set apart as president of the San Marcos Branch, Tula, México.

4. We also find: "Monday, Nov. 12. (1928) In a letter from Bro. Pilar Paez he notes a change in the Genealogical Society there. Flora Carillo succeeded Sister Morales Mexico City as treasurer.

5. Another input: "May 5, 1929 Presiding Elder Isaías Juárez, Mexico assisted by Elders Abel Paez and Bernabe Parra, held a local conference in Pachuca, Hidalgo.....

6. "On Saturday March 8, (1930) President Pratt and Elder Juárez and companions went on from Pachuca to the little town of San Marcos and the day was spent there in visiting with the saints. In the afternoon the Branch President Bernabe Parra drove ......

7. Rey L. Pratt's journal entry of 9 March 1930 list Pilar Paez as the second counselor to Juárez in those early days and Bernabe Parra as president of the San Marcos branch.

8. "November 7, 1930 Brother Pilar Paez, branch President of the Tacubayo [a] D.F. Mexico advises us in his letter of November 6th of the following organization that has been effected in his district:.....

9. It states: "Fri. Nov. 7, (1930) Brother Pilar Paez, Branch President of Tacubayo [a] D.F. Mexico reported that a Sunday School had been organized...

10. Again: "On Dec. 17, (1930) Pres Pratt and Dr. Harris again visited Isaías Juárez in San Pedro and also Pilar Paez who was interviewed and turned over to Pres Pratt tithing and offering money.   11. "Conferences held at San Marcos, Hidalgo, Mexico November 24, 1934 .....Elder Bernabe Parra, Second Councilor in the District Presidency, ...

The district presidency was an unofficial calling made primarily to authorize them to carry out conferences. At the same time three of the four names associated with the district presidency were called to be branch presidents.

T. PAGE 132 CHAPTER 5 NOTE 32: The diary of Consuelo Gomez González indicates on January 10, 1932 entry the following: "Dieron a conocer el Pte Guillermo Canales y el misionero Casillas los acuerdos tomados en la Primera Convención." Dando posible luz que la Primera Convención se llevo acabo el 5 de Enero de 1932 como lo indica el *Informe general*.

Sobre la Segunda Convención el diario de Antoine R. Ivins dice lo siguiente:

Feb 11, 1932 Cashed a check for $100 for emergency, and crossed over to Juárez with BP. Pierce who for one of my checks sold me enough plata to pay for our tickets to Mexico City and buy our food. It cost us 41 cents on the dollar.

Got our tickets, passed the customs inspectors without being asked for our passports and were off to Mexico City as tourists. The trip was interesting though tiresome and the food was poor. Arrived Mexico City Sat. morning the 13th of Feb. and went to the Hotel Regis which BP Pierce had told us was a good hotel. It was not what we would have liked but we took a room for us at twelve pesos and six for Bro. Ballard's. Washed up and called Ambassador Clark for information as to how to get out to our people for Sunday.

Called Ambassador Clark for information as to how to get out to our people for Sunday. He arranged a transfer for us to the Hotel Geneva, a much more satisfactory place at less money, two bed rooms, a toilet with bath, and a sitting room, all for fifteen pesos.

Sunday morning we transferred our luggage to the Geneva and Brother Clark's man drove u off to San Pedro Martyr and dropped us off at the house of Isaías Juárez who is in charge of the work in Mexico. It was a surprise to him, as I had not told him just when we would be there not caring to create any excitement because of the uncertainty of the conditions there.

We went to their Sunday school which was conducted very much as our own and was very well done, surprisingly so.

Sister Juárez served dinner and it was a very good dinner prepared while we had been in Sunday school.

At two o'clock we went back to the Church to the afternoon meeting which was well conducted. We heard several of the local brethren.

As we were not qualified to minister we did not dare take part in the regular meeting and Sunday School services but after it had been adjourned we stood up and talked to them, I did the interpreting for Brother Ballard and Vilate as usual and before I got through speaking Brother and Sister Clark came for us in their car and they came in and talked through me as interpreter. It was all very interesting. The women there are about as much alike as two peas on a pot, the man not quite so much so. All are a distinct Indian type and show practically no ----- spanish blood at all. Brother Clark says he has great faith in these indians but little at all in the mixture he has to deal with in his official capacity.

February 16, Tuesday we met the leading men of the branch at 5 p.m. and at Portales (The Mexican City Branch) regarding the creation of a chapel in Mexico City. They have been urging it upon the Presidency of the Church for same time. We found that they desire a place where perhaps 1,500 people can congregate for conference, coining in from all the surrounding territory, think they can do all the work themselves and raise a good deal of the money by subscription. Coming at this time it is refreshing to see a group of people who are not afraid to tackle such a proposition.

February 17, It had been arranged that we would go to Tecalco for Wednesday and hold meeting with them, Brother Clark furnished the transportation - his small car and driver and gave us a fine lunch to eat on the way. We left Mexico City about 10 o'clock and reached Tecalco about 2:20 to find the home full of waiting Saints.

When we entered I saw what was coming and urged Brother Ballard ahead so that he received a shower of rose petals that they had in dishes. They

11

were lined up, the ladies on one side, the gents opposite, and the children at the far end. It was a rare experience and Brother Ballard was thrilled with it. That is the nearest thing to Hawaii that we have experienced in the mainland. As we entered they sang us a hymn - as I remember it began with "The messengers are coming" or so some expression.

We listened to about six or eight of their Branch Presidents from all the way from Cuautla to Tula and then the meeting was dismissed and we talked to them for a good while. Many of them wept for the joy of seeing an apostle and their new presidents. Among them was Lucas Zuniga whom my father baptized when he was there on a mission years ago.

We had been instructed not to be out on the road after dark so had to leave about four thirty or five and when we did arrive the Clarks were worried that we had not put in an appearance a half hour earlier. This ended our meetings with the Mexicans.

Tuesday, Wednesday, and Thursday we were the guests of the Clarks at the Embassy and this was an experience to be remembered. They are wonderful, hosts. and I enjoyed getting better acquainted with him. He looks for all the war world like a Woolley. I like his attitude towards the Church and towards the political questions that were discussed and personally would like to see his fellow Senator Smoot in the Senate.

Through their courtesy we saw the pyramids of San Juan Teotihuacan, the Snake pyramid, and the Chinampas (floating gardens). At the latter place we had lunch with them on the water in one of the house boats that are so much used there. It was all very enjoyable.........

We saw also the Museum and walked and rode through the Chapultepec wood. It was all very interesting to me to see it after- so many years and find it so little changed. Many of the wonderful stores of Calle San Francisco (now Francisco I. Madero) are vacant and the old buildings look older, . The P. 0. Building which I saw began, is completed and a fine structure. The Teatro Nacional has never been complete and had gone into the ground to the depth of sixteen steps .1 wonder if it will ever stop. I doubt that it will ever be finished.

From this writting we can conclude that Apostle Ballard and President Ivins were not in Mexico because of the first convention. The Museo feels that the second convention did take place as indicated in the *Informe General* on April 3, 1932.

U.   PAGE 159 CHAPTER 6: On the leadership of the first stake organized in Mexico City it states that the clerk was Luis Rubalcava. The two clerks were Roman Alcala and Carlos Alvarez.

Chapter 1

Early Proselyting and Colonizing

The Mormons' initial move into Mexico was motivated principally by two factors: proselyting Indians and exploring for colonization and refuge. Continual efforts to proselyte Indians derived from the Latter-day Saints' religious beliefs about the development of the Lord's Kingdom in the "last days." They were taught that should the "children of Father Lehi," both at home and in Latin America, be converted, their Lord's coming would be hastened.[1] They had a profoundly felt need to preach the gospel to the Indians, to educate them and lift them up economically and culturally in order to bring them into the Kingdom. This was a theme acted upon from the earliest days of the church and was a principal force in Parley P. Pratt's mission to Chile and in later missionary and colonization efforts.

On the other hand, the Mormons' nearly constant exploration since their arrival in Utah Territory was a practical response to a hostile West as well as part of the mission they had set for themselves. They needed to explore in order to know the country intimately in the event they had to flee persecution again. They needed to explore in order to know where best to expand their settlements, and they needed far-flung settlements in order to be economically and politically secure as well as to enhance their proselyting the Indians.[2] Brigham Young soon developed an expansion pattern—first sending missionaries to the Indians, then (sometimes simultaneously) exploring for settlement sites, and then colonizing.

The Mormons' need for security was evident in their original westward movement in 1846–47 as they searched for religious freedom and a place of refuge to protect their lives and their property. Missouri Governor Lilburn Boggs's "extermination order" (rescinded only in 1976) was quite fresh in their minds. The move west, the 1857–58 Utah War, and subsequent federal laws against plural marriage kept the Mormons on the alert for places of refuge. Thus, most of the new colonies stretched from Salt Lake City to the south—toward Mexico, where many thought the ultimate refuge lay.[3] Joseph Smith had reputedly said that the Latter-day Saints would ultimately go to the Great Salt Lake and would build cities in all directions, but "the government will not receive you with the laws that God designed you to live [by], and those who are desirous to live the laws of God will have to go south." Mosiah Levee Hancock, who was present at the time, remembered Joseph pointing to southern Arizona or Mexico on the map as he spoke.[4]

By 1870 the church's settlements extended to the southern border of Utah Territory. With the U.S. Army having defeated the Navajos that year in northern Arizona, and Mexico's political turmoil temporarily resolved, extending the settlements farther south became feasible. The time now seemed right for a new round of exploration, missionary work, and colonization, perhaps throughout Arizona and even into Mexico.

The Missionary Expedition of 1875–76 as an Extension of Early Developmental and Eschatological Ideology

In June of 1874 Brigham Young announced that soon it would be time to take the gospel to Lehi's millions of Mexican descendants.[5] Profound social and political changes were occurring in Mexico, and, since Mexican Catholic tradition and power were deteriorating, the new missionaries to Latin America would find less resistance than had Parley P. Pratt a quarter of a century earlier.

Brigham Young was aware of Mexico's La Reforma, which ultimately would allow the Mormons to return to Latin America in 1876. Like the earlier Chilean revolution that had helped to frustrate Pratt's mission, La Reforma was a struggle between Conservatives and Liberals. But, whereas in Chile the Conservatives had won and essentially closed down the country to religions other than Catholicism, in Mexico it was just the reverse. Events there excited people about religion and enabled non-Catholic churches to function in the open and quite freely. That was part of the Liberals' political agenda, and they were in power.

By the 1830s Mexico's liberal position had evolved from the previous decade's hatred of kings and obsession with decentralized state power to a movement to secularize the courts, education, and marriage vows, and to diminish, if not destroy, the Mexican Catholic church's political power. Finally, in the 1850s, the Liberals gradually realized the need for fundamental social and economic reforms if Mexico were to avoid further dismembering by the United States. The year 1855 saw the beginning of a twenty-one-year reform in which the Liberals promoted laws curtailing the Catholic church's traditional political privileges, and initiated— although abortively—a new economic and social order.

La Reforma included the popular uprising that unseated Santa Ana from the Mexican presidency (he had lost both Texas and the Mexican Northwest to the United States) and the anti-clerical verdicts of 1855 and 1856 that removed the priests' control of public education and bridled them politically. It saw the drafting of a Mexican constitution in 1857; a breathing space in 1861 with constitutional liberties under Benito Juárez (the Zápotec Indian for whom the Mormon colony of Juárez and the Mormons' flagship school in Mexico were named); the armed French intervention the previous year as part of a tripartite invasion with Spaniards and the English under Napoleon III, and the consequent enthronement of a French monarch (Maximilian) in Mexico from 1864 to 1867; the reconstruction of Juárez's presidency from 1867 until his death in 1872; and the rule of the brilliant and circumspect Sebastián Lerdo de Tejada until 1876, the year the Mormon missionaries entered the Mexican Republic to preach the gospel.

Out of all this carnage, deprivation, dislocation, and upheaval two remarkable trends developed that finally opened the doors for the Latter-day Saint missionaries. One was the Catholic church's loss of civil control; the other was the people's increasing interest in religions other than Catholicism—an interest that did not necessarily provoke organized persecution or social disfavor. Between 1871 and 1880 several Protestant religions, including

15

Methodist, Quaker, Presbyterian, Baptist, and Congregationalist, established missions in Mexico and began a vigorous journalistic battle against the Catholics.[6] The government itself sometimes seemed to favor the Protestants, allowing, for example, literature from the London Bible Society to enter the country tax-free while subjecting Catholic publications to a high tariff. Had La Reforma not occurred, Mormons probably would not have entered Mexico as missionaries or as colonists for a long time.

The Mexican turmoil, with its secular and religious opening-up, coincided in part with the U.S. Civil War. Americans, following their dismembering of Mexico in 1848, were largely uninterested in Mexico just before and during that war. But when it was over, Mexico's new economic and social order attracted American industrialists, who once more sought expanding markets and raw resources. American publications (to which Brigham Young no doubt had access and which perhaps he read) widely advertised Mexico's commercial and religious offerings.[7] Consequently, by 1876 scores of Americans had entered Mexico for religious and commercial reasons.[8]

The invasion greatly alarmed the Catholic church, which viewed the Protestant entrance in particular as a "greater threat than the hostile and oppressive measures of the Mexican government."[9] But while the Catholic clergy and their conservative allies could resist and preach against the American presence, they could not totally prevent it. For their part, the Mexican Liberals were delighted for anyone to countervail the Catholic church.

The Liberals favored foreign colonization in order to break the Catholic church's power and also to refurbish a bankrupt national treasury. As early as 1862, Mexico's government had encouraged its citizens to colonize unoccupied northern lands in order to improve the national economy and combat American encroachment. However, since the first such attempts were unrewarding, the Liberals began around 1875 to look for foreigners—mainly Europeans and Americans—to settle northern Mexican lands. This "philosophical positivism"[10] argued for Mexico's need for new blood to break the traditional Mexican power brokers' hold and to build a dynamic commercial and industrial economy.[11] Argentina, the United States, Australia, New Zealand, Canada, and Brazil had been doing it with immigrants.[12] Why not Mexico?

The government encouraged the settlement and redistribution of unoccupied public lands by giving one-third of a tract of land to any individual or colonization company that would survey it properly. In May of 1875, scarcely four months before Mormon missionaries left Salt Lake City for Mexico, the legislature authorized the government to contract with foreign and domestic colonization companies to bring in foreign immigrants. It was a happy day for the Mormons.

The Mormon movement southward, the defeat of the Navajos, the new Mexican accessibility, the many Lamanites in Mexico, the distinct possibility that flourishing settlements could be established—all these things combined to encourage and enable the Mormons to venture into the southern republic. In 1874 Brigham Young asked Daniel W. Jones and Henry Brizzee to prepare themselves for a mission there.

In 1847, when he was only seventeen, Jones had crossed the Plains with volunteers from St. Louis, Missouri, to take part in the war with Mexico. He remained in Mexico for three years, learned enough Spanish to interpret for the army, and "indulge[d] in many of the wild and reckless ways of the people."[13] While he was traveling through Utah during the summer of 1850 on his way to the gold fields in California, he accidentally shot himself and was forced to recuperate that winter in Provo, Utah. There he met Mormons who impressed him. He studied the Mormon faith and on 27 January 1851 was baptized.

Jones was a controversial figure who, in his role as a principal Mormon contact with the Indians, frequently defended them and chastised other Anglo–American Mormons for not following through on the Book of Mormon's mandate to teach them the gospel. Brigham Young especially liked him. But he was abrasive enough that twice attempts were made to deprive him of his membership in the church and, in 1857, after he was ordained to the Mormon priesthood office of seventy, Brigham Young himself had to intercede to get the Provo group to admit him.[14]

Reflecting upon the assignment President Young had given Brizzee and himself, Jones thought it would not be easy. He had fought in the Mexican—American War; he remembered Mexico's religious situation of a quarter century earlier and dreaded speaking against the Catholic church in Mexico. Yet, obediently, he concluded: "This mission has to be commenced by someone, and if it is necessary for the extreme sacrifice to be made, just as well to be me as anyone else."[15]

Both Brizzee and Jones had a working knowledge of Spanish. President Young told them to perfect that knowledge and to translate the scriptures and other documents to take with them on their mission. (Apparently Parley P. Pratt had never completed that task.) But neither Jones nor Brizzee felt especially certain about what to do. Several months' struggle did not build their confidence much—nor did stories of Pratt's experiences twenty-four years earlier in Chile. All Brigham Young had told them was to get ready for their mission by studying Spanish and by translating. But how?

A Philippine immigrant, Melitón González Trejo, soon provided the answer. Trejo, a well-educated former Spanish Army officer stationed in the Philippines for several years, had recently arrived in Salt Lake City. He had been praying for answers to his religious questions and said he had been informed in a dream that he would find his answers by going to Salt Lake City and seeing the Mormons. After resigning his commission he sold his property and set out for Utah, where, looking for someone who spoke Spanish, he met Brizzee. Jones quickly enlisted him to translate the documents President Young had ordered.[16]

They began work at once on approximately one hundred pages of selected Book of Mormon passages. By the end of May 1875, however, Brizzee had withdrawn from the project because (according to Jones) of a disagreement with Brigham Young.[17] And both Jones and Trejo were out of money. Discouraged, Jones visited President Young in June 1875 and explained what both he and Trejo had done and why they could do no more. While there were no church funds for the project, President Young did authorize the men to solicit donations to finance it. If that didn't work, he would see it through with his own personal funds.[18] He advised Jones and Trejo to complete the printing of their hundred-page selection from the Book of Mormon so they could begin their mission in September, before the heavy snows. With five hundred dollars of donated money, they printed fifteen hundred copies of the *Trozos Selectos del Libro de Mormón.*[19]

In late summer and early autumn of 1875, Brigham Young called five other elders—Helaman Pratt, James Z. Stewart, Anthony W. Ivins, Robert H. Smith, and Ammon M. Tenney—to accompany

Daniel Jones to Mexico.[20] Jones also decided to take his teenaged son, Wiley, with him. Only two of the missionaries, Daniel Jones and Ammon Tenney, spoke Spanish.

It must have been an unnerving experience. Just before the missionaries were to take a train to California and from there a steamer to Mexico's west coast, Brigham Young contacted them. Would they mind traveling by horseback, he asked, and going not to California and Mexico City as planned, but south through Arizona to the Mexican state of Sonora? (A round trip of nearly 3,000 miles!) President Young asked them to look for places to settle along the way and to teach the gospel to the Indians. Combined exploration, colonization, and preaching had worked in Utah Territory; now they would try them in Mexico. The missionaries quickly altered their plans.

Brigham Young was concerned about refuge again. The early months of 1875 had brought intense persecution from the federal government and from other non-Mormons over plural marriage. In March President Young was imprisoned for contempt of court. In April George Reynolds was convicted and sentenced for unlawful cohabitation; his appeal was pending when Jones and his party left Utah. James Z. Stewart later recalled that when Orson Pratt (Parley P. Pratt's brother) formally blessed the missionaries before they left, he seemed to feel some foreboding, telling the elders, "I wish you to look out for places where our brethren could go and be safe from harm in the event that persecution should make it necessary for them to get out of the way for a season."[21]

Jones, his son Wiley, Robert H. Smith, James Z. Stewart, and Helaman Pratt (Parley P. Pratt's son) loaded up their thirty horses and pack mules with provisions and their precious translated literature and left Nephi, Utah, in September 1875. Ammon M. Tenney and Anthony W. Ivins (age twenty-three) joined the expedition at Toquerville and Kanab, Utah, respectively. The journey lasted ten months and took them nearly three thousand miles—all by horseback.[22] Mormons in settlement after settlement along the southern route greeted the traveling missionaries enthusiastically, contributing food and clothing, provisions, and more animals, and giving advice, counsel, and encouragement. Clearly, they considered this effort particularly important.[23]

But Brigham Young had still more to say about the nature of the mission. In a telegram delivered by an Indian runner who overtook the missionary party outside of Kanab, he asked the missionaries to explore Arizona's Salt River Valley (present-day Phoenix) as a possible settlement site. The missionaries did, of course, explore and report; Mesa, Arizona, colonized by Mormons, is one of the results. They also visited and preached to the Pueblo and Zuñi Indians of Arizona and New Mexico. For this kind of missionary work Tenney was as suited as Jones; he had been with the 1851 wagon train of Mormons who settled San Bernardino, California, learned Spanish there, and spent years with Jacob Hamblin as an interpreter among the Indians.[24]

In Tucson, Arizona, the missionaries heard about fresh and furious Yaqui Indian wars in Sonora.[25] The Yaquis, who for more than two centuries had resisted first the Spaniards and now the Mexicans, simply would not submit. The missionaries were told there was no safe passage for anyone in the area. Since they had intended to explore and preach in Sonora, this news was troubling. While thinking the matter over for several days, they took advantage of Arizona Governor Anson Pacely Killen Safford's cordial invitation to preach in the Tucson courthouse. Safford encouraged them to bring Mormon colonists to Arizona.

"We want to go to Mexico and see what can be done," Jones wrote. "We hear terrible reports from there. People tell us that our lives are worth nothing. There is war going on. We will keep moving along and trust in God to protect us and leave His Spirit to tell us when to stop."[26] They turned east toward Franklin, Texas, finally crossing from there into Mexico's El Paso del Norte (present-day Ciudad Juárez, in the state of Chihuahua) after nearly four months of travel, exploration, and preaching to the Indians and others along the way.

The mood of the missionaries, who were received warmly and without delay by Mexican customs officials (thanks to La Reforma), changed momentarily to one of exuberance. They had brought the gospel once again to Israel in the Western Hemisphere, ending the twenty-five-year hiatus since Parley P. Pratt's efforts in Chile. Surely, now, among Lehi's descendants, the faith would take root and grow.

The missionaries' euphoria vanished as they quickly sensed El Paso del Norte's political and religious tensions. Local priests warned their congregations not to listen to the Mormons and to bring the missionaries' literature to them, without reading it, so they could destroy it. Given the relatively small amount of literature the horses and pack mules could carry, such procedures could have quickly unburdened the missionaries of all their cargo. But Jones instructed them to hold tightly on to their Book of Mormon selections until they discovered the best way to reach people.

The first major confrontation came on a Sunday, three days after the missionaries' arrival, while they attended Catholic services in El Paso del Norte. After the mass the officiating priest, Padre Borajo, warned the people vigorously and emotionally about the Mormons. From Borajo's perspective, Satan himself had entered Mexico:

> Now of all the plagues that ever visited the earth to curse and destroy mankind we have the worst just come to us and there stand the representatives of this plague. Look at them. Their faces show what they are.
>
> Thanks to God we have been warned in time by the Holy Pope that false prophets and teachers would come among us. These men represent all that is low and depraved. They have destroyed the morals of their own people, and have now come here to pollute the people of this place. They have no virtue. They all have from six to one dozen wives. Now they have come here to extend the practice into Mexico. I denounce them. Yes, here in the presence of the image of the Virgin Mary, I denounce them as barbarians. And I want you all to get their books and fetch them to me and I will burn them.[27]

Not only had the Juárez Liberals attacked the Catholic church politically, but now they had opened the borders to people such as the Mormons who were polluting the country's religion. During the priest's exhortation a large crowd gathered in the entryway and the adjoining courtyard to listen. As the Mormon elders attempted to leave the cathedral, the crowd blocked their way. The moment was tense. Jones wrote, "I began to feel as though it would be best for us to get out of the crowd before the Spirit got too high, as some fanatic might be tempted to slip a sharp knife in among our ribs. We managed to work ourselves gradually out of the crowd which filled the door yard for several feet. When clear we walked straight way to our quarters."[28] Once inside, the elders prepared a report to send to Brigham Young.

The whole city now knew who the Mormons were. As the elders walked through the streets, the women fled or eyed them suspiciously from peepholes in the doors of their houses. And there were the epithets and occasional stone-throwings that had frequently greeted Mormons elsewhere.

Robert H. Smith and Ammon M. Tenney concluded very quickly that not many precious souls would enter the church in El Paso del Norte. Even though Brigham Young had cautioned them against baptizing just yet, requiring only that they explore and preach, they soon became discouraged with Mexico. Politico–religious tensions from La Reforma and the Indian wars to the west in Sonora did not bode well for their efforts.

Disheartened, Smith and Tenney began also to resent Daniel Jones. It seemed that his way was the only right way to do anything. Jones and Smith had quarreled when Jones had obligated Smith to maintain a night watch to avoid having their animals stolen. A special meeting had been held to iron out differences between the two men. Jones told Smith he was a liar and that he should pack up and go home. Smith insisted on finishing his mission, but not in Jones's company. The other elders told Jones he was also treating them harshly and asked him to be more considerate.[29] Personal and political tensions increased and compounded. Tenney and Smith were also, according to some, alarmed at what might happen to them in Mexico. Their anxiety, coupled with Jones's leadership style, sent them packing; they finally asked to be released from Jones's jurisdiction so they could complete their mission among the Pueblo and Zuñi Indians of New Mexico.[30] These Indians had expressed interest in the Mormon message; certainly they seemed more promising than the people of El Paso del Norte. Tenney's departure left Jones as the only missionary able to speak Spanish with the Mexicans.

Smith and Tenney were only partly correct about the Mexican environment. They saw that the missionaries would get nowhere in El Paso del Norte, but they mistakenly assumed that a similar fate awaited them elsewhere in Mexico. Jones, however, suspected rightly that there were greener pastures farther south.

Since the animals were in poor condition, it was unwise to press south right away. So Helaman Pratt and James Z. Stewart returned with most of the animals to Franklin, Texas, to spend the winter where fodder was cheaper. The Joneses and Ivins, who had remained in Mexico, decided to set up a saddlery in El Paso del Norte—a service the city obviously needed and one for which

Jones was skilled. Brigham Young had presented him with a new set of saddlemaking tools before the elders had left Utah, no doubt foreseeing a need such as this.

The three missionaries earned their keep from the saddlery. Even Padre Borajo, impressed by the fine workmanship on the saddles, commissioned the elders to make him two. The missionaries made friends—including the chief political officer, Pablo Paladio, a Liberal who had at first been difficult to deal with. Paladio controlled access to the public because he had authority to grant permission to hold religious meetings; he refused the elders' requests at first but was at last won over by their exemplary conduct. Paladio finally offered the elders a letter of introduction to the governor of the state. On the whole, however, the missionaries maintained a low profile, studied their Spanish, and prepared for further work in Mexico.

Eventually they realized that the Liberals' political attacks on the Catholic church had affected many people. All this was new to Jones despite his previous experience in Mexico. The American visitors soon found that although there were not too many Liberals in El Paso del Norte, those who were there sought the elders out and wished them well. Through these contacts the missionaries discovered a natural alliance between themselves and the Liberals. Both were interested in religious freedom, in Mexican development, in the Indians; and both considered the Catholic church a hindrance. The missionaries quickly learned that individuals who failed to kneel or doff their hats when passing a cathedral (an insolent omission that would have occasioned public outcry, perhaps even jailing, twenty-five years earlier) could be considered friends.[31] "We kept our eyes open for [them]," wrote Jones, "as we were always safe with them."[32]

In early March, nearly two months after Jones and his two companions entered Mexico, they received a letter from Brigham Young expressing his approval of them and offering counsel:

> I feel that it would be wise for you to visit the old original blood as much as possible. Let the Catholic church alone; if its members wish to hear the truth, expound it to them as to any other people, but do not debate with them. . . . Be cautious in your labors and movements; do not court opposition, but move steadily on, presenting the truths of the gospel to those who will hear you, and inviting

23

all to become partakers of the gospel of the Son of God. You have
the faith and prayers of all that you will be able to do a good work,
and I have no doubt but that you will see me again in the flesh
yet many times.[33]

After they received this letter, the missionaries visited some
of the nearby haciendas and ranching estates that employed large
numbers of Indians. But the clergy watched their movements
carefully even outside El Paso del Norte. Moreover, the ranch
owners told the Indians they would expel anyone who listened
to the Mormons.[34] In spite of La Reforma, the interest-marriage
of clergy and landowners remained intact in the Mexican north.
While the Indians hoped for release, for the time being there was
nothing either they or the missionaries could do to effect it. So
the elders bided their time, fattened their animals, studied
Spanish, and worked to pay their bills.

Brigham Young's letter also contained a troubling note. Federal
pressures on Utah polygamists were increasing. President Young
mentioned that he had been imprisoned again for a short while
and that many of the church's leaders were under severe duress.[35]
He also emphasized the importance of exploring well for settlement locations. Should the Mormons be driven out again they
would need to know where to go.

In mid-March Stewart and Pratt rejoined Ivins and Jones and
his son in El Paso del Norte as planned, and on 20 March 1876
they all departed for the interior of Chihuahua. They distributed
several copies of their Book of Mormon selections as they preached
the gospel in various settlements along the way. Passing through
Carrizal and El Carmen—the latter located in a large valley with
abundant water and fertile soil, and suitable for settlement[36]—they
proceeded to Chihuahua City, arriving on 12 April. The Liberals
held political power in Chihuahua City, and Governor Ochoa
readily gave the missionaries permission to hold the first Latter-
day Saint meeting in Mexico.

Chihuahua City authorities furnished them with the Zaragoza
Theatre, which was, aside from the local cathedral, the largest
public gathering place in the city. The missionaries had hand-
bills printed advertising their Sunday afternoon meeting. As soon
as the very popular cockfights were over, Jones arose to address
an audience of about five hundred, some attending because of

24

his announcement, others because curiosity prompted them to remain following the cockfights. Since this was the first public Mormon meeting in Mexico, the media coverage is of interest:

> A few days ago a remarkable event attracted the attention of the public of this place. Daniel W. Jones, a prominent Mormon Apostle, had printed and distributed handbills announcing that he would preach a sermon on Mormonism at the Zaragoza Theatre. Rumors that Mr. Jones and his co-laborers would be stoned [*apedreados*] incited us to attend the meeting. The audience present was very large, and at first complete order reigned. The preaching commenced in the midst of profound silence, which was evidence that the audience was interested. After a little while a few discontented persons commenced to initiate disorder by throwing small stones and pieces of wood at where the speaker stood, but they had few imitators and were frowned down by the good judgment of the majority. The lecture was not very interesting, the audience diverted itself principally by contemplating the constant struggle of the orator with the difficulties of the Spanish language. The performance concluded with a heterogeneous mixture of applause and hisses.[37]

Nevertheless, contacts multiplied as the missionaries approached those who passed by the cathedral without taking off their hats.[38] Almost without exception the Liberals expressed much interest in the Book of Mormon. Jones attributed this to their renewed pride in Mexico's Indian heritage stimulated by La Reforma and Benito Juárez, the movement's chief architect and indefatigable defender.

With kindly assistance from the Chihuahua City postal authorities—some of whom donated their own time to help package the Book of Mormon selections—the elders sent five hundred copies of the selections to prominent men in nearly one hundred of Mexico's major cities. Jones's cover letter informed the recipients of where they could obtain more information and invited them to consider the book's message carefully. Since most of the copies would probably fall into the hands of Liberals, the missionaries expected that their message would not go unnoticed; they spent the rest of their three weeks in Chihuahua City preaching the gospel to whoever would listen and inquiring about possible settlement sites.

While the elders were preaching and distributing literature, Governor Ochoa invited them to his office several times. Having heard of Mormon accomplishments in the Utah desert, he viewed the Mormons as prospective colonizers in Chihuahua. He was solicitous of their welfare, and he wanted them to be completely informed about the availability of suitable land. It was true, he said, that the Mexican government offered lands to prospective colonizers, but there was a problem: the government had no really good lands to offer. All the best tracts were already secured by old grants with perfectly legal titles. Tell Brigham Young, the governor said, that if the Mormon people want to colonize in Chihuahua they should expect to buy lands from private individuals; they should not allow themselves to be swayed by any offers from the Mexican government. The offers look good on paper, and the government may do all it can, but beware.[39]

Leaving Chihuahua City, and having heard that there were many Indians in the mountains, the missionary party traveled west toward the Sierra Madre foothills.[40] They encountered no clerical opposition when they arrived six days later at Concepción de Guerrero. The town's only priest was cooperative, the people were not devoted Catholics, and the chief political officer readily granted them permission to preach and even offered to protect them if necessary. The missionaries rented a house adjacent to a large hall and began arranging meetings. At the first one held in Guerrero, on Sunday, 23 April, Jones preached a sermon on the "United Order," a term Mormons apply to their own unique though unsuccessful attempt at communitarian living. Francisco Rubio, a local man who had become acquainted with the missionaries and their message, explained the Book of Mormon to those in attendance that day and related its account of Christ's visit to the Americas. Jones later wrote, "[Rubio] really understood and believed the Book of Mormon; as once in the meeting he took it in his hand and explained it in a more lucid manner, especially the part relating to the Savior's appearance on this continent, than I had ever heard before. Individually, I received new light from the native."[41]

The elders held more meetings, and the people of Guerrero liked what they heard. Some of the elders visited Arísiachic, a large Tarahumara Indian settlement in the mountains west of Guerrero. After they had told the chief about their message, he gathered his people together to listen to the elders. The Indians seemed pleased with the doctrine they heard and asked the missionaries to return. The elders left several copies of the Book of Mormon selections, and the chief assigned two young men to study them. Jones was so impressed with this visit—which reaffirmed his conviction concerning the church's mission to the Lamanites—that ten years later he wrote:

> From what I have seen now and then among the natives I sometimes think that the people called Latter-day Saints are only half converted. I have seen and felt more warmth of spirit and faith manifested by natives than I ever saw by white Saints. Even the Apaches told me that they would not wait long for the winding up scene, when they once had power and authority from God to act in His name. That faith, which will yet remove the powers of evil from around the Saints, will come largely from the remnants. I think we will need them in our work and should be looking after them some little and not altogether after money.[42]

Spending a day with the Tarahumaras and then returning to their base at Guerrero, in the next three weeks the elders found many people who expressed profound faith in the Book of Mormon's authenticity and also a strong desire for the Mormons to come and live among them.[43]

With Lamanites from all areas virtually clamoring for their message and their association, should the elders extend their visit? Some of them thought not. After several vigorous discussions, Jones reluctantly decided to cut the mission short and return to Utah. Several factors may have influenced this decision.[44] First, the missionaries' financial resources were almost certainly meager. Throughout their mission they depended on small sums Brigham Young sent them. Even with Daniel Jones's earnings from the saddlery, the missionaries had been unable to pay their debts in El Paso del Norte and had delayed their journey southward until they received additional money from President Young. Pratt and Stewart's wintering in the United States, where fodder for their horses was cheaper, only bought them time. In Chihuahua City they had lived on credit amply supplied by the Liberals. Yet before leaving for Guerrero they were obliged to sell one of their horses to pay their bills. At Guerrero one friendly store owner, Eselso González, seeing their plight, refused payment for the meeting hall they had rented from him and for items they had purchased on credit from his store. He even insisted on giving them additional provisions for their journey, softening his largess with the obvious lie that he could not sell the goods anyway.

Second, there was still conflict among the elders. Indeed, during part of the return trip to Utah Jones would travel alone, refusing even to share mealtime with the other elders. For their part, his companions reported that Jones was tyrannical and unfair. And since Jones was the only one who spoke enough Spanish to preach, confer with government officials, or even carry on ordinary daily conversation with the Mexicans, the other elders' ineffectuality may have contributed to their own—and Jones's—impatience and frustration. Jones continued to demand secure night watches, which kept the elders constantly tired and sometimes even exhausted. He felt justified when, while camped at a watering hole (Cantarracio) between El Paso del Norte and Chihuahua City, the elders were delayed two days tracking down their stolen horses.

A third reason Jones's companions pressed him to depart early from Guerrero was that, following Brigham Young's last-minute suggestion not to baptize or found branches, they felt they should get on with their itinerant preaching. This was an era of published proclamations, mass meetings, and public announcements—not the modern door-by-door missionary contact with individual families and groups. These elders saw themselves as ambassadors to a whole nation rather than as teachers of individuals. They considered themselves to be emissaries of the Lord, preparing the way for others by preaching, distributing literature, and making friends. Not even the five hundred potential new Mormons in Guerrero were enough to persuade them to stay on.[45]

Finally, perhaps the most important reason to leave Guerrero was the missionaries' eagerness to report to Brigham Young about the possibility of founding colonies in Mexico. Not only had they found some promising sites, they also had concluded unanimously that before the Mormon church could make very much progress among the Mexicans, Mormons would have to establish colonies in Mexico in order to teach new members the Mormon way of life.[46] They also had the refuge question in mind, which had taken on some urgency given all that was happening back in Utah

Territory. Some of the elders believed that not only would colonies be founded in Mexico but eventually the entire church would be driven there, thus fulfilling Book of Mormon prophesies that converted Gentiles would be numbered with the descendants of Lehi. With the pressures in Utah—Brigham being arrested from time to time and others being harassed—the idea became more and more attractive to the missionaries. Brigham Young's approval of their report confirmed to them the correctness of returning home.[47]

Leaving Guerrero on about the first of May, they traveled northward to Tejolócachic and from there to the mountain villages of Mátachic and Temósachic (both of which have Mormon congregations today), where the villagers received them kindly and welcomed copies of the *Trozos Selectos del Libro de Mormón*. Tomás Tribosa of Mátachic arranged for a congregation to gather in his home, and at Temósachic even the village priest, who was looking for new information about Jesus Christ, welcomed them and called a large number of people together to hear them preach. Many gladly received the Book of Mormon's message. When they returned to Tejolócachic, the missionaries met with equally enthusiastic audiences. Upon the elders' departure the Indians gave them so much corn and beans that they could not carry all the food on their pack animals.

Two days later the missionaries arrived at Namaquipe and camped outside town near a large ranch house, where they purchased meat and left a copy of the *Trozos Selectos*. That evening the master of the ranch house came to the elders' camp. Jones's narrative gives his name as Francisco Vásquez, who said his age was 103. The man's wife had given him the book the elders had left. "I have been reading this book," he told them. "I understand it and know who you are. You are apostles of Jesus Christ, just the same as Peter, James and John, and I know it. And I also know this book is true." Turning to his wife, who had accompanied him to the elders' camp, he continued: "Wife, have I not been telling our neighbors for two years past that apostles having the true gospel would come to this land, and that I would live to see them?"[48] The man said he wanted to be baptized but the elders declined, convinced that they should not do so until Mormon settlements could be established among the people. (The elders seem to have considered such settlements imminent.)

Leaving the foothills and mountains of the Sierra Madre with its people so anxious to hear the Mormon gospel, the missionaries proceeded north through El Valle and into the Casas Grandes Valley that today embraces the Mormon communities of Colonia Dublán and Colonia Juárez. The farther north they proceeded the less inclined the inhabitants were to listen. As they approached Casas Grandes, the people seemed more and more influenced by advance warnings of the missionaries' approach. So the elders again turned primarily to exploring for possible colonization sites.

Arriving in Casas Grandes on 12 May, they found the Apaches at war with the townspeople.[49] Yet the elders explored the area carefully, asking about various tracts of land and the title problems and water rights associated with them, and taking many notes from which to make their report to Brigham Young. They concluded that the area around Casas Grandes was the most desirable place they had seen for establishing colonies.

Three days after they arrived in Casas Grandes they purchased supplies and continued on, camping that evening at Corralitos. The following day they crossed the frontier into the United States and from there pushed on to Salt Lake City, exploring and noting their observations along the way.

In Mexico the mountain villages received the Mormon message well, much more favorably than the cities. It would be that way for more than three generations, quite contrary to the pattern that later would be set in every other Latin American country. The three decades of sparring between Liberals and Conservatives in Mexico's cities had hardened the Conservatives' position, making them virtually unapproachable by the missionaries. The Liberals, for their part, members of the nascent reformist middle class, were pursuing their own political religion and were interested in Mormons more as potential political allies and developers than as bearers of an intrinsically valuable spiritual message. But the Indians, long under the yoke of traditional Mexico, were now influenced by Juárez reformist ideology that endowed them with a new dignity and hope that thrived on the promises to the Lamanites contained in the Book of Mormon.

Further Missionary and Exploratory Movements into Mexico:
The Push of Political Turmoil in Utah Territory

Brigham Young was sufficiently pleased with the missionaries' July 1876 report that within a month he called Daniel Jones to return to the Casas Grandes region with a colonizing company.

To the question of whom President Young should call to accompany him, Jones replied, "Give me men with large families and small means, so that when we get there they will be too poor to come back, and we will have to stay." Brigham's final instructions were to go to Mexico or southern Arizona and settle "where we felt impressed to stop."[50] They decided to make their first settlement in the Salt River Valley of southern Arizona, which Jones had explored the year before en route to Mexico. Although they stopped short of Mexico, the new colonists clearly intended to push on later.

Along the Salt River, at a place the settlers named Camp Utah, they built their cabins and attempted to set up a mission among the Maricopa Indians. In due time some of the Indians, responding to Jones's missionary overtures, came and asked to live with the colonists in their settlements. However, Book of Mormon prophecies notwithstanding, the Indians' eating and bathing customs were too shocking for some of the Anglo–American families, and the whole affair fell apart. Apparently only Jones could tolerate the Indians at close proximity. The colony split up over the issue before it could generate enough strength to push on into Mexico. Indeed, one faction actually petitioned the territorial authorities to drive the Indians out of the area. "It was not long until it became manifest," Jones wrote, "that I would have to either give up the Indians or lose my standing with the white brethren. I chose the natives. . . ."[51]

Despite the considerable prospects of failure, Brigham Young continued the southern expansion, calling colonists to settle in Arizona.[52] Simultaneously he continued the proselyting and exploring of Mexico. While he had been pleased with the 1876 Chihuahua missionaries' report, he wanted more information, especially about Sonora. The Yaqui wars had prevented the first missionaries to Mexico from entering Sonora, so they had moved eastward to Chihuahua. Yet only from the Indians in the western

31

Sierra Madre Mountains bordering Sonora had the missionaries felt complete acceptance. There were also large numbers of Indians in most of Sonora. Another excursion into Mexico would therefore have to be made before Brigham Young could settle his mind about the country and the Indians in it.

For some time, President Young had considered Sonora a possible colonizing site from which to launch missionary labors among the Indians. Intriguing reports continued to filter down from members of the Mormon Battalion who had been in Sonora during the Mexican–American War.[53] And, in 1872, Colonel Thomas L. Kane, one of the Mormons' most famous non-Mormon friends who had helped immeasurably in securing a peaceful settlement to the Utah War, visited Utah again.[54] He and Brigham Young discussed Sonora once more as an area for missionary and colonization activity; their later correspondence emphasized colonization.[55]

For several years Brigham Young's southern movement had given rise to speculation in the local and eastern press about Mormon designs on Mexico. Indeed, rumors began flying soon after Jones and Brizzee's 1874 mission call.[56] Non-Mormons in Utah Territory continued to press the Saints on the matter. In a vibrant sermon at a general conference of the church held in St. George, Utah, on 6 April 1877, Brigham Young unloaded exasperatedly:

> It has been the cry of late, through the columns of the newspapers, that the "Mormons" are going to Mexico! That is quite right, we calculate to go there. Are we going back to Jackson County [Missouri]? Yes. When? As soon as the way opens up. . . . We intend to hold our own here, and also penetrate the north and the south, the east and the west . . . and to raise the ensign of truth. This is the work of God, that marvelous work and a wonder referred to by ancient men of God, who saw it in its incipiency, as a stone cut out of the mountains without hands, but which rolled and gathered strength and magnitude until it filled the whole earth. We will continue to grow, to increase and spread abroad, and the powers of the earth and hell combined cannot hinder it.[57]

While the Mormons' intentions were to expand the Kingdom everywhere, given the time, Mexico might also be something special—a place of refuge. Thus, Brigham Young's disclaimers aside, missionary and colonizing activity continued in the South.

Jones's colonization company had just left; others would follow, as would additional exploratory missionary groups.

By September of 1876, President Young had another group of missionaries ready to explore Sonora.[58] The new party, including James Z. Stewart and his companion Helaman Pratt from the original Chihuahua missionary party, waited until after the October general church conference in Salt Lake City to begin their long journey.

Accompanying Stewart and Pratt were Stewart's brother, Isaac, and George Terry, Louis Garff, and Melitón Trejo, the translator whose *Trozos Selectos* the first missionaries had taken to Mexico. Finally reaching Tucson, they split into two groups. Pratt and Trejo proceeded south to Hermosillo, the capital of Sonora, where they proselyted for a time and baptized the first five members of the Mormon church in Mexico. Pratt and Trejo thereafter returned to their homes.

For their part, the Stewart brothers, Terry, and Garff entered the mountains of Sonora and attempted to proselyte the Yaqui Indians. The Yaquis, they thought, might be able to open up tremendous opportunities among the Lamanites in Sonora. These Indians were proud, stalwart, and indomitable in defense of their families and territory; neither the Spaniards, French, nor Mexicans had ever conquered them. They had permanent homes, lived in large communities, and worked a rich mine—the gold from which they reportedly traded for guns at Douglas, Arizona, to fight the Mexicans.[59] The missionary party entered Sonora fully aware that the Yaquis were at war with Mexico again, as they frequently had been since before the days of Maximilian. Although at this time the battles were particularly fierce,[60] the elders' commitment and their faith overrode their fear. Surely, they reasoned, God would protect them.

The Yaquis' practice was to take all aliens, including non-Yaqui Mexicans, and execute them if it appeared that they had the slightest attachment to Mexico's aggressive policies against them. From the Yaqui perspective, all that aliens had done for more than a century was rape their women, kill and enslave their men, leave their children homeless and parentless, and rob Yaquis everywhere of their property. No amount of commitment to the missionary cause or talk about Book of Mormon prophecies or the redemption of the Lamanites could break through such barriers. The Yaquis detained and bound the missionaries, tormented them, and were about to kill them when a Yaqui head man intervened. He told the elders that he would spare their lives but that they should leave Yaqui territory at once and not return. Next time he might not be around to rescue them.[61]

Stewart and his company quickly returned to the United States, moving along the border from the Tucson area over to El Paso del Norte, where Stewart had been the year before with Daniel Jones. Gordon Irving, who has collected numerous oral histories about Mormonism in Latin America, records a most interesting episode:

> When they got to El Paso they contacted a Mr. J. W. Campbell, who was a miller and owned a store at San Elizario, which is down the Rio Grande from El Paso a little ways. They had apparently met him the year before. Campbell was interested both in Mormonism and in colonization in Mexico. He proposed at this point, 1877, to buy a large tract of land in the eastern part of the state of Coahuila, somewhere near the Texas border. So Stewart wrote to Brigham Young making this proposition to him, but Brigham wrote back that he would prefer a site somewhat closer to the already established settlements in Arizona. Brigham died shortly thereafter, Stewart and company returned to Utah, and the matter was dropped, leaving the initiative for Mexican colonization with the Jones settlement back in Arizona.[62]

The 1879 Expedition to Mexico City

While all these forays into northern Mexico were occurring, news of Mormonism was sparking comment in Mexico City. Two of the Book of Mormon pamphlets that the Daniel Jones party had mailed out in 1876 when they were in Chihuahua City fell into the hands of influential people in Mexico City who were sufficiently impressed to respond. One was Ignacio Manuel Altamirano, the master of letters of nineteenth-century Mexico. An Indian who had started studying Spanish at age sixteen and thereafter mastered it, he was highly receptive not only to the pro-Indian Liberal rhetoric but also to the Mormons' beliefs about the Lamanites' historical importance. Mormon eschatology regarding the Lamanites' future did not go unnoticed either. Altamirano wrote a letter to Salt Lake City thanking the authorities for the book and requesting to know more about the Mormon message.[63]

Later, Dr. Plotino C. Rhodakanaty—who is considered by some Mexicans to be a father of their country's socialist, agrarian, and syndicalist movements as well as a leading thinker whose ideas on freedom and liberty helped to precipitate the Mexican revolution of 1910—also began to correspond with the Mormons.[64] Rhodakanaty, too, had received one of the Book of Mormon pamphlets. Somehow he had learned of Melitón Trejo, who at the time was living in southeastern Arizona with some of the Camp Utah settlers who had moved on when they could not tolerate Jones's decisions on how and where to include the Indians in their original Salt River Valley settlement. Early in 1878, Rhodakanaty wrote to Trejo at Tres Alamos, saying that he wanted to learn more about the Mormon church.[65] For a time he and Trejo wrote back and forth about the matter. Finally, Trejo wrote to President John Taylor, who had led the church since Brigham Young's death in 1877, and included some of Rhodakanaty's letters.[66]

As early as the autumn of 1878, John Taylor sent Rhodakanaty several publications.[67] Soon Salt Lake City authorities learned that their Mexican correspondent had interested many of his fellow citizens in Mormonism, indicating that between fifteen and twenty now believed in the Mormon gospel. Thereafter, Rhodakanaty first requested, then virtually demanded that he and his friends be baptized. "We've found the gospel," he said, "and we want you to give us the Aaronic priesthood [the lesser of the two Mormon priesthoods] so we can begin proselyting in Mexico."[68] A return letter from Salt Lake City informed him that this would occur only if missionaries were sent to Mexico City. Thereafter, during 1879, Rhodakanaty sent many letters asking for missionaries and promising a great response when they should be sent.

Sending missionaries to Mexico City—an idea Brigham Young had first entertained when he called the original missionaries to Mexico in 1874—now seemed appropriate. John Taylor thought highly of James Z. Stewart, by then a veteran missionary and Spanish speaker, and called him to head south. President Taylor asked Melitón Trejo to accompany him.

Whether Trejo was pleased with this new call we do not know, but he delayed his trip from southern Arizona to Salt Lake City. This, and polygamist President Taylor's move underground to avoid federal marshals, allowed the governing Quorum of Twelve Apostles time to rethink the new mission to Mexico. Given Mexico City's dramatic interest in the church, the apostles concluded that this important mission deserved leadership with higher authority than either Stewart or Trejo held. The church might be on the brink of a major breakthrough in Mexico.

Accordingly, the Quorum sent newly ordained Apostle Moses Thatcher to preside over this proselyting venture. Elder James Z. Stewart joined him at Chicago, and Melitón Trejo at New Orleans. The party took a steamer, crossed the Gulf of Mexico, and reached Veracruz on 14 November 1879. Two days later they arrived in Mexico City and lodged in the principal hotel, the Iturbide.

Thatcher and his companions became convinced after only four days that Rhodakanaty and one of his friends should be baptized. Accordingly, on 20 November 1879, Moses Thatcher baptized Plotino Rhodakanaty and Silviano Arteaga. Three days later Trejo baptized six more. Of these, four were given the Mormon priesthood, three of those being made elders.[69] A congregation was organized and Rhodakanaty called to preside over it, with Silviano Arteaga and José Ybarola as his counselors.

At the meeting in which these Mormon ordinances and appointments were performed, Moses Thatcher prayed for blessings upon Porfirio Díaz, president of Mexico since the close of La Reforma in 1876, upon all political authorities, upon all government personnel, and upon all the Mexican people, to the end that the Mormon gospel would flourish among all people in Mexico, Central America, and South America. The missionaries also made some important governmental contacts. During the troublesome years ahead, several of these contacts would help protect the Latter-day Saints in Mexico.

The missionaries became very busy. By the end of 1879 they had baptized sixteen persons. Trejo and Stewart translated more Mormon literature. Then, during January of 1880, they completed their translation of Parley P. Pratt's *A Voice of Warning* and readied it for the printer, and they wrote numerous articles for the local newspapers as well.

The eastern press in the United States continued to speculate about the Mormons' southern movements. When the New York City *Sun* published an article about the mission to Mexico, many

Mexico City papers excerpted portions of it, commenting rather favorably. But the newspaper *Two Republics*, under the headings of "Yankee Diplomacy," "Filibusterism," and "The Spread of Mormonism," vigorously attacked the Mormon people in general and specifically the events in Mexico City. Through *El Tribuna*, Thatcher attempted to refute the *Two Republics*'s accusations.[70]

The newspaper exchange created some interest among upper-class Mexicans and foreigners in Mexico City. Curious about the Mormons' intent, they opened doors to further interviews with higher Mexican authorities. The elders met with Foreign Minister Zárate, Minister of Public Works and Colonization Fernández Leal, and Minister of War Carlos Pacheco, all officials who had already been acquainted with some aspect of the Mormon experience. They cordially encouraged Thatcher to bring his people and settle in Mexico. Leal, who had visited Utah and greatly admired the Mormons' ingenuity and prosperity, said that Mexico would gladly welcome them.[71]

As a consequence of the many interviews that resulted principally from the exchanges in the newspapers, Thatcher and his companions were also introduced to Emelio Biebuyck, an influential Belgian who was familiar with Utah affairs. Biebuyck had visited Utah Territory three times and had been personally acquainted with Brigham Young, having had several interviews with him. Biebuyck held a colonization contract with the Mexican government (in which the government conceded free public lands in any state for colonization) and warmly advocated Mormon colonization in Mexico. Given Thatcher's continuing interest in colonization, the two became fast friends.

Biebuyck told Thatcher that "with the Mormons in Mexico will come stable government and consequent peace and prosperity and, therefore, success to my business, and that is all I ask."[72] His colonization contract with the Mexican government not only included free public lands but also an $80 subsidy for adults; $40 each for children; twenty years' exemption for all immigrants from military duty and taxation; entry free from tariff duty on teams, wagons, agricultural implements, building materials, and provisions pending the establishment of the colony; and numerous other privileges.

Concurrently with all this stimulating talk of colonization, the missionary efforts in Mexico City began to take a turn for the worse. Among other things, the elders were becoming disillusioned with Rhodakanaty, who, rather than simply adopting Mormon ways as did most new Mormons, was attempting to assimilate Mexican Mormons into his own brand of communal living. Before long Thatcher began to agree with Daniel Jones's earlier conclusions that missionary efforts in Mexico would ultimately depend on a careful gathering of Mexican Saints into Mormon colonies so that the new members could be instructed properly. Biebuyck's colonization offer was therefore too appealing to lose. Scarcely two months after organizing the first branch in Mexico, Thatcher determined to lay this stimulating proposition before President Taylor and the Council of the Twelve.

On 4 February 1880, Thatcher left Stewart in charge and returned to Salt Lake City, arriving there on the twenty-second. Ten days later Biebuyck arrived as agreed, and he and Thatcher explained Biebuyck's contract in detail to the Mormon church authorities. After a lengthy discussion, and with due respect paid Thatcher's and Biebuyck's enormous efforts, the Mormon leaders rejected the offer. Perhaps they still remembered Governor Ochoa's cautionary note four years earlier: "Be careful about offers for public lands."

Although colonization for refuge had been on many people's minds, even as late as 1880 preaching the gospel was the prime objective; colonization was primarily a means to that end. By creating a Mexican Mormon community, Thatcher believed he would be moving God's work forward dramatically. Yet, departing somewhat from Brigham Young's earlier views, the new Mormon leaders felt that colonization in Mexico for this purpose was premature.

Perhaps at this point all Mexican ventures seemed of little moment compared to the problems confronting the Mormons in Utah Territory and Arizona. The antipolygamy crusade now threatened homes and entire communities. Many Latter-day Saints had fled to obscure retreats in Montana, Colorado, Nevada, and Arizona. George Q. Cannon, Utah's territorial delegate to Washington, was quoted in a New York City *Sun* interview as saying that Mormons "cannot move to any part of the territory of the United States, and they may be compelled either to abandon one feature of their religion or to fight."[73] While the idea of a "place of refuge" in Mexico had more than crossed Brigham

Young's mind, it evidently was not considered seriously by his successors. It now seemed that colonizing in Mexico for whatever purpose would have to await a resolution of the crisis at home.[74] All available resources had to be carefully preserved, lest collective energy be dissipated in the struggle.

While Moses Thatcher was in Salt Lake City presenting firm offers of Mexican land for colonization, Trejo and Stewart remained in Mexico City and continued their missionary labors. They completed a more extensive translation of the Book of Mormon and also began proselyting in the villages surrounding Mexico City, focusing on Ozumba, where they had some success. But, on the whole, their efforts were unrewarded. Trejo finally left Mexico City in May of 1880 for his home in Arizona, leaving Stewart the sole missionary from "Zion" (the Mormon settlements in Utah and Arizona).

After the Council of the Twelve rejected Thatcher's proposals, the apostle, accompanied by Feramorz L. Young, returned to Mexico City in December of 1880 to begin again. If colonization was not to be implemented, then they would have to find some other way to spread the gospel. Yet there was no hiding the fact that Thatcher was pessimistic about any other method.

The situation began to deteriorate quite rapidly. For one thing, Rhodakanaty now wanted to set up a Mormon "united order." Indeed, it was the Mormons' communitarianism that had first attracted him to the church. He acted as if he thought the Mormon gospel existed to serve the ideal of communitarianism, and when he could not persuade Thatcher to come over to his point of view he dropped out of the church. Most of the new members the elders had already baptized also dropped out for the same reasons. By 1881 Rhodakanaty was writing articles against the church in Mexico City's socialist newspapers.[75]

As their original flock dwindled away over the issue of communitarianism, Thatcher, Stewart, and Young turned their attention to proselyting others. But the era of La Reforma had ended and with it the political excitement that had aided earlier missionaries. The entrance of Porfirio Díaz's army into Mexico City had established order, albeit by the gun and the sword. It was the kind of order that encouraged a reimposition of Mexican tradition; and the Catholic church, in the large cities at least, began to enjoy a new ascendancy.

Thus in 1880 Moses Thatcher became increasingly convinced that Mexico's city-dwellers were so bound by tradition or fear that the elders would not be able to make headway among them. While Protestant missionaries of several faiths seemed to have some success,[76] the elders concluded that this success came because the Protestants gave their tracts away and "bought" their converts with perquisites and stipends, a practice the Mormons would not or could not emulate. Not surprisingly, therefore, the elders could hardly bring in enough from their translated literature to cover printing costs, although somehow they did distribute thousands of copies, paying for much of it themselves.[77] Responding to a complaint on this matter, President John Taylor instructed them to keep trying to sell their literature for whatever few pennies they might bring in. Church headquarters could not help them much financially because of the federal government's assaults on polygamy in Utah Territory.

Discouraged, the missionaries began to think more and more about the Indians and peasants in the small villages surrounding Mexico City, something they concluded the Lord had wanted them to do all along. It was in and around the village of Guerrero, not Chihuahua City or El Paso del Norte, that Jones and his companions had found people willing to listen. Some of the Protestants seemed to have concluded the same thing, for they had moved into the outskirts of Mexico City. So the elders renewed their efforts in nearby villages such as Ozumba, where they baptized people who would be of lasting significance to the church (the Páez family in particular). But, at the time, Thatcher remained pessimistic about the whole enterprise, becoming more and more convinced that Daniel Jones must have been correct about the social and spiritual necessity of colonization.[78]

Mormons had almost frantically pursued the expansion of their faith into Mexico and the Indian-occupied southern U.S. territories. But their interchanges with these Indians seemed to have been mostly negative, producing primarily frustration and anxiety, despite the enormous commitment to the Lamanites of both the Mormon church and its missionaries. Everything seemed to turn to ashes in the missionaries' hands. Daniel Jones would later and somewhat self-righteously remind the church that it could have sent the missionaries back to Guerrero, where scores of Indians had waited in vain for baptism.[79]

Back in Zion, Mormon interest in the Lamanites remained high between bouts with the federal marshals. Numerous spectacular heavenly visitations to the Indians in the Great Plains and the Rocky Mountains had been reported, and many Mormons considered these proof that Jesus Christ's second coming was imminent.[80] A letter from Wilford Woodruff to a Brother Johnson in Salt River Valley, Arizona, on 7 December 1881, describes his information regarding the Indians' reported angelic visitations. All the Indian nations were on the move, with runners traveling from the Great Plains to the Rocky Mountains. In 1881 Wilford Woodruff had reported that "we as the Quorum of the Twelve have been commanded of the Lord to now turn our attention to the Lamanites and preach the Gospel to them, which we are now endeavoring to do."[81] Apostles Brigham Young, Jr., and Heber J. Grant had been sent to Arizona and New Mexico to look further into the Indian question; Apostle George Teasdale was making rounds in Indian territory; Apostle Francis M. Lyman was traveling the Uinta Reservation to the east; and Apostles Lorenzo Snow and Franklin D. Richards were attending to the northern tribes.[82] Apostle Moses Thatcher was in Mexico City again and, because of his substantial commitment to the Lamanite cause, was certain to be impressed with news of the Indians' reported visions.

In April 1881, four months after Thatcher's return to Mexico, he took his missionaries and a handful of Saints (some of whom had remained from the original Rhodakanaty group) and left Mexico City to ascend the great volcano of Popocatépetl, about fifty miles southeast of the city. There, on 6 April, the fifty-first anniversary of the Mormon church's founding, the Mormons held a conference and, in a formal prayer ceremony, dedicated the land for the preaching of the gospel. Because of the volcano's poetic and historical significance to most of Mexico's Indians, the ascent to its summit held enormous symbolic significance. There was no question in the missionaries' minds to whom their gospel message was to be taken. Attending this first Mexican church conference were Thatcher, Young, Stewart, and several Mormons from Mexico—Silviano Arteaga, Fernando A. Lara, Ventura Páez, Lino Zárate, and two other Mexican members whose names are unknown.[83]

As all these efforts slowly began to pay off, additional Latter-day Saints arrived from Zion. August H. F. Wilcken, a European immigrant schooled in Spanish, was one. He helped translate additional tracts and then went to Ozumba with Fernando Lara to proselyte there and in surrounding villages. Other changes occurred quickly: In June, James Stewart was released to return to his home in Utah; two months later Thatcher was released and August Wilcken selected to replace him, and Feramorz L. Young (who would die within days of typhoid fever) and Fernando Lara left with Thatcher for Utah. Lara had been one of the most dedicated and successful missionaries of the new Mexican members. But sixty-one other Mexican members remained, and that was enough to organize the second formal branch of the church in Mexico, in Ozumba, at the base of Popocatépetl. There Wilcken, Arteaga, Páez, Zárate, and a few others carried on the missionary work on their own.

Within a few months, however, the Mexican Saints were pleased to hear of new missionaries' imminent arrival from Zion. Anthony W. Ivins returned accompanied by Nielson R. Pratt, one more in the long line of Pratt descendants who have served the Mormon church. Within months the Mexican and American missionaries added an additional fifty-one members to the church's records.

In due time, when Wilcken left for home, Ivins was made mission president. Rey Pratt, a later Mormon authority in Mexico, tells us that during Ivins's administration "quite a number of native elders were pressed into service, and the work of preaching the gospel and spreading the truth was vigorously pushed."[84] Among those missionaries were Lino Zárate, Julián Rojas, and an Elder Candanosa. More people joined.

Proselyting extended into numerous small villages in the central Mexican plateau: Toluca, Ixtacalco, Tecalco, and Chimal, all in the state of Morelos; and Nopala, in the state of Hidalgo. Isaac J. Stewart, who had accompanied his brother to the Yaquis several years before, soon joined the group. So did Helaman Pratt, another of the original Mexico missionaries. Those whose interest and ability qualified them for missionary labor would serve double duty for as long as Salt Lake City refused to approve colonization in Mexico.

By March of 1884 Helaman Pratt headed the mission. He extended the work to San Marcos, Hidalgo, a community that later became very important to the Mormons in Mexico. And little by little the missionaries advanced their cause. But Pratt soon reached the same procolonization conclusions as had Jones and Thatcher. Just as the first Mormons had gathered into communities, so should the Mexican members. That the Anglo–American observers may have been less sympathetic to the Mexican culture than to their own does not depreciate their insights into the needs of new faith.

Therefore, after being in the mission only a few months, Helaman Pratt raised another question. If Utah Mormons could not come to Mexico, why not send Mexican Mormons into Arizona where Mormon colonies already existed? Pratt proposed that one hundred to one hundred fifty new Mexican members (virtually the entire church membership in and around Mexico City at the time) should gather either in the Arizona settlements or in some new place in northern Mexico where they could live socially, culturally, and economically as a Mormon community. But President John Taylor thought that Arizona could not handle this many new members and suggested sending perhaps ten families. When Pratt relayed the president's response to the Mexicans, they elected to wait and all go together when a settlement could be established in northern Mexico. That opportunity would come three years later, following a massive Anglo–American colonizing movement into northern Mexico.

Notes

1. Gordon Irving tentatively agrees with this point. (See his "An Opening Wedge: LDS Proselyting in Mexico, 1870–1890.")

2. See, for example, Leonard J. Arrington, *From Wilderness to Empire: The Role of Utah in Western Economic History,* and Deseret News, *Utah the Inland Empire.*

3. Blaine Carmon Hardy, "The Mormon Colonies of Northern Mexico: A History, 1885–1912," pp. 32–34, includes specific data showing the extent of the southern colonization.

4. Cited in ibid., p. 32.

5. The point is recorded by Daniel W. Jones in his autobiography, *Forty Years among the Indians: A True Yet Thrilling Narrative of the Author's Experience among the Natives,* p. 220.

6. The *World Christian Encyclopedia,* edited by David B. Barrett, gives the following information on pages 488–89:

Protestant efforts began with the distribution of scriptures by the American Bible Society in 1824; but until the revolution of 1857 Mexico was virtually closed to Protestant missions. Juárez, the new president at that time, encouraged Protestant activities and several independent missionaries entered Monterrey during the late 1850s. Lutheran immigrants formed a German-speaking congregation in 1861, and the following year the first Baptist church was begun. Encouraged by their success, the American Baptist Home Mission Society established a station in 1870; and 2 years later American Board missionaries were also found in Monterrey and Guadalajara. American Presbyterians entered Mexico City in 1872 and the Methodists a year later. . . . The Southern Baptist Convention came to Mexico in 1880, its first Latin American field; and another important early arrival was the Seventh-day Adventist church in 1893. . . . Two marginal Protestant bodies from the USA have built up large constituencies in Mexico during the present century, namely the Mormons and Jehovah's Witnesses who arrived respectively in 1879 and 1893. *Mormons have had spectacular successes among Indians,* with 40,000 baptisms reported in 1976 alone [italics added].

7. One can point to Graham Sumner Abbot's *Mexico and the United States: Their Mutual Relations and Common Interests,* and especially the series of articles under the title "Our Nearest Neighbor" in *Harper's New Monthly Magazine* 44 (1874).

8. Hardy, "The Mormon Colonies," p. 38.

9. Cited in ibid., p. 38.

10. The idea that "foreigners" could do it better was couched in considerable racism with attempts at legitimization through the philosophical writings of Auguste Comte. The positivists accepted Comte's conclusion that society could be saved by the techniques of the social sciences uncorrupted by metaphysics and theology. The problem was that their "science" was not working with Mexico's indigenous population, so they decided to cast that population aside in favor of a more agreeable one. The impact this had on much of Mexico's indigenous population is noted in chapter 5 of this volume.

11. Ernest Gruening discusses the early Mormon missionaries' warm reception in Mexico in light of the influence of positivism and the favor Mexico showed foreign interests. (See Ernest Gruening, *Mexico and Its Heritage,* pp. 50–53 passim.)

12. See Louis Hartz, *The Founding of New Societies: Studies in the History of the United States, Latin America, South Africa, Canada, and Australia.*

13. Jones, *Forty Years among the Indians,* p. 17.

14. Paul Thomas Mouritzen, "Mormon Beginnings in Mexico: The 1876 Missionary Expedition," p. 4.

15. Jones, *Forty Years among the Indians,* p. 220.

16. K. E. Duke, "Melitón González Trejo, Translator of the Book of Mormon into Spanish," p. 714.

17. Jones, *Forty Years among the Indians,* p. 224.

18. The actual cost of refining the translation (after Jones and Trejo had exhausted their personal funds) was met by individual pledges ranging from

ten cents to ten dollars. Entire congregations as well as individuals contributed to the fund that Brigham Young had authorized. Four hundred and eleven individuals donated money, including Feramorz Little, Erastus Snow, J. P. Ball, William Hyde, Orson Hyde, George Q. Cannon, George Teasdale, Mathias Cowley, Anson Call, and several members of the Martineau family. Of these, Little, Snow, Hyde, Teasdale, Cowley, Call, and the Martineau family figured prominently in the expansion of the church into Latin America.

19. Readers interested in translations of Mormon church literature will be intrigued by the method employed in this case to assure that the translation was done properly. Brigham Young had charged Jones with confirming the translation's authenticity. Jones was certain he had divine help; as he and Trejo were reviewing their Book of Mormon translation for the last time, Jones "felt a sensation in the center of my forehead as though there was a fine fiber being drawn smoothly out. When a mistake occurred, the smoothness would be interrupted as though a small knot was passing out through the forehead" (Jones, *Forty Years among the Indians*, p. 232). The two men would then adjust their translation until the "smoothness" returned. All this did not, however, totally convince Brigham Young. Knowing that none of the church's General Authorities was competent to judge the translation's accuracy, he wanted further assurance before asking for approval to publish it. He asked Jones how he proposed to satisfy the General Authorities that the translation was correct:

> My proposition was to take a book in English we, Trejo and I, were not acquainted with, let Trejo translate it into Spanish, then I without ever seeing the book would take his translation and write it into English and compare it with the original. Brother Brigham said that was fair. He asked me if I was familiar with "Spencer's Letters." I said I was not as I had never read them. He sent me to the Historian's office to tell Brother G. A. Smith to let Trejo have a copy and do as I proposed. On furnishing our translation as agreed upon, Brother Smith laughingly remarked, "I like Brother Jones' style better than Brother Spencer's. It is the same in substance, but the language is more easily understood" (Jones, *Forty Years among the Indians*, p. 231).

20. For the next several paragraphs I am indebted to Paul Mouritzen's unpublished narrative, "Mormon Beginnings in Mexico."

21. James Z. Stewart, Journal.

22. Anthony Woodward Ivins, "Letter to James G. Bleak," [18 February 1889, from Mexico City].

23. See, for example, the philosophizing by Jones in *Forty Years among the Indians*, pp. 216 and 273. Additionally, the compiler of the official chronology of the church considered the expedition to be of supreme importance; of some sixty entries for 1876 that deal with events in the entire church, five are of movements of the missionaries into and throughout Mexico. (See Andrew Jenson, comp., *Church Chronology: A Record of Important Events Pertaining to the History of The Church of Jesus Christ of Latter-day Saints.*)

24. Andrew Jenson, *Latter-day Saint Biographical Encyclopedia*, 4:348.

25. Many native peoples, threatened with assimilation by European conquerors, have resisted the loss of their independent identity, their land, and their autonomous community. That so many "new ethnic groups" have emerged

since the 1960s is testament to some people's unwillingness ever to forget their roots. What distinguishes the Yaquis from most others in all this is their persistence, endurance, and remarkable record of success. Above all, theirs is a history of a people struggling to persevere as an autonomous community on its own land, with its own identity. In this respect, the motivation and goal were not all that different from what the Mormons had in mind for their own communities. But, just as the Mormons had trouble with their "neighbors," so also did the Yaquis. With Mexico's independence from Spain in the first part of the nineteenth century, the Yaquis soon found themselves locked in an almost continuous, and most often violent, battle with the new Mexican republic and its foreign supporters for control over land, water, their own labor and, ultimately, their very identity as a community. The territory was the rich Yaqui River Valley; foreign interests were the mining companies that needed inexpensive labor and security; Mexicans were those who had their own ideas on how to establish their own identity as a modern nation and to pursue national social and economic development. The two world views—the Yaqui and the Mexican—were predicated on opposing sets of values and inevitably clashed. International interests applauded the Mexican Republic.

The proudest moment in Yaqui resistance (1875–1885) occurred precisely at the time the Mormon's missionary expedition was underway (1876), and it was understandable that at the time people in Tucson would speak of furious Yaqui wars in Sonora. Chief José María Leyva Cajeme had succeeded in consolidating political control over the eight Yaqui pueblos left from the days of the Jesuits, finally bringing into existence a separate Yaqui state, which earlier Yaqui leaders had struggled to obtain. For ten years the "Yaqui Republic" built forts and stockpiled materiel to defend its communities from anticipated assaults from the Mexican army; its leaders also attended to religious and other matters that created a socializing solidarity of enduring consequences.

While the "furious wars" the missionaries heard about were most certainly not as fierce as during an earlier Yaqui rebellion in the 1830s when the Yaquis systematically sent out raiding parties to depopulate villages of aliens, it is clear that many people feared the worst and probably heard enough credible evidence from time to time to justify their fears. All of it was enough to deter the Mormon missionaries from entering Sonora. (See Evelyn Hu–DeHart for the best treatment of the Yaquis from the vantage of political and social history [e.g., *Yaqui Resistance and Survival: The Struggle for Land and Autonomy, 1821–1910*, and "Sonora: Indians and Immigrants on a Developing Frontier," pp. 184–92]. A noteworthy cultural perspective is Edward H. Spicer, *The Yaquis: A Cultural History*. For a perspective on this matter during the colonial era, see Marie Lucille Rocca–Arvay, *Assimilation and Resistance of the Yaqui Indians of Northern Mexico during the Colonial Period*.)

26. Daniel W. Jones, "A Letter to R. W. Driggs," 18 November 1875.

27. As reported by Jones in *Forty Years among the Indians*, p. 257.

28. Ibid.

29. Anthony Woodward Ivins, Journal entry of 11 November 1875, records the tensions and his advice to Jones to be more understanding of Smith's and Tenney's feelings.

30. Hardy, "The Mormon Colonies."

31. Ibid., p. 45.

32. Jones, *Forty Years among the Indians*, p. 274.

33. Cited in Mouritzen, "Mormon Beginnings in Mexico," p. 13.

34. Daniel W. Jones, Helaman Pratt, and James Z. Stewart, "Mission Report," 5 October 1876, Manuscript History of the Mexican Mission.

35. Jones, *Forty Years among the Indians*, pp. 260–62.

36. Ivins, Journal entry of 28 March 1876. See also Barney T. Burns and Thomas H. Naylor, "Colonia Morelos: A Short History of a Mormon Colony in Sonora, Mexico," p. 142.

37. *El Semanario Oficial* (date and translator unknown), cited in *Deseret Evening News*, 30 June 1876, recorded in Journal History of the Church, 30 June 1876, p. 2.

38. Hardy, "The Mormon Colonies," p. 45.

39. As reported in ibid., p. 277.

40. In dealing with the journey to the mountains I am heavily indebted to Mouritzen, "Mormon Beginnings in Mexico."

41. Jones, *Forty Years among the Indians*, p. 282.

42. Ibid., pp. 282–83.

43. Ibid., p. 284.

44. Mouritzen's "Mormon Beginnings in Mexico" gives insights into several of the factors.

45. James Z. Stewart, Journal, 1 May 1876, cited in Manuscript History of the Mexican Mission.

46. See Blaine Carmon Hardy, "Cultural 'Encystment' as a Cause of the Mormon Exodus from Mexico in 1912," p. 41.

47. Hardy, "The Mormon Colonies," p. 441, and Jones, *Forty Years among the Indians*, p. 283.

48. Jones, *Forty Years among the Indians*, p. 287.

49. See Lucile Pratt's discussion of the fierce Indian wars in the area between 1877 and 1882 in her "A Keyhole View of Mexican Agrarian Policy as Shown by Mormon Land Problems," pp. 19 ff. See also the discussion in note 25.

50. Jones, *Forty Years among the Indians*, pp. 304, 308.

51. Ibid., p. 314.

52. Hardy, "The Mormon Colonies," pp. 32–34.

53. See, for example, Sgt. Daniel Tyler, *A Concise History of the Mormon Battalion in the Mexican War, 1846–48.*

54. Young's feelings about Kane are best captured by the following excerpt: "We shall ever appreciate the good, the generous, the energetic and talented Little Col." (Brigham Young to Thomas L. Kane, 14 January 1859). Kane claimed to be a Gentile, but his dedication to Brigham Young and to the Mormons was so resolute, and the consequences of that dedication so great, that many people of the time suggested that "Kane had been secretly baptized in Council Bluffs when the Saints first gathered for their westward trek in 1847" (Harold Schindler, *Orrin Porter Rockwell*, p. 285; see also, John Hyde, Jr., *Mormonism: Its*

Leaders and Design, p. 146; and Mrs. C. V. Waite, *The Mormon Prophet and His Harem*, p. 52).

55. Irving, "An Opening Wedge," p. 3. Irving's cover sheet to this lecture, entitled "Questions needing further attention," gives the following added information under Point 2: "Chas. Peterson since I gave this talk has directed me to a very interesting letter from Colonel Kane to Brigham which shifts the attention from proselyting to colonization."

56. See, for example, "Mexico: Reported Intentions of Mormons to Migrate to Mexico," *New York Times*, 22 December 1874, p. 1; and "A Threat from Mormondom," *New York Times*, 22 June 1875, p. 6.

57. *Journal of Discourses*, 18:355–56.

58. *Deseret Weekly*, 13 September 1876, p. 521.

59. W. Ernest Young, interview. See also the discussion in note 25.

60. Lucile Pratt, "A Keyhole View of Mexican Agrarian Policy."

61. Franklin Spencer Gonzalez, "The Restored Church in Mexico" (MS 1967), p. 16; see also Stewart, Journal.

62. Irving, "An Opening Wedge," p. 8.

63. Agrícol Lozano Herrera, interview.

64. Rhodakanaty had only a fleeting period with the Mormons, although he was baptized and, had the Mormons desired to pursue their small communitarian agrarian village models (the "United Order") in Mexico, there is no doubt that Rhodakanaty would have invested considerable energies to help bring them about and make them successful. Born in Athens (1828) of an Austrian mother and a Greek nobleman, he received the best education affordable for the time, even pursuing medical studies in Germany after his father's death and his family's return to his mother's homeland. While a student of medicine in Berlin he developed a great interest in political philosophy and became an admirer first of Hegel and then of the French philosophes Fourier and especially Proudhon. Rhodakanaty visited Paris to meet Proudhon and later returned to study. While there he met, among his young socialist friends, a Mexican who inspired him to think of Mexico as a place where his small community agrarian ideas, based on moral principles of a socialist utopia, might be put into practice. That aspect of his desires never materialized, but he did end up in Mexico, where he became the country's first advocate of anarchist doctrine and founder of the first anarchist working-class organizing group in Mexico. He wielded a profound influence on the emerging urban working-class and agrarian movements of the 1860s, 1870s, and 1880s. (See John M. Hart, *Anarchism & the Mexican Working Class, 1860–1931*, pp. 19–28.) At the time Rhodakanaty was corresponding with the Mormons he was founding and nurturing Mexico's first organizing group, La Social. On 1 January 1878, in a speech to this group, he reviewed the principles on which their work was based and on the need for an organic transformation of society (for him nonrevolutionary) that would be supported by all moral and thinking people. "Exploiters and money lenders who traffic in human beings and with their concerns, who rob and impoverish people overcome by their misery, will also see in La Social a powerful lever that will lift up the poor and the disinherited. . . ." (Plotino C. Rhodakanaty, *Escritos*, p. 77; translation mine).

65. This information, which I have not come across elsewhere, is reported by Irving in "An Opening Wedge," p. 10.

66. Ibid.

67. Jenson, *Biographical Encyclopedia*, 1:131.

68. Irving, "An Opening Wedge," p. 10.

69. Mormons understand the priesthood to be of two categories, each with three offices. The highest category or Melchizedek Priesthood, which has power to deal with spiritual matters, contains the offices of high priest, seventy, and elder (the office to which Rhodakanaty was appointed, something of a signal, therefore, of the high esteem in which the missionaries held him). The "lesser" or Aaronic Priesthood, which contains the "keys" for temporal matters within the church, has offices of priest, teacher, and deacon.

70. Jenson, *Biographical Encyclopedia*, 1:132–33.

71. Ibid.

72. Ibid., p. 133.

73. New York City *Sun*, 13 August 1879.

74. Hardy, "Cultural 'Encystment,'" p. 441.

75. Irving, "An Opening Wedge," pp. 12–14.

76. Useful background materials from the point of view of a Cuban theologian may be found in Justo E. González, *Historia de las Misiones*, chapter 9. O. E. Costas discusses a contemporary view of mainline Protestantism in his published doctoral thesis, *Theology of the Crossroads in Contemporary Latin America*.

77. Stewart and Trejo had finished their translation of Parley P. Pratt's *The Voice of Warning* and had managed to circulate a large number of copies. They translated, printed, and distributed 4,000 copies of John Nicholson's "Means of Escape." The missionaries also printed several thousand copies of Stewart's "Coming of the Messiah" and distributed them widely. Numerous other exchanges occurred through the newspapers and were later published in *The Contributor*. (See Jenson, *Biographical Encylopedia*, 1:134.)

78. Hardy, "Cultural 'Encystment,'" pp. 440–41. Hardy cites volume 3, pages 43–44, of Moses Thatcher's journals, which led him to conclude that the motive for Mexican colonization was to provide Mexican converts a new environment separate from the distracting effects of Mexico's non-Mormon society. All these considerations had led Thatcher to subscribe to Daniel W. Jones's earlier conclusion: "We were united in one idea, and that was before any great work could be done in this country it would be necessary to colonize among the people" (Jones, *Forty Years among the Indians*, p. 283).

79. Jones, *Forty Years among the Indians*, pp. 286–87.

80. Mormon leaders and members between 1877 and 1892 were generally impressed with and excited by the reported visions of an Indian named Moroni as well as the visions of chiefs Shivitts, Wovoka, Sitting Bull, and others. Tribes from the Great Plains to the Rocky Mountains became interested in the Mormons and then developed their own "Ghost Dance" (associated with their belief that a Messiah would soon return to the earth and save them from their plight by annihilating the whites and restoring the buffalo). This terrified many non-Mormon whites and alarmed the U.S. federal government, and these two groups

combined to precipitate the now infamous 1890 massacre of Indians at Wounded Knee, South Dakota. (See Dee Brown, *Bury My Heart at Wounded Knee: An Indian History of the American West*; and James Mooney, *The Ghost-Dance Religion and the Sioux Outbreak of 1890.*)

These visions reinforced the Mormons' eschatology, and the church increased its missionary effort among the Indians. Mormons were convinced that the Indian prophets foretold in the Book of Mormon had finally risen and that perhaps the Savior had actually visited them or one or more of the Three Nephites were among them again. Surely the Second Coming was nearly at hand. Indeed, for this reason some accused the Mormons of using the Ghost Dance craze to rid their territory of gentile settlers. (See Lawrence G. Coates, "The Mormons and the Ghost Dance.")

81. Wilford Woodruff to a "Brother Johnson" in the Salt River Valley, Arizona, 7 December 1881.

82. Ibid.

83. Rey L. Pratt, "History of the Mexican Mission," p. 486.

84. Ibid., p. 489.

Chapter 2

A Place of Refuge—
A Place of Gathering

Most residents of today's Dublán and Juárez colonies are non-Mormon ethnic Mexicans. Yet while Mormons are now in the minority, and while they maintain both English- and Spanish-speaking congregations, the settlements' founding culture, architecture, technology, society, and religion are unmistakably Utahan.

The colonies' old, yet well-cared for, two-story, sunbaked brick homes that survived the ravages of Mexico's 1910-17 civil war resemble the sturdy turn-of-the-century houses in Utah's Brigham City or Mt. Pleasant. There are old barns, open-fenced yards, gardens, lawns, orchards, large schools, and churches. All these, and now several modern brick rambler-style houses interspersed among the typical traditional Mexican homes, indicate a cultural implant that once flourished and still survives.

One is not surprised to find along a dirt road in Dublán a manhole cover manufactured by a foundry named "Brigham"; or in Juárez an academy with imposing buildings and grounds reminiscent of Brigham Young Academy in Provo, Utah; or in the surrounding region evidence of irrigation technology and horticulture and food-processing industries that for their time were unusually advanced. Driving into Dublán in early April, before the rains turn the hills of mesquite and chaparral into a cattleman's Eden, one finds a strikingly green valley of mature fruit trees, irrigated fields, and vigorous industry and commerce. All of it indicates that an ambitious and prosperous Mexican and

Anglo–American people still inhabit this valley. How did this come to be? And why?

In the face of intense federal pressures on the Latter-day Saints in Utah and surrounding regions, the Mormon leaders' reluctance to colonize Mexico soon diminished. Although for a quarter-century Mormons had thought they could defend themselves in Utah Territory and eventually win their case in the courts, by 1885 they realized they could not. Lamanites, colonies, economic expansion, and missions all receded into the background given the Latter-day Saints' need to salvage the doctrinal and organizational integrity of their faith. But the government's final response was uncompromising. Supported by the prevailing, often hypocritical American ideology that the country must rid itself of "the twin relics of barbarism—polygamy and slavery,"[1] and encouraged by the profit to be had by reducing the Mormon hierarchy's economic power, the U.S. government was out to break the church's back.

Mormons had publicly affirmed the principle of "celestial marriage" (polygamy) in 1852, although less than ten percent of the married men of the church practiced it.[2] Plural marriage was a highly unusual custom in nineteenth-century America, and few non-Mormons approved of it. Nevertheless, with the Mormons isolated in Utah Territory, the initial attacks, derision, and satire were mostly relegated to cartoons, caricatures, and professional and academic conventions.[3] Abraham Lincoln did not move against polygamist Utah, although legally he could have after the passage of the 1862 Morrill anti-bigamy act.[4] But following the U.S. Civil War, sentiments toward Mormons and Southerners took a new twist. Radical Reconstructionism was in vogue; the Republicans were in power, and now they had both opportunity and means to press their case. They had fulfilled their pre-Civil War pledge to rid the nation of slavery; now they could turn their attention to the other "relic," polygamy. The martial law of Colonel Patrick Conner, who occupied Utah's Fort Douglas from 1862 through November of 1865, was followed by a series of governors and judges equally determined to bring Mormon marriages into harmony with the law. Edward W. Tullidge tells us in his *Life of Brigham Young* that one such judge, James B. McKean, chief justice of the territorial court, said, "The mission which God has called upon me to perform in Utah, is as much above the duties of other courts and judges as the heavens are above the earth, and whenever or wherever I may find the Local or Federal laws obstructing or interfering therewith, by God's blessing I shall trample them under my feet."[5]

He tried, but the outcome was not satisfactory from the Republicans' point of view. They gradually strengthened their laws, notably with the Edmunds Act of 1882, which penalized severely even those who merely "believed" in polygamy.[6] Thus pressures on families were immense even before the passage of the Edmunds–Tucker Act of 1887,[7] which shattered the Mormon church's temporal foundation, abolishing every important LDS institution from the church's governing bodies to its schools—including the right of Mormon women to vote in territorial and federal elections, an opportunity they had enjoyed since 1870, when a Utah woman cast one of the first female votes in U.S. history.

The matter was sufficiently discomforting that in 1884 the church sent a high-level delegation into Mexican Yaqui country to negotiate for lands in Sonora on which to settle some of the persecuted Saints. The Mexicans would not, it seemed, make polygamy into the stressful issue it had become in the United States (an expectation borne out). Apostles Brigham Young, Jr., and Heber J. Grant organized and accompanied an expedition of thirty-three men from the St. Joseph and Salt River Mormon settlements in Arizona. Since at least 1881, Apostles Young and Grant had tried to reach the Indians in the south. Now it was imperative that they try again—this time more for the sake of refuge than for Yaqui converts.

Benjamin F. Johnson, who accompanied this expedition, reported that this time, unlike 1877, the Indians received the Mormons with interest and, in some cases, open arms.[8] All of this was quite a shock to Mexicans, who had warned that the warlike Yaquis would never let the Mormons out alive. In January of 1885 President John Taylor himself, his two counselors Joseph F. Smith and George Q. Cannon, and several of the Quorum of the Twelve traveled to Arizona and dispatched an exploring party into Chihuahua. Then, along with Joseph F. Smith, Erastus Snow, Moses Thatcher, Jesse N. Smith, Lot Smith, Melitón G. Trejo, and James H. Martineau, President Taylor continued into Sonora.[9] In the end he and the other authorities chose the Casas Grandes

Valley of Chihuahua, which Daniel W. Jones and his company had explored and commended to Brigham Young nine years earlier.

Within days Jesse N. Smith had passed the word to the Saints in Woodruff, Arizona: All the men in hiding to escape prosecution should go to Mexico, as a place had been contracted for; and President Taylor himself advised all polygamists to go to Mexico as soon as possible.[10] Within weeks—even before lands had been secured—Mormon wagon trains were crossing the border. By mid-May of 1885 nearly four hundred prospective colonists waited on the banks of the Casas Grandes River, hoping that Mormon church authorities would soon be able to purchase land.

But there were many problems—some of them foreseen nine years earlier by Chihuahua Governor Ochoa, who had warned the Mormons to beware of both fraudulent land titles and worthless land. Apostles Moses Thatcher, Erastus Snow, Brigham Young, Jr., Francis M. Lyman, and George Teasdale worked almost frantically to secure property for the exiles. In late June of 1885 Teasdale, the camp leader, was constantly encouraging the people and urging them not to leave the camp to return home. He worked hopefully and tirelessly to get a place, concocting every scheme imaginable to relieve the tension. But months passed before he succeeded. Joseph Fish, one of the colonists, gives us a picture of the situation:

> Time was dragging heavily on my hands. It is true I was trying to study Spanish some but had little heart for it under the circumstances. We were camped out on the open prairie exposed to the storms and hot rays of the sun, not even being able to get green timber for a bowery as there was but little of it and that belonged to the Mexicans and we were not allowed to take any of it. Under these circumstances I was feeling quite disappointed in our attempt to colonize. I was doing nothing for my family at home and spending every cent that I brought with me. We were going half fed and half clothed, and to add to our anxiety the prospect of getting a place was apparently more distant than the day we arrived here.[11]

The months dragged on with no land on which to plant and no income, with wagon boxes and dugouts serving as homes. Most colonists eventually spent their cash and were thereafter reduced to abject poverty, many of them wearing rawhide sandals strapped to their feet for shoes. Sickness and flaring tempers consumed the camp from time to time, only compensated for or relieved when people were reminded of the higher purpose for which they were sacrificing. Yet, "as the seasons came and matured, hope was transformed to resentment and faith to discouragement."[12]

Still, week after relentless week, as tense and frustrating negotiations continued, the colonists kept coming. Miles P. Romney's second family was typical. They risked traveling from Arizona to Chihuahua through Indian country mostly controlled by the Apache Geronimo, but they were able to bring little of value to help Romney in the camp. Romney had prepared for them a mud-roofed and dirt-floored stockade building into which they put their furniture: a table made by fastening two boxes together, a rude bed, and round logs for chairs. But, said Romney's second wife, Hannah, "I was thankful for it, my dear children and I would be with their father and we could live in peace, with no marshals to molest us or separate us again."[13]

Family ties were equally strong for Eunice Stewart Harris.

> It seemed there were only two courses for us to choose between and be safe. One was to go to Mexico where all the family could go, but where the prospects financially were not very good, or go to Canada where a man could go [but take only one wife] and live in peace the principle which we had entered at so great a sacrifice together. We decided that he [her husband, Dennison], Annie [the second wife], and Emer [Annie's two-year old son] should go to Mexico at once, and that I should return home [to Payson, Utah] and say nothing about where I had been until they were safely out of the country.[14]

Eventually Eunice and her children joined the others in Mexico. Years later Anglo–American Mormons, many of them not polygamists, were enticed to Mexico by reports of prosperity and virtually unlimited opportunity. In 1885, however, there was one pressing point—to escape the U.S. federal marshals and thereby preserve family life. Some of the polygamous Saints would give their lives, if necessary, to preserve their families.

While skeptical local Mexican authorities sometimes mistrusted Mormon intentions and were uncooperative with this Anglo–American influx, holding up wagon trains at the border and causing seemingly interminable delays, the Mexican federal government extended all reasonable help and protection consistent with its policy to colonize vacant land and to encourage the immigration of capable foreigners. Mexico's federal government even countermanded an expulsion order from the acting governor of Chihuahua. President Porfirio Díaz, in particular, was fond of the Mormons, perhaps in part because he considered them proof that his colonization policy was good for the Mexican economy.

In the fall of 1885 the Mormon leaders finally secured land near present-day Colonia Juárez. (The land was later abandoned because of a survey conflict with a neighboring ranch.) Additional lands were purchased both by individual Mormons and by the church. Safe for a time from the U.S. marshals, and protected from local Mexican politicians by the federal government in Mexico City, the Saints recovered from their most recent exodus and began to sink roots once again. By 1912 the Mormons had settled over four thousand people in nine Mexican colonies—seven in the Mexican state of Chihuahua and two in the state of Sonora.

There were the plateau colonies of Juárez (for Benito Juárez), Dublán, and Díaz (for Porfirio Díaz); the mountain colonies of Cave Valley, Pacheco (for Díaz's minister of war who had been so friendly to Moses Thatcher), García (for another helpful minister in the Díaz cabinet), and Chuichupa, all in the state of Chihuahua; and in Sonora there were the semi-tropical colonies of Oaxaca and Morelos.

Although the colonies were bound to each other socially, and to some extent economically, and were not too far apart, travel between them was frequently difficult because of poor roads and rough terrain. The mountain colonies in particular were isolated. Yet within several years of their founding they became economically integrated, trading back and forth the goods, produce, and materials that each produced best.[15] With irrigation (some of the projects followed an ancient canal), farming and associated industries flourished in the plateau colonies of Juárez and Dublán. The mountain colonies of Cave Valley, Pacheco, García, and Chuichupa were all situated in timbered areas of pine and oak. The mountain meadows were excellent for cattle grazing, and soon cattle and timber industries existed side by side. And the semi-tropical Sonoran colonies of Oaxaca and Morelos, situated on the Bavispe River (a tributary of the Yaqui that empties into the Pacific), yielded valuable produce.

The self-selection of some of the church's most able families to participate in this particular colonization effort virtually assured that the communities would be well organized, purposeful, and solid. Indeed, between 1885 and 1895 six of the Mormon church's Twelve Apostles lived in the colonies, most of them in Juárez. Having fled America because of their way of life, the colonists wanted one thing—to preserve that way of life. They had the leaders and the practical skills to do it.

A natural inclination arose, therefore, to stay "isolated" socially and politically (although not economically) from Mexico. True, there was the concern about converting the Lamanites. But in the first colony's initial two years there were also more pressing matters: staying alive; building homes, churches, schools, and an economy; and solidifying the Mormon communities so that thoroughly Mormon children could take their place in the Mormon Kingdom. Not surprisingly, in succeeding generations the colonies produced a striking number of Mormon leaders who rose to become General Authorities of the church.

The Calm in the Eye of the Storm

The Anglo-American Saints had escaped the fury of the U.S. marshals; they did not feel the threats of the Mexican revolutionaries until much later. In this calm they laid a foundation later used to expand the church into all of Latin America, mainly through educating several generations of children in Mormon principles and Latin American language and culture. In the early years, however, they may not have seen their preparation as such, for from 1887 to 1901 the colonists turned their efforts away from missionary endeavors toward founding a cultural and economic bastion of North America in northern Mexico.

Life on the frontier had its heartaches, with a drought in 1890–91 and killing smallpox and diphtheria epidemics that winter. These problems, coupled with the colonists' isolation and their knowledge of the reduced persecution in Utah once the Mormons had made peace with the U.S. government in 1890 by renouncing the practice of polygamy, made many colonists want to return to the United States. The year 1893 saw Moses Thatcher begging colonists to stay, promising them blessings if they did. Most heeded his counsel.

They did receive immense rewards, especially with respect to family life. The Mormons viewed the family not only as useful, convenient, and practical, but also as intrinsically sacred, as a necessary element in their perception of the divine plan. Families were considered potentially eternal. The only way to assure their permanence, however, was to enter as a family into certain required ordinances and covenants, such as the Mormon temple marriage, and then to conduct a proper family life. Many parents, therefore, struggled tirelessly to keep their families united and intact.

Some polygamous families did break up—one wife remaining in Mexico with her children and another returning to the United States or sometimes to Canada—but generally there was an enormous effort to maintain families intact in Mexico, to care for children, and to insure a proper cultural, educational, and economic environment.

Some of the men had fled to Mexico alone to prepare the way for all their families; others, some polygamous, had arrived with one family; still others had come with several. As time passed there were more and more monogamous marriages. All—men, women, children, polygamous or monogamous—had to build houses, set up irrigation systems, lay out town sites, organize and attend schools, build churches, see to spiritual matters, and care for the sick and bereft. They had to plant, harvest, and store crops; develop trade with the Mexicans; build gristmills, tanneries, food processing plants, saddleries, blacksmith shops, general stores, schools, and churches. The community was everything to everyone. Without it they would not survive. With it they, and their families, might.

Their high degree of literacy and technical skills was a great help to the colonists. Among those who fled to Mexico were accomplished farmers, horticulturists, businessmen, teachers, and medical practitioners. There were also amateur scholars, poets, and musicians. Miles P. Romney, for example, knew by heart several Shakespearean tragedies, had studied thoroughly and in detail the military campaigns of Napoleon Bonaparte and Alexander the Great, and was an acknowledged armchair historian. Within fifty-four days of their arrival in Juárez the colonists had built a stockade for a school, in which Romney's wife, Annie, taught. Before its completion, she took children into her dugout for a few hours of classwork each day.

Many of the colonists were already accomplished church leaders. In the first group of 1885, among the thirty-three men and their families from one Arizona settlement, there were seven "bishops" (lay leaders of individual congregations), several who had served as bishops, and many other prominent regional church leaders.[16]

By 1892 the Juárez colonists had built a canning factory for their abundant orchard fruit and tomatoes. A year later that factory, managed by Joseph C. Bentley, an energetic businessman who later figured prominently in the colonies' history, turned out ten thousand cans of fruit. By the close of the century the colonists were even entering the Mexico City food fairs, which greatly pleased Porfirio Díaz. Indeed, Díaz thought he had sufficient evidence in the Mormons to silence his critics. What more could Mexico want than such prosperous, productive people?

"To reach Colonia Juárez," Charles W. Kindrich of the U.S. State Department reported in 1899, "it is necessary to cross the foothills of the Sierra Madre Mountains. The road winds through passes and defiles until the colony, nestling like a green garden in the wilderness, comes suddenly into view." There, he said,

> The gardens are fragrant with flowers, and the blossoms of the peach, apricot, and plum trees glow in the pure air. Clear water from the *Acequia* along the hillside flows down the gutter of each cross street. Neat brick residences are nestled amid grapevines and pear trees. . . . The green stretches of the *alfalfa* below are in striking contrast with the brown summits that shadow them. From this valley the Mormons have extracted in ten years enough wealth to give them independence.
>
> The capital colony is a beautiful village comparable to any in New England. There is every evidence of thrift, cleanliness, industry, comfort, and good management. There is an absence of the vices common to modern communities. There are no saloons, tobacco shops, jails, nor houses of ill fame in the colony. . . . There is a gristmill, a furniture factory, and other industries in Colonia Juárez. There is an academy with five teachers and 400 pupils. It is the policy of the Mormons to erect school-houses before churches and temples.[17]

During their first twenty-five years, all the colonies received new residents frequently. Until 1890 new families fleeing the intense persecution in the United States entered the colonies almost daily. After 1890, however, with the polygamy issue resolved and the colonies visibly prosperous, people continued to arrive, but now more for economic reasons. The church's land agent, the Mexican Colonization and Agricultural Company, began to shift in its dealings with Mormon colonists from the Mormon communal and communitarian concept to private enterprise capitalism. A "stake" (an organizational unit aggregating several "wards" or congregations) of the church was organized in 1895 with Colonia Juárez its center; new schools were built and an academy constructed—mostly through the colonists' own economic and organizational resources.

The colonies' early years saw only two major departures from the pattern of economic development and cultural isolation that the Anglo–American Saints in Mexico had set for themselves. Given the circumstances, perhaps those departures were doomed from the beginning. One of them concerned the Saints near Mexico City who had elected to stay in central Mexico pending a suitable opportunity to colonize in northern Mexico near the rest of the Mormons. The other departure involved Wovoka, Sitting Bull, Shivitts, and other new Indian prophets who spoke again of recent and spectacular heavenly manifestations among various Indian tribes. This was a signal to the Mormons to take up once again their efforts on behalf of the Lamanites, no matter what the opposition.

Both the colonization effort and the renewed work with the Lamanites were entirely consistent with the Mormons' long-range aims for Mexico and all of Latin America. So as soon as the colonists in northern Mexico had their families minimally secure, they began once again to pursue their larger goals.

Colonization in the North

In 1887, with some of the Anglo–American Mormons still living in tents and others in caves carved from the banks of the Piedras Verdes, they began to colonize the Mexican Mormons. Nearly everyone was convinced that these church members needed to "gather" also. Since the Mexican government very much wanted its own nationals to colonize in the north (the government had required all colonization companies to set lands aside for native

Mexican citizens but had never insisted that the companies facilitate settlement), the time was ripe to unite economics and Mormon eschatology. The Mexican government would facilitate the Mormons' Colonization and Agricultural Company's acquisition of additional lands, and it would pay some of the Mexican Mormons' resettlement costs. Established Mormon colonists would give organizational and logistical help.

Helaman Pratt, mission president in central Mexico (1884–87), stated it best: "Lands, water, grass, and timber enough have been purchased to sustain many hundreds of God's people, and be a gathering place for the native Saints, that they may be made free through the principles of the everlasting gospel, one of which is that of gathering." Pratt could also see some potential problems.

> The hardest of my missionary labor is still in the future; that is to care for and look after the native Saints after they are gathered. The manners and customs of the two races are very different, and through misunderstandings that will naturally arise, it will take constant care and prudence to prevent them from clashing. But I hope to succeed through the blessings of God and the patient assistance of our brethren and sisters, for this is a mission devolving upon all, both old and young, male and female, and God has, in my opinion, forced some of our best Saints out here that they may assist in the redemption of His fallen people.[18]

Mexican officials seemed pleased about the whole matter. The subminister of colonization, Fernández Leal, promised to visit the new colony. Favorable comments regarding the established colonies appeared in Spanish, French, and English in the Mexico City press; the *Two Republics* carried some of it, in a rather substantial turnaround from its earlier anti-Mormon position.[19] As invitations went out to local native Mormons, the arrangements were made amid other complex activities. The colonies' Mormons purchased for the Mexican members about twelve thousand more acres of land (cultivatable, but also including grass, fuel, and timber enough for seventy-five families). And they completed arrangements, pending for several years, to obtain title to fifty thousand acres of land near Asunción. At the same time, they had other business to attend to. They were completing a town organization in Juárez, obtaining a grant to colonize their Corrales purchase, seeking permission to open and construct a toll road from Juárez to Corrales and on to Sonora, and petitioning for service to extend mail to the Mormon towns (which service would require the Mormons to create and staff post offices). On top of all this activity, they were preparing to receive the first company of native Mormons into the colonies.

"The first gathering of native Saints from the city of Mexico is expected here about the middle of May," said the correspondent to the Salt Lake City *Herald* in a report published on 24 April 1887. They were expected to arrive by train (with fares paid by the Mexican federal government) at the San José station. The Mormon brethren would meet them there and transport them by wagon and buggy to the Saints' gathering place.

It was not a successful colonization venture. Henry Eyring recorded in his journal that "a Company of our Mexican brethren and sisters arrived in May [1887] from lower Mexico. After staying for a short time, the majority of them returned dissatisfied."[20] The record is silent on how many arrived, or what resources or expectations they had. Were children born en route? Did whole families journey together? Were the travelers young or old, skilled or unskilled? What sacrifices, hardships, and privations did they experience? We do not know.

Several shocks awaited the Mexican Saints at Colonia Juárez. For one thing, whatever their living conditions had been in central Mexico, those in the north were undoubtedly more harsh. In 1887 the Anglo-American Mormons were still struggling for their new existence in the semi-arid land. Their colonies were young and not yet prospering. The first Mormons from the United States, having settled on land later found to belong to a hacienda, had been forced to relocate in a narrow, rocky canyon. In that canyon (now Colonia Juárez) the Mexican Saints could see many of their Anglo-American Mormon brothers and sisters living in tents and dugouts carved from the banks of the Piedras Verdes. This prospect awaited them too until or unless they could become established. It was not an Eden the Mexican Saints were coming to.

Nor could the Mexican Saints feel secure about the prospects for land. Some of them apparently held communitarian ideals, and many had traditionally practiced the ancient Indian village custom of ejido agriculture—common lands held in trust for the benefit of an entire village. But when they were living among the Anglo-American Mormons, who would make the decisions regarding

Mormon community property? The Mormons' Colonization and Agricultural Company, formed under the laws of the U.S. state of Colorado, operated in those days according to the Latter-day Saints' stewardship theory of landholding. This involved purchasing lands with company funds. Lots were then leased out to members in good standing, who were permitted to occupy and use the land so long as they proved willing to do it properly. But by 1887 the immigrants of 1885 had naturally already taken most of the best lands. The Mexican members no doubt wondered where and how they would find security and prosperity in the new lands.

There was another problem for the Mexican Saints equally as shocking as the harsh environment and the insecurity of land tenure. This was something Helaman Pratt had worried about: the ethnic differences that divided the two groups of Mormons. Different languages, ancestral customs, expectations about life, pleasures, and joys—all these were apparent and quite natural. But there was also a restrained element of Anglo–American condescension. The Anglo–Americans had been convinced all along that they needed to proselyte among the natives through colonizing. That might not have been too offensive—many Mexican members felt the same need to colonize—but the matter grew more grave as it became obvious that native Mexicans were needed to validate the land concessions. Some of these unintentionally offensive Anglo–American sentiments have passed to us more or less intact through a granddaughter of Henry Eyring. She felt that most of the Mexicans who had joined the church up to 1887 were poor because they were "living in a manner not in accord with the Mormon idea of industry and thrift." So they were brought to Juárez,

> but instead of imitating the ways of their white brothers they wanted to be fed without the labor of getting food. A large majority of these folks left the Church and returned to their old homes and ways of living. These people told exaggerated tales of woe and disappointment and little headway could be made among the members of the Mexican mission. Nearly all of them [members in central Mexico] believed the false statements about our colony and quite a bitter feeling resulted. . . . New conversions were out of the question. Grandfather's mission [1887–88 when Eyring was president of the mission in Mexico City] was not satisfactory from the point of view of conversions.[21]

Even Rey L. Pratt, a mission president Mexican members loved (he served from 1907 to 1931), could have been misunderstood as being somewhat condescending while trying to shed the best light on the Mexican members.

It may appear to some that they were not very well converted to so soon turn their backs on Zion, and their faces homeward, but when acquainted with all the conditions, it does not seem so strange. They were people taken from a tropical clime, some of them, and others from the unequaled spring-like clime of the Valley of Mexico. In their native homes they were poor, true it is, but for a few cents they could buy in the markets each day what they needed for that day. Then they had their homes in which to live, in some cases, it being only a cane or cornstalk house with a grass roof—but it was the home in which they were born, and in which their fathers had lived before them, and they had no conception of how to start out to make another. Such a thing as laying up anything for the winter had never occurred to them. Just imagine such a people being planted down in such a place as Colonia Juárez was in an early day—and that in mid-winter—where there were no houses, no ditches, no fences, and above all, no "plaza" nor even a store at which to buy, and see if you cannot imagine how they became discouraged.[22]

Aside from the shock of the environment and strained relations, there was another problem: the Mexican members did not have to worry about persecution as did the Anglo–Americans. The Mexicans could return home—perhaps to social ostracism, but to home nevertheless. The Anglo–Americans could return to the United States only on pain of imprisonment or loss of family life. Given their intense feelings about this matter, their motivation to stick it out was decidedly greater than the Mexicans'.

Within months most of the Mexican members had started back home, many of them making the entire three-month journey on foot. A few families remained in Colonia Juárez for four or five years, but eventually all but two or three persons returned to central Mexico.[23]

Yet the ideology of preaching by way of colonization continued. Few would forget Brigham Young's statement to the Quorum of the Twelve when he first considered settling the "far south" (Arizona): "We will form a line of settlements leading into South America, but this shall be the stepping stone."[24] Thus in

1904, Mormons attempted to colonize in Guatemala.[25] And the Mexican mission president, H. S. Harris, traveled to South America in 1906 to look for new colonization country.[26]

Proselyting among the Lamanites

The second major departure from the Anglo–American colonists' pattern of economic development and cultural isolation also came in 1887. In November of that year church authorities asked Charles Edmund Richardson from Colonia Díaz and three others (Ammon M. Tenney, Peter J. Christopherson, and Gilbert D. Greer) to make another attempt among the Sonora Indians there. It was understood that they would also work among Indians in Arizona if opportunity permitted. There was a great deal of religious fervor among the Indians in the American West, and the Mormon church president, Wilford Woodruff, who succeeded John Taylor, felt inspired to give Mexico another try.

Woodruff's decision can best be understood in context. Indians had been continually reporting to the Mormons information about heavenly visions that an Indian named Moroni and also other Indian chiefs had received. Not only did the Mormons send emissaries to the Indians, but Indian delegations from Great Plains and Rocky Mountains tribes came to the Mormons.

Encouraged by the Lamanites' spiritual awakening, the Mormon leaders intensified efforts to reach them with the Mormon gospel, increasing the number of missionaries among the Indians and even assigning apostles to lead and participate in the work.[27] The Mormons taught farming to the Lamanites in Malad, Thistle, Ruby, and Grass valleys in Idaho and in Deep Creek, Nevada. They set up model farms adjacent to the Wind River, Fort Hall, and Umatilla reservations, established branches of the church among the Indians, and sent out official publications encouraging Anglo–American Mormons to reflect on the importance of the Lamanites' manifestations, visions, and baptisms. Finally, the Mormons tried to prepare their Lamanite brethren for their prophetic calling to build a temple in New Jerusalem by taking them through the Utah temples, where they received the holy endowment rites. Thousands joined the church.

By increasing their work among the Lamanites, many Mormons fully believed they were working hand-in-hand with three ancient immortalized Book of Mormon prophets whose identity and significance were explained by the influential Mormon theologian and apostle, Orson Pratt.

> The Lord made a promise to these three [Nephites] that they should administer, as holy messengers in the latter days, for and in behalf of the remnants of the house of Israel, which should fall into a low and degraded condition in consequence of the great wickedness and apostasy of their ancient fathers; that they should be instruments in his hands in bringing these remnants to the knowledge of the truth. We hear that these messengers have come, not in one instance alone, but in many instances. Already we have heard of some fourteen hundred Indians [in southern Utah and northern Arizona], and I do not know but more, who have been baptized. Ask them why they have come so many hundred miles to find Elders of the Church and they will reply—"Such a person came to us, he spoke in our language, instructed us and told us what to do, and we have come in order to comply with his requirements."[28]

So apparent was the interchange between Mormons and Indians that many Americans condemned the Mormons for starting a "Messiah Craze" among the Indians. Just weeks before the U.S. cavalry's infamous massacre of Indians at Wounded Knee, for example, General Nelson A. Miles said: "It is my belief the Mormons are the prime movers in all this [the Ghost Dance craze]. It will [probably not] lead to an outbreak, but when an ignorant race of people become religious fanatics it is hard to tell just what they will do."[29]

In spite of colonization disasters, persecution, and the Edmunds acts, the church simply was not willing to give up its work among the Indians. In January of 1888 Ammon Tenney, the leader of the new missionary group, arrived with his companions in the Salt River Valley, which had first been colonized by the Jones company in 1877. They sought out Encarnación Valenzuela, one of the early Indian members, and rebaptized him for a renewal of his covenants.[30] He, together with a brother Cheroquis, was commissioned to work in the Sonora Indian mission. The two acted as interpreters as well as missionaries, at least as long as the party was among the Pima Indians.

The group set out southward, preaching to the Lamanites, noting several miraculous occurrences along the way. They baptized their converts in holes they dug in the desert and filled with well water. When they reached Mexico, they preached and baptized among the Papago Indians there. In all, so far, they had added more than 270 Lamanites to the church.

Yet the Mormon church president, Wilford Woodruff, was troubled: commitment to the Indians and baptizing them was not enough. The church had to be organized among them, and this was unlikely unless the Indians could be gathered into a community of the Saints. President Woodruff's letter to Tenney, written in the spring of 1888, attests to this. Because it touches on numerous issues of importance to Mormons of the day I cite it entirely.

Dear Brethren:

The subject of your mission among the Lamanites and the recommendations which you have made concerning the improvement of their temporal condition have been considered by the Council of the Apostles very carefully.

We are desirous to do all in our power to redeem these degraded descendants of the House of Israel from their present low estate, and to impart unto them a correct knowledge of the principles of the Gospel, and those arts of true civilization, which will restore them to the favor of the Lord and fulfill the covenants which he has made concerning them. It seems as though the time is fast approaching when the Gospel will be taken from the Gentiles and given to the House of Israel. Your recent success in baptizing these people gives us great delight, and we rejoice in the prospects that are opening up. But as has been said to you in former communications, this work must be followed up by systematic efforts and by thorough organization and the continued labors of experienced men among them. We cannot in justice to them and to the responsibilities which rest upon ourselves, leave them in the condition in which you have found them. Baptism is well enough, and is of the utmost importance, but there is more than this required in their case to relieve us from the responsibility that we are under to our God in connection with these people. They must be reclaimed. In view of all these considerations the Council of the Apostles have decided that you who are now laboring among the Papago Indians in Arizona be instructed to select a suitable place for gathering the Lamanite converts—a place where water can be stored in reservoirs contiguous to a body or bodies of arable land and that one thousand dollars ($1,000) be appropriated from the tithing of the Maricopa and St. Joseph stakes to be expended under the direction of the presidency of the Maricopa Stake and Bro. A. M. Tenney. An order for this amount has been enclosed in a letter to Pres. Robson and Counselors, sent today. It was also decided that we should suggest that four suitable young men be selected by the presidencies of the Maricopa and St. Joseph stakes, to labor with Bro. A. M. Tenney and associate brethren among the Papagos. These brethren ought to prepare themselves by acquiring the Pima language and labor as missionaries among that people. In order that they may be able to do this, financial aid will be extended to them not to exceed $250 per annum, for each of these young men, from the tithing of those stakes. We trust that this action will be attended with the best of effects. We feel it exceedingly important that men should acquire the language of the tribes among whom they are called to labor. Already you have found how inconvenient it is to communicate your ideas to the people through the medium of an interpreter. No permanent results of a satisfactory character can well be expected from the ministry of men who are crippled by a want of a knowledge of the language of the people among whom they labor.

We trust that the Spirit of the Lord will rest down upon some of our young men and that they will devote themselves energetically to the acquirement of this important language. In your cases, you understand the Spanish, and we feel that it is not a proper thing to require you to devote yourselves to the acquirement of this language, as there will no doubt be an abundant field for the exercise of your ability after a while among the peoples who will understand the Spanish language. For the present we think it better for you to continue your labors among these people, as the door shall open, until they can be taken care of or somebody else supply your places and you go on elsewhere.

Trusting that this action of ours will meet your hearty acceptance and good will, and that the results will be all that we can desire, and praying the Lord to bless you in your labors and preserve you from every evil, I remain,

> Your brother,
> W. Woodruff
> Gilbert D. Greer, Recorder[31]

Just to keep matters in perspective, one might reflect on the fact that in 1888 a good carpenter made a dollar per day; so $1,000 equaled 1,000 man-days of skilled labor, or perhaps the equivalent of $80,000 to $100,000 today—all from two stakes' (eight to ten village congregations') tithing![32] Even so, the whole enterprise fell on hard times. In January 1889, on the eve of the "Manifesto"— the document by which Mormons renounced their practice of polygamy—President Woodruff released Tenney from his mission and advised him not to return to his home in St. John, Arizona, but rather to join the other Saints in the Chihuahua colonies. The colonization and mission to the Lamanites in both north and south Mexico had collapsed, another casualty of highly strained church–state relations in Utah Territory.

All the Mormons in Mexico felt the impact of these failures. For example, when the Mexican Mormons who had attempted colonization in the north returned to their homes in central Mexico, most of them were highly disappointed—even bitter— at what they had experienced in the north. Missionary success in central Mexico thereafter fell off perceptibly. The missionaries attributed this to the discontented Juárez Saints. As they remembered their predecessors' fiasco with Rhodakanaty and his group, their opinion of the Mexicans' readiness for Mormonism sagged to an all-time low.

But there were other discouraging factors in central Mexico. For one thing, as a natural consequence of the political and social tensions emerging from the religious controversies of La Reforma, Catholic sentiment among city-dwellers was high. The urban rich, allied with the Catholic church, came down hard on the side of tradition. To court another religion in those days was to flirt with the destroying angel of a defeated political opposition. For the urban poor the matter was a little more practical: poverty left them vulnerable; they could be fired from their jobs. Although Mexico's dignitaries looked favorably upon the Mormons, it was not for their religious message so much as for their potential colonizing efforts in the north. The government's approbation of activities in the north did not make missionary work in Mexico City much easier.

When city people proved uninterested in their message, the missionaries went to the small villages. But there they found potential converts expecting the church to subsidize them as it was said many of the Protestants working in those same villages did. Climate and sickness posed other problems: yellow and typhoid fevers and smallpox, which took the lives of Feramorz L. Young, Sylvester O. Collett, and Elmer Hooks (and, in 1904,

Apostle A. O. Woodruff and his wife Helen, who were touring the Mexico City mission). And there was also the spiritual apathy of many of the Mexican people.

By 1888 disappointment in the endeavor was sufficient to occasion serious talk of closing the Mexican mission. Financial strains back home and the Mormon church's final struggle with the American government eventually did close it. In December of 1888 a highly discouraged Henry Eyring was released as mission president to return to Colonia Juárez. A month later the Indian mission to Sonora was closed. Then, on 3 June 1889, all foreign missionaries were withdrawn and the Mexican mission was closed. The 241 native Mormons in central Mexico and the more than forty northern Mexican Indians were left to take care of themselves as best they could.

The Mormon church was now bankrupt, its leaders in hiding, its hierarchy threatened with imminent destruction. Within months of the missionaries' withdrawal from central Mexico, President Wilford Woodruff issued the 1890 Manifesto. Thereafter the church attempted to reconstruct itself, deal with shattered families, and accommodate itself to a decidedly hostile American environment. But the steam was all gone from the church's work in Mexico.

We do not know what happened to the Indian members who had been converted in the north. Of the work in the south, some of the branches around Mexico City fell apart as the members scattered; others formed "independent religious societies" and tried to live in conformity with the teachings of the Bible. But many remained loyal to the church during its thirteen-year absence (elders did not return until 1901).[33]

It is not a light matter to convert nearly three hundred people and then be forced to abandon them. Nor is it easy to join a new faith and then be abandoned. Yet, despite the missionaries' discouragement and the new converts' disenchantment, it was really the trouble back in Utah that broke the Mormon church's missionary efforts in Mexico.

Still, the Anglo–American colonies in northern Mexico remained intact. Back in those colonies an understandable nativism prevailed—a reverence for, almost a worship of, the U.S. flag. Even given the alternative of U.S. persecution, many parents had worried about their children being in a strange land, under another flag, where people spoke a different language. What effect, they wondered, would this have? As the twentieth century commenced, the Anglo–American Mormons in Mexico were an economically successful but culturally isolated community, one not quite sure of its mission now that polygamy troubles had subsided and their missionary efforts had been frustrated.

Soon the colonists found their answer: to return to what they would have been about had it not been for the U.S. government. Once again, therefore, Mormons began preaching to the Indians. Someone remembered the branches in Mexico City that had been abandoned in 1889. Shouldn't the church try again? The year 1901 seemed a good time to find out.

Notes

1. Samuel Eliot Morison and Henry Steele Commager, *The Growth of the American Republic*, 1:624.

2. See Nels Anderson, *Desert Saints: The Mormon Frontier in Utah*, p. 416.

3. Gary L. Bunker, "Illustrated Periodical Images of Mormons, 1850–1860," *Dialogue: A Journal of Mormon Thought* 10 (Spring 1977):82–94. See also Gary L. Bunker and Davis Bitton, *The Mormon Graphic Image, 1834–1914*.

4. U.S., *Statutes at Large*, XII, Part 1, 501–2 (1862).

5. Edward Wheelock Tullidge, *Life of Brigham Young, or Utah and Her Founder*, pp. 420–21.

6. U.S., *Statutes at Large*, XXII, Part 1, 30–32 (1882).

7. U.S., *Statutes at Large*, XXIV, Part 1, 635–41 (1887).

8. Benjamin F. Johnson, *My Life's Review*, pp. 287–96, gives a striking description of this expedition.

9. Blaine Carmon Hardy, "The Mormon Colonies of Northern Mexico," pp. 49–51, 73.

10. See John H. Krenkel, ed., *The Life and Times of Joseph Fish, Mormon Pioneer, Autobiography*, p. 269. Also, Israel Call, "Autobiography," 1854–1930.

11. Krenkel, *Life and Times of Joseph Fish*, p. 285.

12. Blaine Carmon Hardy, "Cultural 'Encystment' as a Cause of the Mormon Exodus from Mexico in 1912," p. 443.

13. As reported by Lebra N. Foremaster in Kate B. Carter, comp., "The Mormons in Mexico," in *Treasures of Pioneer History*, 3:209.

14. Eunice Stewart Harris, "Autobiography," p. 26. See also Harris's "Autobiographical Sketch of Eunice Stewart Harris (wife of Denison Emer Harris) written by her in 1932," for a slightly different wording.

15. The practice of "comparative advantage" and complementarity in the conventional sense of economic integration was exceptional.

16. Krenkel, *Life and Times of Joseph Fish.*

17. Charles W. Kindrich, "The Mormons in Mexico," p. 704.

18. Helaman Pratt to his brother, Parley, cited in Journal History, 6 February 1887.

19. See Journal History, 13 April 1887, p. 4.

20. Henry Eyring, Journal, 1835–1902, p. 64.

21. Beatrice Snow Winsor, in Carter, "The Mormons in Mexico," 3:204.

22. Rey L. Pratt, "History of the Mexican Mission," pp. 491–92.

23. Ibid.

24. Sullivan Calvin Richardson, "Autobiography."

25. Gordon Irving, "Mormonism in Latin America."

26. Rey L. Pratt, "History of the Mexican Mission," p. 497.

27. Lawrence G. Coates, "The Mormons, the Ghost Dance Craze, and the Massacre at Wounded Knee," pp. 11–12.

28. *Journal of Discourses*, 26 vols., 17:299–300; see also 18:21–22.

29. Cited by Lawrence G. Coates, "The Mormons and the Ghost Dance," p. 91.

30. The practice of rebaptism for specific spiritual and physical blessings was common in the early days of the church. (See D. Michael Quinn, "The Practice of Rebaptism at Nauvoo.") When he met the Saints in California who had sailed from New York and settled in the area now known as San Francisco, Parley P. Pratt also rebaptized a number of them. Their names are entered in his journal under the date of 26 June 1851 and frequently in July 1851.

31. Wilford Woodruff to Elder A. M. Tenney and fellow missionaries, 10 April 1888, cited in Manuscript History of the Mexican Mission.

32. A "stake," presided over by a "stake president," is composed usually of between three and five thousand members and up to a dozen or so "wards" (congregations), which are headed by "bishops." "Branches" are Mormon congregations in mission districts where stakes have not been formed. Mormons in good standing donate ten percent of their income to the church through their ward bishop or branch president.

33. Rey L. Pratt, "History of the Mexican Mission," p. 493.

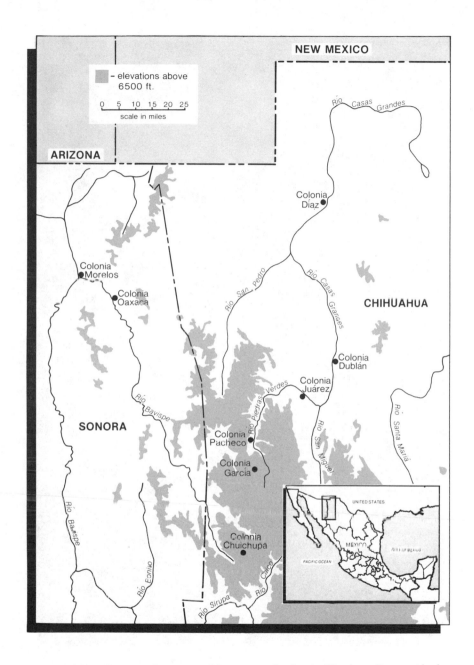

Figure 2.   Nineteenth-century Mormon colonies in Mexico. *Cartography by B. Kelley Nielsen.*

Figure 3.   Anthony W. Ivins, missionary, colonizer, apostle, and indefatigable defender of the Mormons in Mexico, ca. 1905. *Courtesy of LDS Church Archives.*

Figure 4.   Ammon M. Tenney (1844–1925), missionary to Mexico in 1876, 1877–89, and 1901–3. *Courtesy of LDS Church Archives.*

Figure 5.   Porfirio Díaz's *Rurales*, a national police force whose excesses helped precipitate the Mexican Revolution of 1910–17. *Courtesy of Harold B. Lee Library Photo Archives, Brigham Young University.*

Figure 6.   Rafael Monroy, president of the San Marcos branch who was executed by Zapatistas during the Revolution. *Courtesy of LDS Church Archives.*

Figure 7. Rafael Monroy with his daughter, wife, sisters, and mother, San Marcos, ca. 1913. *Courtesy of LDS Church Archives.*

Figure 8. Mormon colonists preparing to flee the ravages of the Mexican civil war, August 1912. *Courtesy of LDS Church Archives.*

Figure 9.   Rey L. Pratt, president of the Mexican Mission, 1907–31, ca. 1906.
Courtesy of LDS Church Archives.

Chapter 3

The Mission Reopened

If the reasons for closing the Mexican mission in 1889 were clear enough to everyone, Anthony W. Ivins, who presided over the Mormon colonies in Chihuahua, found the consequences disagreeable. After years of missionary sacrifices, the sorrowful result was, for whatever justifiable reasons, an abandoned flock in a hostile environment. The Mexican members were not forgotten, however. Ivins could not rest with the knowledge that the Mexican members were left without encouragement. It seemed to him that "if we convert people to the truth of the Gospel and admit them into the Church we ought to take care of them afterward, that is to say, give them all the protection and care in our power to keep them in the path of rectitude and teach them the principles that we know will lead them back into the presence of our Father."[1]

In 1876 Ivins had traveled three thousand miles on horseback to tell the Mexican people about the Book of Mormon. Six years later he had served as a missionary in central Mexico, and then as president of the mission there from 1883 to 1884. He had first-hand experience not only with Mexico's environment but with the open, warm, and gentle spirit of the Mexican people. And he never shrank from his conviction that the church must complete its mission to the Lamanites.

While almost all other Anglo–American Mormons in Mexico were preoccupied with personal survival and development of their own Mormon communities, Ivins continued to brood over the abandoned Mormons in central Mexico, some of whom were his personal acquaintances. Whether he was equally troubled about the many Indian members in northern Mexico who had also been abandoned, we do not know. But he did think and talk much about the church's mission in central Mexico. So it was fortunate indeed for Mexico that Anthony W. Ivins was called in 1895 to leave his comfortable St. George, Utah, home and go to the Chihuahua colonies to preside over all the Mormons in Mexico.

In 1901 Ivins began to focus on the other half of his calling—the Saints in central Mexico. He laid the whole matter before the church's First Presidency during a visit to Utah, speaking not only about the lost sheep who deserved a shepherd, but also about the colonies' young men and women who spoke Spanish and who were acquainted with Mexican customs and culture. In spite of past debacles, things now looked very promising. The pressures from the U.S. government had subsided, in the colonies a new generation had been raised who were both eager and exceptionally qualified to take the Mormon message south once again, and, besides, the colonies' success had brought a surplus of money and manpower to support a new missionary endeavor. In addition, central Mexican members' heartaches had subsided—at least a little. It was a new day, time for a new effort. The First Presidency agreed.

The man that Ivins recommended to head up the southern effort was Ammon M. Tenney, who had accompanied Ivins on the first 1876 expedition into Mexico. He had headed the Mexican Indian mission from 1887 to 1889. Later, taking Wilford Woodruff's advice to leave Arizona for Mexico and settle in the colonies, Tenney had built homes in Díaz and Juárez for his families. In the colonies, and in numerous conversations with Ivins, he had urged that the matter of reopening the southern mission be laid before the First Presidency. When Tenney's appointment came, he was not overjoyed to leave his families again, but he willingly accepted the responsibilities.

This missionary effort was important to church authorities, as had been Apostle Moses Thatcher's venture in 1879. Anthony Ivins and Apostle John Henry Smith accompanied Tenney to Mexico City to see how many of the original members had remained faithful and how they had fared. Ivins knew many of the members personally from his missionary days back in the early 1880s and was anxious to see them again.

The first stop was Cuernavaca. A Mormon hotel operator by the name of H. L. Hall lived there. He was one of those who buoyantly, and apparently effectively, wore his religion for everyone to see.[2] Several of his Mexican employees had joined the church, and he had an immigrant family from Switzerland interested. Hall's hotel afforded the missionaries a base of operations as well as provided a serene location on the evening of 8 June 1901 for Apostle Smith to establish Ammon M. Tenney as president of the Mexican mission. Tenney was under Juárez Stake President Ivins's direct supervision, but there was no doubt that his new title and mandate meant he should begin immediately.

After taking care of preliminary organizational matters and receiving counsel from Hall regarding central Mexican politics, the missionaries again felt a need to call on President Porfirio Díaz. While Díaz was becoming even more politically controversial—and making more enemies—than he had been when the first Mormons in Mexico had sought his help, he was still quite friendly and politically helpful to the Saints. Accordingly, after only two weeks in Mexico, on 17 June, the missionaries asked for and received an audience with the president of the country.

Apostle Smith thanked President Díaz and the Mexican people for their hospitality toward the Mormons. He explained the church's new mission. Díaz expressed great satisfaction—already the northern Mormons' prosperity had gained them a national reputation—and wished the missionaries every success. He asked Apostle Smith to convey his warmest greetings to the Mormon president, Lorenzo Snow, who had succeeded Wilford Woodruff; Smith did, telling President Snow that "no more heroic man stands on God's green earth than the man who stands at the head of the government of Mexico."[3]

Within a decade dark clouds would overshadow Díaz's relationship with the church; but in the meantime Mormons considered the Mexican president their benefactor, and their leaders told him so on every possible occasion. Typical of the Mormons' regard for Díaz at this time was the 24 November 1904 visit of apostles John Henry Smith, Mathias F. Cowley, and Charles W. Penrose. They, along with Richard W. Young, a Dr. Faust, John Beck, D. W. Johnson, and Hyrum S. Harris, congratulated Díaz on behalf of the church and the Mormon colonies in Chihuahua on his election to a new term as president of Mexico.

In 1901 Díaz was a hero to all foreigners in Mexico. He defended them against dissidents within the Mexican political system. The foreigners responded effusively, knowing, as historian Lesley Byrd Simpson explains, that if, "as Disraeli said, one applies flattery to royalty with a trowel, on Don Porfirio Díaz one used a hose." Simpson continues, "He was half-smothered with foreign decorations, each with its appropriate scroll," remarking also that Díaz "listened to speeches that would have upset the stomach of a Santa Anna."[4] None of these speeches surpassed in flattery a toast proffered by U.S. Secretary of State Elihu Root in 1907.

> If I were a poet I should write eulogies; if I were a musician I should compose triumphal marches; if I were a Mexican I should feel that the steadfast loyalty of a lifetime would not be too much to give in return for the blessings he [Díaz] has brought to my country. But as I am neither poet, musician, nor Mexican, but only an American who loves justice and liberty, and hopes to see their reign among mankind progress and strengthen and become perpetual, I look to Porfirio Díaz, the President of Mexico, as one of the great men to be held up for the hero worship of mankind![5]

Hubert Herring, a sympathetic observer of Prussian order, characterized Porfirio Díaz's reign as "an answer to the prayers of a people wearied by a half century of turmoil. The praetorian peace he gave them was the longest period of calm the nation had known since the day Father Hidalgo rang the bell at Dolores."[6]

Not all of Díaz's contemporaries agreed, particularly those who, for whatever reason, either objected to, or were thought to object to, Díaz's vicelike grip over the greatest possible number of Mexican people. His slogan was "Bread and the Club": bread for the army, the bureaucrats, the foreigners, and even the church—and the club for his opponents and the common people of Mexico.[7] When Díaz marched into Mexico City to declare the end of La Reforma in 1876, the nation was suffering from anarchy and fiscal breakdown, banditry, Indians highly disrespectful of monied and propertied Mexicans, and an embarrassing national economic backwardness. But Díaz found his friends: politicians he could cow, an army he could dismember and whose generals he could set against each other, the Catholic church, the Mormons, foreign capital, and the great landholders.

Under Díaz Mexico became a giant feudal fiefdom. His gunmen (*rurales*) were empowered to shoot, no questions asked. Troublesome Indians, striking workers, indiscreet speakers and writers, and honest people declared and treated as bandits by the regime disappeared into the noisome dungeons of the old Belén Penitentiary, or were shot "while attempting to escape." Mexico prospered—that is, the Mexico that mattered to Díaz. Those with titles, money, and real estate were highly pleased. Many other Mexicans were not, but their voices were not heard for another decade. In the meantime the Mormons, knowing they were vulnerable to the vicissitudes of Chihuahua state politics, tried to cover all their political bases, one of which was Don Porfirio. Mormon apostle John Henry Smith was touched by his two weeks in central Mexico. He had found a "gentle and considerate people there, who had been crushed in the past, and the years of serfdom under which they have labored for so many years has killed to a great extent their spirits." It was obvious, however, that Smith did not consider Porfirio Díaz part of the problem. The apostle was convinced that very soon the Mexicans would "enter in at the door designed by their Maker, and would be engaged in building temples to the Lord."[8]

Certainly he and the others were surprised at finding so many Mormon church members in central Mexico whose faith had survived the long interregnum. He talked with some of the old members who had been baptized as far back as 1879, during the Thatcher mission. Ivins himself was "surprised at the thorough understanding both men and women seemed to have of the doctrines and principles of the plan of redemption."[9]

However, when Ivins and Smith returned to their homes, there was no doubting the magnitude of Tenney's assignment to revitalize the missionary work and reorganize the church in Mexico City. As most of the early members had originally been Protestants, they had reintroduced many Protestant customs into their worship during their long separation from the Mormon church. Because Mormonism is pointedly low on public ritual, any deviations or embellishments smack of "sectarianism" or apostasy and may unnerve mainline church members. Certainly, for the most part, the people had maintained religious activity, but in decidedly un-Mormon forms. In addition, many had become sexually promiscuous, a practice highly contrary to Mormon teachings regardless of its acceptability in any given society. Thus Tenney's task was difficult in spite of the favorable recontacts. On top of all this, some members had set up their own congregations and were reluctant to turn them loose, something a centralized religion cannot tolerate. They struggled a bit with Tenney, only relenting when their new mission president promised that the priesthood and the missionaries would never again be withdrawn. (A decade would pass before the Mexican Civil War and the second of three missionary withdrawals would force that promise to be broken.)

Tenney's chronology offers a glimpse into the reopening period. After leaving the other missionaries at the Mexican Central Railroad depot for their trip to El Paso via Chihuahua City, Tenney returned to Cuernavaca to hold more meetings and to learn as much more as he could. Then he left for Amecameca to visit Silvestre López, an old friend of the Mormons there who would do everything for the church except join it.

From Amecameca he went to Cuautla in Morelos, meeting there with Simón Zúñiga, one of the old converts who had been with the Chihuahua colonists in 1887, only to return with his family, disappointed and on foot. Cuautla Mormons welcomed Tenney, and he spent his time reorganizing branches and re-teaching the Mormon church's organizational procedures and fundamental doctrines, emphasizing fasting, tithing, and prayer. While the Mexican Saints had strayed somewhat from conventional Mormon worship and doctrine, all he met seemed willing to learn and to believe. And Tenny baptized six new converts in Cuautla.

From Cuautla Tenney traveled to the foot of Popocatépetl to visit Ozumba. Neither Popocatépetl, Ozumba, nor the surrounding region had changed much from the days in 1884 when missionary Milson H. Pratt had written a description of them. "Ozumba," he had said,

> is nearly south of the city of Mexico, about forty miles distant, and is the centre of several villages overshadowed by the lofty and noted Popocatépetl. It is situated at the southern extremity of the valley of Mexico, which sweeps around and among the hills and mountains like the bed of some large lake, which undoubtedly the greater part of it was, in times gone by. This region has been terribly disturbed by volcanic eruptions, as extinct craters seen in every

direction, abundantly testify. . . . The "gran volcán" Popocatépetl, rising in a cone 17,852 feet above the level of the sea, still emits a small column of smoke, which can be plainly seen on a clear morning from the village of Aclantla, but later in the day it is quite difficult to distinguish on account of the heavy atmosphere.[10]

Later Pratt described the surrounding area, mentioning many of the branches Tenney returned to visit:

The descent from Ozumba to the hot country, or a lower valley just south, called the "tierra caliente," is very rapid, being nearly 3,000 feet in ten miles, and the valley is still over 4,000 feet above sea level. Aclantla lies on the east of Ozumba, San Juán de Guadalupe on the northeast with its large plantation, and Tecalco on the north by west. . . . Chimal, a village of pears and flowers, lies on the south. These settlements are in the immediate vicinity of Ozumba and, what makes them more interesting to us than anything else is that they are all Indian towns, the inhabitants of which are actual Lamanites, Israelites, as there is very little white blood diffused among them, except here in Ozumba. In the other settlements they usually speak the Mexican instead of the Spanish language, although they understand and can speak both. . . . We have also two congregations in the "tierra caliente," one in Coahuixtla and the other in San Andrés de la Cal.[11]

In Ozumba, Tenney met Lino Zárate, who had been a Mormon missionary in 1879 and 1883. On one occasion in 1883 he and Milson Pratt, knowing that all open-air religious meetings were prohibited by Mexican law, had nevertheless been arrested for preaching in Ozumba's central plaza.[12] Now, eighteen years later, Zárate was overjoyed to see Tenney. He was anxious for Tenney to help him heal his sick wife. Zárate and Tenney laid their hands on her head and blessed her according to the Mormon custom. Señora Zárate's rapid recovery thereafter was incomprehensible to all but Tenney and Zárate.

After less than two weeks in Ozumba, Tenney traveled to Atlautla with Zárate and a Mormon man named Camacho. There they found Simón Páez and his family, who had lived in Colonia Juárez for about five years after most of the original colonists from central Mexico had left. Páez received them kindly and wished them well.

With spirits buoyed, Tenney, Zárate, and Camacho next traveled to Chimal and visited the Nicolás Rodríguez family. The family agreed to return to the church on the condition that they would not be deserted again.

Then in Tecalco they found Julián Rojas. The initiative, independence, dedication, and zeal that had made him a success-ful missionary during the days of Thatcher and Ivins now created trouble for the missionaries. Rojas had a congregation and wanted to keep exclusive control of it, reminding the missionaries that for many years his people had been "a sheep without a shepherd." They talked a long time, with Lino Zárate finally exacting an agree-ment from Rojas to reaffiliate with the Mormon church.

A month later, on 18 August 1901, Tenney returned to Tecalco and rebaptized Rojas and seventy-five of his followers into the Mormon church. Rojas demonstrated his sincerity a week later when, after he was advanced to the church's higher priesthood, he watched Febronio Pérez be made president of the newly organized Tecalco branch—Rojas's former congregation. A year later Pérez was released and sent on a mission, and Rojas was installed as president of the Tecalco congregation he had held together for so long.

After reorganizing the Tecalco branch, Tenney returned to Amecameca but found the Mormon church members there resent-ful and rebellious. So he traveled over to Ixtacalco, just outside Mexico City, where he found another Páez family who seemed to sincerely accept his judgment that they had allowed some alien ideas to creep into their religious thinking. And so it went day after day for nearly a year—Tenney working alone, except when accompanied by local members such as Lino Zárate, Ángel Rosales, or Brother Camacho.

In addition to visiting the members and teaching them, Tenney wanted to organize branches as quickly as possible and confer the priesthood on worthy church members. He began as soon as he believed that some of the Saints were able to lead the others under his direction. Next after the branch at Tecalco that Julián Rojas had self-appointedly held together for so many years was one established at San Andrés de la Cal with Francisco Miranda appointed to head it. Needing help, Tenney asked Lino Zárate, Julián Rojas, Juán Méndez, Simón Zúñiga, and Brother Camacho to serve short-term missions to instruct the branches.

Most of these short-term missionaries were married and had many children. Their missions were a service of love and sacrifice.

Soon they were joined by Ángel Rosales, Margarito Bautista, Jacobo Gonzales, and Juán Mairet, son of the Swiss family that H. L. Hall had interested in the church. During the ensuing months, Juán Páez was assigned to preside over the branch at Ixtacalco; José Gonzales was appointed to the same office in Chimal; and the returned missionary Ángel Rosales was placed over the Trigales branch, becoming the first native returned missionary to head a branch of the church among his own people (12 July 1902).

From 1902 through 1910 several consistent patterns emerged in the Mormons' missionary work in central Mexico. First, missionaries with superbly developed Spanish language skills arrived regularly from the northern colonies. Many of these were married and had left spouses and children at home to be cared for by the other Latter-day Saints while they preached.

A second consistent feature, especially during Tenney's presidency and, later, that of Rey L. Pratt, was the increasing indigenous leadership of branches. More native branch presidents and counselors were appointed and trained. Relief Societies (the Mormon church's charitable and educational women's organizations) were organized, headed by local women who learned the arts of compassionate service appropriate for their time as well as skills in health and maternity care. When Lino Zárate died in 1903, for example, he left a wife and seven children. All but his wife and one small daughter were bedridden with the typhoid fever that had taken Zárate's life. The Relief Societies of his own and nearby branches nursed the family back to health and aided them materially and spiritually. And when Apostle A. O. Woodruff and his wife contracted smallpox while touring Mexico City, Juana Páez gave Mrs. Woodruff the competent and caring attention her English nurse could not or would not provide, willingly risking her own life for a dying sister in the faith.

A third consistent feature of the years up to 1910 was the continued attention that authorities in the colonies and in Salt Lake City gave the new mission. Anthony W. Ivins visited frequently to hold conferences and encourage and instruct the local church members and the missionaries. When he was appointed an apostle in 1907, his successor, Junius Romney, did likewise. Numerous apostles (A. O. Woodruff, John Henry Smith, Mathias F. Cowley, Charles W. Penrose, Heber J. Grant, Anthony W. Ivins) made one or more visits between 1902 and 1910. Apostle Cowley even spent an entire month going to each branch organizing Sunday schools and teaching local members basic music skills.

A fourth pattern was the constant attempt to reclaim the abandoned members. Of the nearly three hundred persons converted to the Mormon church by 1889, fifty-five were still Mormons as of 13 August 1902. Many missionaries reviewed the records and contacted the lost ones. Sometimes they were successful, sometimes not. In July of 1903, for example, two elders left for Tula and Nopala to look for several people who had been baptized in those places. In San Sebastián, a village near Nopala, they found José María Yáñez, who, with other members of his family, had been baptized years earlier. He was cool toward the missionaries but showed them photographs of Elders James Z. Stewart, Melitón G. Trejo, and others whom he had known.

Yáñez told the missionaries about his mother's conversion. She had dreamed that some men were publishing a paper that would aid her spiritually. She sent her son Yáñez to find these men. He met Plotino Rhodakanaty, who directed him to where Moses Thatcher was publishing the tracts. After reading the tracts the mother asked the missionaries to come and baptize her. Her son and his wife were also baptized, and later the son was ordained an elder. But he had become disaffected during the long abandonment and had renounced his priesthood. Although they had lost Yáñez, the missionaries found many other members overjoyed to see them again and therefore kept up the effort to find such people.

The final consistent pattern was that many new converts joined the Mormon church. In the fourteen months during which Tenney headed the mission, 175 baptisms were performed, and by 1911 membership had risen to over 1,000. New areas were opened, new branches organized, and the work expanded to include new peoples in new climates.

There was opposition as usual, of course. There were sickness and death, personal problems, sins requiring excommunication, and failings in leadership and performance. Given the impediments to progress, the marvel is that the Mormon expansion went as well as it did. Mexican Mormons have wished that contemporary Anglo–American Mormons, who sometimes have been critical of them, would not lose sight of that fact.

During this period a minor flurry or two harked back to the days of colonization and "gathering." In 1903 H. L. Hall and others strongly advocated setting up a colony of Mormons in Trigales, where a new branch had been organized and the valley and climate seemed perfect to receive the Latter-day Saints in a place of gathering. But Mormon church authorities deferred to the alternative that Helaman Pratt had proposed so many years before—namely, taking a colony of Mormons to the north. Thus five months later, on 15 December 1903, José Zúñiga and his wife left for Dublán to consider colonizing among the Anglo–American Mormons. This got some popular attention in Salt Lake City, with one reporter writing: "As they are the first to immigrate since the reopening of the mission, many of the Mexican Saints are awaiting with interest their reports of the treatment they receive, etc., for several others are thinking of leaving for the colonies soon."[13]

Then, at the 1907 organization of the San Pedro Mártir branch for which Ivins had traveled to Mexico City, he told the congregation that he hoped before long to secure suitable lands near the northern colonies on which to colonize the Mexican Saints.[14] Two years later Ivins, newly appointed an apostle, sat in a meeting of the Quorum of the Twelve in which five thousand dollars was appropriated for land on which to colonize the Mexicans. Apostles Ivins, John Henry Smith, and Francis M. Lyman had made the proposal, recommending that the church purchase land near one of the Mormon colonies already founded by "our people" and "that we do not attempt to colonize them all in one place, but that two small colonies be started."[15] But this effort never gained much momentum.

As the years passed, with the Anglo–American missionaries celebrating each Fourth of July in Tivoli Park and the Mexican members each Sixteenth of September in their own communities, clouds of war were billowing on the horizon. Few important people seemed to see these signs, especially the foreign residents in Mexico. Thus in September of 1910, when Mexico celebrated the hundredth anniversary of Father Miguel Hidalgo's "Cry of Dolores" that had launched the war of independence against Spain, all seemed well to the newspaper writers.

By all accounts, that September celebration was a magnificent occasion. President Díaz spared no expense for the thousands of guests, many of whom were from foreign countries.

In all the wining and dining, and in all the reports sent home, several things were clear: Mexico was the epitome of stability and success in the Western Hemisphere; the country was prosperous, the budget was balanced, and Mexican currency was as strong as the gold that backed it; foreign capital was safe and returned handsome dividends for those who wisely had invested in agricultural lands, oil properties, and mining or railroad stocks.[16] This was a golden age.

Within a year these illusions, long recognized as such by the common Mexicans whose standard of living had plummeted while the national economy rose, were destroyed for the whole world. Mormons in central Mexico and in the northern colonies soon felt the edge of the revolutionary sword.

Notes

1. Anthony Woodward Ivins to Apostle Francis M. Lyman, recorded in Manuscript History of the Mexican Mission, 30 April 1902.

2. John Womack, Jr., very much taken up by the revolutionary Emiliano Zapata, views Hall in a particularly negative light. When the revolution burst loose in the south, Hall scurried all over, including trying to win influence in the United States, to try to save his investments. After the revolution quieted down, he sought to establish a colonization company in the Cuernavaca valley. Womack saw this as just another capitalist move where new landlords would replace the old ones and leave the peasants as bad off as they had become. Womack is scathing: "Among these characters [sharpers, carpetbaggers, pitchmen, hucksters], the jauntiest and most persistent was a New Englander who had spent the last twenty years in Mexico, Hubert L. Hall. A businessman, a Mormon, and an inside-dopester on his adopted country, Hall impressed Americans who met him quite favorably." (See Womack, *Zapata and the Mexican Revolution*, p. 236.)

3. Journal History, 30 June 1901, p. 2.

4. Lesley Byrd Simpson, *Many Mexicos*, p. 292.

5. Ibid. Mexicans whose economic position had been favored by Díaz were equally as effusive in their praise. In direct reference to similar comments about Díaz by Secretary of State Elihu Root on another occasion during his 1907 visit to Mexico, José F. Godoy said in his preface to *Porfirio Díaz, presidente de México, el fundador de una gran república*: "These words, pronounced by Senator Elihu Root . . . amply justify the publication of whatever work may contain valid information and which gives an impartial and truthful account of President Díaz's life. The striking career of this great man, as much for his military prowess as his statesmanship, cannot fail, and has never done so, to capture the attention not only of his countrymen but of everyone in the civilized world" (author's translation).

6. Hubert Herring, *A History of Latin America*, p. 325.

7. For an account of the dictator's method of operations we are indebted to Carleton Beals, one of the earliest American students of Mexico, who later became an eminent lecturer and a prolific writer. See his "Bread or the Club," in Carlos B. Gil, ed., *The Age of Porfirio Díaz*, pp. 61–70. See also John W. Kitchens, "Some Considerations of the *Rurales* of Porfirian Mexico," and Pedro Santoni, "La policía de la Ciudad de México durante el Porfiriato: los primeros años (1876–1884)." Juán Gómez Quiñones in his *Porfirio Díaz, los intelectuales y la revolución* offers an interesting view on changing social policies emerging during the Díaz period. John Hart ("Historiographical Dynamics of the Revolution") and Stuart F. Voss ("The Porfiriato in Time and Space") provide review essays with considerable insight. See also Jesús Romero Flores, *Del porfirismo a la revolución constitucionalista* for an episodic review. The philisophical foundations of the porfiriato are laid out in Leopoldo Zea's *Positivism in Mexico* and in Abelardo Villegas's edited volume *Positivismo porfirismo*.

8. Journal History, 30 June 1901, p. 2.

9. Ivins to Apostle Francis M. Lyman, 30 April 1902.

10. Journal History, 16 February 1884, p. 3.

11. Ibid.

12. Rey L. Pratt, "History of the Mexican Mission," p. 489.

13. Manuscript History of the Mexican Mission, 15 December 1903.

14. Ibid., 19 May 1907.

15. Journal History, 20 January 1909, p. 4.

16. See in general, David M. Pletcher, *Rails, Mines, and Progress: Seven American Promoters in Mexico, 1867–1911*. For a treatise on the penetration of British capital into Mexico during the Díaz period, see Alfred Tischendorf, *Great Britain and Mexico in the Era of Porfirio Díaz*.

Chapter 4

Revolution, Exodus, and Chaos

To speak of Mexico's "third revolution," or *the* Revolution, as Mexicans prefer to call it, is to enter a realm of emotion frequently unbridled by fact. Victors and vanquished perceive such upheavals, their causes and their consequences, differently. For most Mexicans the civil war that began in 1910 and lasted, with periodic respites, into the 1930s, brought both hope and suffering. The hope was to be freed from a rigidly class-based society that usually slighted and often exploited most Mexicans. Yet, as with most revolutions, bigotry was met with bigotry; cruelty replaced cruelty; and banditry, anarchy, and bloodshed reached indiscriminately even into the most isolated villages of the whole land. Would the Revolution amount to no more than out-Heroding Herod?[1] Some Mormons began to wonder, especially the Anglo–American colonists in the north, who were eventually driven into exile once more. They had gone from exile to exile in a single generation, first to Mexico and then back to the United States. Little wonder that these Anglo American Mormons became contemptuous of politicians and politics.

The Revolution, by which all of Mexico's other revolutions pale in comparison, exploded during the last years of Porfirio Díaz and his close advisors, the *científicos*, whose reign legitimized and enforced a tortured species of Social Darwinism in Mexico.[2] The consequence was an acid of discontent that ate away at Mexico's social fabric, yet Porfirio's army and police were able to hold the country together. Thus the *científicos* appreciated Porfirio Díaz as an alternative to anarchy— and their sentiments were shared by many upper-class citizens.

Anglo–American Mormons certainly agreed with Díaz on the question of anarchy. But the *científicos* and the Mormons parted ways over the place of the Indian in Mexican society. While most *científicos* agreed with Díaz "that Mexico's future lay with the white man, that the Indian was useful only as a burden bearer,"[3] the Mormons on all fronts thought otherwise. They had tried for nearly a full century to extend to the Indian the promises contained in the Mormon scriptures. Mormons were offended when the Díaz regime spoke of Indians as mere servants or as a reservoir of cheap labor for Díaz, monied Mexicans, and the foreign individuals, companies, and governments who supported them. But it is also obvious from the record that Mormons liked Díaz immensely because he supported their cause in the north.

On a calm day in September of 1910 Díaz received eulogies from the foreign dignitaries assembled to celebrate Mexico's independence day. But nearby, a mercenary police force known as *rurales* fought the threat of peasant uprisings in the countryside. The legislation behind that police force was a boon to the great land barons (*hacendados*), for it in effect subsidized their operations at the cost of an underpaid and abused peasantry. Peasant cash wages, historian Hubert Herring informs us, had remained "almost unchanged from the last days of the eighteenth to the first days of the twentieth century," but real wages had, at the same time, fallen by more than fifty percent.[4] With the *rurales* in place, that abuse continued unabated.

And justice was largely replaced by the *ley fuga* (fugitive justice), which allowed an arresting officer to shoot any person who "seemed" to be fleeing from "justice." People who offended the sensitivities of the elite were frequently shot in the back whether they were running away or not. As there was no law but the will of Don Porfirio, few worried about even flagrant excesses. To protest meant to die.

Moreover, as Díaz transferred subsoil mineral rights to the Americans and the British, he high-handedly dispossessed thousands of the Indians, who thought cornfields more desirable than oil fields. And by the land law of 1883, as modified in 1894, five thousand Indian communities suffered wholesale confiscation of their ancestral lands, which Díaz transferred to foreign surveying companies and thereafter, for a pittance, to the huge landed estates. "No compensation, no settlement" was dictated with the barrel of a gun. By the end of the Díaz regime fewer than ten percent of the Indian communities had any land whatever. In the ensuing Maya and Yaqui "rebellions," the army and the *rurales* killed thousands; they imprisoned thousands more and sold them into slave gangs to cultivate henequen in Yucatan and tobacco in Oaxaca.

As the politics of Social Darwinism limited access to and control of land, capital, and subsoil mineral rights, the Mexican elite and their European and North American counterparts prospered. Most Mexicans, excluded from meaningful economic participation, became increasingly angry and desperate. In their opinion Mexico had been lacerated and disemboweled, made easy prey for foreign scavengers and for the Mexican national aristocracy who had become "sellouts and expediters." It was not a particularly unbiased view, but it was a prevalent one.[5]

Many Mexicans understandably hated Díaz and the privileged and powerful institutions that supported him and assured the Mexicans' exploitation. Thus the Mormon position was ambiguous: ideological commitment to Mexican spiritual liberation, and political support of an oppressive and economically ambitious regime based on foreign capital and foreign technicians.

Most Mexicans were angry not only with Díaz and his *científicos* but also with the United States, which sixty years earlier had acquired nearly one-half of Mexico as the fruits of the Mexican–American War.[6] One Mormon from Piedras Negras summed up the impact this had on Mexico when he told his North American Mormon visitors, "I love you as missionaries, but I can't forget the fact that your country took my country's territory away."[7] By 1910 many people thought Porfirio Díaz and his *científicos* were giving the country away—an attitude that complicated the Mormons' position in Mexico.

For many years the U.S. State Department, not to mention numerous U.S. citizens interested in oil, minerals, and land, had overtly supported Díaz and sympathized with the *científicos*. To many Mexicans this proved that the United States was preserving Mexico in a drained and vulnerable state. Earlier, the United States had eviscerated Mexico in war, and Mexicans viewed the Americans and other foreigners as no less destructive now; foreign exploitation of Mexican land, Mexican minerals, and Mexican people had simply become more subtle. Porfirio Díaz and his *científicos* permitted—encouraged—all this exploitation. Some Mexicans now described their country as "the mother of foreigners, the stepmother of Mexicans."[8]

The federal and state militia and the *rurales* had quickly suppressed several rebellions against this high-handedness. On the very eve of the Revolution, Mexico seemed stable and peaceful. So, in September of 1910, when Mexico celebrated its first century of independence, "special delegates [from foreign embassies] vied with one another in extolling the virtues and strength of the Díaz regime."[9]

But Díaz had made two serious mistakes. First, since the turn of the century (he had ruled since 1876!), he had progressively reduced the social basis of his regime. As most Mexicans had therefore become unimportant to him, by 1910 he had to rely fo · support almost completely on foreigners or on the *creoles* (mixed European–Indian descent), who prided themselves on being more foreign than Mexican. Virtually no one but they profited from his rule.

Second, in 1908 Díaz had promised publicly to hold free elections in 1910, and he had allowed an opposing political movement to start preparing for those elections. However, when the constitutionalist opposition began gaining immense popular support, an alarmed Díaz suddenly imprisoned opposition leaders and began to intimidate their followers.

In effect Díaz forced his principal opponent, Francisco Madero—a quiet and sensitive man whose main political ideas had been "constitutional government and no reelection"—to become one of the world's most unlikely revolutionaries. Educated, rich, urbane, and campaigning on a constitutionalist platform of law and order, Madero found himself reluctantly sounding a call to arms.

Many Mexicans joined Madero and attempted to destroy the Díaz regime. In the people's eyes, the *porfiriato* (partnership between foreigners and Mexican elite) had gone bankrupt. Many citizens were now ready to commit their lives and personal honor to a campaign for change, even if that campaign meant violence and, ultimately, civil war.

They touched off a revolution that encompassed economic, social, intellectual, and religious traditions at every level of Mexican society. The entire country was disrupted or devastated during the ensuing ten years. Over fifteen percent of Mexico's citizens died of battle wounds or of the disease and starvation that accompanied this internecine and class-based civil war.[10]

In 1913 Madero was assassinated under conditions heavily implicating U.S. Ambassador Henry Lane Wilson.[11] While there is little evidence to suggest that the U.S. government itself was involved, few Mexicans made this distinction. For them Henry Lane Wilson *was* the U.S. government. They pushed the Revolution on.

Ambassador Wilson liked the *porfiriato*, and he worked diligently for its return. He was anxious to secure Victoriano Huerta as Madero's replacement. But Wilson was soon frustrated. He found Huerta besieged on every side, with Zapata, Carranza, Obregón, and Villa each leading a revolutionary wing against him. The civil war went on.[12] The revolutionaries reasoned that Madero's usurper would now benefit the United States and himself by reinstating the *porfiriato*. There was no guesswork because that was how Henry Lane Wilson talked about it. Hence both Huerta the usurper and his supporter, the United States, were considered the enemy.

The year 1916 was the last straw: two columns of U.S. troops entered Mexico under General John Joseph "Black Jack" Pershing on an unsuccessful campaign to capture the romanticized revolutionary, Pancho Villa.[13] In Mexico, Villa's friends and enemies alike hated the Americans. Indeed, Venustiano Carranza, whom the Americans supported in 1916 as a means of undoing Villa, actually turned and fought U.S. soldiers on Mexican soil when they came to get Villa. A great many Mexicans were intensely proud of Carranza's marginal success in the clash. Mexico was for Mexicans, they thought, not for the Spaniards, the French, the Americans, or anyone else. The *porfiriato* would not likely return.[14] The Revolution would go on.

Mormons in central Mexico and in Chihuahua and Sonora were at first largely uninvolved in the Revolution. More than four thousand Anglo–American Mormons lived in the northern colonies; more than sixteen hundred Mexican Mormons lived in central Mexico. Mormon leaders instructed all of them to be conspicuously neutral during the Revolution. But eventually branches were disrupted and members were killed, tortured, and imprisoned by both federal and revolutionary troops. The church lost lands and investments in the north, and the missionaries once again were obliged to abandon their carefully tended central Mexican flock.

Exodus from the Northern Colonies

When Elizabeth Williams and Heber Farr were married in Elizabeth's father's house on Christmas Day 1893 in the Mormon colony of Dublán, Chihuahua, their wedding gifts were not only practical but typical of the Mormons' economic circumstances: two tin plates, two knives and forks, two large spoons, two small spoons, two tin cups, a box of ball blueing, two bars of soap, two chairs, two yards of lace for pillowslips, and a cake stand. Their first home was a tent, and their bed, table, and other furniture were made from shipping crates.[15]

By 1912 wedding gifts were much more lavish and diverse, including not only the standard kitchen utensils but a few luxuries, some household furniture, clothing, livestock, and sometimes even land on which to build a first home. On the eve of the Mormon exodus from Chihuahua and Sonora, in spite of rumored uprisings, the colonies were more prosperous than ever. Eunice Harris, who had left her Payson, Utah, home years before, not expecting much material gain to follow her young family's escape from the U.S. marshals, was understandably happy about the unanticipated economic improvements. Ellen E. B. McLaws wrote from her farm in Sonora in 1912, "This place is growing and improving all the time. Our wheat fields are lovely now. Financial prospects were never better in our lives I guess." In the years before the Revolution, said Thomas Cottam Romney, "we had about all we could wish for."[16]

But for the recently married, as well as their parents, it did not matter much after July of 1912. "I remember our wedding presents," said Luella R. Haws, "some of which had never been unpacked, which we left behind, to be destroyed by the Mexicans who burned our homes."[17] Eliza Tracy Allred added, "We left things for which we had worked 25 years. Our orchards were just bearing fruit. For the first time in my married life we had on hand our year's supply of bread and fruit. We left, piled in boxcars, like animals, with nothing but a few quilts."[18] Alvin M. Larson, one of the Colonia Díaz refugees, remembered how the revolutionaries "burned most of the buildings, drove off the stock and killed all that they didn't take." While five hundred residents were safely away before the revolutionaries came, the city itself was almost completely destroyed. When the Larson family finally arrived in Logan, Utah, in August of 1912, they had "the clothes on our backs and $2.50 in U.S. money."[19] Although they had expected to return shortly and reclaim their lands and property, most of the Mormons eventually reconciled themselves to their loss. Those who returned found the next decade full of trying experiences as the Revolution continued to unfold.

The northern Saints had two liabilities: they were relatively prosperous, and they were Americans. Remaining neutral became an increasingly delicate task as first federal and then revolutionary forces swarmed around the colonies, each claiming to be the "law" that the Mormons must obey and the taxing authority to which they must contribute.

Both the federal forces and the revolutionaries were careful, for a time, not to destroy the colonists' motivation or their wherewithal to produce a surplus that could be confiscated. But as the Revolution continued, so also did demands on the colonists for food, provisions, and services. Aside from that, the unsettled times contributed thefts, personal abuse, plunder, and an occasional murder. Also, neither revolutionaries nor federals could maintain military discipline, although the revolutionaries— especially Pancho Villa—executed several of their men whose petty thefts exceeded the planned plundering of the colonists.

A lively dispute continues today among surviving Anglo-American Mormons who experienced the Revolution, and among their descendants, over whether the exodus was necessary. Were the Saints really in that much danger? Couldn't they have negotiated a little more with the revolutionaries? Couldn't they simply have refused to hand over their weapons, thereby throwing the gauntlet at the rebel ("red flagger") General Salazar as he trained cannons on Dublán? They did have their own militia— couldn't they have fielded it? But the danger to women and children and to many of the men was clear. Junius Romney, the colonies' stake president, ordered the evacuation of Dublán while staring straight into the barrel of one of Salazar's cannons. Not to hand over their weapons—which were numerous—would have meant the bombardment of Dublán and later Juárez. To hand them over with only Salazar's assurances that no further harm would come to the Mormons was too risky.

Within hours the Latter-day Saints were loading hundreds of women and children into open Mexican Central Railroad cattle cars for evacuation to El Paso, Texas. The men followed on horses, bringing what livestock they could. The exodus from the mountain colonies was by horse and buggy to Arizona. Certainly some had misgivings; that is one reason the controversy about the exodus lives on. But once the local church authorities had decided on evacuation, the colonists carried out the plan as quickly as possible.

Among all the Americans in the north, the Mormons suffered least. Both the federals and the revolutionaries treated them less harshly than they did other Americans and the native population. Moreover, in the early stages of the war the revolutionaries plagued them less than the federal troops did, a situation that evoked considerable sympathy among the Mormons for the revolutionaries. Without this information it may be thought a little curious that several colonists eventually arranged to have Mormon temple ordinances done vicariously for one of the most famous revolutionaries—Pancho Villa. Villa had expressed his belief in the Mormon faith to Mormons he had captured and held imprisoned.[20] He did much less damage to Mormons than either his position or his inclination would have allowed; he also announced that he would execute any of his soldiers who violated a Mormon woman. None did.[21]

The Saints' American citizenship became a liability after it became evident that U.S. foreign policy favored Carranza rather than Pancho Villa and that the United States had permitted Carranza's forces to slip behind Villa on U.S. territory and deal him a devastating blow. Loyal to the United States but living in Mexico, the Anglo–American Mormons were fortunate to come off as well as they did.

On 11 September 1912, General Salazar addressed his fellow countrymen and the Mormon colonists who gathered unwillingly at his orders in the despoiled Mormon colony at Morelos. His speech, as interpreted by Moroni Fenn, best illustrates the xenophobic sentiments of the times. According to Fenn, who was one of several captured Mormon colonists conscripted to freight supplies for Salazar's troops, Salazar considered U.S.

President Howard Taft to be a "vile dog," head of a country that had taken the territory of Mexico–Arizona and New Mexico by treason. As recompense, Salazar announced that the revolutionaries were "going to run all the Americans out of Mexico."[22]

Despite Salazar's hyperbole, many Mexicans, especially those around Juárez, respected the Mormons. Although the Revolution nearly destroyed Colonia Díaz and the Mormon mountain colonies, the Juárez colony was relatively unscathed, in part because of local Mexicans' care while the property owners were away. When Junius Romney ordered Dublán and Juárez evacuated, for example, the Juárez bishop, Joseph C. Bentley (who vigorously disagreed with the order but obeyed it nevertheless), and Alonzo Taylor went after dark to Felipe Chávez, the chief government officer in Colonia Juárez, and also to several other Mexicans. Bentley and Taylor charged these men to preserve the colony during the colonists' absence. They placed Chávez in charge of their property and gave him two letters, one addressed to the federals and the other to the rebels, to explain his stewardship to whoever should occupy the settlement. They asked other Mexicans to look after their merchandise, orchards, and cattle. When a few of the colonists returned to Juárez after the exodus, they found that the Mexicans had honored the stewardship in every respect. Mormons in Chuichupa made a similar arrangement that lasted for some time. In Dublán, however, "some of the people were anxious to see the Latter-day Saints go."[23] The colony suffered, to be sure, but the local Mexican residents' care saved it from indiscriminate destruction.

When the Latter-day Saints arrived in El Paso, a heated discussion arose about what they should do next. Treated kindly by El Paso's citizens, some families waited weeks to see if they would be able to return to their homes. Finally, with the U.S. government paying relocation costs, hundreds of Mormons opted to resettle in the United States. President Joseph F. Smith, who had succeeded Lorenzo Snow, closed the Juárez Stake and released its members from their obligations in Mexico. They were free to resettle wherever they could.

In spite of this apparent finality, Apostle Anthony W. Ivins and Bishop Joseph C. Bentley, both of whom were tied emotionally and economically to the Mormon colonies in Mexico, talked often about the possibility of going back. Finally, Bentley and a few

95

others did return, eventually resettling in Juárez, Dublán, and Chuichupa. At times their stay was precarious; at times nearly impossible. During the next few years U.S. President Woodrow Wilson landed Marines at Veracruz, and many Mexicans feared that he would order the sacking of Mexico City (1914).[24] All this was understandably followed by the order of Mormon church president, Joseph F. Smith, for a second evacuation. U.S. General Pershing's futile 1916 expedition into Mexico in pursuit of Pancho Villa also greatly complicated matters for the Saints who had returned. Many dramatic episodes in which life hung perilously in the balance of a quick decision assure that Bishop Bentley and his flock will have a place in the minds of all those who care to think about the Anglo–American Mormon colonies in Mexico.[25] In at least one way, all this was beneficial for the Mormons: In the coming years the colonists would continue to provide critical Spanish language skills for the Mormon missionary efforts elsewhere in Latin America.

Mormons Experience the Revolution in Central Mexico

While Mormons in the north had their burdens with the Revolution, those in the south were also being dislocated. By April of 1911 the Revolution had spread to all parts of the nation, although central Mexico was perhaps quietest. No one had bothered the missionaries or their labors there, although some of the members had a fright from time to time. On 19 April 1911, however, the Ozumba missionaries wrote to Rey L. Pratt, president of the Mexican mission, that the people there and in the surrounding Indian villages where Mormon branches existed were excited by rumors that Zapata would soon attack. Emiliano Zapata, with a few sympathizers in Ozumba and considerably more in the surrounding Indian villages, continued to recruit thousands to the revolutionary cause.[26]

By mid-May Don Porfirio's situation was clearly hopeless. Villa and Orozco had overrun Ciudad Juárez in the north, and between 13 and 17 May, Zapata had fiercely attacked Cuautla, driving out many of its inhabitants and heavily damaging government buildings and installations. Some of the Saints had passed the entire siege within the city. Although no one was injured, the Zúñiga and Aguilar homes were scarred with bullet holes. As the Revolution spread throughout the country, the federal army and even the *rurales* began to collapse like corn stalks in a hurricane. José Yves Limantour, Díaz's brilliant finance minister, saw the inevitable and agreed to Don Porfirio's resignation without even consulting him.

Limantour agreed with Madero that a provisional government should be set up under Francisco de la Barra until Madero could be elected president—an event that was taken for granted. When news of the capitulation broke in Mexico City on 23 May 1911, there was cheering in many homes. The following day huge crowds paraded the streets to the *Zócalo*, Mexico City's enormous central plaza, shouting, "Resign! Resign!" Mobs milled before the National Palace yelling similar phrases not heard freely in public for more than thirty years. Porfirio's answer was to shoot down two hundred on the spot. Others died in their homes—some quickly, some slowly—from wounds no medical doctor dared treat. The missionaries, from their secluded vantage, counted eight dead and noted that the people's joy "knew no bounds" when Díaz resigned on the twenty-fifth.[27] Apparently travel conditions had improved, because the next day the missionaries from several villages gathered to hold church meetings.[28]

Various Mormons had developed impressions of the Revolution. The missionaries and some of the members in Ozumba thought of Zapata as a "southern bandit"; others, in the Indian villages, thought of him as a "southern savior." On the commemoration of Independence Day on the sixteenth of September, the members and six missionaries in Ozumba heard what Zapata had done to Cuautla and believed rumors that he was definitely on his way to Ozumba, although it turned out to be only another scare. They began to hold fewer night meetings but did conduct their scheduled district conference the following February, reporting that their missionary endeavors were generally moving along well.

As Mexican central authority crumbled before the eyes of startled diplomats, anxious foreign businessmen, and alarmed *hacendados*, the Mormons' situation in central Mexico became more confusing and desperate. The Mexican Mormons, like other civilians, were afflicted not so much by bullets and cannon fire as by disease and exposure.[29] Because of the conflict's anti-foreign nature, the Anglo–American missionaries in central Mexico could become targets for assassination.

In April of 1912 President Joseph F. Smith telegraphed Rey Pratt, instructing him to do whatever he thought proper to protect the missionaries. Act in harmony with the American embassy, President Smith told Pratt. Thus the next day all ten missionaries—nearly half of them from the Mormon colonies in Chihuahua—registered with a committee Henry Lane Wilson had appointed to protect Americans in Mexico City. Pratt thereafter contacted all missionaries outside Mexico City, instructing them not to leave their district headquarters overnight. If evacuation should become necessary, he wanted no communication delays.

After taking these precautions, Pratt and his missionaries went about their normal activities. Pratt and Ernest Young (the mission secretary who later contributed significantly to the church in Latin America) finished arranging and publishing a new edition of the Spanish hymnbook that contained compositions and translations made by the missionaries and Mexican members. They expanded their missionary endeavors into the state of Puebla, specifically to Cholula, a place that captured their attention because, as one missionary said, its inhabitants were "a cultured people."[30] They continued their labors in Toluca, San Marcos, Ozumba, and everywhere else except Cuautla. That town, a strategic point of dispute between the Zapatistas and the federal troops, was cut off from visitors for as long as six months at a time.

Careful travel, fewer night meetings, and a little extra caution saw the missionaries through their daily tasks. Then they learned that thousands of Anglo–American Mormons in Chihuahua and Sonora had been forced to flee from their colonies into the United States. Pratt released the affected families' missionary sons from their ecclesiastical duties so they could aid their destitute loved ones. Shortly the Mormon church's First Presidency announced that because of the danger no new missionaries would be sent to Mexico.[31] It was all very depressing for the Mormons.[32]

By 12 August 1912 the situation had become grave in central Mexico as well, where there were more than sixteen hundred Saints.[33] Some of these were driven from their homes in the Toluca district. Elsewhere daily living was disrupted. The federals blamed it all on the Zapatista movement, which had grown considerably during August, swollen by village recruits who saw their chance to free and avenge themselves. For the missionaries to visit any of these insecure southern branches, where several trains had been robbed and burned and the guards killed, became impossible. So the missionaries confined their activities to the "cold country or in the valleys near the conference [district] headquarters, where they [could] work unmolested."[34]

The whipsawing between the federals and the Zapatistas afflicted many Mormon families. Sometimes Mormons could not maintain the appearance of neutrality in the conflict and sometimes the conflict became a pretext to settle old grudges, as in the case of Mormons Camilo Ramos, Modesto Ramos, Leonardo Linares, and Regino García of Cuautla, who were caught in the crossfire between Zapatistas and federals. When, after indiscriminately bombarding an area government troops could find no outside raiders, they saved face by picking up local residents in a fire zone, accusing them of being Zapatistas and imprisoning them. Like many others, these four Mormons had been unfortunate enough to be found where rumors held that Zapatistas would enter. Some may have been Zapatista sympathizers, but they were unarmed.

The federals took the four Mormons to the government's Department of War in Mexico City, which customarily drafted such men into the federal army. Few questions were ever asked about loyalties, since such men were considered cannon fodder anyway: shot from the front by the revolutionaries or from the back by the federals, it did not matter. The barracks at La Canoa received hundreds of them.

Rita Ramos and Sabina Linares stuck as close as they could to their husbands on the trip to Mexico City. Then, understandably desperate, they contacted the mission home and told Rey Pratt what had happened. Everyone knew how the federals treated "suspects." There was not a moment to lose.

Pratt obtained permission to visit the men and also contacted the government's Department of War, where he learned he would have to "prove" the men's innocence. Sabina Linares and Rita Ramos quickly began a return trip to Cuautla to get the required documents. They traveled by train to Ozumba and then walked and hitched rides on mules and burros some thirty miles to their homes in Cuautla, much of which was now rubble. From city officials they obtained the letters and documents that would remove all doubt about the members' involvement with Zapatistas.

Then the wives started back on foot to Ozumba, Rita Ramos carrying a nursing baby and tugging a young son along. From there they continued by train to Mexico City. The ordeal had cost them three days and considerable hardship.

Pratt presented the documents at the office of the secretary of war and also arranged with the military commander of La Canoa that the men not be removed from Mexico City until the question of their liberty had been settled. The assurances were given, but in less than a week the two Mormon men were shipped off to the north without a word to their wives or to Pratt. Pratt again visited the office of the secretary of war. "It's a mistake," he was told, "because conclusive proofs show the innocence of the men."[35] They were to be returned immediately, but they never were. Camilo Ramos died shortly of an "incurable disease" (the federal's description of the cause of his death), leaving his wife and young family to face an uncertain future. Local members cared for the Ramos family—yet during the Revolution so many people were suffering that it was hard for anyone to give much aid.

There were other cases. Someone, reportedly a San Pablo branch member, accused Julia Olivares of that branch of being a Zapatista. Before Pratt could move with the declarations on her behalf, the federals shipped her off to a slave labor camp in Quintana Roo. Federal troops executed Juán Rodríguez of the Chimal branch, as they did Jesús Rojas Enriques from Ozumba when someone accused these men of being Zapatistas. Rodríguez's wife had already died, and he left two children. While Porfirio Díaz had already died, his "law and order" nevertheless lived on. In Ozumba many were settling old grudges by similar means, and when the Zapatistas overran the town they had their turn.[36] The Zapatistas would later execute the Mormons' San Marcos branch president and his trusted friend.

Through all this, Pratt and his remaining seven missionaries continued to travel to accessible branches and help when they could. The most important thing was to keep the branches together so the Mormon community could be activated in time of any single member's need. Mormon Relief Societies continued aiding members all during the civil war.

It was during one of these missionary visits that the Monroy family (Rafael, Jovita, Guadalupe, and their mother, Jesús) of San Marcos was converted and baptized. The missionaries had been proselyting in the state of Hidalgo since the Revolution began, and these were the first new members there since the mission had reopened in 1901. Pratt was fond of Rafael, a relatively wealthy and cultured man who owned a general store, lands, and cattle. The two had long talks, and Pratt invited Rafael and his family to Tívoli Park for the 1913 Fourth of July celebration with the American colony, housing them in the mission home. It was a fateful acquaintance. Because of his Mormon affiliation Rafael Monroy would die in the Revolution.

Central Mexico was becoming a free-fire zone; tensions mounted by the hour in Mexico City. A buildup of revolutionary forces suggested to some that the revolutionaries would try to take the capital in September 1913. As a precaution, Pratt moved his family and the Mexico City missionaries to Veracruz, although they returned for a church conference later in August. On 28 August 1913, however, newspapers printed a request from the U.S. State Department for all Americans to leave the country immediately. Remembering President Smith's earlier instructions, Pratt judged it to be an order for Mormon missionaries too. He notified all his elders in outlying districts to prepare to move to Veracruz.

There were last-minute organizational details to take care of to secure the viability of the branches. Although native members led most of them, this was not true of some of the youngest branches such as San Marcos. Rafael Monroy came to bid the missionaries goodbye, and Pratt ordained him an elder and appointed him to preside over the Mormons in San Marcos, to hold meetings, and to set up the branch there. Pratt, his family, and the missionaries then left.

The Mormons in central Mexico were all alone once more. When Ammon Tenney had promised Julián Rojas and the Páez family in 1901 that the missionaries and the church's priesthood holders would not leave them again, he could not have foreseen September of 1913. But in a sense he had not been completely wrong: the American elders had left, but Mormon leaders remained because ordained Mexican Mormons carried their load and would continue to do so, alone, for more than four years.

When Pratt arrived in Salt Lake City in September 1913, he found the Mormon leaders gravely disappointed about Mexico. They were concerned about the Latter-day Saints in central Mexico and also disturbed about the four thousand members from the northern colonies who had just been expelled from their lands and homes; lives had been lost, and millions of dollars in real and personal property had been destroyed. The leaders had misgivings about ever again being able to preach in Mexico.

Perceiving their feelings, Pratt tried to reassure them. At the October 1913 general church conference held in Salt Lake City he said, "I have the spirit of that mission running through my veins to such an extent that it is almost impossible for me to talk to the people here except I speak in regard to the Mexican Mission."[37]

Again and again Pratt reminded the Anglo–American Saints of the need to maintain a mission to the Lamanites.[38] His daughter, Mary Pratt Parish, thought that some of the authorities got a little impatient with her father for his incessant talk about the work in Mexico. But Pratt's perceptions were accurate; after the Anglo–American Mormons had left Chihuahua the authorities' interest in the work in Mexico noticeably subsided.

What to do now? If we cannot work in Mexico, Mormon leaders reasoned, why not do so among the hundreds of thousands of Mexicans living in the United States? Thus this Mexican disaster spawned the church's Spanish–American mission. Pratt was put in charge. Americans of Mexican ancestry now had a chance to hear the Mormon gospel in their preferred language, Spanish.

Although Pratt wanted to return to Mexico and the church's First Presidency was anxious about leaving the church members alone again, because of the physical danger the authorities finally decided not to send anyone back until the civil war was over. They expressly asked Pratt not to return. He was to correspond with the members and care for them as best he could in that way. The disrupted mail service made this a halting effort at best, but one to which Pratt brought energy and conviction.

Pratt's correspondence with the Mexican members was alternately heartening and distressing. The branch presidents were doing their best to keep their congregations together and to maintain a neutral position among the warring forces (which they were able to do for the most part, except when the Saints were conscripted into one or another of the fighting bands). They held their meetings when peace permitted, and they even did a little missionary work. On the other hand, a few

Mexican Saints, along with many of their fellow citizens, often went hungry. Pratt learned that they were "reduced to scavenging in the streets and eating perhaps once in twenty-four hours. Some of the men had been conscripted into military service, were ill-clothed and poorly paid, their families left to fend for themselves."[39]

Most distressing for Pratt was the letter he received on 16 December 1915 from Jesús Monroy in San Marcos telling of the firing squad execution of her son Rafael and his companion Vicente Morales. Carranza and Zapata had made San Marcos a dueling ground, ripping up railroad beds, setting locomotives and rolling stock aflame, and weekly alternating control of the town. Just as in Ozumba and everywhere else in the Republic, both sides settled personal, political, and religious scores on these occasions. One time, when the Zapatistas held San Marcos, Monroy was denounced for being in league with Carranza and associating with Americans. (Monroy had been nearly obligated, because of the provisions he had in his store, to entertain Carranza's officers when they held the town.) The Zapatistas picked him up, jailed him for a while, found out he was a Mormon, and offered to spare his life if he would denounce his religion. He and Morales declined. In later years the children from the Mormon school *Héroes de Chapúltepec* in San Marcos, Hidalgo, occasionally visited Monroy's and Morales's graves to pay their respects.[40]

For the most part, through all the chaos and bloodshed, the members in central Mexico abided by Pratt's parting counsel: Stick together; stay uninvolved as much as you can; keep the covenants; follow your leaders. They did remarkably well, some of them even managing to save a tenth of their bare subsistence incomes to pay a church tithe.[41]

By November 1917, as the Revolution quieted down, Pratt had received permission to return to Mexico and follow up on his efforts to help. Earlier he had persuaded church authorities to send money for some of the members in Mexico, but no one was sure whether the funds had arrived intact. Now Pratt returned to see who had survived and under what conditions. He realized quickly that many Saints, especially children, had died from exposure and disease during the war. Pratt's reception told him two more things: the Latter-day Saints had tried to keep their church together, and they were overjoyed to see their mission president again.

Pratt noticed that one Indian member, Isaías Juárez, had become an important and widely respected leader among the Mormons in Mexico. Juárez would be even more important in subsequent years, when the Mormon missionaries once more fled Mexico, this time staying absent over ten years while the Mexican national government made its final "peace" with the Catholic church. Once again the Mormon church in Mexico depended on its native leaders to see it through.

Notes

1. It is hard to know just how general this feeling of despair got to be, but certainly by 1914–15 it was widespread. Yet as in other traumas both personal and collective, the despair in Mexico proved to be short run, being ultimately followed by the euphoria of victory. The surviving folk songs about the Revolution are almost all optimistic. However bad the situation was, people somehow chose to remember what they were trying to accomplish rather than what was happening to them in the process. As in anecdotes of the American Revolutionary War, and those of victorious peoples virtually everywhere, despair bathed in the light of victory is seen as courage, strength, and fortitude.

Among foreigners the perceptions are clearly the opposite. One need only study the family records of Anglo–American Mormons who lost their lands and loved ones to the war, for example, to see that to them the victors were evil.

2. In his *A History of Latin America* (p. 328), Hubert Herring may offer the best description of the *científicos*:

> From 1892 on, new faces appeared in the inner circle around Díaz, chiefly creoles in place of the mestizos upon whom he had earlier relied, men who were popularly called *científicos*, scientists. Their political and economic faith owed much to the positivism of Auguste Comte, and they accepted his naive conclusion that society could be saved by the techniques of the "social" sciences uncorrupted by metaphysics and theology. They called themselves liberals, but dismissed the liberalism of Juárez [Mexico's earlier and only Indian president] as visionary and prided themselves upon a tough practicality [one consequence of which was to reduce large sectors of Mexican society to economic exploitation by foreigners and nationals alike]. The *científicos*, never more than a score in number, were often men of considerable idealism, and favored honest administration, impartial courts, and a measure of freedom of speech and press.

The honesty, impartiality, and freedom extended to everyone but the Indians. And it certainly did not bother the *científicos* that Mexico was more Indian than not.

3. Ibid. Herring's bias seems to be that Díaz's mistakes were tactical, not strategic. Any negative comment from Herring about Díaz may therefore be entertained with some confidence as to its validity.

4. Ibid., p. 333. See note 7, chapter 3, for additional bibliographical discussion of the Díaz period.

5. Readers will be interested in the colorful treatment by Anita Brenner, *The Wind That Swept Mexico: The History of the Mexican Revolution, 1910–1942*, pp. 7–36. See also the excellent regional study by Mark Wesserman, *Capitalists, Caciques, and Revolution*; and, for in-depth treatment at a national level, José C. Valadés's *Historia general de la revolución mexicana*.

6. "The Treaty of Guadalupe Hidalgo formally ended the war on February 2, 1848. Mexico received $15 million and the cancellation of all outstanding claims. The United States got Texas (or, more accurately, the assurance of her title to Texas) and the territory that is now California, New Mexico, Arizona, Nevada, Utah, and part of Colorado—about half of Mexico's national domain" (Herring, *History of Latin America*, p. 312). Who caused the war? Answers indict both the Americans and the Mexicans, with a preponderance for single-variable analysis lying most resolutely among expansionist nationalists in the United States and left-wing nationalists in Mexico. For each of these groups the fault was "all the Mexicans' " or "all the Americans'. " The interested reader will want to review Glenn W. Price's *Origins of the War with Mexico: The Polk–Stockton Intrigue*.

7. Lorenzo A. Anderson, Oral History, interview by Gordon Irving, p. 70.

8. The quote comes from Martin C. Needler, ed., *Political Systems of Latin America*, p. 18. Díaz welcomed foreign capital to such an extent that it dominated the economic life of the nation. Herring observes that "the Americans and the British owned the oil wells and mines. The French controlled most of the growing textile business and many of the large shops. The Germans controlled the trade in hardware and drugs. The Spaniards (and especially the *gallegos* from Galicia) were grocers and other retail merchants. The public utilities—trolley lines, power companies, water companies—belonged to the English, the Canadians, the Americans, and various other outsiders. The Mexicans, untrained in modern techniques, were, in effect, aliens in their own land" (Herring, *History of Latin America*, p. 331).

9. Charles Curtis Cumberland, *Mexican Revolution: Genesis under Madero*, p. 3.

10. See, in general, William Weber Johnson, *Heroic Mexico: The Violent Emergence of a Modern Nation*.

11. Marquez Sterling has observed that (as cited in Herring, *History of Latin America*, pp. 340–41, n. 3):

Mexicans generally charge Ambassador Wilson with moral responsibility for the final tragedy of Madero's murder. That he was indiscreet is clear. Secretary of State Philander Knox warned him to use "circumspection." His colleague, the Cuban ambassador, reported that Wilson convened the diplomatic corps after Madero's arrest and proudly informed them: "Mexico has been saved. From now on we shall have peace, progress and prosperity. I have known about the plans to imprison Madero for three days. It was slated to occur this morning." [Herring then observes that

105

Madero and his vice president] signed their resignations on Huerta's promise of safe conduct from the country; Madero's wife and many others
appealed to the American ambassador to persuade Huerta to keep his
promise—but without success, for that diplomat had become one of the
most fervent supporters of the new regime. On February 22 [1913] Madero
and Pino Suárez were murdered by guards who were transferring them
to the penitentiary.

While Wilson is alleged to have been implicated in Madero's assassination and
therefore quite in favor of the military coup that brought General Victoriano
Huerta to power, the German ambassador, Paul von Hintze, favored keeping
Madero alive as a counterweight to United States influence in Mexico. However
one looks at the matter, there was considerable international intrigue in the
whole affair. Two previously unpublished and unknown accounts—one from
Wilson's own hand, the other a memo to Wilson from William F. Buckley—of
these events give an interesting insight into Wilson. (See W. Dirk Raat and
William H. Beezley, eds., *Twentieth-Century Mexico*, pp. 104–14; see also Friedrich
Katz, *The Secret War in Mexico: Europe, the United States and the Mexican Revolution*.)

12. The best general work on Zapata is still John Womack, Jr., *Zapata and
the Mexican Revolution*. On Carranza, see Douglas Richmond, *Venustiano Carranza's
Nationalist Struggle, 1893–1920*; Linda B. Hall has written a very readable and
informative work on Obregón (*Alvaro Obregón: Power and Revolution in Mexico,
1911–1920*); and Jim Tuck has captured the colorful Pancho Villa in his *Pancho
Villa and John Reed: Two Faces of Romantic Revolution*. Considerable "revisionist"
literature is now coming out on the Revolution and the roles each of the above
played in it. See Barry Carr's bibliographical discussion, "Recent Regional
Studies of the Mexican Revolution." Illustrative of some of the new regional
work are James C. Carey, *The Mexican Revolution in Yucatan, 1915–1924*, and
Víctor Raúl Martínez Vásquez, ed., *La revolución en Oaxaca, 1900–1930*.

13. General Pershing's campaign was allegedly in response to Villa's having carried out a raid on Columbus, New Mexico. The U.S. government had
let Mexican federal troops use American soil to slip up on Villa's "protected
flank." Villa thus considered the United States to have forfeited its neutrality
in the war; it was therefore no longer immune to attack.

Many observers have noted that Pershing's campaign in Mexico was less
designed to capture Villa than to put new military equipment to actual field
test prior to what was considered a certain entrance of the United States into
World War I. David Johnson, a colonies Mormon who sold supplies to the U.S.
Army at its field camp near Colonia Dublán in the state of Chihuahua, has
described the wholesale field testing of gun-mounted, cloth-winged aircraft, the
controversial motorized armored vehicles, and automatic gunnery. All this was
being done under conditions patently removed from any pretense of a campaign
to capture Villa (personal interview).

14. According to historian Frank Brandenburg, "Nobody acquainted with
Mexico and the Mexicans can deny that a deep current of antiforeign sentiment runs through the width and breadth of the Revolution. Mexican history
since 1910 is replete with manifestations of xenophobia, chauvinism, and strong
nationalism. Mexican laws contain antiforeign, markedly nationalistic provisions" (*The Making of Modern Mexico*, p. 327).

15. Elizabeth Williams Farr, cited in Kate B. Carter, comp., "The Mormons
in Mexico," *Treasure of Pioneer History*, 3:215.

16. Cited by Blaine Carmon Hardy, "Cultural 'Encystment,' as a Cause of the Mormon Exodus from Mexico in 1912," p. 451.

17. Luella R. Haws, cited in Carter, "The Mormons in Mexico," 3:212.

18. Mary Eliza Tracy Allred, "Autobiography, 1874–1920," p. 13.

19. Cited in Carter, "The Mormons in Mexico," 3:251.

20. The temple work was done in the Mesa temple, 1 March 1966. (See W. Ernest Young, "A Brief Sketch of Lives of Francisco [Pancho] Villa and Felipe Ángeles"; folder also contains correspondence with J. H. Whetten concerning the temple work.)

21. It is often noted that Villa's near fanaticism on the matter of "violations of sexual honor" derived from the brutal gang rape of his sister years before by sons of a rancher for whom his family was obligated to render services. That was also one of the events, it is said, that turned him into a revolutionary.

22. Cited in Barney T. Burns and Thomas H. Naylor, "Colonia Morelos: A Short History of a Mormon Colony in Sonora, Mexico," pp. 175–76.

23. Franklin Spencer González, "The Restored Church in Mexico," p. 106.

24. Many military personnel, having landed and secured Veracruz after considerable bloodshed due to the unexpected Mexican resistance, were anxious to move on to Mexico City. However, such an order was never given. President Woodrow Wilson wanted to avoid any more bloodshed; it was clear that he was surprised and appalled at the slaughter that had occurred in Veracruz. (See Robert E. Quirk, *An Affair of Honor,* and Arthur S. Link, ed., *Woodrow Wilson and a Revolutionary World, 1913–1921.*)

25. Relevant works consulted for this section include B. H. Roberts, *A Comprehensive History of The Church of Jesus Christ of Latter-day Saints*; Burns and Naylor, "Colonia Morelos"; Thomas Cottam Romney, *A Divinity Shapes Our Ends as Seen in My Life Story*; Karl E. Young, *Ordeal in Mexico. Tales of Danger and Hardship Collected from Mormon Colonists*; Thomas Cottam Romney, *The Mormon Colonies in Mexico*; Nelle Spilsbury Hatch, *Colonia Juárez: An Intimate Account of a Mormon Village*; Annie R. Johnson, *Heartbeats of Colonia Díaz*; Journal of John Jacob Walser (1849–1933); Eunice Stewart Harris, "Autobiography"; Joseph Charles Bentley, Journal; Junius Romney, "Remarks Made in the Garden Park Ward Sacrament Meeting, Salt Lake City, Utah, 31 July 1966"; Elizabeth H. Mills, "The Mormon Colonies in Chihuahua after the 1912 Exodus"; Raymond J. Reed, "The Mormons in Chihuahua: Their Relation with Villa and the Pershing Punitive Expedition, 1910–1917"; W. Ernest Young, Oral History, interview by Gordon Irving.

26. See, in general, Womack, *Zapata.*

27. Manuscript History of the Mexican Mission, 25 May 1911.

28. Ibid., 27 May 1911.

29. Ibid., 16 November 1917.

30. Ibid., 19 July 1912.

31. Ibid., 21 October 1912.

32. The sentiments are recorded by an on-the-scene observer, W. Ernest Young, "Diary of My Life," pp. 72–73.

33. Dale F. Beecher, "Rey L. Pratt and the Mexican Mission," p. 300.

107

34. Manuscript History, 5 August 1912

35. Ibid., 2 May 1913.

36. Womack, *Zapata*, pp. 263, 281.

37. Cited in Beecher, "Rey L. Pratt," p. 301.

38. See Rey L. Pratt, "The Mission to the Lamanites."

39. Beecher, "Rey L. Pratt," p. 301. See also Rey L. Pratt's reports in the Manuscript History of 18 October 1916.

40. The symbolism ought not to be lost on North Americans. While Mormon missionaries attended Independence Day celebrations in Tívoli Park during which they heard eulogies honoring the American soldiers who had died in the Mexican–American War of 1846–48 (see for example, Young, Diary, pp. 67–68, as well as the annual entries of the Fourth of July celebrations in the Manuscript History), Mexican Mormons were naming their first indigenous school after their own heroes from the same war. Every Mexican school child learns that the young cadets of the military academy at Chapúltepec preferred death by a suicidal leap from the castle walls to surrendering to the invading American Army storming the city during the Mexican–American War.

41. Rey L. Pratt, "Review of the Mission Labor among the Lamanites."

Chapter 5

Development in Isolation*

By 1913 the Mormon church was sufficiently established in key central Mexican areas to survive the civil war. Although the war disrupted church activities, including missionary efforts, it did not close them down altogether.

During this anarchy and bloodletting, several Mormons—Rafael Monroy and Vicente Morales, for instance—were executed for political and religious reasons. Many of the church's first converts struggled not only to preserve their families' lives but also to establish themselves in a cruel yet promising world.

Among the Mexicans, Mormonism had gone first to the villages and rural outskirts of Mexico City and Puebla rather than to the cities, as it would later in every other Latin American country. Here people had first cheered the Revolution's promises but later feared its methods. The simplicity and poverty of San Marcos, Ozumba, Cuautla, Tecalco, San Andrés de la Cal, San Pedro Mártir, Ixtacalco, and Atlautla contrasted dramatically with downtown Mexico City and its luxurious residential surroundings on the hills of Chapúltepec. That those early Mormons survived in these isolated villages without missionaries from the north is a tribute to their faith and their resourcefulness.

---

*This chapter is based on an unpublished manuscript, "Mormonism in Mexico: Leadership, Nationalism, and the Case of the Third Convention," coauthored with Elizabeth Hernandez.

The first two generations of Mexican Mormons were mostly small-scale rural merchants or farmers who lived in small homes and, like the earlier Mormons who had come to Utah, still struggled to provide their children with basic necessities. There were exceptions, of course: the Monroy and Parra families of San Marcos were not only merchants but also landed proprietors; the Hernández family of Santiago was sufficiently well off to be able to employ seasonal laborers; the Bautista, González, Páez, and Balderas families of Ozumba, Tierra Blanca, Puebla, and the Mexican Federal District had relatives in the United States—some even in Salt Lake City. But most early Mexican Mormons lived with hard work and dependence on uncertain weather. The biggest social events were visits from uncles, aunts, and cousins; church meetings; and Relief Society bazaars and some community fiestas. Once in awhile a Mormon child would have an opportunity to progress through the fifth grade of elementary school.

The early Mexican Mormons were intensely religious. An unusual number of them had gravitated from Catholicism first to Protestant sects, where they had sought but not found answers to their religious questions and so had moved on to Mormonism. Now their questions were about Mormon doctrine. Who were the Lamanites? In light of the Book of Mormon, who were the Mexicans? Who were the Gentiles? What was the Mormon theory of the afterlife? What, in the eyes of God, constituted repentance? As with every group there were those who joined and stayed with the Mormon church because it was easier to follow than to resist; but among the early members their number was not significant. The Mexican Mormons' searching prompted their organizing Bible-study classes, doctrinal discussion groups, and other intellectually stimulating programs, all of which took place in improvised housing. There was no church-funded or church-administered building program; the early Mexican Saints did their own building. Frequently a family expanded its home to make a large enough room for church meetings.[1]

Mormonism in Mexico was growing up. The distance from church headquarters, the political instability in Mexico, and the lack of missionaries during certain periods all augmented the Mexican Mormons' leadership responsibilities. The most trying time, of course, was between 1913 and 1917, when the church was alone in Mexico with inexperienced leaders and members buffeted by war and the hunger and disease that accompanied it. Two significant events accelerated the Mexican Mormons' independence from 1924 to 1935. One was Rey L. Pratt's 1925 appointment to help open the Mormons' South American mission in Argentina, temporarily removing him from his duties in Mexico. The other was the Cristero rebellion, which disrupted Mexico's religious life for nine years.

In 1924 Pratt learned that he would soon leave Mexico for Argentina. He would be separated from both his family and the Mexican members for more than a year. In preparation he conscientiously fostered the development of Mexican ecclesiastical leadership. Again he selected and authorized Mexican members to lead all the central Mexican branches, entrusting them with complete responsibility for their respective congregations. Observers reported that these Mexican leaders functioned so well that the American missionaries could spend all their time proselyting new members.[2] For the most part, Mexican leadership improved, operating in a way that Pratt considered encouraging. Considering Pratt's high expectations, that was no small accomplishment. In Pratt's absence American missionaries and Mexican members worked overtime together to keep their religion alive and growing.[3]

The Mexican members' development was timely because in 1926 the Mexican government deported all foreign clerics from the country, including Mormon missionaries. The North Americans' abrupt departure, like that of the Spaniards and the Italians, was one of the unexpected consequences of the Cristero movement, a vigorous and sustained effort by some Catholic clerics and numerous members to challenge the government and win back ecclesiastical prerogatives lost in the 1910–17 revolution.[4] These clerics wanted nothing less than de facto control of the Mexican government. Smelling a plot hatched by Spanish clerics and Mexican puppets, the angry federal government decided to enforce the Revolutionary Constitution's prohibition of all foreign clerics. And so the North American Mormon missionaries, being both law-abiding and practical, left with great speed.

This forced absence necessarily limited Rey Pratt's activities south of the Rio Grande. Far from giving up on the Mexican Saints, however, he appointed Mexicans to direct and supervise the branch leaders and charged them with efficiently presiding over the Mexican district of the church's mission. In effect, Mexicans thereafter did what Pratt had done—they coordinated, advised, preserved the Mormon doctrine, and enhanced the faith and brotherhood that it encompassed.

Isaías Juárez was appointed to preside over the Mexico district, with Abel Páez and Bernabé Parra acting as his counselors or assistants.[5] These three men brought stability and confidence to the small church groups in central Mexico. Already staffed with local leaders and now enjoying continued direction and encouragement from Juárez and his counselors, the small branches survived, and some even flourished.

There were exceptions to this generally positive trend, of course. After 1934, when North American missionaries slowly began to filter back into Mexico, they found ineptly kept membership records, inadequately prepared statistical forms, and so forth. In their formalistic zeal, some of these missionaries failed to note that religious meetings had been held, spiritual needs attended to, and an organization maintained in spite of political disruption, communication difficulties, and lack of direction from central church authorities. The church survived and grew in the hands of its Mexican leaders—baptisms increased, missionary efforts were launched, and meetinghouses were constructed.

Narciso Sandoval headed one of the flourishing early branches. He had been a Mormon for only four years when the Cristero eruption brought about the third evacuation of all foreign Mormon missionaries. Sandoval thereafter invited all the church members in Puebla to his home for religious study classes. By July 1927, less than a year after its inception, his group had grown enough to require a larger meeting place. With their missionary zeal and Sandoval's enthusiasm, they considered building a chapel of their own. They could then attract even more people to the church, because in a land of many cathedrals, having a suitable meeting place was important.

But the Puebla Mormons had to plan realistically. They could not build a chapel of North American proportions or materials, nor did they particularly want to do so. Instead, they designed a meetinghouse they could build and pay for themselves. Most members contributed financially and shared in both sweat and enthusiasm at the construction site. They built walls and partitions with adobe blocks made by time-proven native techniques. They had no funds for a roof, so Juárez and his counselors stepped in and gave financial assistance—apparently with authorization from Pratt, who now had to spend most of his time in the United States. Within two weeks the roof was in place.

Although the help the Puebla members received from general Mormon church funds was small compared to the almost total contribution the church now makes toward new buildings, it was enough to complete their chapel. The experience unified, strengthened, and encouraged them, and over the next few years the church in the Puebla area grew significantly. Indeed, within four years there were four relatively strong branches in the state of Puebla. Mormon church members were building meeting-houses, carrying out missionary activities, and increasing their membership.[6]

Branches in several other parts of Mexico also grew and progressed during this period. Mormons in Tecomatlán, for example, built a hewn volcanic stone chapel which Rey Pratt called "a credit to the faith of the people."[7] Although there were relatively few Mormon chapels, no full-time missionaries, very little church literature in Spanish, and almost no church programs from Salt Lake City headquarters, the Mormon church in Mexico generally continued to function.[8] Lacking outside help—other than the low-key though watchful aid Pratt was able to give from afar—the Mexican Mormons drew strength from within, from the occasional counsel Pratt could spirit through the political barricades, and from their God. As most were first-generation Mormons, the Latter-day Saint gospel was new and vital to them. In spite of their troubled circumstances, they were anxious to share it with others. Like the early Mormon pioneers, they built their meetinghouses and preached the gospel through a locally sponsored missionary system. By 1930, six Mexican missionaries were out proselyting.[9] Mormonism in Mexico was certainly not stagnating.

Franklin S. Harris, president of Brigham Young University, visited Mexico in 1930 and commented that in his wide travels as a scientist and educator he had never met a better group of Latter-day Saints than those in Mexico.[10] He was not, of course, talking about prosperity, spacious buildings for worship and recreation, or level of knowledge and experience—all of which were, by 1930 Salt Lake City standards, quite deficient.[11] What

Harris did note was the Mexican Mormons' uncommon zeal and earnestness.

Rey Pratt was quite pleased with the Mexican portion of his Spanish-speaking mission. He was convinced that the Mexican Mormons were dedicated to their church and were therefore more able to stand alone than ever before.[12] He was quite aware, for example, that the church's membership growth in Mexico was far exceeding that of the U.S. Spanish-speaking portion of his mission, even though the American side had help from numerous American missionaries.[13] Attendance at the 1931 district conferences also pleased Pratt. As many as 278 people attended a single session of these conferences, which were held in Mexico City and presided over by local Mexican leaders.[14]

Such progress must be credited largely to the constancy and fidelity of numerous Mexican members, both leaders and followers, and to Pratt's own careful overseeing of delegated authority. He maintained contact, counseled, and advised, but did not usurp delegated authority. Admittedly, political conditions constrained him from doing so. But careful delegation was also his preference and his plan for developing local leadership. Rey Pratt called the local leaders "wise and eloquent defenders of the truth"[15] and praised their followers' "inspired expositions of the Gospel."[16]

Pratt worked hard to be worthy of his Mexican flock, traveling frequently—and, necessarily, unofficially—to Mexico to encourage the Mexican Mormons and to aid their small building projects financially. In 1927 he began sending a monthly pamphlet to Mexico which he entitled *El Evangelio Restaurado* (The Restored Gospel), drafting most of the newsletter himself. *The Restored Gospel* evidences his great ability.[17] Now, a half-century since its final publication, the little pamphlet project is still remembered by some of its recipients.[18]

Rey Pratt had uncommon language and literary skills in both Spanish and English. He had another talent, easily felt but difficult to describe—an ability to use language to motivate and to inspire his followers. Effective use of language is something much deeper than technical mastery. Rey Pratt had this profundity, a charismatic, persuasive power. "He had a gift," a Mexican member recalls, "a gift for converting people and strengthening them spiritually."[19]

Pratt's numerous visits to Mexico, including his stops in all the villages where Mormon congregations met, demonstrated these qualities. In spite of legal restrictions, he contacted as many Mormons as possible and attempted, as best he could, to help them. As religious meetings came to a close, Pratt, who after 1926 never sat on the podium because of the restrictions on foreign clerics, would immediately walk to the meetinghouse door and there shake hands with all the members as they departed, expressing to them his love and concern for their well-being. In return, he received, through a touch of the hand or a teary eye, their commitment to push on. Pratt's conviction and love were apparent enough to be warmly received as unhypocritical and without guile or hidden agenda.[20]

Not many people could even appear to be sincere in such a blanket exchange of love. It was his rare sincerity, however, that was Pratt's "gift."[21] The Mexican Mormons reciprocated, the children in the branches sometimes strewing his path with flowers as he entered to attend a conference. Indeed, the only other person to be so honored by the Mormons in Mexico was President George Albert Smith, the Mormon prophet (1945-51).[22]

But then disaster. On 14 April 1931, following an operation for intestinal rupture, Pratt died.

New Links with Utah Mormons

Because of their constitutional problems and Rey Pratt's death, the Mexican Saints were anxious to hear from Salt Lake City. Soon they learned that Antoine R. Ivins had been appointed to succeed Pratt as president of the Mexican mission.[23] The *Deseret News* carried the First Presidency's announcement on 23 April 1931, nine days after Pratt's death.

Like Pratt, Ivins was simultaneously called to be a General Authority of the church and president of the Mexican mission. At the time of the appointment Ivins was in Hawaii supervising a church plantation. He did not arrive in Utah to acquaint himself with his specific responsibilities until 1 July 1931, whereupon he hurriedly made preparations to leave for the mission headquarters in Los Angeles.[24]

Antoine Ivins's father, Anthony W. Ivins, a gregarious man who had spent much of his life working to build Mormonism

in Mexico, was now a member of the church's First Presidency;
Antoine Ivins's uncle, Heber J. Grant, was the church's president.
So the Mexican Mormons probably expected Ivins to help them
as substantially as had his father and Rey L. Pratt. After all, with
such a family heritage, President Ivins could be nothing other
than extraordinary.

In August of 1931, four months after Pratt's death, Antoine
R. Ivins formally took up his new mission duties.[25] He knew Mexico
well, having spent his teenage years in the Chihuahua colonies.
Then, after graduating from the University of Utah and studying law for a year at the University of Michigan, he had gone for
two and one-half years to the National School of Jurisprudence
in Mexico City. After that he had stayed on an extra year at
Mexico's School of Commerce, concentrating on Spanish. His
father, himself bilingual, was particularly anxious that his eldest
surviving son be so too.

After receiving much of his higher education in Mexico, Ivins,
a quiet and introspective person, returned to his hometown,
St. George, Utah, where he managed some of his father's farms.
Later he worked one year at the Lund School for Boys in
Centerville, Utah, and then spent ten successful years as a
manager of the church's Laie Plantation in Hawaii. From that
position, which his father hoped would give him additional
maturity and confidence, Ivins had been appointed to serve the
church in Mexico.[26] Ivins had immersed himself in Mexico at one
point in his life, but then had left. Now he was returning.

In 1931 the Mexican Mormons eagerly waited for Ivins to intro-
duce himself and bring encouragement, guidance, greetings. Nothing
happened. Ivins did not visit the Mexican Saints, write to them, or
send them monthly pamphlets. References to Mexico dropped out
of the mission's manuscript history, and extensive tours of the southwestern U.S. part of the mission always failed to include Mexico.[27]

To be sure, Mexican law still restricted foreign clerics, but that
had never stopped Rey Pratt from operating legally in an unofficial capacity—taking care never to conduct a meeting or sit on the
podium while in Mexico. Antoine Ivins could have done the same.
But perhaps he felt the American side of his mission required
his complete attention. The Mexicans had been doing well without North American missionaries.[28] Or perhaps Ivins had personal reasons.[29] Regardless, the Mexican Mormons felt neglected.

The Mexican Mormons met in late 1931 or early 1932 under district president Isaías Juárez to discuss their problems, such as the lack of missionaries in Mexico and the inadequacy of church literature in Spanish. However, at the moment their main concern was Ivins. His neglect had created a vacuum between the Mexican district of the Mormon church and the General Authorities in Salt Lake City. Some of the Mexican Mormons, feeling a need to take the initiative in something, deliberated and prayed together at a meeting which has come to be known as the "first convention."[30] Then, by letter from Mexico City, they requested that the Salt Lake City authorities give them a mission president of their own nationality who could function legally in Mexico. This was reasonable, they concluded, since their need for a full-time mission president was very real. They did not want to break with Salt Lake City but merely to have a Mexican mission president to represent them to the authorities so that their unique needs could be understood.

While it seemed rational, beneath the surface ran a strong current of emotion. Historically abrasive relations with North Americans made the Mexican Saints sensitive—one might say even touchy. Ivins's lack of attention had fanned the fires of Mexican nationalism. Such neglect, even for a month, would have been offensive to the Mexicans; but it had been much longer than that. Ivins's lack of attention was humiliating to the entire Mexican Mormon church. The North Americans, by ignoring their southern brothers, appeared to be saying that the Mexicans did not matter. Thus the Mexican Saints sought a mission president of their own nationality not only out of practical necessity, but because they thought it would foster self-respect rather than continued dependence.[31]

Neither Ivins nor any other authority in Salt Lake City answered the Mexican members' letter. The Mexican Saints met again and this time renewed their request through a formal written petition. This meeting, probably held in the early spring of 1932, has become known to history as the "second convention."[32]

Ivins did not appreciate the Mexican Saints' actions.[33] In early 1932, about seven months after he had moved into the Los Angeles mission headquarters and nearly a year from the time of his mission appointment, he traveled with Apostle Melvin J. Ballard to Mexico City to meet with the Mexican Latter-day Saints involved

117

in the first and second conventions.[34] He reprimanded their
assertiveness, their holding of extra-official meetings, and their
drafting of petitions. Talking with the district presidency (Isaías
Juárez, Abel Páez, and Bernabé Parra), he explained fundamental
principles of Mormon church government, telling the Mexicans
that a mission president was the First Presidency's representative
to the mission, not the mission's ambassador to the First Presidency. Furthermore, he informed the Mexican members that petitions of the sort they had sent to Salt Lake City were out of order.
Unlike the Mexican political system, which encourages the gathering of signatures for petitions to capture the attention of aloof
public bureaucrats, the Mormon church viewed such procedures
as offensive and inappropriate. But Ivins assured the Mexican
Mormons that with the Lord's inspiration the First Presidency
would meet Mexico's leadership needs in due time. In the meantime the Mexican Mormons were obligated to support the president of the church in his decisions and actions.

Despite the argument's logic, many of the Mexican Latter-
day Saints felt rudely chastised. Their understanding of the
Mormon gospel led them to believe that they had both a right
and an obligation to seek God's will in matters of church leadership, and that is what they had done.[35] Mexican Mormons
concluded that Ivins was ill informed about their country and
therefore incapable of knowing their best interests.[36] Ivins considered the Mexicans ill informed about Mormon church
authority and government.

Yet Mexican Saints were not so bitter as to drop out of their
church. In time they seemed to set the whole leadership problem
aside, carrying out their normal church activities for the entire
period of Ivins's 1931–34 administration. Life with Ivins, while
not what the Mexicans had hoped for, was tolerable. He did
not help, but neither did he hinder by interfering with the
Mexican Saints or their programs. The silent arrangement
between Ivins and district president Juárez seemed, in the short
run, acceptable to all parties. If church leaders in Salt Lake City
wanted the Mexican Saints to quiet down and respect authority,
they did. If Ivins did not want to be bothered by perplexing
Mexican problems, he was not. Most apparently, the Mexican
Saints wanted Mexican leadership, and they had it—Juárez, Páez,
and Parra.

While officially the Mexican section of the mission remained under President Ivins's leadership, in actuality, Isaías Juárez continued to lead the Mexican Saints as he had before the death of Rey L. Pratt. Juárez, however, found himself more alone after the expulsion of all foreign clerics, and his responsibilities were heavier, too, because he did not have a mission president to offer advice and encouragement. Moreover, he was not working full time for the church or being paid, and he was not independently wealthy. Like almost all Mormon leaders, he earned his own living aside from his ecclesiastical responsibilities. Without sufficient time and money, he could not visit all the branches of the mission frequently or regularly, and so Mormonism in Mexico began to suffer from inadequate attention.

Mexican Mormons felt a lack at two levels. They longed for a leader who could salve their wounded pride and make them feel competent and important to the Salt Lake City authorities, and they needed a leader who could dedicate all his energy to the church work in Mexico. Leading the Spanish-speaking mission north of the border was a full-time job, as President Ivins's actions attested. Yet, as Juárez's problems demonstrated, so was leading the mission in Mexico. Following Antoine R. Ivins's departure as mission president in 1934, Salt Lake City leaders moved to meet these needs by appointing Harold W. Pratt, Rey Pratt's half-brother, as the new mission president.

Harold Pratt's dedication and high principles made his severe trials as a mission president seem both unfortunate and unjust. One problem he stepped into, apparently unknowingly, was the functioning but not entirely satisfactory local church leadership arrangements that had developed over the years.[37] He was puzzled and dismayed by the gulf that seemed to separate the American and Mexican halves of his new responsibility. Yet his good faith and his intention to eradicate this gulf destroyed but did not adequately replace the delicate leadership arrangements that had preserved the Mormon church in Mexico during Ivins's administration.

The Mexican Saints did not have to wait for Harold Pratt as they had for President Ivins; within a few weeks of his appointment in 1934 he came to Mexico. Using his Mexican citizenship to advantage, he registered himself as a minister with governmental authorities in Chihuahua, where he had operated a water-well

equipment company earlier. Mexico's improved political conditions as the Cristero rebellion waned made this possible. Since
the war had ended five years earlier, animosities between church
and state had gradually declined. Indeed, when Pratt began work
Mexican priests were operating openly again, and Pratt also began
to do so.

Having registered in Chihuahua as a cleric, as prescribed by
Mexican law, Pratt proceeded to tour the Mexican part of his
mission. He worked efficiently, forcefully, and very visibly in his
church position—presiding over conferences and reorganizing branches, purchasing land for chapels, directly resolving
numerous ecclesiastical problems. He handled many long-
standing problems that Juárez had lacked time and travel money
to resolve.

Harold Pratt spent a great deal of time in Mexico making
what he considered necessary changes. He also assigned a few
American missionaries to Mexico City and Monterrey. But here
Pratt moved cautiously; he did not want trouble with the Mexican authorities over the foreign cleric issue. Since most of his
missionaries were not colonies Mormons with Mexican citizenship, he explicitly instructed them not to proselyte. Instead, the
new missionaries were to help the local Mormons by developing programs and strengthening and encouraging the Mexican
church members. Pratt clearly saw that Mexico needed a strong
pastoral leader.

Harold Pratt's actions were different from those of Antoine
Ivins. Some have said it was because he had an extraordinary love
for the land and its people; certainly he was generous with both
time and money.[38] He moved quickly to help the Mexican Saints,
bringing new information, auxiliary programs, and full-time
church workers from the United States, and reducing Mexico's
isolation from Salt Lake City. Pratt and the new American
missionaries were hardworking.

Harold Pratt and his missionaries were doing much more
than the Mexican Mormons had been able to do, filling many
needs in missionary endeavors, pastoral care, and organizational
development that had gone unmet for more than two decades.
But their efforts went beyond that; soon the enthusiastic outsiders
were doing what the Mexican Saints had been able to do. By
handling almost all church-related problems himself, Pratt

prevented his Mexican brothers from doing so. Because he presided and conducted—and because he was present so much—local leaders had to give way. This did not help Mexican Mormons feel more important and competent; indeed, it struck to the core of the anxieties about their standing with the Americans, hurting some Mexicans' personal and national pride.

Without Pratt's sensing the dilemma, his dramatic assumption of leadership in the mission rapidly constricted the local leaders' activities, a matter they began to resent. First Ivins did not give the Mexican Saints much help; then Harold Pratt came along and gave too much. Local leaders were frustrated and confused, and tension was developing between them and Pratt.[39]

Unaware of these growing frustrations, Pratt was stimulated by what he saw happening in Mexico. The members seemed energetic and enthusiastic about the gospel, and they seemed to be responding quickly to his leadership. Keenly motivated, Pratt threw himself into church work and began planning a new chapel in Mexico City that would meet Salt Lake City's building standards—and not be simply one raised up by local initiative. In addition, just as had Ivins, he was still overseeing the church's mission to Spanish-speaking people in the United States.

Pratt realized that the job that had been too much for Antoine Ivins and Isaías Juárez, combined with his commitment to the building program, was too much for him too. So he requested that the Salt Lake City authorities divide the mission and appoint someone else to run things in the northern areas, freeing him to devote himself to Mexico.

When the Mexican Mormons heard that the mission might be divided, they were stimulated at the prospect of having their own mission. They did not, however, prefer Harold Pratt as the head of that mission. Many of the Mexican Saints openly hoped that the division would bring increased and approved leadership opportunities for their own people. Surely the church would appoint a real Mexican to head the new mission, they thought. To them the timing seemed perfect, and their assumption was that the church's growth in Mexico now clearly required that the country have its own mission organization with its own mission president.

Their optimism was not without reason. Mormonism had begun painfully and slowly in their homeland. But now, in 1935, the endeavors had gained important momentum despite past problems. Several new chapels had been built. Membership had grown substantially, to more than twenty-eight hundred.[40] Parts of the sacred book of Doctrine and Covenants had been translated. A new hymnal was being printed. A beautiful modern chapel was planned for only five miles from the center of Mexico City. It seemed the Mexican Mormons had arrived.

Margarito Bautista, Mexican Nationalist

Not all Mexican Mormons believed that dividing the mission would mean a Mexican mission president, and Margarito Bautista was one of the most articulate. Bautista was a longtime Mormon experienced in the church and an ordained high priest. He had known and admired Rey L. Pratt.[41] Bautista was an uncommonly literate man and a gifted orator who had worked to educate himself, even studying English and living for many years in Salt Lake City, where he taught the Spanish–American branch's Sunday School class. He had observed Mormon church government over a number of years. He had also done a great deal of ordinance work in the Salt Lake Temple and, like many temple workers, had become an expert genealogist.[42] After 1934 he was back in Mexico helping the Mexican Saints trace their ancestry.[43]

An avid scriptorian, Bautista agreed with Rey Pratt and many other Mormon leaders who had preceded him that the Mexicans, their Lamanite history, and the promises to them in the Book of Mormon were inseparable.[44] Pratt had often expressed this theological concept to the Mexican Saints, many of whom took great pride in their mighty Lamanite ancestors. Bautista, stimulated by Rey Pratt's sentiments, decided to write a book correlating Book of Mormon teachings with the Old Testament. Pratt, who was anxious to see more literature become available to the Mexican members, encouraged Bautista.[45] Even after Pratt's death, Bautista persisted, completing his manuscript three years later.[46]

Bautista proudly presented his manuscript to the Salt Lake City authorities, expecting the church to publish it. Apparently they had been unaware of his efforts, and they were surprised to receive his lengthy work. Since it was in Spanish, and most of them could not even read it, they sought the recommendations of various Spanish-speaking Mormons.

One of these was Harold Pratt. He did not have to read too far to know that the Mormon church could not publish the book. It was very polemical, and many of its conclusions had been derived from apocryphal literature such as the Book of Jasher. Moreover, Bautista went beyond official Mormon church doctrine in many cases, as, for example, in his mapping of Book of Mormon locations on the American continent.[47] Following Pratt's recommendation, the Salt Lake City authorities advised Bautista of their decision not to publish the manuscript.[48]

Bautista was stunned. His feelings toward Harold Pratt, whom he knew, were now not exactly affectionate. Since his book, like any artistic work, was an extension of the artist, Bautista was sensitive about it and also felt wounded and misunderstood. These feelings pressed in on him as he packed his bags to return to Mexico, where he felt that he would be more appreciated.[49]

Arriving in Mexico City some time between April and June of 1934, Bautista arranged to have Apolonio B. Arzate, a Mormon who owned a printing establishment, publish the manuscript for him. Bautista's book rapidly gained wide circulation among Mexican Mormons and became a sort of mini-best seller.[50] By this time Harold Pratt was the mission president in Mexico. Alarmed lest the Mexican Saints confuse Bautista's doctrines with those of the Mormon church, Pratt issued a circular letter proclaiming that the church had not authorized the book and that its contents were not in any way church doctrine.[51] Later, Pratt's missionaries counseled all members "not to buy the book and not to read it."[52]

Many Mexican Mormons had donated time and money to publish and distribute the work. Bernabé Parra, a counselor in the Mexican district presidency, had contributed heavily (his picture was printed in the book with an acknowledgment), and most of the Puebla area members had helped fund the work's publication.[53] Surveying the situation, Pratt became concerned. His eventual decision to discourage the circulation of Bautista's book did not derive from a personal vendetta against Bautista, as the book's author had supposed, but rather from his alarm over the book's impact. One missionary of the time remembers that many Saints preferred to quote from Bautista's work than from the Book of Mormon.[54]

Bautista was angered when the book's sales declined after Pratt and the missionaries had discouraged church members from reading it. Many Mormons hesitated to buy a work the church had more or less spoken against.[55] Relations between Bautista and Harold Pratt continued to deteriorate, and their discussions were often very heated. Bautista threatened to sue Pratt for the damage he felt the circular letter was causing. Pratt offered to retract any part of the letter that Bautista could point out was false. Much to his frustration, Bautista could point to nothing in it that was patently false. Elsewhere Pratt referred to Bautista as an apostate and a wolf among sheep.[56] Later, Bautista accused Pratt of trying to kill Abel Páez, Bautista's nephew, explaining subsequently that he had meant Pratt had tried to kill Páez's spirit.[57]

Why did the book cause all this furor? Whatever else one might say about it, the work is certainly fascinating in a speculative way. Bautista wove his tales very skillfully, drawing from the Old Testament, the Book of Mormon, the Book of Jasher, the writings of Abraham and Joseph Smith, and other sources, and he developed his characters fully from frequently dry sources. He brought biblical characters to life for mid-twentieth-century Mexicans.[58] And the maps! Speculation about the location of Book of Mormon cities and regions has fascinated generations of Mormons. That fascination created even more interest in Bautista's theological thought.

Margarito Bautista's book is lengthy and haphazardly organized. He wrote over five hundred pages to bring his characters to life and recapitulate most of the Book of Mormon's historical portions using various integrated sources. Part of the book's problem is its scope. In his long title, Bautista proposes to discuss both Mexico's history (including its original settlers and later European intruders) and the future destiny of Europe and America. Trying to handle such a huge chunk of material made the manuscript longer and longer and had a crippling effect on its organization.

Its length notwithstanding, Mexican Mormons did not read Bautista's book in the detached way most North Americans then and now would read it, but fully emotionally, as if they were reading their own family history. Searching for a proud national heritage, they welcomed grand stories of the noble Aztecs and Mayas and of their ancestors who had formed great, civilized, chosen nations.[59] And most of all, welcoming Bautista's interpretation of Book of Mormon prophecies, they wanted to know that Mexico would be mighty again.[60] Bautista focused on the history and heritage of the American peoples and emphasized the impressive future prophesied for Israel's American descendants.

No one questioned the book's substantial impact on Mormons in Mexico, or the Americans' alarm at that impact. But why were the book's effects so profound? Why were Mexicans so keen on national pride and personal dignity, so preoccupied with their ancestral heritage? Since the turn of the century few North American Mormons had been interested in those subjects. They had forgotten the post-revolutionary nationalism that followed the U.S. Revolutionary and Civil wars, a nationalism very much alive in Mexico, and so did not understand the book's popularity in Mexico. Consequently, like the pioneer stories Utah Mormon children recite in Sunday School, accounts of the Mexican Revolution and the Cristero period—and the Mormons' role in them—have inspired five generations of Mexican Mormon children and their parents. In these stories the United States and Spain do not fare well.

In many ways sending a North American mission president and missionaries to Mexico could be compared to sending Yankee overseers into Alabama to preside over the religious education of Anglo–Americans a decade after Lincoln's emancipation proclamation. Suspicion, distrust, and prejudice had to be overcome each time a new North American Mormon entered Mexico on behalf of the church. Remarkably, many Mexican Saints grew to love the foreign Mormon missionaries!

Margarito Bautista and his book fit perfectly with this growing Mexican nationalism. Mexican Mormons thrilled as they read the Book of Mormon's promises to them. Margarito touched these people, giving them a proud past and a glorious future.

Why did the book cause Anglo–American Mormons such difficulty? Aside from the doctrinal problems, it spiritedly argued a strong but, for some, discomforting position. The "chosen people," Bautista held, were none other than the Latin Americans and particularly the Mexicans. "Gentiles," those not of the House of Israel, were somehow second-class. Orthodox Mormonism teaches that one can belong to the House of Israel either through bloodline or by "adoption." Bautista's emphasis was quite unorthodox. To be a son or daughter of Israel by direct descent (which members of American Indian lineage, however diluted, were thought to be) was decidedly better, he maintained, than being adopted (like most North American Mormons). It was this racial prestige and sense of belonging that Margarito Bautista sought to give his countrymen. He wanted to inspire and motivate them with their future greatness. At the same time he attached a certain stigma to the lineage of the North Americans and the despised Spaniards.[61]

Thus, in addition to its doctrinal unorthodoxy, Bautista's effort to build up the Mexican Mormons was driving a wedge between them and the North American authorities. Since this could only hinder the church's work in Mexico, Harold Pratt opposed it. Pratt was attempting to build faith and testimony among members that would unite all Mormons into one people, not numerous fragmented "national Mormon churches." Bautista, however, interpreted the opposition personally and ethnically—as directed not only against himself but against the whole Mexican people. The Mormon leaders did not call a Mexican mission president during the Revolution and the Cristero Rebellion, Bautista reasoned, because they were afraid to turn the work over to a Mexican. Why? Because they did not want Mexican leaders to develop. Why? Because they were afraid such Israelite leaders would challenge them for the highest positions in the church.[62]

Perceptive and observant, Bautista could see how well Mexican leadership had developed, and he felt that the development had occurred in spite of the Salt Lake City authorities. He judged that the church leaders, being intelligent men, also saw this and so were sending Americans to take over Mexico once more so they could stunt any further growth of Mexican leadership. This belief embittered and drained him. He did not see anything good about the Mexican mission's impending division; he feared it would only bring more Americans and thereby diminish the role of Mexican leaders.

Bautista was not alone in his feelings. Although very few people agreed that the Salt Lake City authorities were conspiring against Mexican Saints to keep them from progressing spiritually, many *did* see a Mexican mission president as essential to their progress. In the words of one Mexican Saint, "It would be a most splendid privilege for our people to have a man of our own race to govern the affairs of the church in this choice part of the continent." The feelings and words poured out: "If the church does not give us the means as well as open the way for us to officiate with authority among our own people for their complete development, we will never be able to carry forth this important work for ourselves and our people . . . [;] it will be impossible for us to make the necessary progress without this leadership opportunity."[63] Many Mexican Saints did not want increased American presence and trusted that the authorities in Salt Lake City would be sensitive to their desires and needs. Others, however, like Bautista, both expected and feared it.

Once people knew that the mission might be divided, it was clear that their views about what that would mean for Mexican Mormons diverged widely. Bautista and those like him feared the division while most Mexican members looked forward to it; all waited to see whether an ethnic Mexican would be selected as mission president. It was clear that whatever the choice, the implications would be substantial.

In April of 1936 the church divided the Mexican mission into the Mexican and Spanish–American missions, with the Rio Grande forming their common border. Harold W. Pratt would preside over the new Mexican mission. He would arrange for new mission headquarters in Mexico City.

Notes

1. Santiago Mora González, interview by F. LaMond Tullis.

2. William Walser, Oral History, interview by Gordon Irving, p. 23.

3. This does not mean to say, of course, that the usual problems associated with missionary labors did not remain, or that extraordinary ones did not become evident. For example, Rey L. Pratt was aware that after his departure to Argentina some of his missionaries were being deported by the government, and others were breaking mission rules. He communicated both his awareness and concern to his family by letter under date of 20 April 1926.

4. The best and most comprehensive treatment of the Cristero period is in Jean Meyer's monumental works, two volumes of which are *The Cristero Rebellion: The Mexican People between Church and State, 1926–1929* and *La cristiada: los cristeros.* An important and perceptive regional analysis is Jim Tuck's *The Holy War in Los Altos: A Regional Analysis of Mexico's Cristero Rebellion.* A well-focused regional study is *El movimiento cristero: sociedad y conflicto en los altos de Jalisco* by José Díaz and Ramón Rodríguez. See also Ramón Jrade's "Inquiries into the Cristero Insurrection against the Mexican Revolution."

5. Abel Páez and Bernabé Parra are those generally recognized as being the *first* chosen to assist Isaías Juárez. Rey L. Pratt's journal entry of 9 March 1930 lists Pilar Páez as the second counselor to Juárez in those early days and Bernabé Parra as president of the San Marcos branch. So there is some confusion. Nevertheless, Parra was president of the branch, of that there is no doubt; and equally without question is the fact that Parra did become Juárez's counselor. But when? After Pilar Páez? But Pilar is a woman's name unknown among contemporary Mexicans as ever being given to a man. Did Pratt make a mistake in his journal entry? Did he call a woman as a counselor to Juárez? This is very unlikely, for it would have broken the church's priesthood leadership tradition. Did a man have a woman's name? We wish we had the answer. A clue may reside in the excommunication trials of 1937, in which the name of Pilar Páez appears. I have not had access to the minutes of those trials.

6. I have relied on two main sources for information on the development of the church in the Puebla areas: Cruz González de la Cruz, Oral History, interview by Gordon Irving; and Santiago Mora González, interview by F. LaMond Tullis.

7. Manuscript History of the Mexican Mission, quarter ending 31 March 1930. During this period there were two relevant records the church missions were required to keep: the Manuscript History noted above and the Mexican Mission Historical Record. In Mexico's case they overlap a great deal. However, the Historical Record tends to contain minutes of official meetings, while the Manuscript History records movements of personnel and additional miscellaneous facts of interest to the record keeper. Both are only as reliable as were the mission secretaries, and the quality is highly varied.

8. Church literature available in Spanish at the time, in addition to the Bible, consisted of the Book of Mormon, two pamphlets, and the words to several hymns provided by Rey L. Pratt himself, along with a Spanish hymnal prepared in 1904.

9. Manuscript History, quarter ending 31 March 1930.

10. Rey L. Pratt, Journal, entry of 30 November 1930.

11. They were deficient by standards of the Salt Lake City area but not necessarily by standards of some rural communities in southern and eastern Utah, where poverty and hard work also went hand in hand. In some areas of Utah the meetinghouses and the Mormon villages surrounding them now stand in complete decay, austere witnesses to the communal struggles of a people whose children were overtaken by opportunity and affluence in larger urban centers.

12. Manuscript History, quarter ending 31 March 1930.

13. *Deseret News* (Salt Lake City, Utah), "Church News," 19 March 1932.

14. Manuscript History, quarter ending 30 June 1931. In the conference held at San Pedro Mártir there were six sessions (4–5 April 1931) with the following numbers in attendance: 71, 107, 157, 153, 172, and 133. In the six sessions held at the conference in Tecalco (11–12 April 1931), the attendance figures were 101, 164, 232, 223, 278, and 107.

15. Rey L. Pratt, Journal, 9 March 1930.

16. Manuscript History, quarter ending 31 March 1930.

17. Copies of *The Restored Gospel* are available in the LDS Church Archives. Rey Pratt's other works include unpublished poetry and journal materials, numerous hymns in Spanish translation (over sixty are in the church's current Spanish hymnal), two pamphlets still in print—*La Restauración*, and "*. . . y la verdad os hará libres*"—and personal letters, all in the Church Archives.

18. González de la Cruz, Oral History.

19. Ibid., Oral History, as translated by the author from the original tape.

20. In this section we try to describe Rey L. Pratt as we think the Mexican Saints perceived him. While reality and perceptions of reality may in fact coincide, in a study such as this it is the latter that is significant. It is the Mexican Saints' *perception* of Pratt that helps explain his ultimate impact on these members.

21. The technical point raised here deals with *charismatic* leadership, elements of which, we argue, Pratt enjoyed. What is a charismatic leader's special relationship with the masses that makes his whole operation so convincing? One begins by noting that the relationship refers to an extraordinary quality of person, regardless of whether that quality is actual, alleged, or presumed. The legitimacy of such a leader's rule rests upon his followers' belief in extraordinary powers, revelations, and hero worship. This is very different from traditional rule that tends to be both authoritarian and conservative and, if respected, also feared.

Cultural factors (for example, traditional personalistic leader–follower identities in Latin America) may facilitate the appearance of charismatic leaders, but they do not, in the strictest sense, provide the necessary conditions for their emergence. Such leaders arise in societies where *personalismo* and its related "strongman" attractions do not exist as a dominant cultural trait. While Latin America has long been noted for its *caudillos* and *caciques*, the legitimacy of their rule tends to derive from traditional, not charismatic, authority.

But consider Rey L. Pratt. Was he a traditional *caudillo* or *cacique?* It has been argued that he fell quite neatly into the Mexican's need to make a personal psychological commitment to a leader. (See Dale F. Beecher, "Rey L. Pratt and the Mexican Mission," p. 294.) Yet this would not seem to explain completely the relationship of Pratt to the Mexican Saints or shed much light on the nature of his authority. Where the Mexican culture looked for domineering strength, Pratt was weak; where it approved of harshness, he responded with kindness; where Mexicans were used to a ruler's iron hand, Pratt persuaded through pleading, personal contact, genuine interest, and above all, an unabashed expression of love. If Mexicans enjoyed Pratt because he was "personal," it is also true that his personal authority base was as much charismatic as it was traditional. For further discussion of these points as well as a review of Max Weber, refer to my *Politics and Social Change in Third World Countries*, pp. 79–85.

The Mexican Mormons' understanding of the matter was that Pratt was expressing the pure love of Christ which, by living in harmony with divine, eternal principles, made possible his power to change lives.

22. González de la Cruz, Oral History. John Hawkins noted in a personal conversation that, in Guatemala, flower-spreading is common symbolism for the receiving of saints in Catholic ritual. Insofar as this same symbolism existed in Mexico, the Mormons were in effect honoring Pratt with cultural sainthood.

23. Manuscript History, quarter ending 30 June 1931.

24. *Deseret News,* "Church News," 1 July 1931.

25. Manuscript History, quarter ending 30 September 1931.

26. Information about Antoine R. Ivins's character and insights into his relationship with his father were obtained from an interview with his sister, Augusta Wells.

27. Manuscript History, quarters ending 30 September 1931 and 30 June 1932.

28. *Deseret News,* "Church News," 19 March 1932.

29. Because I was unable to avail myself of any of Antoine R. Ivins's papers for the 1932 period, I do not know whether his papers for other periods are available in the LDS Church Archives. As oral interviews on his 1932 administration have not provided much information, I therefore can shed little light on why Ivins ignored the Mexican part of his mission.

Some tentative clues may be gleaned from an address Ivins gave to a congregation of more than eight thousand assembled in the historic tabernacle on Temple Square, Salt Lake City, at the October 1931 general conference of the church. In an unofficial capacity he brought greetings from thirteen thousand members in the Pacific Isles. Then, in his official capacity of a new mission president he conveyed "greetings of not quite so many, but a kindred people who are living nearer to us, the Mexican people. There are quite a number of them in the Church, and they are faithful and sincere and reasonably energetic in the performance of their duties" (Ivins, in Conference Report, Oct. 1931, p. 72).

He reminded the audience that missionary work to the Mexicans was begun in 1875 when a party of half a dozen men (including his father as a junior member) rode their horses from St. George, Utah, as far south as the city of Chihuahua, Mexico. This opener of his speech permitted Ivins to review missionary work in Mexico and praise, quite lavishly, the work of Rey L. Pratt, expressing hope that he (Ivins) could measure up to the standard that Pratt had set.

When Ivins gave his speech he had been in the mission only about six weeks and so still had not had the "good fortune to meet them all [the missionaries]." But he hoped to be able to visit all the mission within several weeks.

At this point in his speech, Ivins gives us, I believe, an important clue as to why he ignored Mexico. "It seems that the people of the Church are not entirely clear as to what the Mexican mission at present consists of," he said. He then reviewed the episode of the withdrawal of foreign missionaries from Mexico and announced that at the time only one ordained missionary was working in Mexico—a local Mexican brother working in Monterrey. "All of the other work that is being done by missionaries [there were forty-one under his jurisdiction] is being done in the United States. Our mission covers a length of two thousand miles, from Los Angeles to Brownsville, Texas. In addition to that we have a very thrifty and vigorous [Spanish-speaking] branch in this city [Salt Lake City], and we have organized branches that are laboring under the guidance of native branch presidents in various cities in and around the valley of Mexico" (Ivins, in Conference Report, p. 73). By "we," Ivins meant the church and Rey Pratt, who had set it up that way in Mexico. Ivins still had not been there.

Thereafter Ivins seems to identify completely with the American side of his mission, implying that Mexico was more or less a de jure but not a de facto part of his concern. We have the impression that Ivins, in his own mind, considered himself to be a "missionary president" rather than a "pastoral president." For him it seems to have been important to concentrate his efforts where his missionaries were, not where they could not be.

30. Sources of information on the first convention include González de la Cruz, Oral History; William Walser, Oral History, pp. 26–27; Santiago Mora González, Oral History, interview by Gordon Irving; Harold Brown, Oral History, interview by Gordon Irving, pp. 31–32; Julio García Velázquez, Oral History, interview by Gordon Irving, pp. 4–34; *Informe general de la tercera convención*, LDS Church Library, Historical Division, Salt Lake City; and Santiago Mora González, interview by F. LaMond Tullis.

31. "That the white race is our tutor we do not deny, but it is also true that at some point in time our tutor, by a humanitarian act, must set us free to develop our own selves. . . . The success or fruits of sixty years of our church's labor among us cannot be recognized until the moment that it [the church] has sufficient faith to confer upon us the responsibility of guiding our own destinies for the development of our spiritual life and the redemption of our people . . ." (*Informe general de la tercera convención*, p. 20; translation from the Spanish by F. LaMond Tullis).

It is now commonplace throughout the world that ethnic groups undergoing rapid value changes (such as rural Mexicans adopting a new religion of hope and expectation) tend to seek equality with their associates in both form and substance. They tend to develop an unbounded sensitivity to their dignity and personal worth, and they struggle for the day in which others will respect them as much for what they hope to become as for what they are. These are some of the new conditions that contribute to a rejection of paternalism, actual or implied. Almost all forms of cultural, social, or economic dependency, and, in general, any position that may imply "the rear seat on the bus" are repudiated. I have summarized much of the new literature in this area in "Ethnicity and Ethnic Conflict."

32. In describing and analyzing the first and second conventions, I have had considerable trouble collating the information from the sources. There are very little concrete data available on this time period—some oral histories recorded long after the fact, some materials printed by Third Conventionists in 1936, a record of visits to Mexico by Apostle Melvin J. Ballard and Antoine R. Ivins. Accordingly, I have had to put together a picture of reality for this time period with very few puzzle pieces. The gaps have been filled by extrapolations from the pieces available.

To help the reader evaluate what I have said, I will illustrate my reasoning and "piecing together" with the dating and placement of the first two conventions from data tabulated on the following page.

It does not seem possible, given what we know about the first convention, that it took place before April 1931, when Rey L. Pratt died in Salt Lake City. After all, it convened, in large measure, to handle problems occasioned by Pratt's death. On the other hand, both conventions must have occurred by March of 1932 when Apostle Melvin J. Ballard and President Antoine R. Ivins visited Mexico. Otherwise, given what we know of Isaías Juárez, he would not have led or even participated in the second convention. But we know that he did participate in both the first and the second conventions.

Referring to the sources, it seems that we must rely on the *Informe general* as being the most accurate, since it was written approximately thirty years earlier

Source	Convention	Date Occurred	Location
Cruz González–OH	1st	Feb. 1931	San Pedro Mártir
Cruz González–OH	1st	After the death of R. L. Pratt	?
Cruz González–OH	2d	Sept. 1931	San Pedro Mártir
Julio García–OH	1st	After the death of R. L. Pratt	?
Julio García–OH	1st	While R. L. Pratt was president	Mexico City
Julio García–OH	2d	While A. R. Ivins was president	?
Narciso Sandoval–OH	1st	1932	
Informe general, p. 16	1st	5 Jan. 1932	Nativitas, Mexico City
Informe general, p. 16	2d	3 Apr. 1932	San Pedro Mártir

than the taping of the oral history interviews and gives the most exact dates. I therefore accept its location of the conventions. However, the date for the second convention must be in error—perhaps simply a printing or editorial error. We might hazard a guess that the correct date for the second convention is 3 March 1932. Although this is only a month earlier, it would make a tremendous difference because this date would place the second convention immediately prior to the visit to Mexico of the North American authorities. If this is the case, then the puzzle pieces fall together nicely. If not, then we have no explanation.

33. In any chain of authority a complaint tendered directly from the rank-and-file to the top leadership puts middle-level leaders in an uncomfortable position. This is one reason why middle managers put such an emphasis on "going through channels." It is also suggestive of why those channels are nearly always "clogged." The fact is that, aside from rendering service, middle-level managers—e.g., mission presidents—are also obliged to protect themselves from recrimination. Therefore, as Antoine Ivins reacted, he moved in good faith to resolve a troublesome problem but also in a way designed to legitimize his own position. And his was a particularly delicate position, for he had to give an accounting directly to both father and uncle.

34. Apostle Ballard reports on his trip in the *Deseret News*, "Church News," 19 March 1932.

35. Mexican Saints could have looked to the example of Brigham Young, who admonished Mormons to take an active part in confirming that they were led by inspired men. He stated:

I am more afraid that this people have so much confidence in their
leaders that they will not inquire for themselves of God whether they are
led by him. I am fearful they settle down in a state of blind self-security,
trusting their eternal destiny in the hands of their leaders with a reckless
confidence that in itself would thwart the purposes of God in their salva-
tion, and weaken that influence they could give to their leaders, did they
know for themselves, by the revelations of Jesus, that they are led in the
right way. Let every man and woman know, by the whispering of the Spirit
of God to themselves, whether their leaders are walking in the path the
Lord dictates, or not. (Brigham Young, *Discourses of Brigham Young*,
comp. John A. Widtsoe, p. 135, as cited in The Church of Jesus Christ of
Latter-day Saints, *A Royal Priesthood, 1975–76: A Personal Study Guide for the
Melchizedek Priesthood Quorums of The Church of Jesus Christ of Latter-day Saints*,
pp. 37–38.)

36. My information on the feelings of the Mexican Saints about
President Ivins's visit derives from the *Informe general*, and the Oral Histories
of Harold Brown, William Walser, and Santiago Mora González.

37. Manuscript History, 28 February 1934.

38. E. LeRoy Hatch, Oral History, interview by Gordon Irving; and
Ana Marie Pratt, Oral History, interview by Gordon Irving.

In his business dealings, Harold Pratt would suffer a loss rather than ask
(much less demand) payments on debts from people he knew were having a
hard time financially (John Floyd Walser, interview by F. LaMond Tullis).

39. This analysis draws on a large body of social science literature dealing with social movements. (Refer to my *Politics and Social Change*, pp. 61–85, and
Lord and Peasant in Peru.)

40. This figure is an extrapolation. Official membership records for the
mission before it was divided show the following: 1933, 4,045; 1934, 4,219;
1935, 4,245; 1936, 4,317. For 1937, the year after the division, the figures show
2,854 for Mexico. Assuming constant ratios between the Mexican and United
States sections of the mission before division, Mexican membership in 1935
would have been approximately 2,800.

41. My information on the relationship between Rey Pratt and Margarito
Bautista derives from the Julio García Velázquez, Oral History, p. 15.

42. W. Ernest Young, Oral History, interview by Gordon Irving, p. 33. Young
is a good source on Bautista because he knew him quite well. It is from Young
that we learn that Margarito Bautista was knowledgeable concerning both church
and nonchurch matters. It is also from Young that we learn of Bautista's interest
in and experience with temple work and genealogy. Young corroborates our
impression that Bautista was a gifted man, as is certainly evidenced by his
writing.

Accepting the biblical suggestion (1 Cor. 15:31–32) that all people, living
and dead, require baptism for their exaltation, Mormons search out the names
of their ancestors and submit those names to one of the temples so that the
living, by proxy, may perform the ordinances for them.

43. Both Julio García Velázquez (Oral History, p. 60) and William Walser
(Oral History, p. 24) state that the First Presidency sent Bautista to Mexico to
train Mexican Mormons in genealogical matters. While Bautista may have been

encouraged by some General Authorities, we do not know that he was directly commissioned to do this work. More likely he was doing it on his own due to his intense interest in the whole matter, although Walser (Oral History, p. 24) does state that Harold Pratt objected to Bautista's "being sent."

44. Mary Pratt Parrish, Oral History, interview by Gordon Irving, p. 19. In this interview we learn additional matters relating to Rey Pratt's interest in both the Lamanites and the promises extended to them through the Book of Mormon. Pratt did considerable work with the Book of Mormon; by 1929 he had translated into Spanish the chapter headings, the references, the index, and other materials.

45. García Velázquez, Oral History. In addition, from reading Rey Pratt's writing in "The Restored Gospel," we know that he was fascinated by the possible connections between Latin American Indians and the peoples of the Book of Mormon. In his writing Pratt speculated on these connections, closely paralleling some things that Bautista later wrote in his book.

46. The lengthy book, including illustrations and maps, is entitled *La evolución de México: Sus verdaderos progenitores y su origen y el destino de América y Europa.* Copies are available in the Special Collections division of the Harold B. Lee Library, Brigham Young University, Provo, Utah, and in the LDS Church Library, Historical Division.

47. Bautista's maps, whatever else they may be, are fascinating. He has two folded insets near the end of the book. One opens out to a world map, showing the paths that Book of Mormon peoples may have taken in traveling to America as well as various cities and regions mentioned in the scripture. The second map, a detailed outline of Central America, shows the purported locations of a large number of Book of Mormon settlements as well as routes taken by intracontinental expeditions noted in the Book of Mormon. There is a small engraved imprint of the American continent on the cover of the book. On it North America is labeled "Mulek," South America "Lehi." Maps like these are certainly not doctrinal, but they do make very interesting study for people who by inclination have an intellectual curiosity. Bautista had just such an inclination.

48. William Walser, Oral History, pp. 23–24. Walser talks about the church's actions in relation to Bautista's book and states that Harold Pratt did not have to read very far into the book to make his decision. As soon as he got to the argument in favor of state religion, he knew that the church could not possibly publish the book.

49. We do not know that Bautista left the United States in 1934 solely because of this frustration. Indeed, he may have been commissioned to do genealogy work in Mexico (see note 43). However, it is also instructive to know that Bautista was one of between three and five hundred thousand people of Mexican ancestry who returned or emigrated to Mexico between 1931 and 1934. Some were homesick, many were unemployed and destitute, many were harassed and pursued by U.S. federal agents. They were crossing the border into Mexico en masse. America was in the throes of the worst depression of its history. A combination of Mexican heartbreak in "the promised land" and U.S. protectionism of the employment possibilities of its own citizens combined to produce, as Andrés C. González, Jr., reports in an interview, "trainload after trainload of Mexicans crossing over into Mexico at the El Paso border crossing." Thousands were returning at the other international crossings as well. Some of those who

were being deported were, in fact, Mexican–Americans holding valid U.S. citizenship. (See, for example, the notes by Rodolfo Acuña, *Occupied America: The Chicano's Struggle toward Liberation*, pp. 190–95.)

Whether Bautista was primarily a *repatriado*, or primarily a man commissioned to do genealogical work, or, as later asserted, one mainly intent on fomenting rebellion in the church, we find difficult to judge. A complex combination of motives, not all of them neatly laid out beforehand, no doubt were at work in his decision to return to Mexico.

50. García Velázquez, Oral History. In addition, the title page of the book bears the name of Apolonio Arzate as the printer.

51. Harold W. Pratt, Journal, 30 April 1936.

52. Andrés C. González, Jr., a missionary in Mexico at the time, made this statement in an interview with F. LaMond Tullis.

53. Santiago Mora González, interview.

54. Andrés C. González, Jr., interview.

55. This was the analysis given by Abel Páez and recorded in Harold Pratt's Journal, 3 May 1936.

56. Information on the conflicts between Harold W. Pratt and Margarito Bautista comes from a number of sources: Harold Pratt, Journal, April, May, June 1936, passim; Manuscript History, quarter ending 30 June 1936; García Velázquez, Oral History, pp. 4–11; and Brown, Oral History, pp. 31–42.

57. The accusation that Harold Pratt had tried to kill Abel Páez was made in a letter Bautista wrote to Ester Ontiveros, a missionary working in Monterrey at the time. That letter is transcribed in the Mexican Mission Historical Record under the date of 22 April 1936.

58. Such endeavors are not new, then or now, as a casual survey of Mormon religious works will quickly show any observer. These works are not, however, generally sponsored by the church, although many have received encouragement from one or another General Authority. Bautista himself was not working in total isolation on this point, even in the 1920s and 1930s. An earlier work by Louisa L. Greene Richards, *Branches That Run over the Wall: A Book of Mormon Poems and Other Writings*, had set the Book of Mormon in blank verse and had added romance, names of wives, and historical embellishment to the narrative. The effort received warm congratulations from Anthon H. Lund and George Reynolds, two General Authorities. As the work had gained great popularity in the Salt Lake Valley, it is doubtful that it would have escaped Bautista's attention.

59. Andrés Iduarte, who grew up in the revolutionary period (ca. 1910–40) of Mexican history, wrote of the feelings Mexicans had as they studied their country's past.

> The elementary school made chauvinists of us. We hated the Spaniards as Spaniards, and reserved a special loathing for Pedro de Alvarado, the perpetrator of the cruel Indian massacres; we adored Cuauhtémoc, who defended the great Tenochtitlán (Mexico City) and who, when forced to surrender to Cortés, asked the latter to kill him with his own dagger; and Cacamatzín, who stoned countless Spaniards to death. We blushed with repugnance at the very mention of Montezuma, the Aztec emperor who

surrendered Mexico City to the Spaniards; of Malinche, the concubine of Cortés; of the treacherous Indians who supported Cortés against the Aztecs and so betrayed their country. We were at once indignant and distressed by the intelligence and audacity of Hernán Cortés.

Mexicans felt that " 'the damned Spaniards never had anyone as valiant and cultured as [their] heroes.' [There was] hatred for the despicable Spaniards as Spaniards, love for the Mexicans as Mexicans; happiness over the slaughter of Spaniards, sadness over the death of [Mexican] patriots; an unreasoning zeal very similar to religious fanaticism: passion, bloodshed, and fire to nourish [their] fantasies" (*Niño: Child of the Mexican Revolution*, pp. 66–67).

60. We see the same thing happening in the new nations of Africa. Perhaps the most striking evidence of this phenomenon is the renaming of countries. Mali, for example, has taken its name from an ancient African kingdom in the area. Further examples are the Republic of Zaire, Zambia, and Zimbabwe.

61. There has been little love lost between Mexicans and Spaniards. The colonial relationship between the two was broken off with merciless bloodletting and much bitterness. As recently as 1975 the two countries had very strained relations.

62. Brown, Oral History, p. 32.

63. Enrique González, quoted in the *Informe general*, p. 18, translated by F. LaMond Tullis.

136

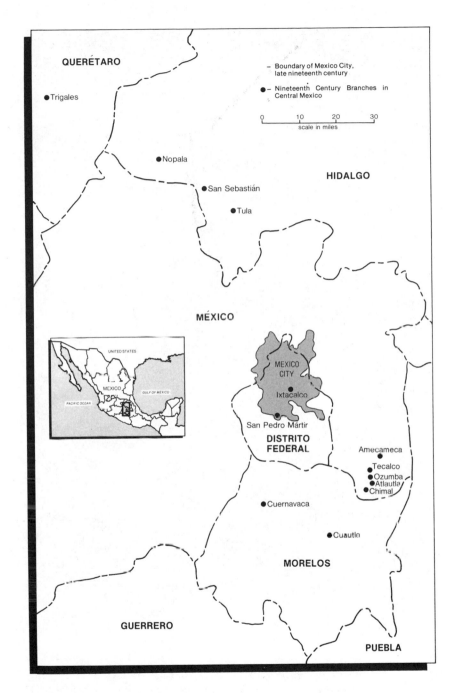

Figure 10.   Early branches in central Mexico. *Cartography by B. Kelley Nielsen*

Figure 11.   Mission President Rey L. Pratt and Isaías Juárez (seated) with
David Juárez, Benito Panueya, Narciso Sandoval, and Tomás
Sandoval, ca. 1927. (The man wearing the hat is unidentified.)
Courtesy of LDS Church Archives.

Figure 12.   David O. McKay, who made efforts to reunify the Mormon church
in Mexico while counselor to President George Albert Smith,
ca. 1935. *Courtesy of Harold B. Lee Library Photo Archives, Brigham
Young University.*

Figure 13.   Abel *Páez*, leader of the Third Convention, speaking at the reunification conference attended by President George Albert Smith, 1946. *Courtesy of LDS Church Archives.*

Figure 14.   Mexican mission leaders, ca 1947. First row, Isaías Juárez. Arwell L. Pierce, Abel Páez, and Bernabé Parra. (Second row is unidentified.) *Courtesy of LDS Church Archives.*

Figure 15. Abel Páez, J. Reuben Clark, Jr. (U.S. Ambassador to Mexico), and Isaías Juárez, ca. 1931. *Courtesy of LDS Church Archives.*

Figure 16.   Church President George Albert Smith, who presided over the
reunification conference that brought the Third Convention back
into the mainline church, ca. 1951. *Courtesy of Harold B. Lee Library
Photo Archives, Brigham Young University.*

Figure 17.   Group constructing benches at the first chapel in San Marcos, Hidalgo, ca. 1930. Bernabé Parra is standing. *Courtesy of LDS Church Archives.*

Chapter 6

The Third Convention*

Soon after news of Harold W. Pratt's appointment reached Mexico City, Abel Páez, first counselor in the Mexican district presidency, was at work. Spurred on by his uncle, Margarito Bautista, he summoned the Saints to a crisis conference now called the Third Convention. Those attending the conference decided once more to petition the First Presidency for a Mexican mission president. The petition and ensuing events occasioned a split in the Mexican district of the Mormon church that lasted ten years. The eventual reconciliation, which saw Mormon prophet George Albert Smith travel to Mexico City to preside over a reunification conference, is a testament to how boundaries of language, ancestral custom, ethnicity, and national identity can be crossed within a single faith even when nationalistic sentiments make people touchy, defensive, or insensitive.

The authorities had denied the Mexicans' request twice. Now, rebellious and angry, some of the Mexican Mormons became even more convinced that their mission leader should be able to understand them and their needs, and that they had had no such leader since Rey L. Pratt. Their sensitivity, pricked by ethnic pride and their own declining leadership opportunities, was further heightened by their frustrated hopes.

---

*This chapter is based on an unpublished manuscript, "Mormonism in Mexico: Leadership, Nationalism, and the Case of the Third Convention," by F. LaMond Tullis and Elizabeth Hernandez.

Sensing his people's mood, Isaías Juárez, president of the mission's Mexican district, was alarmed by their preparations for the Third Convention. He could see the implications perhaps better than anyone, having struggled through nine years and many storms to lead the mission. Juárez had learned to read the pulse of the Mexican Saints accurately. He knew this would be no simple petition; quite a few Mexican Mormons were determined to settle for nothing less than a Mexican leader, however unusual— even odd—such a demand was for Mormons, whose authorities are always appointed from above, never "selected" by the congregation. Juárez also sensed accurately the mood of the authorities in Salt Lake City: he knew there would be no Mexican mission president forthcoming. The church, he reasoned, would not succumb to pressure politics, and he foresaw an unfortunate and inevitable clash.

Juárez remembered the first and second conventions and Antoine R. Ivins's teachings that such conventions and petitions were unacceptable in the Church of Jesus Christ. And, although he was as frustrated as many other Mexican Saints, he realized that another convention must ultimately part ways with the church. He refused to align himself with it.

Customarily among the Mormons, leaders at the top try to sense the needs both of a people and their organization, making fitting appointments according to their best judgment as influenced by their conscious effort to seek the will of the Lord. Local leaders are not "elected" as such; rather, once leaders are appointed, local members are asked to "sustain" them. Juárez clearly understood, therefore, the inevitable conflict. He probably also understood the church's traditional position of sending in "outsiders" where the faith is young, gradually trusting new members, as they become "seasoned," to assume the most significant leadership responsibilities.

Juárez was no passive fence-sitter. Having taken a position against the Third Convention, he then tried to soothe and persuade the Mexican Saints. Finally he issued a circular letter explaining that the meeting was unauthorized and out of order and that those who participated in it would be considered rebellious and therefore run the risk of excommunication. He contacted Harold Pratt posthaste and tried to sensitize him to the impending trouble and its roots. He met repeatedly with Abel Páez, trying to dissuade him.

Isaías Juárez bewildered and angered Páez. Twice before, Juárez had subscribed to meetings like the Third Convention, even helping to draft an earlier petition. But now he wanted to avoid a break with the authorities in Salt Lake City. Páez, on the other hand, seemed confused, uncertain what to do, for he did not see the matter in the same light as did Juárez. Initially he wavered under pressure from Juárez, agreeing that the convention was not only out of order but futile, and promised to call it off. Later, however, Páez reversed himself, declaring that the effort was worth any risk.

Abel Páez had labored diligently and faithfully in the church for years. As he meditated on his own experiences,[1] Margarito Bautista's arguments began to make a lot of sense to him. If the Mexican Saints did not stand up for themselves now, when would they? Tired of what he perceived as paternalism, unnerved by what he considered second-class treatment in the kingdom of God, and convinced that the Conventionists' desires were just, Abel Páez finally supported and agreed to preside over the Third Convention. With Bautista's help, he set out to organize the proceedings.

Amidst considerable discussion among Mexican Mormons—given Juárez's circular letter against the convention—approximately one hundred and twenty members nevertheless convened on 26 April 1936.[2] Guadalupe Zárraga came as an observer to take notes for Presidents Juárez and Pratt. The Conventionists quickly decided that the Salt Lake City leaders had misunderstood their previous requests. Even though Harold Pratt had come from the Mormon colonies and was a Mexican citizen, he was not one by blood and race and certainly not one culturally. The Saints' new petition was intended to convey their desire for a president who was Mexican by blood and spirit (*de raza y sangre*).

Reasoning that the church's General Authorities might not be aware of qualified Mexican members, the Third Convention decided to nominate a candidate. They considered several men, including Narciso Sandoval and Margarito Bautista.[3] In the end, however, the convention settled on Abel Páez. They did not intend to demand Páez's appointment but rather to clearly inform the Salt Lake City authorities that qualified Mexicans were available.

After making their main decision, the Conventionists strengthened their petition in two ways. First, wanting their leaders to recognize their intense seriousness, they agreed to gather

139

signatures for the petition. Second, the Conventionists authorized a commission composed of Abel Páez, Narciso Sandoval, and Enrique González to travel to Salt Lake City and personally present the petition and supporting documents to the Mormon church's General Authorities. Its business concluded, the Third Convention then adjourned.

Harold Pratt was stunned. Having rushed to Mexico City just two days before the convention, he had feared the worst but hoped for less; he had not believed Páez would go through with proceedings so out of character for Mormons as to be totally incomprehensible to the mainline church except in terms of apostasy. Páez had agreed at one point to cancel the convention. In light of this agreement, and in order to avoid more dissension, Juárez and Pratt had stayed home and out of sight. Then Guadalupe Zárraga brought the shocking news. Isaías Juárez wept when he heard that his counselor of many years had betrayed him.[4]

Harold Pratt realized that the Mexican brethren would soon implement their decisions. Seeking to prevent that, Pratt immediately contacted Abel Páez. They set a meeting for 30 April, the Thursday following the convention.[5]

On the appointed day Abel Páez met with Pratt, Juárez, and Bernabé Parra, the second counselor in the district presidency. After a long discussion, the men agreed on four points: first, Páez would terminate the Third Convention's activities, including the gathering of signatures for the petition. Moreover, Páez would thereafter take no unilateral action on any matter without the district presidency's consent, a hallowed leadership practice within the Mormon faith. Second, to show their unity and harmony, the four leaders— Páez, Juárez, Parra, and Pratt—would together visit all the local branches. Third, each would send a separate report of the Third Convention to the First Presidency of the church. Fourth, all would prepare to visit Salt Lake City soon to discuss the Mexicans' feelings and desires with the General Authorities. The upcoming October general conference was set as a tentative date for the trip.[6]

Abel Páez left the meeting satisfied. The Third Convention had accomplished something after all: Harold Pratt now seemed to take Mexican desires quite seriously, and now the Mexican Mormons would be able to present their case in person to the General Authorities. Surely such a trip would prompt positive action. Páez felt that the Third Convention's purposes would now be carried out within the church structure and that therefore his actions were appropriate.

But Páez was to be disappointed. As the district presidency visited the various branches, Pratt and Juárez seemed to equivocate on their position. Pratt said that he alone would take the petition to Salt Lake City at conference time. Then, instead of assuring church members that Third Convention desires would be enacted through regular church channels, Juárez and Pratt made it increasingly clear that both the convention's procedures and its goals were out of order. They suggested that Páez and his colleagues were wolves among the Lord's sheep and warned all members against listening to them.[7] Mainline Mexican Mormons—approximately two-thirds of the membership—had made their anti-Third-Convention opinions known to Juárez and Parra, and no doubt Pratt had received communications on the issue from Salt Lake City. In any case, Conventionists were incensed. They wondered how Páez could believe that Pratt would do anything but present the Third Convention's case negatively.[8]

Abel Páez was in a delicate position with respect to his own followers. He had agreed to work with the district presidency and Harold Pratt, and he had announced this decision to all the Saints involved in the Third Convention. Now the Conventionists felt betrayed, themselves chastised and their goals scorned by the very men with whom their leader was supposedly working. They judged Páez a traitor to their cause, unworthy of his nomination for mission president. However, despite their dismay, the Third Conventionists abided by their earlier decisions.

Abel Páez, of course, felt no less betrayed. After working with Pratt and Juárez to determine their intentions regarding the Third Convention, he reached an irreversible position. With a note of finality he claimed all responsibility for the Third Convention and its activities, stating publicly his determination to implement its decisions. These, he felt, were too beneficial and necessary to the mission's well-being to now be ignored.[9] If "proper channels" were closed, he would work outside those channels.

With equal finality the Salt Lake City authorities carried out their plan to divide the Mexican mission, investing Harold Pratt with complete stewardship over the church's activities in Mexico

141

City. The new president entered Mexico with his wife and five children to begin a long ordeal.

The Third Convention Breaks from the Church

And so the battle lines, however reluctantly and unintentionally drawn, were firm. Páez and more than eight hundred Mexican Saints aligned themselves with the Third Convention (by now an institution with its own organized structure) and adamantly demanded a Mexican mission president. President Pratt and more than two thousand Saints who opted to remain with the mainline Mormon church (despite the objections of even some of them to the missionary system and leadership arrangements) continued with the blessings of the church's General Authorities.

In November of 1936 the First Presidency replied formally to the Conventionists. J. Reuben Clark, Jr.,[10] a member of the First Presidency and former U.S. ambassador to Mexico and undersecretary of state, prepared a carefully written letter to be read in all the congregations.[11] In that letter Clark declared that the people who signed the convention's petition were entirely out of order; that the mission president was not the representative of the members to the president of the church but of the president to the people, and that this representative should therefore be acquainted with all the church procedures in order to prevent disorder and disruption; that none of the church's missions were presided over by any other than men from the bosom of the church; that if the president of the church ever felt so inspired he would appoint one of their number to preside over them; that Mexicans had an unusual number of their own people in responsible positions anyway; that the Mexicans were not exclusively (among Mormons) of the blood of Israel, and that both Mexicans and North American Mormons were from the same family (that of Joseph); that all of the Book of Mormon's promises applied as well to one people as to another, and so on for fourteen typescript pages.[12] As Isaías Juárez had foreseen, there would be no Mexican mission president in the near future.

The church's presiding authorities had hoped that Clark's sensible response would put an end to the Third Convention. But generally, it did not.[13] For most Third Conventionists, the letter only confirmed what they had suspected all along: that Harold Pratt had presented their case negatively at the October general conference in Salt Lake City and that the leaders therefore did not yet understand the nature of the problem.

The First Presidency themselves learned quite soon that the letter had solved nothing. No doubt somewhat exasperated by this time, the authorities decided to send Antoine R. Ivins to Mexico one more time to attempt a reconciliation. Although Ivins was considered the church's frontline expert on Mexico, his previous trips there had been largely unsuccessful because, as he perceived, the Mexican Mormons did not respect his authority.[14] So Apostle George F. Richards, one of the senior members of the Council of the Twelve Apostles, was appointed to accompany Ivins.

When Elders Ivins and Richards reached Mexico City in February of 1937, it was clear that they misunderstood the Mexican position. The Americans interpreted the Third Conventionists' demand to be twofold: a Mexican mission president, *and the right to name him themselves*.[15] The nomination of Abel Páez seems to have caused this confusion. The Third Convention had not in the beginning intended to demand the right to name a mission president. Páez's nomination was only intended to inform the Salt Lake City authorities that there were potential Mexican leaders and that the people did prefer them. But Conventionists meant to leave the appointment up to Salt Lake City, a prerogative they acknowledged as proper and necessary within the Mormon faith. What the dissidents did insist, however, was that their president, whoever he was, should be a Mexican by race and thereby able to fulfill both the spirit and letter of Mexican laws and also, in their opinion, better understand the needs of Mexican Mormons.

In this spirit Páez, as the convention's official representative, had written to the First Presidency just a month after the convention, asking the presiding brethren to grant Mexican Mormons a mission president of pure Mexican race.[16] Yet Elders Ivins and Richards and also David O. McKay, a counselor to the church president, Heber J. Grant, seemed to assume that Páez was demanding his own appointment as president of the Mexican mission.[17] In any event, to them all this flurry of activity over leadership appointments smacked of pressure politics if not outright apostasy.

143

The Mormon church's First Presidency could not become—or even to appear to become—a rubber stamp for anyone, nor could it succumb to any group's pressures generated outside the church's established channels for dealing with such matters. Thus their misunderstanding of the Third Convention's effort to help the church's leaders reach a judicious decision put them on the defensive. In response they took the offensive, sending Ivins and Richards to Mexico to settle the issue once and for all.

Ivins and Richards went to present the First Presidency's position one more time, to point out vigorously that faithful church members sustain the word of the prophet in matters of dispute.[18] No one in Salt Lake City considered that Ivins and Richards should negotiate or compromise with the Conventionists in Mexico. When Third Convention leaders learned of the impending visit and its purpose, they refused to meet privately with the visitors, asking Ivins and Richards to address all the people in a general meeting. The visiting brethren agreed, even though it meant spending an extra week in Mexico.

As the meetings began on 14 February 1937, two government officials entered the hall and sat down. Third Conventionists later said these men were interested in becoming Mormons and were quite harmless, but Harold Pratt did not know that.[19] In fact, before the meeting he had heard rumors that the Conventionists might provoke an arrest. Naturally he began to get a little nervous; as foreigners, by law neither Ivins nor Richards should have been officially addressing a Mexican religious congregation. And so, his apprehension growing by the minute, President Pratt called one of his missionaries aside and instructed him to put Elders Ivins and Richards on a train for the United States. The last thing he wanted was the arrest of two General Authorities.[20]

The leaders' swift exit without any speeches at all disappointed the Mexicans. Later, convention hardliners complained that if the visitors had been like the apostles of old they would not have feared government officials or anyone else, but would have stayed and presented their talks, having faith that everything would work out. After all, they reasoned, the Third Convention would not have been so foolish as to invite people who would antagonize the General Authorities of the church.[21]

Nevertheless, the authorities were antagonized. In due time Ivins and Richards made their report to the First Presidency. The tactics they described understandably displeased the presiding brethren. David O. McKay, in particular, was greatly distressed. This perceived attempt to arrest the First Presidency's representatives was the last straw, and he urged that excommunication procedures against Third Convention leaders begin at once.[22]

Harold Pratt circulated the text of Apostle Richards's planned talk in which he stated unequivocally that the Mexican Saints were erring and fast falling into apostasy and demanded that they humble themselves and return to full church fellowship by supporting Harold Pratt and in every other way obeying presiding authorities' counsel. If they failed to do so, they would risk excommunication. Richards's talk also demanded that the Conventionists discontinue their unauthorized publications and stop their translating (which included portions of the Doctrine and Covenants not yet published in Spanish, as well as the Pearl of Great Price, "Joseph Smith's Teachings," and two additional sacred Mormon writings).[23] The text, however correct and proper, was counterproductive: thereafter Third Conventionists *explicitly demanded the right to decide for themselves who their mission president should be.*[24] The earlier misunderstanding had become a self-fulfilling prophecy.

By May of 1937 the breach was obviously absolute. The church began excommunication proceedings against all Third Convention leaders. On 6, 7, and 8 May 1937, courts were convened in San Pedro Mártir and the sentences handed down. Conventionist leaders were excommunicated for rebellion (having worked against the mission authorities), insubordination (having completely disobeyed the orders of mission authorities), and apostasy (having failed to recognize the Mormon church's authority).[25]

As the leaders' excommunication rang to them with a note of aggressive finality, Mormons who sympathized with the Third Convention realized that now they must define their own positions. One could belong to the Third Convention or to the Mormon church, but not both. Each individual had a difficult decision to make. As a Conventionist, how could one participate in the Mormons' temple ordinances, an integral part of the religion and one available only to Mormons in good standing?[26] Would God accept and recognize baptisms and other ordinances performed by Third Conventionists? Looking ahead, what would Third Convention members need to do if they ever decided to reenter the mainline Mormon church? Most importantly, did God approve of the Third Convention? To participate in the activities that North American Mormon leaders did not authorize or approve of was one thing; it was quite another to associate with an apostate group and thereby relinquish one's church membership.[27]

Most Mexican Mormons felt that a complete loss of association with the church was a heavy price to pay for a Mexican mission president. The church was important to them; they did not want to lose it. They wanted to go along with the church in all respects—but not under Harold Pratt's leadership.[28] Some members felt that God's will must decide the dilemma. For many it became a question of exercising their right—as the Mormon faith teaches—to personal revelation. If God felt their cause was ju: t and approved of their position, they would opt for the Third Convention. Rebellion against the church was acceptable, they reasoned, as long as it did not entail rebellion against God. When the count was in, nearly a third of the Mexican Mormons, deciding that God was with them and the Third Convention, cast their lot with the rebellious group.

Yet, significantly, two-thirds of the Mexican Mormons disagreed. God could not, they argued, approve of the Third Convention or any other group that rebelled against his church. Feeling that the issue was largely racial or nationalistic, they chose to remain true to the mainline church. For some this required submission to leadership conditions which they personally found disagreeable.[29] But that was necessary, in their eyes, to keep faith with the Lord.

Of course, there were other reasons for joining or not joining the Third Convention. Family members influenced each other, with spouses joining mates and children their parents.[30] Expediency reigned in other minds: they met with a Third Convention congregation because it was nearest to their homes, or, likewise, they met with a regular Mormon congregation.

But the Mexican Mormons did not emphasize these motives; adult members remained with or departed from the mainline church because they considered it the right thing to do. Feelings were intense and sometimes impassioned. Faithful mainline members condemned Third Conventionists as heretics and looked upon them almost as devils. If a Third Conventionist came into a chapel held by a mainline congregation and sat down, the pew would empty. Third Conventionists, for their part, accused loyal church members of giving in and betraying the cause of Mexican leadership.[31] Aside from shouting at each other from time to time, the two sides generally severed their relations.

The Third Convention as a Countergroup

And so the break was complete. The Third Convention went its own way, taking with it a large number of people, some chapels, furniture, and records. But the going was not easy. Within weeks Margarito Bautista challenged the convention's leadership on a number of doctrinal points. Some people thought Bautista was using doctrinal issues simply to camouflage his own jockeying for leadership in the convention.[32] The more likely truth is that Margarito was substantively serious. He advocated the reestablishment of polygamy and the United Order, Mormonism's own largely abandoned cooperative economy.[33]

The Third Conventionists' quarrel with Salt Lake City was not a doctrinal one, and they had no intention of letting such questionable issues as polygamy and the United Order separate them even more from the mainline church. The tensions soon became unmanageable, and the convention expelled Margarito.[34] Bitter and scornful, Bautista left the Third Convention to its "darkness" and went to Ozumba, Mexico, where he set up his own colony, the "New Jerusalem."[35] While Bautista's group was not totally isolated (he kept in touch with other Mormon fundamentalist and apostate groups), they were largely rejected by Conventionists and non-Conventionists alike. In the beginning, Bautista had provided impetus for concerns most considered justifiable. Now the memory of his contribution was replaced with a troublemaker's image. Mainline Mormons said they had figured that out long ago.

Thus the Third Convention continued without Margarito Bautista, polygamy, a vision of an economic utopia, or any other doctrines radically different from those of the official Mormon church.[36] It also soon developed an organizational structure parallel to that of the mainline church. After all, its doctrinal base was the same, and its leaders were experienced and dedicated former Mormon church officials. As if to underline their intention

to remain doctrinally pure, the Conventionists called themselves
The Church of Jesus Christ of Latter-day Saints (Third Convention). They organized Sunday Schools, conducted sacrament
meetings, established "mutual improvement associations" (MIA,
the church's youth organization), and functioned very much like
a normal Mormon congregation. Like the mainline church, they
blessed infants, baptized children, and ordained men to the
priesthood.[37]

Since missionary work was especially important to Third
Conventionists, they trained their youth in public speaking, an
art especially appreciated in Mexico.[38] Young Conventionist men
and women were thereafter sent out to "preach the word" to all
who would listen. And perennial missionary Narciso Sandoval
kept up his efforts, too.

Missionary work was far from being the Third Conventionists'
only concern, however. In order even to survive, Conventionists
knew they had to house a viable and living organization. Thus,
in addition to emphasizing missionary activity and developing
all the other Mormon church programs they knew about, convention members launched an ambitious building program.[39]
Donating land, labor, and capital, they constructed at least six
new meetinghouses and, in accordance with Mormon custom,
dedicated them to their Lord.[40]

The Third Convention also produced some religious
literature—for example, a magazine entitled *El Sendero Lamanita*
(The Lamanite Path), which contained articles such as "How the
Gospel Came to Mexico" and "The Blessed Gentiles about which
the Scriptures Speak," and reports of various convention conferences and activities.[41] Apolonio B. Arzate, the publisher of
Margarito Bautista's book, edited *El Sendero Lamanita*. The Third
Convention also published a report of events leading to the
group's establishment—a lengthy document prepared expressly
for the General Authorities, which contained transcripts of letters,
minutes of various official meetings, and other materials.[42]

Learning English was another Third Convention-sponsored
project. Offhand this seems strange, since Conventionists were
openly nationalistic. However, anxious to learn more about the
gospel, they were impatient with the slow pace of Salt Lake City's
translation work. They wanted to be able to read more than the
thirty (out of 136) sections of the Doctrine and Covenants that

had been translated under Antoine R. Ivins, and they wanted to read and study Mormon Apostle James Talmage's *The Articles of Faith* and *Jesus the Christ*, both noncanonical but fundamental Mormon works.[43]

Regardless of its ill-advised separatist strategy, it is evident that the Third Convention accomplished some remarkable things. Among these were the training of indigenous leaders, expanding a missionary program to include their own sons and daughters, development of educational opportunities for their children, and expanding doctrinal literature available in Spanish translation.[44] Abel Páez excelled as its president, getting to know the names and concerns of almost every member. He worked diligently for his people and they reciprocated in kind, with convention members trusting him and accepting his judgments with uncommon confidence. In the early years, before internal leadership struggles began, Abel Páez and the Third Convention came to be synonymous. In fact, mainline church members called the dissidents the "Abel Páez Third Convention group."[45]

The convention continued to operate for ten years, from April of 1936 to May of 1946, growing and progressing alongside mainline church groups. While mainline members did not have an indigenous Mexican mission president, they nevertheless did receive considerable material and organizational help from Salt Lake City, Harold Pratt working as hard as he could on their behalf. Thus both Mormons and not-so-Mormons grew in stature and organization, parallel in sentiment and structure but passionately divided over who their mission president should be.

Harold Pratt labored long to establish permanent mission headquarters in Mexico City. He set up a program of action for his twenty-five missionaries and visited every mainline congregation as often as he could. But he was often ill, and his heavy work schedule weakened him further. Mainline Mexican Mormons could have helped Pratt more, but he thought that he should do as much as he could by himself. He was finally released in 1938 for health problems and was succeeded by A. Lorenzo Anderson.[46]

Anderson, also a colonies Mormon, accepted the call very reluctantly. Among other things, he was worried about how his wife would respond. Some people thought that she had always disliked Mexicans and did not think much good would come out of Mexican Mormons. Anderson rightly wondered if he would be well received in Mexico City.[47]

Rumor reaching Mexico City had it that in the Chihuahua colonies some American Mormons were delighted with Anderson's appointment because they thought Anderson would do what Harold Pratt had not: get those members back in line, show them who was boss, and put them in their place. Third Convention? What an outrage![48]

Whether true, exaggerated, or false, as this unfortunate rumor flew, Third Conventionists dubbed President Anderson "El Domador de Salvajes Mexicanos" (The Tamer of Mexican Savages).[49] Because of the resulting animosity and distrust, there was little contact between the Third Convention and the church during Lorenzo Anderson's presidency. No matter what Anderson and his wife did, the situation was stacked against them. Anderson managed to lead the mission for four years, treading water and holding the line. Finally, in May of 1942, he was replaced by Arwell L. Pierce.[50]

Diplomacy, Persuasion, and the Art of Reunification

Pierce was no Mexican, either by race or birth. Special arrangements had to be made for him to be president of the Mexican mission since he was not even a colonies Mormon.[51] But he was an ecclesiastically experienced man, a diplomat, and a politically sensitive leader. He developed a greater sense of propriety with respect to the society of Mexican Mormons than anyone the church had sent to Mexico since Rey L. Pratt.

But Pierce's work in Mexico was not easy. After evaluating the missionaries he was appointed to lead, he concluded that they understood the gospel insufficiently and were not teaching very effectively what they did know. He immediately set up a strict regimen of work and study for them. Eventually winning their respect and admiration, Pierce worked enthusiastically and vigorously, changing procedures and establishing new policy guidelines.[52]

Arwell L. Pierce dealt with the Third Convention—in fact, the task was his particular calling. In appointing Pierce as mission president, J. Reuben Clark, Jr., had given him a special charge to work for the reunification of the church.[53]

The Third Convention genuinely puzzled Pierce. The more he looked into it the more he realized that its members were vitally and energetically carrying out Mormon church programs. The twelve hundred members had fifteen functioning branches, six constructed chapels, and a small corps of missionaries.[54] They were teaching Mormon doctrine strongly and faithfully. Their reasons for apostasy, he concluded, were certainly not doctrinal—yet Conventionists were outside the community of the church. As he studied the situation, he wondered how brotherhood could have decayed so completely.

Over the years the issues had become clouded, memories diffused or altered, and passions changed. If Pierce could not initially see the issues involved, he had no difficulty in recognizing that the convention would bring great strength to the church in Mexico if its members could be brought back into the fold. And so, slowly and painstakingly, he put all his diplomatic skills to the task. Realizing that feelings had been hurt in the past, the new president set out first to heal the wounds and then to treat the scar tissue. Although initially he was abused, that response soon changed—first to respect, later to admiration.[55]

Pierce began by attending Third Convention meetings and conferences. Slowly, carefully, he introduced himself and built friendships with Third Convention members and leaders. He even tried to assist the convention in its own programs, inviting its members to the mission home to pass on information from Salt Lake City, giving advice when asked, and distributing recently translated church literature.[56] And he talked with Abel Páez and his wife, with Othón Espinoza, Apolonio Arzate, Julio García, and even Margarito Bautista. Always ready to listen and to see, he extended hospitality and acceptance unconditionally.

After weighing all he had heard, Pierce concluded that the Third Convention problem had been poorly handled. Given the circumstances, he even thought that some of the convention's complaints were justified.[57] While having a Mexican mission president was the Third Conventionists' primary concern, they also wanted a building program for chapels as the Americans had, the same kind of church literature that the Americans had, an educational system for their children (as the American Mormons had for theirs in northern Mexico), and an opportunity for their young people to go on missions, as the Americans also did. Was there anything wrong with that? Yes and no, Pierce realized; he did not object to the goals, although one could legitimately wonder how programs to achieve them could possibly have been funded in the 1930s. On the other hand he saw how the Third Conventionists' methods had brought them trouble.

Pierce could not approve of the Third Convention's rebellion and withdrawal from the Mormon church, but he did not for the most part object to the convention's goals. He understood how its members could have reached their decision to leave the mainline church, and because of his understanding, for the first time in nearly a decade disagreeing men were discussing the issues rather than shouting about them.

That the issues were now somewhat understandable did not nullify or simplify them. But things had changed in ten years. The Mormon church was now able to be much more committed to Mexico. It had much more literature in translation and still more forthcoming. Now that World War II was over, it was developing a strong missionary program, and more missionaries would soon be called.

In the meantime the Conventionists had generally maintained doctrinal purity, had done vigorous proselyting, and had promoted much interest in the Book of Mormon. Given all of these factors, reunification seemed possible. Certainly it was desirable.

So Pierce listened, persuaded, argued, lectured, sympathized, and worked long hours, because he felt the convention should return to the church. Arwell Pierce loved the Mormon gospel and he loved Mexico. He was confident that Mormonism could now make giant strides in Mexico if only the Mormons would unite, and he dedicated his tenure as mission president to that end.[58]

In time, Pierce's efforts began to pay off. The convention recognized him as a friend, its leaders even asking him to speak in convention conferences. He did so, carefully honoring the confidence by avoiding sensitive issues, speaking instead on "neutral" subjects like prayer.[59] He spoke of his own desire for reunification only when such talk was appropriate. In return, Third Conventionists began to visit mainline church meetings, and Pierce, graciously, asked them to sit near the front.

It was not just soothing actions that brought the convention around to Pierce's point of view, however. After they had accepted him, Pierce began engaging them in various ways. He usually took Harold Brown, his special assistant, on his speaking engagements and often instructed Brown to give them the word.[60] The "word" was hardheaded and tough. Then Pierce would follow with his "sweet, loving, come-unto-Zion talk." Thus Brown, as the "tough man," absorbed the Third Convention's anger, and Pierce, as the "loving and understanding man," received a positive response.[61]

Circumstances within the convention itself aided Pierce's wooing of its members. The condition of Abel Páez, who had long suffered from a severe case of diabetes, was perhaps most important. As he was responsible for the spiritual welfare of more than a thousand people, he worried about what would happen to them after he died. Pierce could see this thought weighing heavily upon Páez's mind and began to appeal to his sense of responsibility. Who was going to lead the people after Páez died? If the convention was a temporary way of bringing about Mexican leadership, how would the people get back into the church after Páez was gone? Would future generations be deprived of the church's blessings, and would Páez want to bear the responsibility for that?[62] Finally, Páez began to soften and to warm up to Pierce, and the reluctant warrior started to think with cautious enthusiasm about reunification.

Meanwhile, the mainline church in Salt Lake City was changing. President Heber J. Grant had died and was succeeded in 1945 by George Albert Smith. This leadership change was significant: President Smith began his ministry with a sensitive awareness of the Saints throughout the world. He preached love and forgiveness to members who had recently been on opposing sides in the World War. This same pervading influence of loving kindness had an effect in Mexico.[63]

George Albert Smith especially trusted David O. McKay, the senior ranking member of the church's Quorum of Twelve Apostles and also a counselor to the former president, Heber J. Grant. President Smith asked David O. McKay to continue on as a counselor in the First Presidency. This augured well for the Mormons' Mexican mission, since Apostle McKay had toured the Mormon church in Mexico extensively and happily two years earlier. Among other things, he wanted to begin a major building program in Mexico and so had spent time examining possible sites for chapels.

He had also met, become friends with, and counseled individual Saints, and had listened to their hopes and aspirations for the church in their native land. While listening he refrained from arguing. He accepted their proffered hospitality gracefully, even going to the home of Third Conventionist Othón Espinoza to bless his infant granddaughter.[64] Mexican Mormons were impressed. Conventionists were overwhelmed. Salt Lake City, through the person of David O. McKay, now seemed more attentive.[65] If others were extending the olive branch of peace, why not respond in like spirit? So reasoned many Third Conventionists.[66]

As the church became more attractive to all the Mexican Saints, the convention became correspondingly less so. And in spite of the greatness of Páez, by 1945 serious leadership quarrels had developed within the convention. Some members who had previously supported Páez had begun to shift their allegiance. Othón Espinoza, a staunch convention member and one of the excommunicated leaders, found himself confused and undecided about his future course, and Apolonio Arzate, owner of the printing press, had stated as early as 1943 that he was "pretty well disgusted with the whole situation and about ready to quit."[67] While he did not, his sentiment expressed the shift of support from Páez to Pierce.

Well aware of this, Pierce kept up the initiative. He took church literature to Apolonio Arzate to be printed—and then used the occasions to have long talks with him. He chauffeured Third Convention leaders in his car, talking all the while. He reasoned, argued, and pleaded—all the time and anywhere.[68]

And Arwell Pierce was as self-effacing as he was vigorous in helping Third Conventionists to contain and to understand their own pride. This perhaps more than any other single characteristic enabled him to deal successfully with the Third Convention, for he never claimed credit for accomplishments, but always said, "Not I alone, but I with your help and with the help of the Third Conventionists—together we can bring to pass a great work."[69] Never vindictive, punitive, or perceptibly worried about his own pride, he could take abuse without returning it.[70] For that reason Conventionists remembered him as "a wise man, a very good man, very diplomatic; one who knew how to deal with people of all kinds in the world."[71]

As Third Conventionists began to trust Pierce, his arguments rang true. "I don't understand why you want a mission president of Mexican blood," he would say.

A mission president is actually only a representative of the First Presidency of the church. He is only in charge of the missionaries and the proselyting work. Mission presidents and missionaries only supervise branches until they are strong enough and numerous enough to be organized into a stake. What you really need here in Mexico is a stake organization, the same as the Hawaiians".[72] A stake is an independent unit indirectly under the supervision of the First Presidency of the church. But we cannot have a stake in Mexico until we are more united. Let's all unite under the leadership of the First Presidency of the church, strengthen our branches and prepare to become a stake. We will never achieve this so long as we are divided and so few in number.[73]

Pierce would then drive his point home, advising his listeners that the church would never give the Third Conventionists a Mexican mission president while they persisted in rebellion. Their cause was hopeless. And, at any rate, their goal was undesirable. If they wanted Mexican leadership, they should seek a Mexican *stake president*. And to build a stake they should rejoin the mainline church and build the kingdom in Mexico. Pierce further stated that Mexico could rapidly qualify for a stake once the Third Convention had returned to the church.[74]

Given the evolving circumstances, this argument made a lot of sense to convention members. Moreover, Pierce supported his words with action that would prepare a new generation of Mexican leaders. He got the priesthood manuals and other leadership materials translated, mimeographing some and hiring Apolonio Arzate to print others. He organized new districts under local leadership. He held leadership seminars and told the Mexican Saints that they must begin taking care of matters on their own rather than coming to the mission president with every little problem. People began to notice that Pierce was achieving the Mexicans' goals.[75] And they felt that their Lord was with him.

Pierce was effectively diffusing the leadership question, which was now perceived as the only genuine Third Convention issue remaining. Arwell Pierce was an attractive leader implementing an equally attractive program. Moreover, the Salt Lake City authorities now seemed more open and favorable toward Mexico. On the other hand, there was internal leadership dissension among the Conventionists, and Abel Páez's health was deteriorating. Accordingly, for many Third Conventionists the central issue began to shift from "Should we reunite ourselves with the church?" to "How can we reunite ourselves with the church without losing our personal dignity?"

Pierce understood this dilemma and the role that personal dignity (*dignidad*) plays in the Mexican culture. A severe loss of dignity would have been so irredeemably devastating that thereafter people would not have been able to function in the church. Should that have occurred, strong and faithful members who also happened to be Conventionists—and their descendants—would have been lost to the church forever. Pierce energetically sought to avoid that, "even if some extraordinary measures have to be taken . . . as far as the Church is concerned."[76]

Pierce tried in several ways to help Third Convention leaders preserve their *dignidad*. One of these ways involved face-saving rationalizations. After all, he argued, Third Conventionists were not "selling out" on the idea of Mexican leadership—they were taking steps toward it. They could reason that the Third Convention had made its point and that Salt Lake City was now listening. After the reunification, the church in Mexico would develop rapidly, and thereafter a stake would be organized with local leadership presiding.[77]

Perhaps Arwell Pierce's crowning achievement was his initiation of an ecclesiastical review of the excommunication of the Conventionist leaders. In April 1946, the First Presidency of the church changed the verdict to disfellowshipment, a much less onerous sanction which made reentry of the Conventionists into the church much easier.[78] This decision was no doubt influenced by President George Albert Smith's view that the church's trouble in Mexico seemed more like a big family quarrel than apostasy.[79] In any event, the change from excommunication to disfellowshipment meant a lot in terms of *dignidad*. Most conspicuously, Third Convention leaders did not have to be rebaptized to come back into the church (although all ordinances performed by them while outside the brotherhood of the church were repeated). Less obviously, the change implied that the church recognized that it might have made some errors in dealing with the Third Convention episode. Mexican Saints recognized all these implications, and this change smoothed the path of reunification.[80]

The church made another face-saving move in dealing with convention members who had been baptized without Mormon church-sanctioned authority. They were told not that they had to be rebaptized, which would ordinarily have been the case, but rather that a restitution or ratification of their former baptisms would have to be made. Rebaptism, restitution, ratification—the effect was the same: members were rebaptized by those holding the proper Mormon priesthood authority.[81] But the terminology preserved *dignidad*, as did the fact that Pierce himself performed most of the rebaptisms.[82]

George Albert Smith's 1946 visit to Mexico was another important move. Mainliners and Conventionists alike were immensely proud and honored to receive the man all Mormons recognized as Prophet, Seer, and Revelator (the president's official title). For President Smith's visit to the Tecalco conference, the home of the Third Convention, they spread flowers along the lane leading into the chapel and stood on each side in long lines singing "We Thank Thee, O God, for a Prophet" as the president walked along the flower-strewn path.[83]

Despite his illness while in Mexico, George Albert Smith was a striking success. People pressed in from all sides wanting to shake his hand or just to be near him, and they were thrilled that he would sit at their tables and share their food. Of course, many also wanted to receive him in their homes. He accepted the Mexicans' hospitality graciously, much as David O. McKay had three years earlier.[84]

The Mexico City conference under George Albert Smith's direction saw approximately twelve hundred Third Conventionists return to the fold. Tension was high as the conference began. No one was sure what President Smith might say. He might speak in a condemning tone, chastising Third Conventionists. He might point an accusing finger. But he did not; his love and kindness soon dispelled the tension. Harold Brown, who translated for him on this occasion, said the tension eased and people relaxed and began to smile and respond. Brown remembered the occasion as a most extraordinary one.[85]

The prophet spoke in both the morning and afternoon sessions, stressing the need for harmony and unity. The Third Convention choir, comprising more than eighty voices, provided the music.[86] President Smith asked Abel Páez to speak to the congregation, and the Third Convention leader expressed his joy at being able to return to the church and his happiness about the work that would now be accomplished.[87] Pictures were taken, and an article of considerable length, with the pictures, was published in the *Deseret News*.[88] Obviously, the Third Convention's return to the church was an important and happy event for nearly everyone.

There were a few malcontents. Some accused the church of giving Páez $25,000 to betray the Third Convention.[89] Others, echoing Margarito Bautista, accused Páez of delivering the sheep of Israel to the Gentiles.[90] And Margarito Bautista and his own group remained in Ozumba, appearing only occasionally to hurl epithets—"Gentiles! Sons of Egyptians! Fathers of obscurantism!"[91] Some American Saints were also upset, feeling that Pierce had soft-pedaled the Third Convention group and brought its members back into the church on false pretenses.[92]

Be that as it may, the Conventionists, seeing the hand of the Lord in the matter, came back. Pierce, making good his declared intention of developing local leadership, put people to work right away. By special permission of the First Presidency, on 19 June 1946 he selected and organized a Comité de Consejo y Bienestar (Counsel and Welfare Committee). Guadalupe Zárraga, Abel Páez, Bernabé Parra, Apolonio Arzate, and Isaías Juárez—strong leaders with highly diverse backgrounds—were called to serve on this committee.[93]

Zárraga, Harold Pratt's original "spy," had remained faithful to the mainline church through the troublesome years. Parra had remained loyal to Mormon church authorities even though he had been excommunicated for moral infractions unrelated to the Third Convention.[94] He had recently been returned to full membership. Páez and Arzate were, of course, former convention leaders. And Isaías Juárez? The former district president of Mexico had become inactive during Harold Pratt's presidency.[95] First he had been exiled to Guatemala for political activities, but then, in keeping with his principles and leadership talents, he had returned to Mexico to help found his country's national peasant union (Confederación Nacional Campesina).[96] That effort, and his work with the Mexican federal government's Agrarian Department, had kept him traveling virtually every Sunday.[97] Although frustrated with Anglo–Mormon leadership in Mexico, he sought other outlets for his talents and had kept in close touch with many church members.

As different as these men were, they now came together in a new spirit of brotherhood and worked harmoniously in the Mormon church. They counseled and advised the mission president, assisted in branch and district conferences, and worked in every way possible to prepare Mexico for a stake. And so did Narciso Sandoval, who, while in his fifties and after the reunification, left to serve still another mission for the church.[98] Many problems remained, of course, but all of them were overshadowed by two facts: the church was together again, and there was a buoyant spirit of peace and optimism about the future.

Fifteen years would pass before the new vineyard would mature, however; the first stake for Mexican Mormons was not organized until 1961, sixty-six years after the organization of the first stake in Mexico at Colonia Juárez in 1895. And even then it was not presided over by Juárez, Parra, Hernández, or López, but by Harold Brown. Brown, a colonies Mormon like so many previous higher authorities in Mexico, was cast in the mold of Rey Pratt and Arwell Pierce. He quickly opened up leadership opportunities for his Mexican brothers. His first counselor was none other than Julio García Velázquez, a former Conventionist leader. Gonzalo Zaragoza served him as second counselor and Luís Rubalcava as clerk.

In 1986 Mexico had eight missions and eighty stakes functioning. Mexicans by birth and race preside in almost all the stakes and missions. Leadership in Mexico started to come of age in the 1930s; now it has matured.

But let us return to Mexico City in 1946, where there were a number of Americans and Mexicans, each deeply individual, conflicting less in their perceptions of self, others, duty, religion, and world than they had ten years earlier. Foremost on the American side was Arwell L. Pierce, experienced president of the sorely tried but newly united Mexican mission. Over forty-five North American missionaries filled the ranks. On the Mexican side, there was Isaías Juárez, an astute politician and gifted leader. There was Abel Páez working forthrightly in the mission. And there were others—Julio García, Bernabé Parra, Apolonio Arzate, Guadalupe Zárraga, Narciso Sandoval, Othón Espinoza and several Mexican missionaries, all brought together by the reunification of the Third Convention and the church. Almost everyone was pleased.

Notes

1. Abel Páez had also served as a missionary in the Mexican mission when it still included the southwestern part of the United States. His service was primarily in Texas, where he learned a great deal of English (Harold Brown, Oral History, interview by Gordon Irving, p. 34).

2. Harold W. Pratt, Journal, 27 April 1936.

3. Julio García Velázquez, Oral History, interview by Gordon Irving, p. 9. This informant also mentioned the name of Andrés González as having been placed in nomination, although Andrés González, Jr., in a personal interview (1976), expressed doubts as to the accuracy of this. As he carried his father's name and was in Mexico as a missionary at the time of the Third Convention, he is certain that someone would have called the episode to his attention. Interestingly, the name of Andrés González had also been raised by Antoine R. Ivins as a likely candidate for mission president in the event Harold Pratt should be replaced (Antoine R. Ivins to the First Presidency, 2 September 1936). González had immigrated to the United States and spoke English, but he also had maintained close contact with Mexico.

Andrés González, Jr., mentioned in a personal interview that his father had actually been approached by Apostle Melvin J. Ballard respecting a call to head the mission, but both agreed that it would not be possible because of substantial business debts that González was working to retire at the time.

4. Pratt, Journal, 27 April 1936. Third Convention leaders viewed the tears of Juárez in a different light. They accused him of being a sellout, better, a "copout," to the North Americans. (See *Informe general*, p. 41.)

5. Pratt, Journal, 27 April 1936.

6. Mexican Mission Historical Record, 22 April 1936. (Entries for May were placed on this date.)

7. *Informe general*, passim.

8. García Velázquez, Oral History, pp. 8–9, 13.

9. Mexican Mission Historical Record, 22 April 1936. (Entries for May were placed on this date.)

10. J. Reuben Clark, Jr., a U.S. Mormon, had lived among the Mormons in Mexico when he was the U.S. ambassador there from 3 October 1930 to 3 March 1933. Mexican Saints liked and respected Ambassador Clark. (See Martin B. Hickman, "The Ambassadorial Years: Some Insights," in Ray C. Hillam, ed., *J. Reuben Clark, Jr.: Diplomat and Statesman*, pp. 175–84, and Frank Fox, *J. Reuben Clark, Jr.: The Public Years.*)

11. Pratt, Journal, 11 November 1936.

12. As summarized by Antoine R. Ivins in a letter to Harold W. Pratt, 27 October 1936. A copy of the First Presidency's letter was placed in the LDS Church Archives, but at this writing archival personnel had not been able to locate it. I therefore could not review it.

13. Conventionists had previously agreed to abide by any decisions the First Presidency might make. By implication, they would therefore support Harold Pratt if their petition were denied. Now, however, they considered the

previous agreement to be null and void because their own leaders had not been allowed to present the petition to the authorities in Salt Lake City. Conventionists figured that Pratt, who had presented it, had done so with prejudice. (See Santiago Mora González, Oral History.)

Bautista had agreed to abide by the First Presidency's decision if it went against the Third Convention. A decision either for or against would not be in vain, he thought. If the First Presidency acted favorably on the petition, "we will get our desires fulfilled. If they do not, the petition will nevertheless motivate Harold Pratt to pick up the work of the Mission and get it off dead center" (as reported by Santiago Mora González in an interview, 1975).

When the negative answer finally came, however, Bautista was most adamant in his reversal. This occasioned the first split in the convention's ranks. On this issue the members of the branch at La Libertad (Puebla) withdrew and asked Harold Pratt what they would have to do to be reinstated in the church. Their great concern was that in staying with the convention they would lose out on temple work, be prevented from keeping records that would be acceptable to the Lord, be hard put to enlarge the missionary work, and be obliged to take custody of tithing funds that should be submitted to the church.

Pratt journeyed to the Puebla area where the La Libertad branch was located and sat down with the branch president, Santiago Mora González, to talk the matter out:

> "We were in the Convention," the branch president said, "but have now withdrawn and are no longer members of it. We now need to know what your conditions are, or the conditions of the church, so that we can return to full membership in it."
> Pratt responded: "Has one of you received the priesthood in the Convention?"
> "No."
> "Has one of you been baptized in the Convention?"
> "No."
> "Then you are still members of the church. There are no conditions for you. Just return to faithfulness." (Santiago Mora González, interview.)

14. Antoine R. Ivins had previously made two trips to deal with the problem of Mexican leadership. In 1932 he traveled with Apostle Melvin J. Ballard. Then, in the summer of 1936, he went to help Harold Pratt (Manuscript History, 30 June 1936). Mexican Saints did not welcome him on either occasion. In a letter to the First Presidency dated 11 December 1936, President Ivins confided that while in Mexico he sensed the Saints felt him to be hardly competent.

15. "Mensaje del Presidente George F. Richards para ser leída en el culto en Tecalco el Domingo 14 de Febrero de 1937," p. 4.

16. Letter is cited in the George F. Richards, "Mensaje," p. 5. The Spanish reads as follows:

> El verdadero objeto de dichas convenciones fue llegar a un acuerdo con los presidentes de las ramas, hermanos del Sacerdocio, y miembros de la iglesia quienes estaban presentes, a pedir a la Primera Presidencia de la Iglesia, a concedernos el favor de nombrar a un presidente de raza pura mexicana para dirigir los destinos de la Misión primero, a causa de la necesidad existente, y segundo, a causa del verdadero espíritu de la ley

existente del país, como seguramente sabrán Uds. lo que es el requisito de la ley en asuntos de culto actualmente, por consiguiente fuímos obligados a tomar ese curso.

My English translation of the above text follows:

The true objective of the above mentioned conventions was to come to an agreement with branch presidents, priesthood brethren, and [other] church members in attendance to ask the First Presidency of the church to grant us the favor of naming as our [mission] president a pure ethnic Mexican to direct mission affairs, first because of existing needs, and second because of the true spirit of this country's laws because, as you surely know, such is the requirement of the current law on religious worship, and so we were obligated to take this course.

17. "Mensaje del Presidente George F. Richards," p. 6.

18. Ibid., pp. 13–14.

19. García Velázquez, Oral History, pp. 24–25; Harold Brown, Oral History, p. 32; and E. LeRoy Hatch, Oral History, interview by Gordon Irving, p. 12.

20. Hatch, Oral History. President Pratt's perceptions, justifying his precipitous actions, are found in the Mexican Mission Historical Record, 14 February 1937. See also Manuscript History, quarter ending 31 March 1937.

21. García Velázquez, Oral History, pp. 24–25; Brown, Oral History, p. 32; episode described in Hatch, Oral History, p. 12.

22. Ivins to Harold Pratt, 25 February 1937.

23. "Mensaje del Presidente George F. Richards," p. 16. The Doctrine and Covenants and the Pearl of Great Price are, of course, two of the four canonical works of the church, the others being the Book of Mormon and the Bible. Only portions of the Doctrine and Covenants had been made available in Spanish and none of the Pearl of Great Price. "Joseph Smith's Teachings" (not to be confused with the *Teachings of the Prophet Joseph Smith*, which appeared in English two years later) was a key doctrinal work that had received wide circulation among English-speaking members, but also had not been translated into Spanish. Objections to freelance translations were grounded in previous bad experiences with literature circulated in Europe. (See Ivins to A. Lorenzo Anderson, 27 December 1938.)

24. *Informe general*, p. 36.

25. The minutes of the proceedings are found in the Mexican Mission Historical Record for 6, 7, and 8 May 1937. See also notes 13 and 65 of this chapter.

26. Endowments, sealings, and baptisms for the dead held a hallowed spot in the hearts of many Mexican members even though most had never done any temple work. This sensitivity comes out in the Santiago Mora González interviews, is alluded to in the *Informe general*, and is a topic that came up repeatedly during the later Pierce presidency.

27. In that sense the fears were quite unfounded. Only eight excommunications were ever made. Most dissidents were simply considered "inactive" as far as official records were concerned.

28. Mora González, Oral History, interview by Gordon Irving.

29. Ibid., and also González de la Cruz, Oral History, interview by Gordon Irving; also Cirilo Flores Flores, Oral History, interview by Gordon Irving.

30. A. Lorenzo Anderson, Oral History, pp. 83, 90.

31. García Velázquez, Oral History; Brown, Oral History, p. 35.

32. Brown, Oral History, pp. 33–34. Brown states that Margarito Bautista felt himself to be the logical choice for mission president before the convention split with the church. Bautista did not like being passed over by church authorities. (He was a high priest; Harold Pratt a seventy and thus, in his eyes, of "lower rank.") His continued jockeying for leadership after the schism may have proven to be an insupportable challenge to Third Convention leaders, who were, after all, just then in a difficult process of organization. This view, however, must be balanced by the minutes of the initial Third Convention meeting, which state that Margarito Bautista turned down a proffered nomination for mission president (*Informe general*, pp. 18–19).

33. The technically correct term, *polygynous*, is not used here because it is not ordinary usage. All references to *polygamy* or *polygamous* should be understood as referring to polygynous relationships.

34. Mora González, Oral History; Walser, Oral History, p. 27; Brown, Oral History, pp. 27, 86; García Velázquez, Oral History, p. 14.

35. Eran A. Call, Oral History, interview by Gordon Irving.

36. "Doctrinal Purity" was a goal from the very beginning. (See Mora González, Oral History, and García Velázquez, Oral History.)

37. The blessing certificate of Virgilio Aguilar Páez, dated 13 November 1938 and prepared by the Third Convention, reads as follows: "BENDICIÓN DE NIÑOS, Expedido por la Tercera Convención, Rama de Atlautla México. El presente certifica que el niño Virgilio Aguilar ha sido bendecido en la Iglesia de Jesu Cristo de los Santos de los Últimos Días de la Misión Mexicana el día 13 del mes de Noviembre de 1938 por el Anciano Felipe Barragán." Signed by Abel Páez as president and Othón Espinoza as secretary. The logo is of Temple Square, Salt Lake City. Gordon Irving made available to the author a copy of the certificate.

38. García Velázquez, Oral History, p. 92.

39. Call, Oral History; Hatch, Oral History.

40. Call, Oral History.

41. Brown, Oral History. A few copies of *El Sendero Lamanita* are available in the LDS Church Archives.

42. García Velázquez, Oral History. The report, entitled *Informe general de la tercera convención*, is in the LDS Church Archives.

43. García Velázquez, Oral History.

44. In light of contemporary trends in the church, one is forced to the conclusion that almost the only thing wrong with Third Convention goals, aside from the strategy used to achieve them, was their timing (and the misunderstanding of the role of authority). Consider that the Third Conventionists sought (1) indigenous leadership, (2) expanded missionary programs that would include

their own sons and daughters, (3) educational opportunities for their children, (4) a complete line of doctrinal literature, and (5) opportunity for temple work. In Mexico today virtually all ecclesiastical divisions (branches, wards, stakes, missions) are headed by native members; among the most productive missions of the church, now staffed by hundreds of native as well as North American youth, have been those in Mexico; the Church Education System in Mexico has been hailed from every quarter as a landmark accomplishment not only for the church but for the whole country; translation services producing volumes of literature for the Mexican members are functioning in Mexico, Salt Lake City, and at Brigham Young University; regular temple excursions were promoted by the church to its Mesa, Arizona, temple where thousands of Mexican visitors have been attended to by North American Mormons; the Mexican members now have their own temple in Mexico City. All of the programmatic goals of the Third Convention have been realized in Mexico.

45. Mexican Mission Manuscript History, quarter ending 30 November 1942.

46. Pratt, Journal, 6 August 1938. Harold Pratt had suffered from chronic appendicitis since April 1937, and in December 1937 he submitted to an appendectomy. Shortly after recovering from this operation, however, he began suffering from what he called "kidney colic" and eventually had to have a kidney removed. He was released when he returned to the United States for that operation.

47. Pratt, Journal, 6 August 1938; Andrés González, Jr., personal interview by F. LaMond Tullis.

48. García Velázquez, Oral History, p. 26.

49. Ibid.

50. Mexican Mission Manuscript History, quarter ending 31 May 1942.

51. I do not know of the exact arrangements, only that Pierce took great care to work them out "properly." The Third Conventionists had previously hired a lawyer in Salt Lake City to look into Harold W. Pratt's military training service at Utah State Agricultural College in Logan, Utah. They had attempted to use this information as a basis for getting Pratt expelled from Mexico, but Mexican authorities would not buy their argument because Pratt was a bona fide Mexican citizen—a condition they considered not to have been changed by obligatory military training at an American university. However, church authorities in Salt Lake City felt certain that if Conventionists discovered that Pierce had been born in the United States, they would work for his ouster too (A. Lorenzo Anderson to Arwell Pierce, 16 April 1942). There was some irreverent speculation about Pierce's having paid *mordidas* (bribes) and J. Reuben Clark's subsequent disgust concerning any such activity (Anderson, Oral History, p. 103).

52. Mexican Mission Manuscript History, quarter ending 31 March 1943.

53. Arwell Lee Pierce, "The Story of the Third Convention," p. 1.

54. See García Velázquez, Oral History.

55. Brown, Oral History, pp. 34–35.

56. Pierce's predecessor, A. Lorenzo Anderson, had refused to give the Third Convention any literature. The perceived correctness of this hard-line

approach in dealing with dissidents was confirmed by Antoine R. Ivins in his 3 July 1939 letter to Anderson.

57. Brown, Oral History, p. 34.

58. Some colony Mormons vigorously objected to Pierce's efforts, even accusing him of deceiving David O. McKay into believing that the Conventionists had not apostatized from the church (Walser, Oral History, p. 28).

59. See, for example, Manuscript History, 30 November 1942.

60. In 1946 Brown had given a speech in a district conference in Cuautla that analyzed the ideological errors of the Third Convention, documented and based on scriptures the Conventionists themselves had been using. It was a major address that formed the basis for many of Brown's speeches as he accompanied Pierce, and it was later published in the *Liahona* under the title of "Ephraim esparcida entre los Gentiles."

61. It appears that the men may have been doing something similar to the technique of "whipsawing." Paul H. Hahn, in *The Juvenile Offender and the Law*, p. 233, describes an interrogation technique in which "tough" and "soft" officers alternately question a suspect. In time the suspect tends to fear and reject the "tough" officer but respond to the "kind" one. Whether Pierce was consciously using a variant of this technique we do not know, but the effect was apparently the same. (See Brown, Oral History, p. 38.)

62. Ibid.

63. Mormons have long noted substantial differences in the operating styles and programmatic emphases of their leaders.

64. Manuscript History, quarter ending 31 December 1943.

65. In the early days of the difficulty, David O. McKay, then counselor to the church president, Heber J. Grant, had taken a hard-line, punitive approach to the Convention leaders. Following his return from Mexico, however, he apparently viewed things differently. He asked Antoine R. Ivins to research the Third Convention correspondence to see if there might be anything that would preclude the First Presidency's reconsidering, or reviewing, the cases of those who had been excommunicated. (See Ivins to David O. McKay, 9 March 1944.)

66. García Velázquez, Oral History.

67. Manuscript History, quarter ending 30 September 1943.

68. Brown, Oral History, pp. 34–36; Call, Oral History; Mexican Mission Historical Record, passim, for this period; Manuscript History, passim, for this period, with specific illustrations in the entries for the quarter ending 31 March 1943.

69. González de la Cruz, Oral History.

70. Brown, Oral History, pp. 34–36.

71. Flores Flores, Oral History, with corroboration from the oral histories of Mora González and González de la Cruz.

72. Harold W. Pratt had earlier spoken to the Third Conventionists about a stake, but when he reported as much to the First Presidency, those authorities responded by cautioning "about your promising them a stake organization or even the possibility of one of their number presiding over the mission. The

privilege of their receiving the Gospel should merit their appreciation and support of those who have been sent down, appointed, and set apart to preside
over that Mission. The Lord will dictate when reappointment or reorganiza-
tion should be made. In the meantime it is the duty as well as the privilege
of members to conform to the teachings and requirements and the ideals of
the Church." (The letter was signed by Heber J. Grant and David O. McKay and
entered in the Manuscript History for the quarter ending 30 June 1936.)

73. Reconstructed from the Manuscript History, quarter ending 31 March
1943. A "stake," presided over by a "stake president," is comprised usually of
between three and five thousand members and up to a dozen or so "wards"
(congregations), which are headed by "bishops." "Branches" are Mormon congregations in mission districts where stakes have not yet been formed.

74. Narciso Sandoval Jiménez, Oral History, interview by Gordon Irving.

75. Brown, Oral History, p. 36.

76. Ibid., p. 34.

77. By late 1975 there were twelve stakes in Mexico City alone (Aragón,
Arbolillo, Camarones, Churubusco, Ermita, Zarahemla, Industrial, Villa de las
Flores, Satélite, Tacubaya, Moctezuma, Netzahualcoyotl) and fourteen stakes elsewhere in the country. Through 1983 six additional stakes were formed in Mexico
City (Azteca, Chapúltepec, Iztapalapa, Linda Vista, Tlalnepantla and Tlalpan),
along with forty additional stakes elsewhere in the country (total, seventy-two).
Most were presided over by local nationals. This has been a trend that continued
through August 1986, with the addition of Mexico City North and Mexico City South
stakes, and an additional six elsewhere in Mexico, for a total of eighty. Interestingly
and not surprisingly, names of two of the stakes in Mexico City derive from
famous Aztec personalities and one from the name of a Book of Mormon city.

78. In February 1937, the First Presidency (Heber J. Grant, David O. McKay,
J. Reuben Clark, Jr.) instructed Harold W. Pratt to convene an ecclesiastical trial
for Third Convention leaders (Harold Pratt, Journal, 27 February 1937). However,
the First Presidency's notification letter to the leaders of the convention was
signed by Antoine R. Ivins and George F. Richards, so that the position of the
First Presidency would not be compromised in the event of an appeal (A. R.
Ivins to the First Presidency, 27 February 1937; and Ivins to Harold W. Pratt,
2 March 1937). Pratt convened his appointed court on 6, 7, and 8 May 1937,
and it voted to excommunicate Margarito Bautista, Abel Páez, Narciso Sandoval,
Pilar Páez, Othón Espinoza, Apolonio Arzate, Felipe Barragán, and Daniel Mejía.
(The minutes are recorded in the Mexican Mission Historical Record for 6, 7,
and 8 May 1937.) A majority of those excommunicated were branch presidents,
and Abel Páez was a member of the district presidency.

Shortly thereafter David O. McKay made an inquiry of Harold Pratt, asking whether it would be a good idea to invite the disaffected leaders to El Paso
to meet with some of the brethren there. Perhaps a rehearing of their trials
could be held (Harold Pratt, Journal, 18 May 1937). This seemed to suggest that
if the men were just to develop a contrite spirit, the "lower" court's decision
might be reversed. If the invitation was ever extended, the men did not accept
it (none of them even went to the original trial) because they considered Pratt's
court to have operated unrighteously. They therefore concluded that the verdict was null and void in the eyes of God (Manuscript History, quarter ending
30 June 1943; also quarter ending 31 December 1943).

In "The Story of the Third Convention," Arwell Lee Pierce picks up the narrative:

President George Albert Smith, in a special meeting I had with him and his counselors in the First Presidency's office in April of 1946, had me read the appeal to the First Presidency of the Church translated from the Spanish into the English and, also, the Mission President's recommendation to the First Presidency about the appeal. My recommendation as Mission President was that we accept the appeal as presented and I recommended that the action taken against these men in the beginning, excommunication from the Church for rebellion, be changed from excommunication to disfellowshipment because I thought excommunication was too severe in view of all the circumstances. . . . President Smith then asked for one of his counselors to make a motion and President McKay moved that the appeal, as presented, be passed upon favorably. . . . This was passed on favorably by the First Presidency with President Pierce, by request of President Smith, voting with them.

79. Pierce, "Story of the Third Convention," p. 5.

80. Brown, Oral History, p. 36.

81. García Velázquez, Oral History.

82. Manuscript History, quarter ending 30 September 1946.

83. Hatch, Oral History; García Velázquez, Oral History.

84. García Velázquez, Oral History.

85. Brown, Oral History.

86. *Deseret News*, "Church News," 15 June 1946.

87. González de la Cruz, Oral History.

88. *Deseret News*, "Church News," 15 June 1946.

89. García Velázquez, Oral History.

90. Daniel Mejía, as cited in González de la Cruz, Oral History.

91. Brown, Oral History.

92. Walser, Oral History.

93. Manuscript History, quarter ending 31 December 1946. Pierce made public announcement of the action in "Anuncio de Interés a la Misión Mexicana," pp. 405, 439, and strongly urged the members to support these men in their callings.

94. Anderson, Oral History, p. 61.

95. Pratt, Journal, 15 September 1937; Manuscript History, 31 March 1943.

96. Agrícol Lozano Herrera, interview; García Velázquez, Oral History. While the Revolution had been fought and reforms implemented, most workers and peasants never really benefited to the extent they desired. Union organizing activity among them continued long after the guns were quiet, and sometimes that activity earned its participants the enmity of the government they may have fought to help to install. Isaías Juárez was one such organizer. (For general background, see Ann L. Craig, *The First Agraristas: An Oral History*

of a Mexican Agrarian Reform Movement and, for a regional emphasis, Heather Fowler Salamini, *Agrarian Radicalism in Veracruz, 1920–38,* and Romana Falcón, *El agrarismo en Veracruz: La etapa radical [1928–1935].)*

97. Manuscript History, 31 March 1943.

98. Lozano Herrera, interview by F. LaMond Tullis.

Primera Parte

Los Cimientos Históricos de la Experiencia Mormona en México

Capitulo 1

PROSELITISMO Y COLONIZACIÓN

Fueron dos los factores principales que motivaron la incursión inicial de los mormones en México: efectuar proselitismo entre los indígenas, y explorar para realizar una posible colonización y obtener refugio.

Los esfuerzos continuos para predicar el evangelio a los indígenas se derivaron de las creencias religiosas de los mormones sobre el desarrollo del reino de Dios en los 'últimos días', pues se les enseñaba que si los 'hijos del padre Lehi' fueran convertidos, tanto en Estados Unidos como en Latinoamérica, la venida de su Señor sería apresurada.[1] Así, tenían una profunda necesidad de predicar el evangelio a los indios, educarlos y ver que progresaran tanto económica como culturalmente para poder introducirlos en el reino. Este fue el tema que se manejó desde los primeros días de la Restauración, convirtiéndose en la fuerza principal de la misión de Parley P. Pratt a Chile, así como de las obras misional y de colonización que realizó posteriormente la Iglesia.

Por otro lado, además de ser parte de su objetivo original, la continua exploración de los mormones desde su llegada al Territorio de Utah fue una respuesta práctica a un oeste que se mostraba hostil. Debían explorar y familiarizarse totalmente con el lugar, estando así preparados para huir en caso de presentarse una nueva persecución. También necesitaban explorar para saber hacia dónde convenía más extender sus campamentos, pues requerían poblados satélites que les garantizaran la estabilidad económica y política suficientes para poder hacer proselitismo entre los indígenas.[2] Brigham Young pronto desarrolló un patrón de expansión, enviando primero misioneros a los indios, luego -- en ocasiones simultáneamente-- explorando para buscar lugares dónde acampar y finalmente colonizándolos.

La necesidad de los mormones de tener seguridad se

evidenció en su movimiento original hacia el oeste en los años 1846 y 47, cuando buscaban libertad religiosa y un lugar de refugio para proteger sus vidas y propiedades. La orden de exterminio del gobernador de Misuri, Lilburn Boggs (abrogada hasta 1976), permanecía fresca en sus mentes. El traslado al oeste, la guerra de Utah de 1857-58 y las leyes federales subsecuentes en contra del matrimonio plural, mantuvieron alerta la búsqueda de sitios en los cuales los miembros de la Iglesia pudieran resguardarse. Así pues, la mayoría de las nuevas colonias se extendían desde Salt Lake City hacia el sur, ya que muchos pensaban que México sería el lugar de su refugio final.[3] Se dice incluso que en cierta ocasión el profeta José Smith afirmó que los Santos de los Últimos Días irían finalmente al Gran Lago Salado y construirían ciudades en todas direcciones, pero que "el gobierno no los recibiría con las leyes que Dios designó para vivir, y aquellos que estuvieran deseosos de vivir las leyes de Dios tendrían que ir al sur". Mosiah Levee Hancock, testigo de la escena, dijo haber visto cómo José Smith, mientras hablaba, señaló el mapa en dirección a Arizona o México.[4]

Para 1870 las colonias mormonas llegaban a la frontera sur del Territorio de Utah y era viable el poder extenderlas aún más en la misma dirección, ya que en ese año el ejército estadounidense había derrotado a los indios *navajo* en el norte de Arizona y, a su vez, la agitación política mexicana parecía estar temporalmente resuelta Las condiciones eran, por consiguiente, idóneas para una nueva ola de exploración, trabajo misional y colonización probablemente no sólo en Arizona, sino también en el vecino país del sur.

LA REFORMA EN MÉXICO: ANTECEDENTE DEL DESARROLLO INICIAL LA EXPEDICIÓN DE 1875 - 1976

En junio de 1874, Brigham Young anunció que pronto sería el tiempo de llevar el evangelio a los millones de mexicanos descendientes de Lehi.[5] Profundos cambios sociales y políticos ocurrían en México, y como las tradiciones y el poder de la Iglesia Católica se estaban deteriorando, los nuevos misioneros enviados a América del

Sur enfrentarían una resistencia menor que la que un cuarto de siglo atrás encontrara Parley P. Pratt.

Manteniéndose al tanto del movimiento de Reforma suscitado en México, Young sabía que ese cambio permitiría que para 1876 los mormones regresaran a los países latinoamericanos. Al igual que en la lucha revolucionaria que frustrara la misión de Pratt en Chile, en el territorio mexicano la contienda se daba entre los bandos conservador y liberal. Pero mientras que en el país sudamericano los primeros habían ganado y esencialmente cerrado las fronteras a religiones ajenas a la católica, en México la situación era totalmente contraria: los acontecimientos provocaron gran excitación en la gente con respecto a la religión, y permitieron a las iglesias no católicas funcionar abierta y libremente. Lo cual de hecho formaba parte de la agenda política de los liberales, que ahora estaban en el poder.

Durante la década de 1830 la posición liberal había evolucionado sobre la que prevalecía diez años antes -- caracterizada por el odio a los monarcas--, transformándose en un movimiento obsesivo que pugnaba por la descentralización de los poderes del Estado, la secularización de las cortes, el derecho a la educación, los convenios nupciales, y al mismo tiempo por disminuir, si no destruir, el poder político de la Iglesia Católica Mexicana. Finalmente, en un proceso gradual, los liberales reconocieron la necesidad de contar con reformas sociales y económicas fundamentales que ayudaran a México a evitar que Estados Unidos se apropiara de una parte mayor de su territorio.

El año 1855 vio el comienzo de una reforma que cristalizaría hasta 1876, cuando los liberales promovieron leyes que limitaron los tradicionales privilegios políticos de la jerarquía católica e iniciaron, aunque de manera embrionaria, un nuevo orden económico y social.

El movimiento de Reforma incluyó un levantamiento popular que resultó en la caída del presidente mexicano Antonio López de Santa Anna, quien había cedido el territorio de Texas y el noroeste mexicano a los Estados Unidos; asimismo, en los años 1855 y 56 se dictaron los veredictos que eliminaron el control que hasta entonces el clero mantenía sobre la educación pública, frenándolo políticamente y suprimiendo también el fuero militar. A partir de esa primera disposición reformista, que daría lugar a la *Constitución de 1857*, se sucedió una serie de notables acontecimientos en México: el inicio, a partir de 1861, de un período de libertades constitucionales bajo el gobierno de Benito Juárez; la intervención armada de Francia como parte de la invasión que efectuó en conjunto con españoles e ingleses, encabezada por Napoleón III, y que tuvo como consecuencia la coronación del emperador Maximiliano de Habsburgo (1864-1867); la reconstrucción de la presidencia de Juárez en un nuevo período, que inició en 1867 y concluyó en el año de su muerte, 1872; y por último, el gobierno del brillante Sebastián Lerdo de Tejada que se prolongó hasta 1876, justo la fecha en que los misioneros mormones ingresaron a la República Mexicana para predicar el evangelio.

Todo ese período de matanza, depravación y conmoción social dio surgimiento a dos tendencias sobresalientes que hicieron que se abrieran finalmente las puertas a los misioneros Santos de los Últimos Días: la pérdida del control civil por parte de la Iglesia Católica, y el creciente interés de la población en diversas religiones ajenas al catolicismo --atracción que no necesariamente provocó una persecución organizada o resistencia social.

Entre los años 1871 y 1880 varias denominaciones protestantes establecieron misiones en México, dando inicio en la prensa a una vigorosa batalla en contra de los católicos;[6] la lista incluía a metodistas, cuáqueros, presbiterianos, congregacionistas y bautistas. El gobierno mismo a veces parecía favorecer a los protestantes, a quienes permitía, por ejemplo, que importaran al país literatura de la *Sociedad Bíblica de Londres* sin el pago de impuestos, en tanto que al mismo tiempo imponía una alta tarifa aduanal a las publicaciones católicas. Si la Reforma no hubiera ocurrido, probablemente los mormones no habrían podido entrar a México por un largo tiempo, ya fuera como misioneros o colonizadores.

Ese torbellino político en el que se dio la apertura secular y religiosa, coincidió en parte con la Guerra Civil estadounidense (1861-1865). Enterados de la adquisición de territorio mexicano que su país había logrado en 1848, la mayoría de los norteamericanos se encontraban desinteresados en México antes y durante dicho conflicto armado. Mas cuando éste terminó, la nueva economía y el nuevo orden social mexicanos despertaron el interés de los industriales, quienes una vez más buscaban tanto mercados en expansión como materias primas. Diversas publicaciones estadounidenses, que sin duda Brigham Young tenía a su disposición y tal vez leía, hacían una extensa propaganda de las ofertas comerciales y religiosas existentes en México,[7] mismas que hicieron que para 1876 un numeroso grupo hubiera ya ingresado al territorio mexicano.[8]

Esa invasión alarmó grandemente a la Iglesia Católica, que en lo particular veía la entrada de los protestantes como una "amenaza mayor que las medidas hostiles y opresivas del gobierno mexicano".[9] Si bien el clero católico y sus aliados conservadores eran capaces de resistir y predicar en contra de la presencia estadounidense en el país, no podían prevenirla totalmente. Por su parte, los liberales de México estaban encantados de que alguien más se opusiera a la Iglesia Católica.

Los liberales favorecieron la colonización extranjera con la mira tanto de destruir el poder católico como de rescatar el tesoro nacional, que se hallaba en bancarrota. Ya desde 1862, con el fin de mejorar la economía y combatir la incursión norteamericana en su territorio, el gobierno de México había motivado a los ciudadanos para que colonizaran las tierras desocupadas en el norte del país. Sin embargo, puesto que desde el principio dichos intentos resultaron infructuosos, por el año 1875 los liberales comenzaron a buscar extranjeros --principalmente europeos y estadounidenses-- para que se establecieran en esos territorios. Este 'positivismo filosófico'[10] argumentaba la necesidad de sangre nueva para romper el tradicional dominio de poderes en México, así como para dar cauce a una dinámica economía comercial e industrial.[11] Si Argentina, Estados Unidos, Australia, Nueva Zelandia, Canadá y Brasil lo habían estado logrando con inmigrantes,[12] ¿por qué no México?

El gobierno fomentaba la ocupación y redistribución de tierras públicas deshabitadas, dando la tercera parte de una parcela a cualquier individuo o compañía colonizadora que estuvieran dispuestos a definir sus límites apropiadamente. En mayo de 1875, a escasos cuatro meses de que los misioneros mormones salieran de Salt Lake City rumbo a México, los legisladores mexicanos autorizaron a su gobierno para contratar compañías colonizadoras nacionales y extranjeras que llevaran inmigrantes al país. Ese fue un día feliz para los Santos de los Últimos Días.

El movimiento mormón hacia el sur; la derrota de los indios *navajo* a manos del ejército estadounidense; la Reforma mexicana que dio acceso a nuevas doctrinas; la existencia de muchos lamanitas en México, y el hecho singular de que ahí pudieran ser establecidos promisorios asentamientos, fueron elementos que se combinaron para permitir que los mormones se aventuraran en la república del sur. De hecho, ya en 1874 Brigham Young había pedido a Daniel W. Jones y Henry Brizzee que se prepararan para salir en una misión a ese país.

En 1847, cuando sólo tenía diecisiete años, Daniel W. Jones había cruzado las planicies con voluntarios de San Luis, Misuri, para participar en la guerra contra México, país en el que permaneció tres años y donde aprendió lo suficiente del idioma español como para servir de traductor al ejército norteamericano. En sus propias palabras, participó "en muchas de las actividades desenfrenadas y sin juicio de la gente".[13]

Durante el verano de 1850, mientras viajaba por el estado de Utah rumbo a los 'campos de oro' californianos, se disparó accidentalmente a sí mismo y, para recuperarse, se vio forzado a permanecer en Provo durante el invierno. Fue ahí donde conoció a los mormones, quienes lo impresionaron. Estudió su fe y fue bautizado el 27 de enero de 1851.

Jones fue un personaje controvertido que, en su papel de *contacto principal de la Iglesia con los indios, frecuentemente los defendía y al mismo tiempo amonestaba a otros mormones angloamericanos por no seguir el mandato de enseñarles el evangelio, tal como estaba asentado en el

Libro de Mormón. A Brigham Young le caía especialmente bien. Pero Jones era tan áspero que en dos ocasiones se intentó despojarlo de sus privilegios como miembro de la Iglesia --y en 1857, tras haber sido ordenado al oficio de *setenta* en el sacerdocio, Brigham Young tuvo que interceder personalmente ante el grupo de Provo para que lo aceptaran.[14]

Reflexionando sobre la asignación que el presidente Young les había encomendado a Brizzee y a él, Jones pensaba que ésta no sería fácil. Él había peleado en la guerra entre Estados Unidos y México, recordaba la situación religiosa que prevalecía en ese país un cuarto de siglo atrás y le atemorizaba el tener que hablar en México contra la Iglesia Católica. Pero obedientemente, concluyó: "Esta misión ha de ser iniciada por alguien, y si es necesario que deba hacerse el sacrificio extremo, tan bueno es que lo haga yo como cualquier otro".[15]

Brizzee y Jones poseían ambos un rudimentario conocimiento del español, así que Brigham Young les dijo que lo perfeccionaran y tradujeran las escrituras y otros documentos para llevar consigo en la misión --al parecer Parley P. Pratt nunca completó esa tarea. Pero ni Jones ni Brizzee se sentían especialmente seguros de lo que debían hacer. El esfuerzo de varios meses no fortaleció mucho su autoconfianza, ni lo hicieron las historias sobre las experiencias que Pratt tuvo veinticuatro años antes en Chile. Todo lo que el presidente Young les había dicho era que estuvieran listos para su misión, estudiando español y traduciendo. Pero ¿cómo?

Pronto proveyó la respuesta Melitón González Trejo, quien recientemente había llegado a Salt Lake City. Hombre bien educado y ex oficial del ejército español asignado durante varios años en Filipinas, Trejo había estado orando para obtener una respuesta a sus preguntas sobre la religión; dijo que en un sueño se le había informado que si iba a Lago Salado y veía a los mormones, las hallaría. Después de renunciar a su comisión en las islas Filipinas, vendió sus propiedades y partió a Utah, donde al buscar a alguien que hablara español, se topó con Brizzee. Rapidamente Jones lo reclutó para traducir los documentos que el presidente había ordenado.[16]

De inmediato comenzaron a trabajar en aproximadamente cien páginas de pasajes seleccionados del Libro de Mormón. Sin embargo, para fines de mayo de 1875 Brizzee se había retirado del proyecto como consecuencia -- según Jones-- de un desacuerdo con el presidente Young;[17] y ambos, Jones y Trejo, carecían de dinero. Desanimado, en junio de 1875 Jones visitó a Brigham Young y le explicó lo que Trejo y él habían hecho, así como la razón por la que no podían hacer más. Puesto que la Iglesia no contaba con fondos para el proyecto, el presidente los autorizó para solicitar donativos con los que se financiara la traducción; si eso no funcionaba, él la apoyaría con sus fondos personales.[18] Les aconsejó que terminaran la impresión de las cien páginas seleccionadas para que pudieran iniciar su misión en septiembre, antes de las fuertes nevadas. Con los 500 dólares donados, Jones y Trejo imprimieron 1,500 ejemplares de los *Trozos Selectos del Libro de Mormón*.[19]

Al finalizar el verano y comenzar el otoño de 1875, el presidente Young llamó a otros cinco élderes para que acompañaran a Daniel W. Jones a México: Helaman Pratt, James Z. Stewart, Anthony W. Ivins, Robert H. Smith y Ammon M. Tenney.[20] Jones decidió llevar también consigo a su hijo adolescente, Wiley.[A] De los seis misioneros, únicamente Jones y Tenney hablaban español.

Aquella debe haber sido una experiencia desalentadora. Justo antes de que los misioneros tomaran el tren a California, donde abordarían un buque de vapor que los llevaría hasta la costa occidental mexicana, Brigham Young los contactó. ¿Les importaría viajar a caballo y no ir a California ni a la ciudad de México, como estaba planeado, sino hacia el sur, cruzando Arizona para llegar al estado de Sonora? El presidente les pidió que en el trayecto buscaran lugares de asentamiento, y enseñaran el evangelio a los indios. La combinación de exploración, colonización y predicación había dado buen resultado en el Territorio de Utah; ahora lo intentarían en México. Rápidamente, los misioneros modificaron sus planes.

De nuevo, a Brigham Young le preocupaba el refugio.

Durante los primeros meses de 1875 se había intensificado la persecución del gobierno federal y de grupos antimormones por la práctica del matrimonio plural. En marzo fue encarcelado el presidente Young por rebelarse ante un tribunal, y en abril George Reynolds fue apresado y sentenciado por cohabitar ilegalmente --su apelación estaba aún pendiente cuando Jones y su grupo salieron de Utah. James Z. Stewart recordaría después que cuando Orson, el hermano de Parley P. Pratt, bendijo formalmente a los misioneros antes de que se fueran, pareció tener un presentimiento, diciendo a los élderes: "Deseo que ustedes busquen lugares a los que nuestros hermanos puedan ir y estar a salvo, en caso de que la persecución hiciera necesario que ellos tuvieran que apartarse por una temporada."[21]

Jones, su hijo Wiley, Robert H. Smith, James Z. Stewart y Helaman Pratt --hijo de Parley P.-- cargaron sus treinta caballos, prepararon mulas con provisiones y su preciosa literatura traducida, y salieron de Nephi, Utah, en septiembre de 1875. Ammon M. Tenney y Anthony W. Ivins, de veintitrés años, se unieron a la expedición en los poblados de Toquerville y Kanab, Utah, respectivamente. La jornada duró diez meses, en los que recorrieron casi cinco mil kilómetros de ida y vuelta, todo a caballo.[22] Por los poblados que pasaban en su marcha hacia el sur --todos ellos comunidades mormonas--, los misioneros recibían entusiastas contribuciones de alimentos, ropa, provisiones, animales y, por supuesto, también información, consejo y ánimo. Claramente, los hermanos y amigos veían esa misión como un esfuerzo sumamente importante.[23]

Pero Brigham Young tenía más que decir sobre la naturaleza de esta misión. En un telegrama, entregado por un corredor indio que alcanzó al grupo en las afueras de Kanab, les pidió que exploraran el valle del Río Salado, hoy área de Phoenix, Arizona, como un posible lugar para colonizar. Naturalmente, los misioneros investigaron y rindieron su informe. (La zona de Mesa, Arizona, colonizada posteriormente por miembros de la Iglesia, es uno de los muchos resultados de aquella exploración.) También visitaron y predicaron a las tribus de los indios *pueblo* de

Arizona y *zuñi* de Nuevo México. Para este tipo de trabajo misional, Tenney era tan capaz como Jones, ya que había estado en 1851 en la *Caravana Mormona* que pobló San Bernardino, California, tiempo en el que aprendió español, sirviendo durante varios años a Jacob Hamblin como intérprete entre los indios.[24]

En Tucson, Arizona, los misioneros escucharon que en Sonora había nuevas y furiosas guerras con los *yaqui*,[25] que no querían someterse tras resistir por más de dos siglos primero a los españoles y ahora a los mexicanos. Se les dijo a los misioneros que no había paso seguro para nadie en esa área, y dichas noticias eran preocupantes porque precisamente su intención era explorar y predicar en Sonora. Mientras meditaban el asunto unos días, aprovecharon la cordial invitación de Anson Pacely Killen Safford, gobernador de Arizona, para predicar el evangelio en el Palacio de Justicia de Tucson --quien los animó también a que llevaran colonos mormones al estado.

"Queremos ir a México y ver qué es lo que se puede hacer allá", escribió Jones. "Escuchamos informes terribles de por allá. La gente nos dice que nuestras vidas no tienen valor en ese lugar. Se está llevando a cabo una guerra. Vamos a mantener nuestro movimiento y confiar en Dios para que nos proteja, y que Su Espíritu nos indique cuándo debemos parar."[26] Cambiaron la dirección hacia el este y se dirigieron a Franklin, Texas. Habían pasado casi cuatro meses desde el inicio de su viaje, explorando y predicando a los indios y a otros que encontraban en su camino, cuando finalmente cruzaron a México en el lugar llamado El Paso del Norte, hoy Ciudad Juárez, Chihuahua.

El ánimo fatigado de los misioneros, quienes fueron recibidos calurosamente y sin demora por las autoridades aduanales mexicanas --gracias a la Reforma--, cambió momentáneamente a uno de exuberancia: ellos habían llevado una vez más el evangelio a los israelitas del hemisferio occidental, terminando así con una pausa de veinticinco años desde los esfuerzos de Parley P. Pratt en Chile. Seguramente ahora la fe echaría raíz y crecería entre los descendientes de Lehi.

Mas la euforia de los élderes desapareció tan pronto

como percibieron la tensión religiosa y política existente en el lugar. Los sacerdotes católicos locales amonestaron a sus congregaciones para que no escucharan a los mormones y también para que, sin leerla, trajeran toda la literatura misional que se les diera, con la finalidad de que ellos pudieran destruirla. Dada la cantidad limitada de literatura que los caballos y mulas transportaban, ese procedimiento podría hacer que su cargamento desapareciera rápidamente y sin ningún beneficio. Así, Jones los instruyó para que fueran extremadamente cuidadosos con sus ejemplares de *Trozos Selectos,* hasta encontrar la mejor forma de hacerlos llegar a la gente.

El primer enfrentamiento importante sucedió tres días después de la llegada de los misioneros a El Paso del Norte, un domingo en que asistían a los servicios católicos. Al terminar la misa, el sacerdote que oficiaba, de nombre Borajo, amonestó a la gente en forma vigorosa y emocional sobre los mormones. Desde su punto de vista, Satanás mismo había entrado a México.

Ahora, de todas las plagas que han visitado la tierra para maldecirla y destruir a la humanidad, nos ha llegado la peor, y allí se encuentran los representantes de ella. Véanlos. Sus rostros demuestran lo que son. Gracias a Dios hemos sido advertidos a tiempo por el Santo Papa de que falsos profetas y maestros vendrían entre nosotros. Esos hombres representan todo lo que es bajo y depravado. Han destruido la moral de su propia gente y ahora han venido para contaminar a la gente de este lugar. Carecen de virtud. Todos ellos tienen de seis a una docena de esposas. Ahora han venido aquí para extender esta práctica en México. Yo los denuncio. Sí, aquí en presencia de la imagen de la Virgen María, los denuncio como bárbaros. Y quiero que todos tomen sus libros, me los traigan, y los quemaré.[27]

No sólo los liberales de Juárez atacaban a la Iglesia Católica políticamente, sino que ahora también habían abierto sus fronteras a personas como los mormones, que estaban 'contaminando' la religión de su país. Durante la exhortación del sacerdote, un numeroso grupo de personas se reunió en la entrada y en el patio contiguo para escuchar. Cuando los élderes intentaron salir de la catedral, la multitud bloqueo su camino. El momento era tenso. Jones escribió: "Empecé a sentir que sería mejor para nosotros salir de entre el gentío antes de que el ambiente se agitara, ya que algunos fanáticos podrían estar tentados a deslizar su navaja entre nuestras costillas. Gradualmente conseguimos desplazarnos entre la multitud que llenaba el patio de la entrada. Cuando estuvimos libres, nos dirigimos directamente a nuestra vivienda."[28] Una vez dentro, los misioneros prepararon un informe para enviarlo a Brigham Young.

Ahora toda la ciudad sabia quiénes eran los mormones. Al caminar por las calles, las mujeres huían de ellos o los veían sospechosamente a través de mirillas en las puertas de sus casas. Y hubo insultos, así como los ocasionales apedreos que frecuentemente habían recibido los Santos de los Últimos Días en otros sitios.

Los élderes Robert H. Smith y Ammon M. Tenney llegaron rápidamente a la conclusión que no muchas almas preciosas se unirían a la Iglesia en El Paso del Norte. Aun cuando el presidente Young les había prevenido para no bautizar todavía,[B] pidiéndoles que se limitaran a explorar y predicar, México pronto los desanimó a ambos. Las tensiones político-religiosas producto de la Reforma, y las guerras indígenas al oeste, en el estado de Sonora, no fueron un buen augurio a sus esfuerzos.

Descorazonados, los dos misioneros empezaron a resentirse contra Daniel W. Jones, pues parecía que la única forma correcta de hacer las cosas era la suya. Smith y Jones tuvieron una discusión en la que el primero lo acusaba de haberlo obligado a vigilar de noche para prevenir que los animales fueran robados. Se llevó a cabo una reunión especial con el fin de apaciguar las diferencias entre los dos. Jones le dijo a Smith que era un mentiroso y que debería reunir sus cosas e irse a casa. Éste insistió en terminar su misión, pero no en compañía de aquél. Los demás élderes le dijeron a Jones que su trato hacia ellos era también muy

severo, suplicándole que fuera más considerado.[29] Las
tensiones personales y políticas se incrementaron y
mezclaron. Según algunos, Tenney y Smith también estaban
preocupados por lo que les pudiera pasar en México. Su
ansiedad, junto con el estilo de liderazgo de Jones, los hizo
reflexionar y finalmente pidieron ser relevados de su
jurisdicción para terminar su misión entre los indios *pueblo* y
zuñi de Nuevo México.[30] Estos grupos habían expresado
interés en el mensaje mormón, y ciertamente se veían más
promisorios que la gente de Paso del Norte. Con la salida de
Tenney, Jones quedó como el único misionero capaz de
hablar en español con los mexicanos.

Smith y Tenney estaban sólo parcialmente en lo
correcto con respecto al ambiente en México. Se dieron
cuenta de que los misioneros no llegarían a ningún lado en El
Paso del Norte, pero equivocadamente supusieron que el
mismo destino los esperaba en cualquier otro lugar del país.
En contraste, Jones suponía con acierto que había pastos
más verdes hacia el sur.

Puesto que los animales se encontraban en malas
condiciones, no era inteligente emprender de inmediato la
salida hacia el sur, así que Helaman Pratt y James Z. Stewart
regresaron con la mayoría de los animales al poblado de
Franklin, para pasar el invierno donde el forraje era más
barato. Jones, el hijo de éste e Ivins, que permanecieron en
México, decidieron instalar una talabartería en Paso del
Norte, servicio que obviamente la ciudad necesitaba y para el
cual Jones estaba capacitado --sin duda anticipando una
necesidad así, Brigham Young se había presentado con un
juego de herramientas para fabricación de sillas de montar
antes de que los élderes salieran de Utah.

Los tres misioneros pudieron ganar su sostén con la
talabartería. Aun el padre Borajo, impresionado por el fino
trabajo de las sillas, les encargó que le hicieran dos. De esa
manera fueron haciendo amigos, entre ellos el principal
oficial político, Pablo Paladio, liberal al cual inicialmente
había sido difícil tratar. Paladio, quien controlaba el acceso al
público por su autoridad para permitir la celebración de
reuniones religiosas, rehusó las primeras peticiones de los
élderes, pero finalmente fue ganado por su conducta

ejemplar y les ofreció una carta de presentación para la cita que sostendrían con el gobernador del estado. No obstante, durante todo el tiempo los élderes se mantuvieron en un segundo plano, estudiando español y preparándose para el trabajo que más adelante realizarían en México.

Comprendieron, con el tiempo, que los ataques de los liberales a la Iglesia Católica habían afectado el pensamiento y la forma de ser de mucha gente. Para Jones, en contraste con su experiencia previa en el país, todo eso era nuevo. Pronto los misioneros se dieron cuenta de que aun cuando no eran muchos los liberales en Paso del Norte, aquellos que existían los buscaban y les deseaban éxito. Y fue mediante esos contactos que descubrieron una alianza natural con los liberales, pues les interesaba la libertad religiosa, el desarrollo de México, los indios, y ambos consideraban como un estorbo a la Iglesia Católica. Los norteamericanos pronto aprendieron que las personas que no hacían caravanas ni se quitaban el sombrero al pasar frente a la catedral --omisión insolente que apenas veinticinco años atrás hubiera sido motivo de protesta pública y aun encarcelamiento--, podían ser considerados como amigos.[31] "Mantuvimos nuestros ojos abiertos hacia ellos", escribió Jones, "ya que con ellos siempre estábamos seguros."[32]

En los primeros días de marzo, a casi dos meses de que Daniel W. Jones y sus dos compañeros entraran a México, recibieron una carta del presidente Young en la que les ofrecía consejo y expresaba su aprobación.

> *Siento que sería juicioso que ustedes visitaran lo más posible la sangre nativa. Dejen a la Iglesia Católica en paz; si sus miembros desean escuchar la verdad, expóngansela como a cualquier otra persona, pero no mantengan debates con ellos... Sean precavidos en sus labores y movimientos; no busquen oposición, pero muévanse firmemente hacia delante, presentando las verdades del evangelio a aquellos que deseen escucharlos, e invitando a todos a que sean participantes del evangelio del Hijo de Dios. Ustedes tienen la fe y oraciones de todos para que sean capaces de hacer un buen trabajo, y no tengo*

duda de que me verán de nuevo en la carne todavía muchas veces.[33]

Después de recibir la carta, los misioneros visitaron algunas de las haciendas cercanas y ranchos que empleaban grandes cantidades de indios. Pero los curas vigilaban sus movimientos sigilosamente, incluso fuera de Paso del Norte. Además, los propietarios de ranchos dijeron a los indígenas que desocuparían a cualquiera que escuchara a los mormones.[34] A pesar de la Reforma, el lazo de unión entre el clero y los terratenientes permanecía intacto en el norte de México: mientras que los indios deseaban la liberación, no había nada que ellos o los misioneros pudieran hacer a tal efecto. Así, los élderes esperaban el tiempo oportuno alimentando a sus animales, estudiando español y trabajando para pagar sus cuentas.

Pero la carta de Brigham Young también contenía una nota preocupante: la presión federal en contra de los polígamos de Utah se estaba incrementando. El Presidente Young les mencionó que había sido encarcelado una vez más, aunque por corto tiempo, y que muchos de los líderes de la Iglesia se encontraban bajo severa coacción.[35] Volvió a enfatizar la importancia de una buena exploración para identificar campamentos. Si los mormones iban a ser obligados a abandonar sus hogares, tenían que saber a dónde ir.

A mediados de marzo de 1876, como estaba planeado, Stewart y Pratt se unieron nuevamente a Ivins y los Jones en Paso del Norte, y el día 20 partieron juntos hacia el interior de Chihuahua. En el camino, distribuyeron copias de *Trozos Selectos del Libro del Mormón* al predicar en algunos poblados. Tras pasar por El Carrizal y El Carmen --lo último localizado en un extenso valle de abundante agua y tierra fértil, ideal para un asentamiento--,[36] continuaron hasta la ciudad de Chihuahua, a la que llegaron el 12 de abril. Los liberales tenían el control político en esa capital estatal, y el gobernador Antonio Ochoa Carrillo rápidamente concedió permiso a los misioneros para que efectuaran la primera reunión de Santos de los Últimos Días en México.

Las autoridades de Chihuahua les proporcionaron el *Teatro Zaragoza*, que era, junto con la catedral, el sitio más amplio de reunión pública en la ciudad. Los misioneros tenían volantes impresos que anunciaban su reunión vespertina del domingo.[c] Tan pronto como terminó la muy popular pelea de gallos, Jones se levantó para dirigirse a un auditorio de cerca de quinientas personas, algunas presentes a causa de la publicidad, otras porque la curiosidad las hacía permanecer acabada la pelea. Ya que esta era la primera reunión pública de mormones en México, resulta interesante su cobertura por parte de la prensa:

> *Hace algunos días, un suceso extraordinario atrajo la atención del público de este lugar. Daniel W. Jones, un prominente Apóstol Mormón, imprimió y distribuyó volantes anunciando que predicaría un sermón sobre el mormonismo en el Teatro Zaragoza. Los rumores de que el Sr. Jones y sus colaboradores serían apedreados, nos incitaron a asistir a la reunión. El auditorio presente era muy numeroso, y al principio reinaba un completo orden. La prédica dio inicio en medio de un profundo silencio que evidenciaba el interés de los presentes. Poco después, unos cuantos descontentos comenzaron el desorden aventando pequeñas piedras y trozos de madera hacia donde se encontraba el predicador, pero tuvieron sólo unos cuantos imitadores y fueron mal vistos por el buen juicio de la mayoría. El sermón no fue muy interesante; el auditorio se divirtió principalmente al contemplar el esfuerzo constante del orador con las dificultades del español. La presentación concluyó con una heterogénea mezcla de aplausos y silbidos.[37]*

No obstante, los contactos se multiplicaron conforme los misioneros se acercaban a aquellos que no se quitaban el sombrero al pasar frente de la catedral.[38] Casi sin excepción, los liberales expresaron gran interés en El Libro de Mormón. Jones atribuyó esto al renovado orgullo por la herencia del indio mexicano, estimulado por la Reforma y su principal arquitecto e infatigable defensor, Benito Juárez.

Con la amable asistencia de las autoridades postales de Chihuahua --algunas de las cuales donaron su propio tiempo para ayudar a empacar los *Trozos Selectos*--, los élderes enviaron quinientas copias a hombres prominentes en casi cien[D] de las principales ciudades de México. La carta de presentación que Jones preparó informaba a los destinatarios sobre dónde podrían obtener mayor información, invitándolos a considerar detenidamente el mensaje del libro. Puesto que probablemente la mayoría de los ejemplares caería en manos de liberales, los misioneros esperaban que su mensaje no pasara inadvertido; pasaron el resto de sus tres semanas en Chihuahua predicando el evangelio a cualquiera que los escuchara, y preguntando sobre posibles lugares de asentamiento.

Mientras los élderes estuvieron predicando y distribuyendo literatura, en varias ocasiones el gobernador Ochoa los invitó a su despacho. Habiendo oído de los logros conseguidos por los mormones en el desierto de Utah, los veía como futuros colonizadores en el estado de Chihuahua. El gobernador procuraba su bienestar y quería que estuvieran completamente informados sobre la disponibilidad de tierras adecuadas. Les dijo que era cierto que el gobierno mexicano ofrecía tierras a los posibles colonizadores, pero existía un problema: en realidad el gobierno no tenía buenas tierras que ofrecer, pues las mejores regiones estaban ya todas aseguradas por viejos acuerdos y títulos perfectamente legales. "Díganle a Brigham Young que si el pueblo mormón quiere colonizar en Chihuahua, tendrán que comprar tierras de los particulares; no deben dejarse llevar por ninguna oferta del gobierno mexicano. Las ofertas se ven bien en papel y el gobierno podrá hacer todo lo que pueda, pero estén alertas", les dijo Ochoa. [39]

Dejando la ciudad de Chihuahua, el grupo de misioneros viajó hacia el oeste en dirección a las colinas de la Sierra Madre, pues sabían que había muchos indios en la montañas.[40] Cuando seis días después llegaron a Concepción de Guerrero, no encontraron ninguna oposición clerical. El único sacerdote era cooperativo, los pobladores no eran católicos devotos, y el principal oficial político rápidamente les autorizó a predicar y hasta ofreció protegerlos si fuera necesario. Los élderes rentaron una casa junto a un amplio salón y empezaron a preparar reuniones. En la primera, efectuada el domingo 23 de abril, Jones predicó un sermón sobre la *Orden Unida,* término que los mormones aplicaban a su propio --aunque inexitoso-- intento de vida comunitaria. Francisco Rubio, un hombre local, que había conocido a los misioneros y su mensaje, explicó el Libro de Mormón a los asistentes, y relató la visita de Cristo a las Américas. Jones escribiría más tarde: "Rubio en verdad entendió y creyó en el contenido del Libro de Mormón; como cuando durante la reunión lo tomó en su mano y lo explicó de la manera más lúcida que yo jamás hubiera oído antes, especialmente la parte que relata la aparición del Salvador en este continente. En lo personal, yo recibí nueva luz del nativo."[41]

Los élderes realizaron más reuniones, y a la gente de Concepción Guerrero le gustó lo que escuchaban. Algunos de los misioneros visitaron Arísiachic, una población grande que se encontraba en las montañas al oeste de Guerrero, habitada por los indios *tarahumara.* Después de haber informado al jefe sobre su mensaje, éste reunió a su gente para que juntos escucharan a los élderes. Los indios parecieron contentos con la doctrina que oyeron y pidieron a los misioneros que volvieran. Dejaron varias copias de los *Trozos Selectos* y el jefe asignó a dos jóvenes para estudiarlos. Tan impresionado quedó Jones con esa visita, la cual reafirmó su convicción de la misión de la Iglesia hacia los lamanitas, que diez años más tarde escribiría:

> *De lo que he visto ahora y entonces entre los nativos, a veces pienso que la gente llamada Santos de los Últimos Días está sólo parcialmente convertida. He visto y sentido más calidez de espíritu y fe manifestada por los nativos, de la que jamás ví entre los santos de raza blanca. Incluso los apaches me dijeron que ellos no esperarían mucho el desenlace final, una vez que tuvieran el poder y la autoridad de Dios para actuar en Su nombre. Esa fe, que todavía removerá los poderes del mal de entre los santos, vendrá principalmente de los remanentes. Yo pienso*

que los necesitaremos en nuestro trabajo, y que
deberíamos preocuparnos por ellos un poco, y no
tanto por el dinero.[42]

Tras pasar un día con los *tarahumara* y regresar a su base en Guerrero, los élderes encontraron durante las siguientes tres semanas muchas personas que expresaron profunda fe en la autenticidad del Libro de Mormón, así como un fuerte deseo de que los mormones fueran a vivir entre ellos.[43]

Con los lamanitas de todas las áreas virtualmente clamando por su mensaje y asociarse con ellos, ¿deberían los misioneros extender su misión? Algunos de ellos pensaban que no. Después de varias discusiones acaloradas Jones decidió, de mala gana, reducir la misión y regresar a Utah. Diversos factores pueden haber influido en esa decisión.[44] En primer lugar, los recursos financieros de los élderes ciertamente estaban casi agotados. A lo largo de su misión dependieron de las pequeñas sumas que Brigham Young les enviaba. Aun con los ingresos de Daniel W. Jones en la talabartería, habían sido incapaces de pagar sus deudas en El Paso del Norte, retrasando su salida hasta recibir dinero adicional del presidente Young. La estancia de Pratt y Stewart en Estados Unidos durante el invierno, donde el forraje para sus caballos era más barato, sólo les dio tiempo. En la ciudad de Chihuahua habían vivido de un amplio crédito concedido por los liberales, aunque antes de partir hacia Concepción Guerrero se vieron obligados a vender uno de sus caballos para pagar las deudas. En Guerrero, el amistoso tendero Eselso González, viendo su apuro, rehusó que le pagaran por el salón de reuniones que les había rentado, así como por los artículos que habían adquirido a crédito en su tienda; y hasta insistió en darles provisiones adicionales para el viaje, disfrazando su generosidad con la obvia mentira de que 'de todas formas no iba a poder vender la mercancía'.

El segundo factor fue que todavía existían problemas entre los misioneros. De hecho, Daniel W. Jones viajaba solo durante el trayecto de regreso a Utah, rehusando incluso compartir tiempo durante las comidas con los otros élderes;

además, sus compañeros reportaron que era tiránico e injusto. Ya que Jones era el único que hablaba suficiente español para predicar, conferenciar con las autoridades del gobierno y hasta sostener conversaciones rutinarias con los mexicanos, inconscientemente sus compañeros pudieron haber contribuido a su propia impaciencia y frustración, así como a la del mismo Jones. Éste continuó exigiendo veladas seguras por las noches, lo que contribuyó al cansancio y agotamiento constante de los demás misioneros. Se sintió justificado cuando en cierta ocasión, mientras acampaban en un dique (Cantarracio) entre Paso del Norte y la ciudad de Chihuahua, los élderes perdieron dos días por tener que buscar sus caballos que habían sido robados.

La tercera razón con que los compañeros de Jones lo presionaban para dejar Guerrero antes de tiempo, era que -- siguiendo la última sugerencia de Brigham Young en el sentido de no bautizar o crear ramas-- debían continuar con su predicación. Fue esa una era de proclamaciones impresas, reuniones en grupo y anuncios públicos, a diferencia de la moderna costumbre misional de ir puerta tras puerta contactando familias y grupos. Y es que los élderes se veían a sí mismos como embajadores a toda una nación, y no como maestros de individuos; se consideraban enviados del Señor, preparando el camino, predicando, distribuyendo literatura y haciendo amigos para que en su momento otros vinieran a dar seguimiento a la labor. Ni siquiera los quinientos posibles conversos en Guerrero fueron suficiente para que los misioneros permanecieran ahí más tiempo.[45]

Finalmente, quizá la razón más importante para dejar Concepción Guerrero era la ansiedad de informar a Brigham Young sobre la posibilidad de fundar colonias en México. Jones y sus compañeros no sólo habían encontrado algunos posibles sitios, sino que también concluyeron unánimemente que antes de que la 'Iglesia Mormona' pudiera progresar mucho entre los mexicanos, tendrían que establecerse colonias en ese país con el fin de enseñar a los miembros nuevos la forma de vivir el mormonismo.[46] También estaban preocupados por el problema de refugio, que había tomado urgencia por todo lo que estaba ocurriendo en el Territorio de Utah. Algunos de los misioneros creían que no sólo se formarían colonias mormonas en México, sino que eventualmente la Iglesia entera sería llevada a esos lugares, cumpliendo así las profecías del Libro de Mormón de que los gentiles convertidos serían contados con los descendientes de Lehi. Conociendo la presión que existía en Utah --con Brigham Young encarcelado de vez en cuando y otros miembros de la Iglesia siendo agobiados--, la idea era más y más atractiva para los élderes. La aprobación que el presidente Young dio a su informe, confirmó la buena decisión de regresar a casa.[47]

Partiendo de Guerrero el primero de mayo del mismo año, viajaron hacia el norte rumbo a Tejolócachic y de allí a las aldeas montañosas de Mátachic y Temósachic --sitios que en la actualidad cuentan con congregaciones mormonas--, donde los habitantes recibieron gustosamente a los misioneros y las copias de *Trozos Selectos*. En Mátachic, Tomás Tribosa hizo los arreglos para que se reuniera una congregación es su hogar, y en Temósachic aun el mismo sacerdote del pueblo, quien buscaba más y nueva información sobre Jesucristo, les dio la bienvenida, juntando a un buen número de personas para escucharlos. Al regresar a Tejolócachic, los misioneros reunieron auditorios igualmente entusiastas; cuando partieron, los indios les dieron tal cantidad de maíz y frijol que sus animales no podían cargarlo todo.

Dos días después los misioneros llegaron a Namaquipe y acamparon en las afueras del pueblo, cerca de un rancho donde compraron carne y dejaron un ejemplar de *Trozos Selectos*. Esa tarde, el mayordomo de la casa vino al campamento de los élderes. La narración que preparó Jones le da el nombre de Francisco Vásquez, un hombre de 103 años de edad, según sus propias palabras. La esposa de Vásquez le había dado el libro que los élderes habían dejado. El mayordomo les dijo: "He estado leyendo este libro. Yo lo entiendo y sé quiénes son ustedes. Ustedes son apóstoles de Jesucristo, así como lo fueron Pedro, Santiago, y Juan; y yo lo sé. Y yo también sé que este libro es verdadero." Volteando hacia su esposa, quien lo había acompañado al campamento de los misioneros, continuó: "Esposa, ¿no es cierto que yo les he estado diciendo a los vecinos por más de dos años, que apóstoles teniendo el Evangelio verdadero, vendrían a estas tierras, y que yo viviría para verlos?"[48] El hombre dijo que deseaba ser bautizado pero los élderes no aceptaron, convencidos de que no lo deberían hacer hasta que entre la gente pudieran establecerse poblados mormones --al parecer Jones y los demás consideraban que tales poblados eran inminentes.

Dejando los cerros y montañas de la Sierra Madre junto con su gente tan deseosa de escuchar el evangelio mormón, los misioneros continuaron hacia el norte por El Valle y entraron en el Valle de Casas Grandes, en donde actualmente se encuentran las comunidades mormonas de Colonia Dublán y Colonia Juárez. Mientras más hacia el norte viajaban, encontraban menos personas interesadas en escuchar su mensaje. Al acercarse a Casas Grandes, diversos avisos advertían a la gente sobre la llegada de los misioneros. Así que éstos de nuevo se dedicaron a explorar con el fin de hallar sitios adecuados para colonizar.

Llegando a Casas Grandes el 12 de mayo, se encontraron con la noticia de que los indios *apache* estaban en guerra contra ese pueblo.[49] Sin embargo, los élderes exploraron el área cuidadosamente, preguntando sobre ciertas parcelas de terreno, así como acerca de los problemas de escrituración y derechos de agua asociados con dichas tierras; tomaban muchas notas, que usarían para preparar su informe a Brigham Young. Concluyeron que el área en torno a Casas Grandes era el lugar más apropiado que ellos habían visto para el establecimiento de colonias.

Tres días después de llegar a Casas Grandes, compraron provisiones y siguieron adelante, acampando en Corralitos. La jornada siguiente cruzaron la frontera, entrando a los Estados Unidos y dirigiendo sus esfuerzos a Salt Lake City, explorando y anotando sus observaciones de viaje.

En México, los poblados en las montañas recibieron el mensaje mormón en una forma más favorable que en las ciudades. Lo mismo sucedería por más de tres generaciones, en contraste con el patrón que más tarde sería establecido en los otros países de Latinoamérica. Las tres décadas de lucha entre liberales y conservadores en las ciudades de

México, habían endurecido la posición de los últimos, haciéndolos mucho más inaccesibles para los misioneros. Por su parte, los liberales --miembros de la naciente clase media reformista-- andaban en búsqueda de su propia religión política, y sólo estaban interesados en los mormones como un posible aliado político y colonizador, sin verlos como poseedores de un valioso mensaje espiritual. Y los indios, que por mucho tiempo habían estado bajo el yugo del México tradicional, eran ahora influenciados por la ideología reformista de Benito Juárez, quien les dio una dignidad y esperanza nuevas que se apegaba a las promesas dadas a los lamanitas en el Libro de Mormón.

OTRAS EXPEDICIONES EN MÉXICO. EL CAOS POLÍTICO EN EL TERRITORIO DE UTAH

Brigham Young se encontraba tan complacido con los reportes misionales de julio de 1876, que antes de un mes volvió a llamar a Daniel W. Jones para que regresara a la región de Casas Grandes con un grupo de colonizadores.

A la pregunta del presidente Young respecto a quiénes debería llamar para que lo acompañaran, Jones contestó: "Deme hombres que tengan familias numerosas y pocos recursos, para que cuando lleguemos sean tan pobres que no puedan regresar y tengamos que permanecer allí". Las instrucciones finales de Brigham Young fueron que deberían ir a México o al sur de Arizona, y acampar "donde fueran inspirados a hacerlo".[50] Decidieron hacer el primer poblado en el Valle del Río Salado, parte sur de Arizona que Jones había explorado en la misión del año anterior. Pero aunque pararon antes de llegar a México, los nuevos colonos tenían toda la intención de más tarde continuar adelante.

En los linderos del Río Salado, en el sitio que ellos llamaron *Campamento Utah,* construyeron cabañas e intentaron establecer una misión entre los indios *maricopa.* En su debido tiempo algunos de los indios, respondiendo a la prédica misional de Jones, llegaron y preguntaron si podían vivir en su campamento. Sin embargo, a pesar de las profecías del Libro de Mormón, las costumbres indias en cuanto a comer y bañarse fueron muy escandalosas para algunas de las familias angloamericanas, y todo lo logrado se desintegró. Aparentemente solo Jones podía tolerar la proximidad de los nativos. Así, el campamento se dividió sobre el asunto antes de poder generar fuerza para continuar hacia México. De hecho, uno de los grupos formalmente hizo una petición a las autoridades del territorio para que sacaran a los indios de su área. "No pasó mucho para hacer evidente que tendría que despegarme de los indios o perder mi posición entre los hermanos blancos. Yo escogí a los nativos...", escribió Jones.[51]

A pesar de las considerables posibilidades de fracaso, Brigham Young continuó con la expansión hacia el sur, dando llamamiento a colonos para que asentaran colonias en Arizona.[52] Al mismo tiempo, continuó explorando y haciendo proselitismo en México. Aunque había estado complacido con el informe misional de Chihuahua en 1876, el presidente deseaba mayor información, especialmente sobre Sonora. Las guerras de los *yaqui* habían impedido que los primeros misioneros a México entraran en Sonora, teniendo que desviarse hacia el este llegando a Chihuahua. Pero únicamente con los indios que vivían en la parte occidental de la Sierra Madre, que colindaba con Sonora, habían sentido una aceptación total. Por otro lado, había también numerosos poblados indígenas en la mayor parte de ese estado. Así que otra excursión a México tendría que realizarse antes de que Brigham Young tomara una decisión sobre el país y los indios que en él vivían.

Por algún tiempo, el presidente Young había considerado a Sonora como un posible lugar para colonizar y desde el cual lanzar la obra misional entre los indios. Continuaban llegando a sus manos inquietantes informes de miembros del *Batallón Mormón,* que habían estado en Sonora durante la guerra México-Estados Unidos.[53] Ya en 1872 el Coronel Thomas L. Kane, uno de los más famosos amigos de los mormones y quien había sido instrumento en llegar a un acuerdo pacífico para la Guerra de Utah, visitó de nuevo el Territorio de Utah.[54] Él y Brigham Young hablaron entonces sobre Sonora como un posible lugar para colonización y trabajo misional. En su correspondencia posterior se enfatizaba el colonizar Sonora.[55]

Por varios años, el movimiento hacía el sur que encabezaba Brigham Young había dado lugar a especulaciones por parte de la prensa --tanto local como en el este de Estados Unidos-- sobre los diseños que los mormones tenían para ese lugar. Dichos rumores se propagaron tan pronto como Jones y Brizzee recibieron su llamamiento misional en 1874.[56] Los colonos no mormones que vivían en el Territorio de Utah continuaban presionándolos. Durante un vibrante discurso en la Conferencia General de la Iglesia que se llevó a cabo en Saint George, Utah, el 6 de abril de 1877, Brigham Young habló exasperadamente:

> *Últimamente se ha notado un escándalo, en las columnas de los periódicos, en el sentido de que los 'mormones' se van a México. Esto es correcto: calculamos ir allá. ¿Vamos a regresar al Condado de Jackson, Misuri? Sí. ¿Cuándo? Tan pronto como se abra el camino... Intentamos mantener lo nuestro aquí, y al mismo tiempo penetrar el norte y el sur, el este y el oeste... y levantar el estandarte de la verdad. Esta es la obra de Dios, esa obra grande y maravillosa referida por hombres antiguos de Dios, que la vieron incipiente, como una piedra cortada de la montaña no por mano, pero la cual rodó y adquirió fuerza y magnitud hasta que llenó toda la tierra. Continuaremos creciendo y propagándonos en el extranjero, y ni todos los poderes de la tierra ni del infierno podrán detener esta obra.[57]*

Mientras que las intenciones de los mormones eran expandir el reino en todo lugar a su debido tiempo, México podría ser algo especial: un lugar de refugio. A pesar de las aclaraciones de Brigham Young, la actividad misional y de colonización continuó en el sur. La compañía que encabezaba Jones acababa de salir. Seguramente otras le seguirían, así como más grupos misionales exploratorios.

Para septiembre de 1876, el presidente Young ya tenía un nuevo grupo de misioneros para explorar Sonora,[58] que incluía a James Z. Stewart y su compañero Helaman Pratt --

participantes en el primer grupo de misioneros que visitaron Chihuahua. Esperaron hasta después de la Conferencia General de octubre para emprender su larga jornada.

Los que acompañaron a Stewart y Pratt fueron el hermano de Stewart, de nombre Isaac, George Terry, Louis Garff y Melitón Trejo --el traductor de los *Trozos Selectos* que habían llevado consigo los primeros misioneros a México. Cuando finalmente llegaron a Tucson, Arizona, se separaron en dos grupos.[E] Pratt y Trejo continuaron al sur rumbo a Hermosillo, la capital de Sonora, donde hicieron proselitismo durante un tiempo y bautizaron a los primeros cinco miembros de la Iglesia de Jesucristo de los Santos de los Últimos Días en México. Pratt y Trejo regresaron entonces a sus hogares.

En contraste, los hermanos Stewart, Terry y Garff se dirigieron a las montañas de Sonora e intentaron evangelizar a los *yaqui*. Pensaban que ese grupo indígena podría ayudar a abrir grandes oportunidades entre los lamanitas de Sonora, pero eran orgullosos, leales e indomables en defensa de sus familias y su territorio; ni los españoles, franceses o mexicanos los habían conquistado. Tenían hogares permanentes, vivían en comunidades grandes, y trabajaban una mina rica --usando el oro para conseguir armas en Douglas, Arizona, para pelear contra los mexicanos.[59] Los misioneros entraron a Sonora conscientes de que los *yaqui* estaban de nuevo en guerra contra el gobierno mexicano, como lo habían estado frecuentemente desde los días del emperador Maximiliano de Habsburgo. Aun cuando a esas alturas los enfrentamientos ya eran particularmente feroces,[60] la convicción y fe de los élderes hicieron que sus temores se apaciguaran. Ciertamente, razonaron, Dios los protegería.

La práctica del pueblo *yaqui* era tomar presos a todos los extranjeros --incluyendo a aquellos mexicanos sin su sangre-- y ejecutarlos si había cualquier evidencia de que estuvieran aunque fuera ligeramente conectados con las políticas en contra de ellos. Desde su punto de vista, lo único que habían hecho esos extranjeros durante más de un siglo era violar a sus mujeres, matar y encarcelar a sus hombres, dejar a sus hijos huérfanos y sin hogar, y en todas partes robar sus propiedades. Ningún cometido de la obra misional o plática sobre las profecías del Libro de Mormón y la redención de los lamanitas, podría penetrar tales barreras. Aprehendieron y ataron a los misioneros, los torturaron y estaban a punto de matarlos cuando uno de sus jefes intervino. Dijo a los élderes que les perdonaría la vida, pero que deberían salir de su territorio y jamás regresar. La próxima vez quizá no estaría presente para rescatarlos.[61]

Stewart y sus compañeros rápidamente regresaron a los Estados Unidos, viajando a lo largo de la frontera desde el área de Tucson hasta llegar a El Paso del Norte, sitio donde antes él estuviera con Daniel Jones. Gordon Irving, quien ha coleccionado numerosas historias orales sobre el mormonismo en Latinoamérica, registra este interesante episodio:

> *Cuando llegaron a El Paso contactaron al señor J.W. Campbell, quien era molinero y dueño de una tienda en San Elizario, población que se encuentra a cierta distancia de El Paso y colinda con el Río Grande. Aparentemente lo habían conocido el año anterior. Campbell estaba interesado tanto en el mormonismo como en colonizar en México. Les propuso en esa ocasión, 1877, comprar una parcela grande en la parte este del estado de Coahuila, cerca de la frontera con Texas. Así que Stewart le escribió a Brigham Young para presentarle esta proposición, pero el presidente le contestó que preferiría un lugar más cercano a las colonias ya establecidas en Arizona. Brigham murió un poco después y Stewart y sus compañeros regresaron a Utah. Así terminó este asunto, dejando la iniciativa para colonizar México en manos de Jones, quien se encontraba en Arizona.[62]*

LA EXPEDICIÓN DE 1879 A LA CIUDAD DE MÉXICO

Mientras que todos estos intentos de penetrar el norte de México ocurrían, las noticias sobre el mormonismo generaron comentarios en la ciudad de México. Dos de los ejemplares del Libro de Mormón que el grupo de Daniel W.

Jones había mandado por correo en 1876, mientras se encontraban en Chihuahua, cayeron en manos de personas influyentes de la Capital, quienes se interesaron lo suficiente para leer y desearon más información. Uno de ellos fue Ignacio Manuel Altamirano, el maestro de Letras del México del siglo XIX. Indio que había empezado a aprender el español a la edad de dieciséis años para después dominarlo, Altamirano fue suficientemente receptivo no sólo a la retórica liberal que favorecía a los indios, sino también a las creencias mormonas sobre la importancia histórica de los lamanitas. La escatología mormona respecto al futuro de los lamanitas tampoco le pasó desapercibida. Altamirano escribió una carta a Salt Lake City, en la que agradecía a las autoridades por el libro y solicitaba mayor información sobre el mensaje mormón.[63]

Poco después, el doctor Plotino C. Rhodakanaty entabló correspondencia con los mormones.[64] Considerado por algunos mexicanos como el padre de los movimientos sociales, agrarios y sindicales de la nación, así como sobresaliente pensador cuyas ideas de libertad y derechos ayudaron a precipitar la Revolución Mexicana de 1910, Rhodakanaty también había recibido uno de aquellos ejemplares de los *Trozos Selectos del Libro de Mormón.* Por alguna razón sabía de Melitón Trejo, quien estaba viviendo en el sureste de Arizona con algunos de los colonos del *Campo Utah* que se habían separado del campamento original llamado '*Valle del Río Salado',* a raíz de ya no poder tolerar las decisiones de Jones con respecto a cómo y dónde incluir a los indios en su campamento. A principios de 1878 Plotino Rhodakanaty le escribió a Trejo a la población de Tres Álamos, indicándole que deseaba saber más sobre la 'Iglesia Mormona'.[65] Durante algún tiempo hubo correspondencia entre los dos sobre este asunto. Finalmente, Trejo le escribió a John Taylor --quien dirigía la Iglesia desde la muerte de Brigham Young, acaecida en 1877-- e incluyó algunas de las cartas de Rhodakanaty.[66]

Ya para el otoño de 1878, el presidente Taylor le había mandado a Rhodakanaty varias publicaciones sobre la Iglesia.[67] Las autoridades de Salt Lake City pronto se dieron cuenta de que su interlocutor en México había interesado en

198

el mormonismo a muchos de sus conciudadanos, indicando que entre quince y veinte ahora creían en el 'Evangelio Mormón'. Poco después Rhodakanaty primero solicitó, y luego prácticamente demandó que se les bautizara a él y a sus amigos. "Hemos encontrado el Evangelio, y deseamos que ustedes nos den el Sacerdocio de Aarón (el menor de los dos sacerdocios en la fe mormona) para que así podamos empezar la prédica en México", les dijo en una de sus misivas.[68F] La respuesta de Lago Salado fue para informarle que eso sólo sucedería si se mandaban misioneros a donde él y sus compañeros se encontraban. Durante el año de 1879 Rhodakanaty envió muchas cartas solicitando misioneros y prometiendo gran éxito cuando fueran enviados.

El mandar misioneros a la ciudad de México --cosa que Brigham Young tenía en mente cuando extendió el llamamiento a los primeros misioneros a México, en 1874-- era una idea que ahora parecía ser apropiada. John Taylor estimaba a James Z. Stewart, quien para entonces era ya un misionero experimentado y hablaba el español, y lo llamó para que se dirigiera al sur, pidiendo a Melitón Trejo que lo acompañara.

No es posible saber si Trejo estaba contento con ese nuevo llamamiento, pero demoró su viaje de Arizona a Lago Salado. Esto, aunado a la necesidad que tuvo el presidente Taylor de pasar a la clandestinidad para evitar a los comisarios federales que perseguían la poligamia, le permitieron al grupo gobernante --el Quórum de los Doce Apóstoles-- volver a pensar esta nueva misión hacia el país del sur Dado el gran interés por la Iglesia demostrado por aquellos en la ciudad do México, los apóstoles concluyeron que para esa misión tan importante era necesario un liderismo con mayor autoridad que la que tenían tanto Stewart como Trejo. La Iglesia podía estar a la puerta de su mayor oportunidad en México.

Por lo tanto, el Quórum de los Doce mandó al recién ordenado apóstol Mosses Thatcher para presidir sobre esta importante misión. El élder James Z. Stewart se le unió en Chicago, y Melitón Trejo en Nueva Orléans. El grupo entonces tomó un buque de vapor para cruzar el Golfo de México, arribando a Veracruz el 14 de noviembre de 1879.

Dos días después llegaron a la ciudad de México[G] y encontraron alojamiento en el hotel principal, llamado *Iturbide.*

Después de escasos cuatro días, el apóstol Thatcher y sus compañeros se convencieron de que Rhodakanaty y uno de sus compañeros debían ser bautizados. Así que el 20 de noviembre de 1879, Thatcher bautizó tanto a Plotino Rhodakanaty como a Silviano Arteaga; tres días después, Trejo bautizó a otras seis personas. De esos primeros conversos, a cuatro se les confirió el sacerdocio --tres de ellos en el oficio de élder.[69] Se organizó una congregación y se llamó a Rhodakanaty para presidirla, con Silviano Arteaga y José Ybarrola como sus consejeros.

En la reunión donde se llevaron acabo estas ordenanzas y llamamientos, Mosses Thatcher ofreció una oración pidiendo una bendición especial sobre Porfirio Díaz --el presidente de México desde el cierre de la Reforma, en 1876--, las autoridades políticas, el personal que trabajaba para el gobierno, y sobre todo el pueblo mexicano, con el fin de que el evangelio pudiera florecer entre toda la gente de México, Centroamérica y América del Sur. Los misioneros también cultivaron contactos gubernamentales importantes que más tarde, durante años difíciles para los miembros de la Iglesia, les ayudarían a proteger a los Santos de los Últimos Días en el país.

Los élderes llegaron a estar bastante ocupados. Para fines de 1879 habían bautizado a dieciséis personas.[H] Trejo y Stewart también tomaron tiempo para traducir más literatura mormona. En enero de 1880 terminaron el folleto *Una Voz de Amonestación,* de Parley P. Pratt, y lo prepararon para la imprenta; al mismo tiempo escribieron numerosos artículos para la prensa local.

Por su parte, la prensa en el este de los Estados Unidos continuaba especulando sobre el movimiento mormón hacia el sur. Cuando el diario neoyorquino *The Sun* publicó un artículo sobre la misión a México, muchos de los periódicos de la capital mexicana reprodujeron fragmentos y dieron comentarios ligeramente favorables. Pero el diario *Dos Repúblicas*, bajo los encabezados 'Diplomacia Yanqui', 'Obstruccionistas', y 'Propagación del Mormonismo', atacó vigorosamente al pueblo mormón en general --y en particular a los eventos específicos en la ciudad de México. Utilizando el periódico *La Tribuna*, Thatcher hizo el intento de aclarar las acusaciones aparecidas en *Dos Repúblicas*.[70]

El intercambio de artículos en los diarios llamó la atención de los mexicanos pertenecientes a la clase alta y de los extranjeros que radicaban en la Capital. La curiosidad sobre los propósitos de los mormones abrió puertas para realizar entrevistas con las autoridades más influyentes. Los misioneros se reunieron con el ministro de Relaciones Exteriores (Zárate), el Ministro de Obras Públicas y Colonización (Fernández Leal) y el Ministro de Guerra (Pacheco), todos ellos ya enterados de la experiencia mormona. Cordialmente invitaron a Thatcher a traer a su gente y establecerse en México. Leal, quien había visitado Utah y miraba con agrado su ingenio y prosperidad, dijo que México con gusto les daría una bienvenida.[71]

Como consecuencia de las muchas entrevistas suscitadas principalmente por el intercambio de artículos en los diarios, el apóstol Thatcher y sus compañeros tuvieron la oportunidad de conocer a Emelio Biebuyck, un influyente belga que estaba familiarizado con los asuntos de Utah. Biebuyck había estado tres veces en el Territorio de Utah, conociendo personalmente a Brigham Young en varias entrevistas que le fueron concedidas. Biebuyck era dueño de un contrato de colonización que había hecho con el gobierno mexicano, en el cual se le concedía tierras públicas sin costo en cualquier estado de la República, si eran para fines de colonización, y calurosamente abogaba por la colonización mormona en México. Dado el interés continuo de Thatchor por colonizar, los dos se hicieron amigos rápidamente.

Biebuyck le dijo a Thatcher que "con la colonización de los mormones en México vendría un gobierno estable, y en consecuencia paz y prosperidad; por lo tanto mis negocios prosperarían, eso es todo lo que pido"[72] El contrato de colonización que él tenía con el gobierno mexicano no sólo incluía tierras libres de costo, sino también un subsidio de 80 dólares por adulto y 40 por cada niño; exención por veinte años del servicio militar e impuestos para cada inmigrante; entrada libre de impuestos para su equipo, carretas, artículos agrícolas, materiales de construcción, y provisiones para facilitar el establecimiento de sus colonias -- además de otros numerosos privilegios.

Simultáneamente a toda esta plática estimulante de colonización, las actividades misionales en la ciudad de México empezaron a empeorar. Entre otras cosas, los élderes comenzaron a desilusionarse con Rhodakanaty, quien en vez de simplemente aceptar el estilo mormón --como lo hacían la mayoría de los nuevos conversos--, estaba intentando asimilar a los mormones mexicanos a sus propias ideas en cuanto a una vida comunal. No tardó mucho para que Thatcher estuviera de acuerdo con la conclusión previa de Daniel W. Jones en el sentido de que los esfuerzos misionales únicamente tendrían éxito con un cuidadoso recogimiento de santos mexicanos en colonias mormonas, a fin de que fueran adecuadamente instruidos. Así pues, la oferta de colonización propuesta por Biebuyck se veía muy atractiva para perderla. No habían pasado dos meses desde la organización de la primera rama en México, cuando Thatcher se propuso presentar esa proposición al presidente Taylor y el Quórum de los Doce.

El 4 de febrero de 1880 Thatcher dejó a Stewart encargado y regresó a Salt Lake City, a donde llegó el 22 del mismo mes. Diez días después, como habían previamente acordado, Biebuyck llegó y entre los dos explicaron en detalle a las autoridades de la Iglesia sobre el contrato que Biebuyck tenía con el gobierno mexicano. Tras una larga discusión y con el debido respeto dado a los esfuerzos de Thatcher y Biebuyck, los líderes mormones rechazaron la propuesta. Tal vez todavía recordaban el consejo que el gobernador Ochoa les había dado cuatro años antes: "Tengan cuidado con ofertas que incluyan tierras públicas".

Aunque el propósito de colonizar para que fuera un lugar de refugio había estado en la mente de muchos, hasta finales de 1880 la predicación del evangelio era el objetivo principal. El colonizar era un medio para lograr ese fin. Creando una comunidad mexicana mormona, Thatcher creía que él estaría impulsando y adelantando el trabajo de Dios en una forma dramática. Sin embargo, desviándose de las ideas previas de Brigham Young, los nuevos líderes de la Iglesia sentían que ese tipo de colonización en México, y con tal propósito, era algo prematuro.

Tal vez entonces los intentos mexicanos parecían ser de poca importancia en comparación con los problemas que enfrentaban los mormones de Utah y Arizona. La cruzada antipolígama amenazaba hogares y comunidades enteras, por lo que muchos Santos de los Últimos Días se habían mudado a retiros escondidos en Montana, Colorado, Nevada y Arizona. A George Q. Cannon, quien era el delegado en Washington del Territorio de Utah, se le atribuyó haber dicho en una entrevista con el diario neoyorquino *The Sun* que los mormones "no tenían a donde irse en todo el territorio de Estados Unidos, y tal vez serían compelidos a abandonar una parte de su religión, o bien a pelear."[73] Mientras que la idea de 'un lugar de refugio' en México había más que cruzado la mente de Brigham Young, evidentemente no fue considerada como seria por quienes lo sucedieron en el gobierno de la Iglesia. Ahora parecía que colonizar México tendría que demorarse hasta que la crisis en casa fuera resuelta.[74] Todos los recursos disponibles tenían que ser cuidadosamente preservados para que no se dispersara la energía colectiva en dicha lucha.

En tanto que el élder Mosses Thatcher estuvo en Salt Lake City presentando ofertas firmes de tierras mexicanas para colonizar, Trejo y Stewart permanecieron en la capital mexicana y continuaron su obra misional. Concluyeron una traducción más extensa del Libro de Mormón e iniciaron la predicación en poblaciones vecinas a la ciudad de México, enfocando sus esfuerzos en Ozumba, donde tuvieron algo de éxito. Pero en general sus esfuerzos misionales se vieron sin recompensa. Trejo finalmente salió de la Capital en mayo de 1880 para regresar a su casa en Arizona, dejando a Stewart como único misionero de *Sión* --nombre dado a los asentamientos mormones de Utah y Arizona.

Después de que el Consejo de los Doce Apóstoles rechazara la propuesta de Thatcher, éste regresó a la ciudad de México en diciembre de 1880 para recomenzar, acompañado por Feramorz L. Young. Si la colonización no iba a llevarse a cabo, entonces tendrían que encontrar otra manera de propagar el evangelio --aunque resultaba evidente que la actitud de Thatcher era pesimista sobre el éxito de cualquier otro método.

La situación empezó a deteriorarse rápidamente. Por un lado, Rhodakanaty quería establecer una *'Orden Unida'* mormona. Ciertamente, fue ese concepto mormón del comunitarismo lo que primeramente le llamó la atención, y cuando no pudo convencer a Thatcher de adaptar su punto de vista, se retiró de la Iglesia. La mayoría de los nuevos conversos se apartaron también por la misma razón. Ya para 1881, Rhodakanaty escribía artículos contra de la Iglesia en los periódicos socialistas.[75]

Al ver que el redil original disminuía por la idea del comunitarismo, Thatcher, Stewart y Young orientaron su atención a hacer nuevos prosélitos. Pero la era de Reforma había terminado, y con ella la emoción política que había ayudado a los primeros misioneros. La entrada del ejército de Porfirio Díaz a la ciudad de México estableció el orden, aunque por pistola y espada. No obstante, fue un tipo de orden que fomentó una reimposición de las tradiciones mexicanas, con lo que la Iglesia Católica --al menos en las ciudades grandes-- empezó nuevamente a gozar de ascendencia.

En 1880 el apóstol Thatcher se convenció de que los residentes de la capital mexicana estaban tan amargados por la tradición o el temor, que los élderes no podrían tener gran éxito entre ellos, en tanto que algunos misioneros protestantes de varias denominaciones parecían tener algo de éxito.[76] Los élderes concluyeron que se debía a que aquellos regalaban sus folletos y 'compraban' a sus conversos con favores y remuneraciones, y dicha práctica no podía ser emulada por los mormones. Es sorprendente, por lo tanto, que a pesar de no poder cubrir el costo de impresión de su literatura traducida, los misioneros encontraran la manera de distribuir miles de copias, pagando ellos mismos el costo.[77] El presidente Taylor, en respuesta a este asunto, les indicó que continuaran vendiendo la literatura por cualquier cantidad posible: la sede de la Iglesia no podía darles gran ayuda financiera por causa de los problemas que enfrentaba con el gobierno federal sobre poligamia en el Territorio de Utah.

Desanimados, los misioneros empezaron a pensar más y más en los indios y campesinos de los pequeños poblados circunvecinos a la ciudad de México, algo que, concluyeron, era lo que el Señor deseaba que hicieran desde el principio. No había sido en la ciudad de Chihuahua ni en El Paso del Norte, sino en los alrededores y en el poblado de Concepción Guerrero, en donde Daniel W. Jones y sus compañeros habían encontrado gente ansiosa por escuchar. Algunos grupos protestantes se dieron cuenta de la misma situación, por lo que habían enfocado su atención en las orillas de la capital mexicana. Así, los élderes reanudaron sus esfuerzos en los poblados cercanos, como Ozumba (Estado de México), donde bautizaron a gente que más tarde llegaría a ser prominente para la Iglesia --en particular la familia Páez. No obstante, en ese tiempo Mosses Thatcher permaneció pesimista sobre el esfuerzo, convenciéndose más y más de que Jones debió estar en lo correcto en cuanto a las necesidades sociales y espirituales de colonización.[78]

Los mormones se habían dedicado frenéticamente a la expansión de su fe en México y las tierras ocupadas por los indios en la parte sur de los territorios de Estados Unidos. Pero sus experiencias con estos indios habían sido en su mayoría negativas, produciendo principalmente frustración y ansiedad a pesar del enorme cometido de la Iglesia y sus misioneros hacia los lamanitas. Todo parecía volverse ceniza en las manos de los élderes. Más tarde y a manera de autojustificación, Jones recordaría a la Iglesia que podría haber mandado a los misioneros al poblado de Concepción Guerrero, donde multitud de indios habían estado esperando en vano su bautismo.[79]

En Sión, el interés en los lamanitas permaneció como prioridad a pesar de los encuentros con los comisarios federales. Numerosas y espectaculares visitaciones celestiales fueron reportadas por los indios de las planicies y las Montañas Rocallosas, y muchos de los miembros de la Iglesia consideraban esto como prueba de que la Segunda Venida de Jesucristo era evidente.[80] Wilford Woodruff le escribió el 7 de diciembre de 1881 una carta al hermano Johnson, en el Valle del Río Salado, Arizona, donde describe la información que él tenía concerniente a dichas visitaciones angélicas reportadas entre los indios. Todas las naciones indígenas estaban en movimiento, enviando corredores desde aquellos lugares. Ese año, Woodruff había informado: "Nosotros, como Quórum de los Doce, hemos sido ordenados por el Señor a dedicar ahora nuestra atención hacia los lamanitas y a predicarles el Evangelio, y ahora estamos haciendo ese esfuerzo."[81] Los apóstoles Brigham Young, hijo, y Heber J. Grant, habían sido asignados a Arizona y Nuevo México para poder entender mejor la situación entre los indios; George Teasdale visitaba el territorio indio; Francis M. Lyman viajaba a la Reserva de Uinta, que se encontraba al este, y los también apóstoles Lorenzo Snow y Franklin D. Richards atendían a las tribus del norte.[82] El apóstol Thatcher se encontraba en la ciudad de México nuevamente, y por razón de su compromiso substancial hacia la causa lamanita, ciertamente iba a impresionarse al escuchar las noticias de las visitaciones informadas por los indios.

En abril de 1881, cuatro meses después de su regreso a México, Thatcher dirigió a una congregación de santos -- algunos de los cuales habían permanecido del grupo original de Rhodakanaty--, y saliendo de la capital mexicana ascendieron el gran volcán Popocatépetl, ubicado a 80 kilómetros al sureste de la ciudad de México. Ahí, el 6 de abril, a cincuenta y un años de que la Iglesia de Jesucristo de los Santos de los Últimos Días fuera organizada, los mormones realizaron una conferencia, y en una ceremonia formal de oración, dedicaron el país de México para la predicación del evangelio. Por razón del enorme y simbólico significado que para la mayoría de los indios mexicanos tenía el Popocatépetl, la ascensión a su cumbre cobraba un significado profundamente simbólico. No había duda en la mente de los misioneros con respecto a quiénes debía llevarse el mensaje. Aquellos que asistieron a esta primera conferencia de la Iglesia en México fueron Thatcher, Young, Stewart y algunos mormones de la ciudad de México -- Silviano Arteaga, Fernando A. Lara, Ventura Páez, Lino Zárate y otros dos miembros cuyos nombres se desconocen[831] Todos estos esfuerzos empezaron lentamente a dar resultados, y otros Santos de los Últimos

Días comenzaron a llegar de Sión. Uno de ellos fue August H.F. Wilcken, un inmigrante europeo educado en el idioma español. Wilcken ayudó a traducir otros folletos, y posteriormente fue a Ozumba con Fernando Lara para hacer proselitismo ahí y en los poblados circunvecinos.

Otros cambios ocurrieron rápidamente: en junio, James Stewart fue relevado para regresar a su casa en Utah; dos meses después Thatcher fue relevado y August Wilcken seleccionado para reemplazarlo, y Feramorz L. Young --quien a los pocos días moriría de tifoidea-- y Fernando Lara salieron junto con Thatcher rumbo a Utah. Lara había sido uno de los más dedicados y exitosos misioneros de entre los mexicanos. Sesenta y un miembros de ese país permanecieron, lo cual fue suficiente para organizar formalmente la segunda rama de la Iglesia en el pueblo de Ozumba, justo en la base del Popocatépetl. En ese lugar, Wilcken, Arteaga, Páez, Zárate y otros continuaron solos la obra misional.

Unos meses después, los santos de México se llenaron de gozo al saber de la inminente llegada de nuevos misioneros de Sión. Anthony W. Ivins regresó acompañado por Nielson R. Pratt, uno más en la larga lista de los de ese apellido que han servido a la Iglesia. Al poco tiempo, los misioneros mexicanos y estadounidenses agregaron cincuenta y un miembros más a los registros de la Iglesia en México.

A su debido tiempo, cuando Wilcken regresó a su casa, Ivins recibió el llamamiento como presidente de Misión. Rey Pratt, quien más tarde sería una autoridad de la Iglesia en México, dijo que durante la administración de Ivins "un buen número de élderes nativos fueron llamados al servicio misional, y el trabajo de la predicación del Evangelio y de extender la verdad fue vigorosamente encarrilado.[84] Algunos de estos misioneros locales fueron Lino Zárate, Julián Rojas, y un élder apellidado Candanosa.[J] Más gente se unió a la Iglesia.

El proselitismo se extendió a numerosos pero pequeños poblados en la meseta central mexicana: Toluca, Ixtacalco, Tecalco y Chimal, todos ellos en el estado de Morelos; y Nopala, en el estado de Hidalgo. Isaac J. Stewart, quien acompañó a su hermano en la visita a los *yaqui* unos años atrás,^K no tardó en unirse al grupo. De igual manera lo hizo Helaman Pratt, otro de los misioneros originales enviados a México. Indudablemente, todos aquellos cuyo interés y habilidad los calificaban para la labor misional, servirían en doble capacidad mientras que en Lago Salado se rehusaban a aprobar la colonización en México.

Para marzo de 1884, Helaman Pratt dirigía la Misión. Extendió la obra a San Marcos --en Hidalgo--, una comunidad que más tarde llegaría a ser parte muy importante para los mormones en el país. Paso a paso los misioneros avanzaron la causa. No tardó mucho para que Pratt se sumara a la opinión de pro-colonización que Jones y Thatcher habían expuesto: así como los primeros mormones se habían reunido en comunidades, así deberían hacerlo los miembros mexicanos. Que los observadores anglosajones hayan sido menos comprensivos hacía la cultura mexicana que a la de ellos mismos, no disminuye su percepción ante las necesidades de una nueva fe.

Así, después de estar en la misión unos pocos meses, Helaman Pratt propuso un nuevo plan: Si los mormones de Utah no podían venir a México, ¿por qué no mandar a los mexicanos a Arizona, donde ya existían colonias mormonas? Su propuesta era que se unieran, ya fuera en Arizona o el norte de México, entre 100 y 150 de los nuevos miembros mexicanos --prácticamente toda la membresía de la Iglesia en la ciudad de México y sus alrededores en ese entonces. Ahí podrían vivir social, cultural y económicamente como una comunidad mormona. Sin embargo, John Taylor opinaba que Arizona no podría manejar dicha cantidad, y sugirió que se mandaran tan solo unas diez familias. Cuando Pratt notificó la respuesta del presidente Taylor a los miembros mexicanos, éstos decidieron mejor esperar hasta que se pudiera establecer un poblado en el norte del país. Esa oportunidad vendría tres años más tarde, después de una colonización masiva de angloamericanos en el norte de México.

NOTAS:

1. Gordon Irving con un poco de duda acepta este punto. (Vea su libro "An Opening Wedge: LDS Proselyting in México, 1870-1890.")

2. Como ejemplo vea los siguientes libros de Leonard J. Arrington, *From Wilderness to Empire: The Role of Utah in Western Economic History*, y en el diario Deseret News, *Utah the Inland Empire*.

3. Blaine Carmon Hardy, "The Mormon Colonies of Northern Mexico: A History, 1885-1912," pp. 32-34, incluye datos específicos indicando el grado de la extensión de la colonización hacia el sur.

4. Citado en ibid., p. 32.

5. Este punto esta registrado por Daniel W. Jones en su autobiografía, *Forty Years among the Indians: A True Yet Thrilling Narrative of the Author's Experience among the Natives*, p. 220.

6. *The World Christian Encyclopedia*, editada por David B. Barrett, da dicha información on las páginas 488-89: Esfuerzos Protestantes empezaron la distribución de las escrituras de la Sociedad Bíblica de América en 1824; pero México estaba prácticamente cerrado para actividad religiosa Protestante hasta la revolución Mexicana de 1857. Juárez, el nuevo presidente en ese tiempo, animó a que hubiera actividades Protestantes y algunos misioneros independientes entraron a Monterrey durante la década de 1850. Inmigrantes Luteranos formaron una congregación de habla Alemana en 1861, y el siguiente año se estableció la primera Iglesia Bautista. Animados por los resultados, la Sociedad Hogareña Misional Bautista Americana se estableció en 1870; dos años después misioneros de la Mesa Directiva Americana también se encontraban en Monterrey y Guadalajara. Los Presbiterianos americanos también se establecieron en la Ciudad de México en 1872 y los Metodistas un año después......La Convención de los Bautistas del Sur llego a México en 1880, su primer campo en Latino América; y otra llegada importante fue la de los Adventistas del Séptimo Día en 1893....Dos organizaciones Protestantes de los EUA han levantado grandes delegaciones en México durante el siglo presente, los Mormones y los Testigos de Jehová, quienes llegaron en 1879 y 1893 respectivamente. *Los Mormones han tenido resultados espectaculares entre los nativos*, con mas de 40,000 bautismos reportados solo en 1976 (cursiva agregadas).

7. Uno puede mencionar los escritos de Graham Sumner Abbot titulado *México and the United States: Their Mutual Relations and Common Interests*, y especialmente una serie de artículos bajo el titulo de "Our

Nearest Neighbor" que se encuentra en la revista de *Harper's New Monthly Magazine*, página 44 (1874).

8. Hardy, "The Mormon Colonies," p. 38.

9. Ibid. Citado p. 38.

10. La idea de que los "extranjeros" podían hacerlo mejor se formuló en un racismo considerable con intentos de legitimación a través de los escritos filosóficos de Auguste Comte. Los positivistas aceptaban las conclusiones de Comte de que la sociedad podía ser rescatada por las técnicas sugeridas por las ciencias sociales siempre y cuando fueran incorruptibles por las ciencias de metafísica y teología. El problema radicaba en que la "ciencia" no estaba trabajando entre la población indígena, así que decidieron hacer esa población a un lado a favor de una mas agradable. El impacto que esto tuvo en la población indígena de México se encuentra en el capitulo cinco de este volumen.

11. Ernest Gruening trata el tema de la recepción amistosa que los primeros misioneros Mormones a México recibieron en contraste a la influencia del positivismo y la preferencia que México demostró hacia los intereses extranjeros. (Vea Ernest Gruening, *México and its Heritage*, pp. 50-53 passim.)

12. Vea Louis Hartz, *The Founding of New Societies: Studies in the History of the United States, Latin America, South Africa, Canada and Australia*.

13. Jones, *Forty Years among the Indians*, p. 17.

14. Paul Thomas Mourtizen, "Mormon Beginnings in México: The 1876 Missionary Expedition," p. 4.

15. Jones, *Forty Years among the Indians*, p. 220.

16. K.E. Duke, "Melitón González Trejo, Translator of the Book of Mormon into Spanish," p. 714.

17. Jones, *Forty Years among the Indians*, p. 224.

18. El costo real de refinar la traducción (después que Jones y Trejo habían agotado sus fondos personales) se completo con promesas individuales desde diez centavos hasta diez dólares. Congregaciones enteras así como individuos contribuyeron al fondo que Brigham Young había autorizado. Cuatrocientos once personas donaron dinero, entre ellos Feramorz Little, Erastus Snow, J.P. Ball, William Hyde, Orson Hyde, George Q. Cannon, George Teasdale, Mathias Cowley, Anson Call, y varios miembros de la familia Martineau la cual también influyo grandemente en la expansión de la Iglesia en Latino America.

19. Aquellos lectores que se interesen en las traducciones de literatura de la Iglesia Mormona, estarán intrigados por los métodos que se

utilizaron y en particular en este caso para asegurar que la traducción se llevara acabo correctamente. Brigham Young había comisionado a Jones para que confirmara la autenticidad de la traducción. Jones estaba seguro de tener ayuda divina ya que mientras él y Trejo repasaban la traducción del Libro de Mormón por última vez, Jones "sintió una sensación en el centro de su frente que parecía que hubiera una fibra fina interminable. Cuando ocurría un error la suavidad de la fibra se interrumpía y parecía ser que un pequeño nudo pasara por la frente" (Jones, Forty Years among the Indians, p. 232). Los dos entonces modificaban la traducción hasta que la suavidad de nuevo regresaba. Todo esto no convenció a Brigham Young en su totalidad. Sabiendo que ninguna de las Autoridades Generales era competente para juzgar la exactitud de la traducción, él deseaba aseguranza adicional antes de aprobar su publicación. El le pregunto a Jones como era que iba a satisfacer a las Autoridades Generales que la traducción era correcta.

> Mi propuesta fue de seleccionar un libro en Inglés con el cual ni Trejo ni yo estuviéramos familiarizados y dejar que Trejo lo tradujera al español, después de su traducción yo lo tomaría y sin jamas haber visto el original lo escribiría en inglés y lo compararíamos. El hermano Brigham indico que esto era justo. Me pregunto si yo estaba familiarizado con "Spencer's Letters." Le dije que no, ya que jamas las había leído. El me mando a las oficinas del Historiador para que le dijera al Hermano G.A. Smith que le diera una copia a Trejo y hacer lo que yo había propuesto. Al entregarle la traducción como se había acordado, el Hermano Smith, con una sonrisa nos dijo, "Me gusta mas el estilo del Hermano Jones mas que el del Hermano Spencer. Es la misma esencia, pero el lenguaje es mas fácil de entender" (Jones, Forty Years among the Indians, p. 231).

20. Por los siguientes pasos estoy endeudado a un narrativo de Paul Mourtizen que no se ha publicado, "Mormon Beginnings in Mexico."

21. Del diario de James Z. Stewart.

22. Anthony Woodward Ivins, "letter to James G. Bleak," (18 de Febrero de 1889 enviadas de la ciudad de México."

23. Como ejemplo vea la forma en que Jones en su libro Forty Years among the Indians, pp. 216 y 273 filosofa sobre este punto. Además, el compilador de la cronología oficial de la Iglesia considera la expedición de suma importancia; de aproximadamente sesenta anotaciones para el año

1876 que tratan los eventos en la Iglesia en su totalidad, cinco de ellos son sobre movimientos misionales a y a través de México. (Vea la compilación de Andre Jenson, *Church Chronology: A Record of Important Events Pertaining to the History of The Church of Jesus Christ of Latter-day Saints.*)

24. Vea Latter-day Saint Biographical Encyclopedia, 4:348 por Andrew Jenson.

25. Mucha gente nativa, amenazados con asimilación por conquistadores Europeos, han resistido la perdida de su identidad independiente, sus tierras, y sus comunidades autónomas. El hecho de que muchos otros "nuevos grupos étnicos" han surgido desde el año 1960

es testamento que algunas personas no están dispuestas a olvidar sus raíces. Lo que distingue a los Yaquis mas que ha otros en este aspecto es su persistencia, resistencia, y su récord excepcional de éxito. Sobre todo, hay una historia de una gente luchando con dificultades para preservar como una comunidad autónoma en sus propias tierras, con su propia identidad. En este aspecto, la motivación y metas no eran tan diferentes de las que los Mormones tenían en mente para su propias comunidades. Pero así como los Mormones tenían problemas con sus "vecinos," así mismo los Yaquis. Con la independencia que México había recibido de España al principio del siglo diecinueve, los Yaquis se vieron envueltos en casi una continua, y por su mayoría violenta, batalla con la nueva República Mexicana y su soporte extranjero con el fin de controlar tierras, agua, su propia mano de obra, y finalmente su propia identidad como comunidad. El Territorio era el fértil Valle del Rió Yaqui; intereses foráneos donde las compañías mineras necesitaban mano de obra barata y además seguridad; Se les llamaba Mexicanos a aquellos que tenían sus propias ideas de como establecer su propia identidad como nación moderna y en búsqueda de un desarrollo nacional social y económico. Los dos puntos de vista - la de los Yaquis y los Mexicanos - estaban basados sobre valores completamente opuestos e indudablemente chocaron. Los intereses extranjeros aplaudieron a la República Mexicana.

El momento de mayor gloria para la resistencia Yaqui (1875-1885) ocurrió precisamente al tiempo en que las expediciones misionales Mormonas se emprendían (1876), y es entendible que en ese tiempo la gente de Tucson hablara de furiosas batallas en Sonora. El Jefe José María Leyva Cajeme había logrado éxito en consolidar a los ocho pueblos Yaquis que habían permanecido desde los días de los Jesuitas, y finalmente trajo a la existencia un estado Yaqui nuevo, que anteriormente otros líderes Yaquis habían fracasado en conseguir. Por diez años la "República Yaqui" construyó fuertes y almacenó materiales para defender a sus comunidades de asaltos anticipados del ejército Mexicano;   Sus líderes también administraron los asuntos religiosos y otros que crearon una solidaridad de consecuencias duraderas.

Mientras que "las furiosas batallas" de las cuales los misioneros escucharon, ciertamente no fueron tan furiosas como las que ocurrieron en una rebelión Yaqui en 1830, donde los Yaquis sistemáticamente enviaron redadas para despoblar comunidades donde vivían extranjeros, es claro que mucha gente temía lo peor y probablemente habían escuchado bastante evidencia meritoria de cuando en cuando para justificar sus temores. Todo esto fue suficiente para disuadir a los misioneros Mormones entrar a Sonora. (Vea el libro de Evelyn Hu-DeHart para la mejor explicación de los Yaquis desde el punto de vista político e historia social (e.g., *Yaqui Resistance and Survival: The Struggle for Land and Autonomy*, 1821-1910, y "Sonora: Indians and Immigrants on a Developing Frontier," pp. 184-92). Una perspectiva cultural digno de mencionar es la de Edward H. Spicer, *The Yaquis: A Cultural History*. Una perspectiva sobre este asunto en la era de colonización, vea el libro de Marie Lucille Rocca-Arvay, *Assimilation and resistance of the Yaqui Indians of Northern Mexico during the Colonial Period*.)

26. Daniel W. Jones, "A letter to R. W. Driggs," 18 de Nov. de 1875.

27. Según lo reporto Jones en su libro *Forty Years among the Indians*, p. 257.

28. Ibid.

29. En el diario de Anthony Woodward Ivins con fecha de 11 de Noviembre de 1875, registra la tensión y su consejo a Jones para que tuviera mas paciencia y considerara mas los sentimientos de Smith y Tenney.

30. Hardy, "The Mormon Colonies."

31. Ibid

32. Jones, *Forty Years among the Indians*, p. 274.

33. Se cita en Mortizen "Mormon Beginnings in Mexico," p.13.

34. Daniel W. Jones, Helaman Pratt, y James Z. Stewart, "Mission Report," 5 de Octubre de 1876, Manuscript History of the Mexican Mission.

35. Jones, *Forty Years among the Indians*, pp. 260-262.

36. En el diario de Ivins con fecha del 28 de Marzo de 1876. Vea también el libro de Barney T. Burns y Thomas H. Naylor, "Colonia Morelos: A short History of a Mormon Colony in Sonora, Mexico," p. 142.

37. *El Semanario Oficial* (fecha y traductor desconocido) se cita en *Deseret Evening News*, del 30 de Junio de 1876, y se encuentra registrado en el "Journal History of the Church con fecha del 30 de Junio de 1876, p. 2.

38. Hardy, "The Mormon Colonies," p. 45.

39. Como se reporta en ibid., p. 277.

40. Al tratar el tema de la jornada a las montañas me encuentro grandemente endeudado con el libro de Mourtizen, "Mormon Beginnings in Mexico."

41. Jones, *Forty Years among the Indians*, p. 282.

42. Ibid., pp. 282-283.

43. Ibid., p. 284.

44. El libro de Mourtizen, "Mormon Beginnings in Mexico" nos da una perspectiva sobre estos factores.

45. El diario de James Z. Stewart, fechado el 1 de Mayo de 1876, se cita en el "Manuscript History of the Mexican Mission."

46. Vea el libro por Blaine Carmon Hardy, "Cultural 'Encystment' as a Cause of the Mormon Exodus from Mexico in 1912," p. 41.

47. Hardy, "The Mormon Colonies," p. 441, y Jones, *Forty Years among the Indians*, p. 283.

48. Jones, *Forty Years among the Indians*, p. 287.

49. Vea las discusiones de Lucile Pratt sobre las feroces guerras Indias de la era entre 1877 y 1882 en su libro "A Keyhole View of Mexican Agrarian Policy as Shown by Mormon Land Problems," pp. 19 en adelante. También vea la discusión en la nota 25.

50. Jones, *Forty Years among the Indians*, pp. 304, 308.

51. Ibid., p. 314.

52. Hardy, "The Mormon Colonies," pp. 32-34.

53. Vea por ejemplo el libro del Sgt. Daniel Tyler, *A Concise History of the Mormon Battalion in the Mexican War, 1846-1848*.

54. Los sentimientos de Young hacia Kane son mejor capturados por el siguiente extracto: "Siempre vamos a apreciar lo bueno, lo generoso, al enérgico y talentoso Coronel Little." (Brigham Young a Thomas L. Kane, 14 de Enero de 1859). Kane reclamaba ser un gentil, pero su dedicación hacia Brigham Young como a los Mormones era tan resuelta, y la consecuencia de esa dedicación era de tanto impacto, que muchos contemporáneos sugerían que "Kane había sido secretamente bautizado en Council Bluffs cuando los Santos por primera vez se reunían para iniciar su viaje hacia el Oeste en 1847" (Harold Schindler, *Orrin Porter Rockwell*, p. 285; vea también el libro de John Hyde, Jr., *Mormonism: it's Leaders and Design*, p. 146; y el libro de la Sra. C.V. Waite, *The Mormon Prophet and His Harem*, p. 52.

55. Irving, "An Opening Wedge," p. 3. La portada de esta conferencia de Irving, titulada "Questions needing further attention," da la

siguiente información adicional bajo el punto 2: "Chas. Peterson desde que di este discurso me ha señalado una carta muy interesante que escribió el Coronel Kane a Brigham Young que cambia la atención de proselitar a colonizar."

56. Vea por ejemplo, "Mexico: Reported Intentions of Mormons to Migrate to Mexico," *New York Times*, 22 de Dic. de 1874, p. 1; y "A Threat from Mormondom," *New York Times*, 22 de Junio de 1875, p. 6.

57. *Journal of Discourses,* 18:355-56.

58. *Deseret Weekly*, 13 de Septiembre de 1876, p. 521.

59. Entrevista con W. Ernest Young. Véase también la explicación en la nota 25.

60. Lucile Pratt, "A Keyhole View of Mexican Agrarian Policy."

61. Franklin Spencer González, "The Restored Church in Mexico" (MS1967), p. 16; también vea el diario de Stewart.

62. Irving, "An Opening Wedge," p. 8.

63. Entrevista con Agricol Lozano Herrera.

64. El período de Rhodakanaty con los Mormones fue fugaz, y aunque fue bautizado y tenía el deseo Mormón de llevar acabo el modelo de un poblado agrario en común (el Orden Unido) en México, no cabe duda que Rhodakanaty haya dedicado considerable energía para poder llevarlo acabo y lograr el éxito. El nació en Atenas (1828) de madre Austríaca y un noble Griego, él recibió la mejor educación permitida para su tiempo, aun dedicarse a estudios médicos en Alemania después de la muerte de su padre y el regreso de su familia a la tierra nativa de su madre. Mientras estudiaba medicina en Berlín desarrollo un gran interés en filosofía política y llego a ser un admirador, primeramente de Hegel y después de los filósofos franceses Fourier y especialmente de Proudhon. Rhodakanaty visito París para ver a Proudhon y después regreso para estudiar. Mientras se encontraba allí conoció, entre sus amigos jóvenes socialistas, a un Mexicano quien lo inspiro para que pensara de México como un lugar donde sus ideas de un poblado agrario pequeño, basado en principios morales de una utopía socialista, pudiera ponerse en practica. Los aspectos de sus deseos nunca se realizaron, pero si llego a México, donde llego a ser el primer defensor en el país de la doctrina anarquista y fundador del primer grupo de trabajadores en México. Ejerció una influencia profunda en el nacimiento de una clase urbana trabajadora y movimientos agrarios de las décadas 1860, 1870, y 1880. (Vea el libro de John M. Hart, Anarchism & the Mexican Working Class, 1860-1931, pp. 19-28.) Durante el tiempo en que Rhodakanaty estaba correspondiendo con los Mormones, organizaba y nutria el primer grupo en México, La Social. El 1 de Enero de 1878, en un

discurso dado a dicho grupo, repasó los principios sobre los cuales sus obras estaban basadas y sobre la necesidad de una transformación orgánica de la sociedad (para él no revolucionaria) que seria apoyada por toda la gente moral y pensadora. "Explotadores y prestadores de dinero los cuales trafican con seres humanos y sus negocios, quienes roban y empobrecen a la gente agotada por su miseria, también verán en La Sociedad una palanca poderosa que levantara al pobre y el desheredado...." (Plotino C. Rhodakanaty, Escritos, p. 77.

65. Esta información, la cual no la he visto en ningún otro lugar, es reportada por Irving en su libro "An Opening Wedge," p. 10.

66. Ibid.

67. Jenson, *Biographical Encyclopedia*, 1:131.

68. Irving, "An Opening Wedge," p. 10.

69. Los Mormones entienden que el sacerdocio se compone de dos categorías, cada cual con tres oficios. El mas alto o el Sacerdocio de Melquisedec, el cual tiene el poder para tratar cosas espirituales, se compone de los oficios sumo sacerdote, setenta, y elder (el oficio al cual Rhodakanaty fue ordenado, y por lo tanto una indicación de la estima que los misioneros tenía hacia él). El "menor" o Sacerdocio de Aarón, el cual encierra las llaves de asuntos temporales dentro de la Iglesia, tiene los oficios de presbítero, maestro, y diácono.

70. Jenson, *Biographical Encyclopedia*, 1:132-33.

71. Ibid.

72. Ibid., p. 133.

73. New York City Sun, 13 de Agosto de 1879.

74. Hardy, "Cultural 'Encystment,'" p. 441.

75. Irving, "An Opening Wedge," pp. 12-14.

76. Material útil e informativo desde el punto de vista de un teólogo Cubano, se puede encontrar en el libro de Justo E. González, *Historia de las Misiones*, en el capitulo 9. O.E. Costa presenta en forma contemporánea un punto de vista del Protestantismo principal en la publicación de su tesis doctoral, *Theology of the Crossroads in Contemporary Latin America*.

77. Stewart y Trejo habían terminado la traducción del folleto *La Voz de Amonestación* de Parley P. Pratt y habían logrado circular un buen numero de copias. Tradujeron, imprimieron, y distribuyeron 4,000 copias del folleto de John Nicholson "Means of Escape." Los misioneros también imprimieron miles de ejemplares "La Venida del Mesías" escrito por Stewart y los distribuyeron extensamente. Numerosos intercambios de prensa se llevaron acabo y mas tarde fueron publicados en el diario The Contributor. (Vea Jenson, Biographical Encyclopedia, 1:134.)

78. Hardy, "Cultural 'Encystment,'" pp. 440-441. Hardy cita el volumen 3, páginas 43-44 de los diarios de Moises Thatcher, de donde le hizo concluir que el motivo de colonizar México era de proveer a los conversos Mexicanos un nuevo ambiente separado de los efectos contrastantes que la sociedad no - Mormona de México proporcionaba. Todas estas consideraciones habían guiado a Thatcher a estar de acuerdo con la conclusión previa de Daniel W. Jones: "Unánimes estábamos en una idea, y esa era que antes de que se pudiera llevar acabo una gran obra en el país, seria necesario colonizar entre la gente" (Jones, *Forty Years among the Indians*, p. 283).

79. Jones, *Forty Years among the Indians*, pp. 286-87.

80. Los líderes y miembros Mormones de los años 1877 a 1892 en su mayoría estaban impresionados con y exitados por los reportes de visones de un Indio llamado Moroni así como las visiones de los jefes Shivitts, Wovoka, Sitting Bull, y otros. Tribus desde los Grandes Planicies hasta las Montañas Rocosas se interesaron en los Mormones y entonces desarrollaron su propio "Baile Fantasma" (asociado con sus creencias de que un Mesías pronto regresaría a la tierra y los salvaría de su grave situación aniquilando a los blancos y trayendo de nuevo al búfalo). Esto aterrorizo a mucho blancos no - Mormones y alarmo al gobierno federal de los E.U.A., y estos dos grupos se unieron para precipitar lo que ahora se considera el infame masacre de los Indios de 1890 en Wounded Knee, South Dakota. (Vea el libro de Dee Brown, *Bury My Heart at Wonded Knee: An Indian History of the American West*; y el de James Mooney, *The Ghost-Dance Religion and the Sioux Outbreak of 1890*.)

Estas visiones reenforzaron la escatología Mormona, y la Iglesia acelero su esfuerzo misional entre los Indios. Los Mormones estaban convencidos que el profeta Indio predicho en el Libro de Mormón finalmente se había levantado y que tal vez el Salvador mismo los había visitado o uno o mas de los Tres Nefitas estaba entre ellos nuevamente. Ciertamente la Segunda Venida estaba por llegar. Por esta razón, algunos acusaban a los Mormones de usar dicha ceremonia para sacar a los gentiles de su territorio. (Vea el libro de Lawrence G. Coates, "The Mormons and the Ghost Dance.")

81. Wilford Woodruff a un "Hermano Johnson" en el Valle de Río Salado, Arizona, el 7 de Diciembre de 1881.

82. Ibid.

83. Rey L. Pratt, "History of the Mexican Mission," p. 486.

84. Ibid., p. 489.

CAPITULO 2

UN LUGAR DE REFUGIO Y RECOGIMIENTO

La mayoría de los residentes de las actuales colonias Dublán y Juárez son mexicanos no mormones. Pero aunque éstos son minoría y se reúnen en congregaciones de habla inglesa o castellana, la cultura fundadora de esos asentamientos, su arquitectura, tecnología, sociedad y religión, son inequívocamente 'estilo Utah'.

Las casas de dos pisos de estas colonias --viejas pero bien cuidadas--, hechas de ladrillo cocido al sol y que sobrevivieron los destrozos provocados por la guerra civil de México de 1910-1917, recuerdan a los caserones de final del siglo en Brigham City o Mount Pleasant, Utah. Hay viejos graneros, patios sin cercas, jardines, pastos, huertas, grandes escuelas e iglesias. Todo esto y las modernas casas tipo *rambler* se entremezclan con las tradicionales casas mexicanas, lo que indica un implante cultural que una vez floreció y aún sobrevive.

Uno no se sorprende de encontrar al lado de un camino de tierra, en Dublán, una alcantarilla fabricada en la fundidora llamada 'Brigham'; o en Juárez una academia con edificios imponentes y jardines parecidos a los de la *Academia Brigham Young* de Provo, Utah; o evidencias, en las regiones circunvecinas, de la tecnología de irrigación, horticultura y las industrias de procesado de alimentos usualmente avanzadas para su tiempo. Al entrar a Dublán a comienzos de abril, antes de que las lluvias transformen las lomas de mezquite y chaparral en un edén para los ganaderos, el visitante encuentra un impresionante valle verde con maduros árboles frutales, campos de riego, y comercio e industria vigorosos. Todo lo cual indica que un ambicioso y próspero grupo de mexicanos y angloamericanos continúan habitando el valle. ¿Cómo fue que esto se dio, y por qué?

A la vista de las intensas presiones federales sobre los Santos de los Últimos Días en Utah y sus zonas aledañas, la renuencia de los líderes mormones a colonizar México pronto se desvaneció. Aunque por un cuarto de siglo los mormones pensaron que podrían defenderse en el Territorio de Utah y eventualmente ganar su caso en las cortes, para 1885 concluyeron que eso ya no era posible. Lamanitas, colonias, expansión económica y misiones pasaron a segundo término ante la necesidad de los miembros de la Iglesia de rescatar la integridad doctrinal y organizativa de su fe. Pero la respuesta final del gobierno era inflexible. Apoyado en la predominante y muchas veces hipócrita ideología norteamericana de que el país debía deshacerse de "las reliquias gemelas del barbarismo: poligamia y esclavitud",[1] y entusiasmado por el beneficio que obtendría al reducir el poder económico de la jerarquía mormona, el gobierno estadounidense decidió romper el sostén de la Iglesia.

En 1852 los mormones habían afirmado públicamente el principio del "matrimonio celestial"[2] (poligamia), aun cuando menos del diez por ciento de los hombres casados de la Iglesia lo practicaban. El matrimonio plural era una costumbre altamente inusual en los Estados Unidos del siglo XIX, y sólo unos cuantos no mormones lo aprobaban. Pero con los Santos de los Últimos Días aislados en el Territorio de Utah, los ataques iniciales, la mofa y la sátira quedaron relegados a los chistes, las caricaturas y las convenciones profesionales y académicas.[3] Abraham Lincoln no se opuso a la poligamia de Utah, aunque legalmente pudo haberlo hecho después de ser aprobada en 1862 la *Ley Morrill* anti-bigamia.[4] Sin embargo, al cabo de la Guerra Civil de Estados Unidos, los sentimientos hacia los mormones y sureños tomaron un nuevo giro. El 'Reconstruccionismo' radical estaba en boga; los republicanos se hallaban en el poder y ahora tenían la oportunidad y los medios para presionar su causa. Habían cumplido con su promesa previa de liberar a la nación de la esclavitud, y ahora podían centrar su atención en la poligamia --la otra "reliquia". La ley marcial del coronel Patrick Conner, que ocupara el *Fuerte Douglas* en Utah desde 1862 hasta noviembre de 1865, fue seguida por una serie de gobernadores y jueces que compartían la determinación de hacer que los matrimonios mormones armonizaran con la ley. Edward W. Tullidge nos dice en su libro *Vida de Brigham Young* que uno de esos jueces, James B. McKean, jefe de justicia de la corte territorial, dijo: "La misión a la que Dios me ha llamado para desarrollar en Utah, está con mucho sobre los deberes de otras cortes y jueces, así como los cielos son más altos que la tierra; y donde sea y cuando sea que yo llegue a encontrar las leyes locales o federales obstruyendo o interfiriendo, con la bendición de Dios las pisotearé bajo mis pies."[5]

McKean trató, pero los resultados no fueron satisfactorios desde el punto de vista de los republicanos. Gradualmente fortalecieron sus leyes, principalmente con la *Ley Edmunds* de 1882, que penalizaba severamente aun a aquellos que simplemente "creyeran" en la poligamia.[6] Así que la presión sobre las familias fue inmensa incluso antes de la aprobación de la *Ley Edmunds-Tucker* en 1887,[7] que echó por tierra la fundación temporal de la Iglesia, aboliendo cada institución importante de los Santos de los Últimos Días --desde el cuerpo gubernamental de la Iglesia hasta sus escuelas--, así como el derecho que las mujeres mormonas tenían de votar en elecciones territoriales o federales (una oportunidad que ellas habían gozado desde 1870, cuando una mujer de Utah realizó uno de los primeros votos femeninos en la historia de los Estados Unidos.)

El asunto fue tan desagradable que en 1884 la Iglesia envió una delegación de alto nivel al *territorio yaqui* de México para negociar tierras en Sonora, a fin de que en ellas se asentaran algunos de los miembros perseguidos. Parecía que los mexicanos no harían de la poligamia un tema tan escabroso como lo era en Estados Unidos --y así fue. Los apóstoles Brigham Young, hijo, y Heber J. Grant organizaron y acompañaron una expedición de 33 hombres provenientes de los asentamientos mormones de Saint Joseph y Salt River, en Arizona. Desde por lo menos 1881, Young y Grant habían tratado de contactar a los indios en el sur. Ahora era imperativo que lo intentaran de nuevo, pero esta vez más por buscar refugio que por hacer conversos.

Benjamín F. Johnson, quien acompañó a la expedición, informó que en esa ocasión, a diferencia de 1877, los indios recibieron a los mormones con interés y en algunos casos hasta con los brazos abiertos.[8] Ello fue una enorme sorpresa para los mexicanos, quienes les habían advertido que los violentos *yaquis* jamás permitirían que los mormones salieran con vida. En enero de 1885 el mismo presidente John Taylor, sus consejeros Joseph F. Smith y George Q. Cannon y algunos del Quórum de los Doce, viajaron a Arizona y despacharon un grupo explorador a Chihuahua. Entonces, junto con Joseph F. Smith, Erastus Snow, Moses Thatcher, Jesse N. Smith, Lot Smith, Melitón G.

Trejo y James H. Martineau, el presidente Taylor continuó hacia Sonora.[9] Al final, él y otras de las autoridades escogieron el valle de Casas Grandes, en Chihuahua, que había sido explorado y recomendado a Brigham Young por Daniel W. Jones y su compañía nueve años antes.

En cosa de días Jesse N. Smith había corrido la voz a los santos en Woodruff, Arizona: Todos los hombres que estuvieran escondidos para poder escapar a la persecución deberían ir a México, ya que un lugar había sido contratado para eso; y el propio presidente Taylor aconsejó a todos los polígamos que fueran a México lo más pronto posible.[10] Pocas semanas después --incluso antes de que las tierras hubieran sido aseguradas-- caravanas mormonas cruzaban la frontera. A mediados de mayo de 1885, cerca de 400 posibles colonizadores aguardaban en las orillas del Río Casas Grandes, deseando que las autoridades de la Iglesia pudieran pronto adquirir tierras.

Pero hubo muchos problemas --algunos previstos nueve años antes por el gobernador de Chihuahua, quien había dicho a los mormones que se cuidaran mucho de los títulos fraudulentos y las tierras inservibles. Los apóstoles Moses Thatcher, Erastus Snow, Brigham Young, hijo, Francis M. Lyman y George Teasdale trabajaron denodadamente a fin de asegurar propiedades para los exiliados. A finales de junio de 1885 el líder del campamento, Teasdale, estaba constantemente animando a la gente y pidiéndoles que no regresaran a sus hogares. Trabajó lleno de esperanza e incansablemente para obtener un lugar, ideando las más inimaginables argucias para disminuir la tensión. Pero pasaron meses antes de que el apóstol Teasdale tuviera éxito. Joseph Fish, uno de los colonos, da una imagen de la situación:

> *"El tiempo escurría pesadamente en mis manos. Es cierto que yo trataba de estudiar algo de español, pero tenía poco corazón para ello dadas las circunstancias. Estábamos acampados en la pradera abierta, expuestos a las tormentas y los quemantes rayos del sol, sin siquiera poder obtener un tronco verde para que sirviera como enramada, ya que sólo había unos cuantos y no se nos permitía tomar ninguno pues pertenecían a los mexicanos. En esas circunstancias, me sentía bastante*

*decepcionado por nuestro intento de colonizar.
Nada estaba haciendo por mi familia que se
encontraba en casa, y gastaba cada centavo
que había traído conmigo. Nos hallábamos
medio alimentados y a medio vestir, y se
sumaba a nuestra ansiedad la idea de que el
obtener un lugar estaba aparentemente más
distante que el día en que llegamos ahí.*"[11]

Los meses pasaron sin que recibieran tierras en
donde sembrar y sin ingresos, con las cajas de sus carretas
sirviendo como hogares. Eventualmente la mayoría de los
colonizadores gastó su efectivo y se vieron reducidos
después a la más abyecta pobreza, usando muchos de ellos
como zapatos unas sandalias de cuero amarradas a los pies.
Las enfermedades y los violentos temporales azotaban el
campamento de vez en cuando, compensados únicamente
cuando se le recordaba a la gente el objetivo superior por el
que estaban sacrificándose. Sin embargo, "así como las
estaciones venían y maduraban, la esperanza se transformó
en resentimiento y la fe en desánimo."[12]

No obstante, semana tras semana los colonos
indefectiblemente seguían llegando, mientras las frustrantes
negociaciones continuaban. La segunda familia de Miles P.
Romney es un ejemplo típico. Se arriesgaron a viajar de
Arizona a Chihuahua a través del territorio indio controlado
en su mayoría por el apache Gerónimo, pero pudieron traer
pocos valores para ayudar a Romney en el campamento. Él
les había preparado una empalizada de estuco, con techo de
lodo y pisos de tierra dentro de la cual pusieron sus
pertenencias: una mesa hecha con dos cajas amarradas, una
cama dura y troncos redondos como sillas. Pero Hanna, la
segunda esposa de Romney, dijo: "Yo estaba agradecida por
ello, mis queridos niños y yo estaríamos con su padre y
podríamos vivir en paz, sin comisarios que nos molestaran o
separaran otra vez."[13]

Para Eunice Stewart Harris los vínculos familiares eran
igualmente fuertes.

*"Parecía que únicamente había para nosotros
dos caminos entre los cuales escoger y estar
seguros. Uno era ir hacia México, donde toda la
familia podía estar pero donde la perspectiva
financiera no era muy buena; o ir a Canadá,*

donde un hombre podía ir (pero con sólo una esposa) y vivir en paz el principio por el cual habían entrado juntos en tan gran sacrificio. Decidimos que (mi esposo) Dennison, Annie (su segunda esposa) y Emer (el hijo de dos años de Annie) deberían ir a México de inmediato, y que yo regresaría a mi hogar en Payson, Utah, sin decir nada sobre dónde había estado hasta que ellos se hallaran a salvo fuera del país."[14]

En su oportunidad, Eunice y sus hijos se reunieron con los demás en México; y años más tarde los mormones angloamericanos --muchos de ellos no polígamos-- serían atraídos al país por las noticias de prosperidad y oportunidades prácticamente ilimitadas que había en él. Sin embargo, en 1885 había un punto de presión: escapar de los comisarios federales estadounidenses y de esa forma preservar la vida familiar. De haber sido necesario, algunos de los miembros polígamos habrían dado la vida para preservar a sus familias.

En tanto que localmente las autoridades mexicanas se mostraban escépticas y desconfiaban de las intenciones mormonas, sin cooperar con el influjo de los angloamericanos y deteniendo sus carretas en la frontera --con las interminables demoras correspondientes--, el gobierno federal les extendía toda la ayuda y protección razonables, congruente con su política de colonizar tierras deshabitadas y apoyar la inmigración de extranjeros capaces. El gobierno mexicano llegó incluso a revocar una orden de expulsión del entonces gobernador de Chihuahua. En lo particular, el presidente Porfirio Díaz simpatizaba con los mormones, en parte porque quizá consideraba que ellos probaban que su política de colonización era buena para la economía mexicana.

Finalmente, en el otoño de 1885 los líderes mormones aseguraron tierras cerca de donde actualmente se encuentra la Colonia Juárez --aunque el sitio fue abandonado más tarde por un conflicto territorial con un rancho adyacente. Tanto la Iglesia como diversos miembros adquirieron tierras adicionales. Temporalmente a salvo de los comisarios estadounidenses y protegidos por políticos locales y el gobierno federal en la ciudad de México, los Santos de los Últimos Días se recuperaron de su más reciente éxodo y una vez más empezaron a echar raíces. Para el año de 1912 los mormones habían ubicado más de cuatro mil personas en nueve colonias mexicanas: siete en el estado de Chihuahua y dos en Sonora.

Estaban las que se encontraban en la meseta, como *Colonia Juárez* (llamada así en honor al presidente Benito Juárez); *Colonia Díaz* (por Porfirio Díaz) y *Colonia Dublán;* las colonias montañesas de *Valle Cave, Pacheco* y *García* (por el ministro de Díaz que fue tan amistoso con Moses Thatcher, y por otro ministro que también ayudó), y finalmente la *Colonia Chuichupa* --todas ellas en el estado de Chihuahua. Y en Sonora estaban las colonias semitropicales de *Oaxaca* y *Morelos.*[L]

Aun cuando las colonias tenían nexos sociales --lo que en algunos casos llegaba al aspecto económico--y no se encontraban muy retiradas entre sí, el viajar de una a otra resultaba usualmente difícil debido a los pobres caminos y el terreno escabroso. Las colonias montañesas se encontraban particularmente aisladas. No obstante, pocos años después de haber sido fundadas se integraron económicamente, intercambiando los bienes, productos y mercancías que cada una producía mejor.[15] Con la irrigación (algunos de los proyectos seguían un canal antiguo), la agricultura y las industrias afines, las colonias de Juárez y Dublán florecieron en las planicies. Las montañesas del Valle Cave, Pacheco, García y Chuichupa estaban situadas todas en zonas donde abundaban pinos y cedros; a su vez, las praderas montañosas eran excelentes para pastar ganado, lo que hizo que rápidamente las industrias maderera y ganadera existieran una al lado de la otra. Por último, las colonias semitropicales de Oaxaca y Morelos --situadas en el *Río Bavispe*, afluente del *Yaqui* que se vacía en el Océano Pacífico ofrecieron una valiosa producción.

La auto-selección de algunas de las familias más capaces de la Iglesia para tomar parte en este esfuerzo de colonización, virtualmente aseguró que las comunidades estuvieran bien organizadas, llenas de propósito y solidez. De hecho, entre 1885 y 1895 seis de los doce apóstoles de la Iglesia vivieron en ellas --la mayoría en Colonia Juárez. Habiendo salido de Estados Unidos debido a su estilo de vida, los colonos deseaban una sola cosa: preservar esa manera de vivir. Y contaban con los líderes y la habilidad práctica para hacerlo.

Surgió entre ellos, sin embargo, una inclinación natural para permanecer 'aislados' social y políticamente de México --aunque no en lo económico. Cierto, existía el interés de convertir a los lamanitas, pero en los dos años iniciales de esas primeras colonias hubo también otros asuntos más urgentes: permanecer con vida; construir casas, iglesias y escuelas, así como una economía, y solidificar las comunidades mormonas para que sus niños pudieran tomar su lugar en el Reino. Sin que fuera sorpresa, en las generaciones subsecuentes las colonias produjeron una asombrosa cantidad de líderes que se alzaron para convertirse en Autoridades Generales de la Iglesia.

CALMA EN EL OJO DE LA TORMENTA

Los Santos de los Últimos Días de origen angloamericano habían escapado de la furia de los comisarios estadounidenses, y no sintieron las amenazas de la Revolución Mexicana sino hasta mucho después. En ese ambiente calmado pusieron los cimientos de algo que más tarde se utilizaría para expandir la Iglesia en toda la América Latina, principalmente mediante la educación de varias generaciones de niños con principios mormones y el idioma y la cultura de esos países. En sus primeros años, sin embargo, los colonos pueden no haber visto esa preparación como tal, ya que de 1887 a 1901 sus esfuerzos hicieron a un lado la obra misional y se dedicaron a fundar un bastión cultural y económico estadounidense en el norte de México.

La vida en las llanuras tenía sus sinsabores, con una sequía en 1890-91 y epidemias asesinas de viruela y difteria en ese mismo invierno. Tales problemas, combinados con su aislamiento y las noticias de que la persecución en Utah había disminuido una vez que los mormones hicieron las paces con el gobierno en 1890 --renunciando a la práctica de la poligamia--, hicieron que naciera en muchos colonos el deseo de regresar a Estados Unidos. En 1893 Moses Thatcher les suplicaba que permanecieran, prometiéndoles bendiciones si lo hacían. La mayoría siguió su consejo.

Sí, recibieron incontables recompensas, especialmente con respecto a la vida familiar. Los mormones veían a la familia no sólo como una necesidad --conveniente y práctica-- sino también como una institución intrínsecamente sagrada: un elemento esencial en su percepción del plan divino. A las familias se les consideraba como potencialmente eternas; no obstante, la única manera de asegurar su permanencia era entrar conjuntamente en ciertas ordenanzas y convenios tales como el matrimonio en el templo, y luego llevar una vida familiar apropiada. Muchos padres, por tanto, luchaban incansablemente para mantener la suya unida e intacta.

Ciertas familias polígamas llegaron a separarse --una esposa permanecía en México con sus hijos y la otra regresando a los Estados Unidos u ocasionalmente a Canadá. Pero generalmente existía un esfuerzo enorme para que permanecieran intactas en México, a fin de cuidar a los hijos y asegurar un adecuado ambiente cultural, educativo y económico.

Algunos hombres habían huido solos a México para preparar el camino a sus familias; otros --varios polígamos-- habían llegado con solo una familia, en tanto que otros más arribaron con varias. Con el paso del tiempo se fueron dando cada vez más matrimonios monógamos. Todos: hombres, mujeres y niños (polígamos o monógamos) tenían que construir casas, establecer sistemas de riego, planificar poblaciones, organizar y asistir a las escuelas, construir iglesias, ver por los asuntos espirituales y cuidar por los enfermos y necesitados. Debían sembrar, cultivar y almacenar las cosechas; establecer comercio con los mexicanos; construir molinos, tenerías, fábricas de víveres, talabarterías, herrerías, tiendas de abarrotes, escuelas e iglesias. La comunidad era todo para todos. Sin ella no podrían sobrevivir; con ella, tanto ellos como sus familias podrían lograrlo.

Sus habilidades técnicas y buen nivel escolar fueron para los colonos una gran ayuda. Entre los que huyeron para México se encontraban competentes agricultores, hombres de negocios, maestros y practicantes de medicina; había también eruditos aficionados, poetas y músicos. El citado Miles P. Romney, por ejemplo, sabía de memoria varias tragedias de Shakespeare, había estudiado a fondo y en detalle las campañas militares de Napoleón Bonaparte y Alejandro Magno, y se le reconocía como investigador histórico. En los 54 primeros días de su llegada a Colonia Juárez, los colonos construyeron una empalizada que sirvió como escuela en la que Annie, la esposa de Romney, enseñó. Antes de que terminara la construcción, diariamente ella llevaba a los niños a su casucha para darles unas cuantas horas de instrucción.

Muchos de los colonos ya eran experimentados y competentes líderes de la Iglesia. En el primer grupo que llegó de uno de los poblados de Arizona en 1885, compuesto por 33 hombres y sus familias, había siete *obispos* --líderes de una congregación individual--, otros que antes lo habían sido, y muchos más prominentes líderes regionales de la Iglesia.[16]

Para el año de 1892 los colonos de Juárez habían construido una fábrica enlatadora para sus abundantes cosechas de fruta y tomates. Un año más tarde esa misma fábrica, dirigida por el enérgico hombre de negocios Joseph C. Bently --que más tarde destacaría en la historia de esas comunidades--, produjo diez mil latas de fruta. A finales del siglo XIX las colonias participaban ya en las ferias de la ciudad de México, lo que agradó bastante al presidente Porfirio Díaz. Ciertamente él pensaba que en la actividad de los mormones tenía la suficiente evidencia para acallar a sus críticos: ¿que más podía desear el país que gente próspera y productiva?

Charles W. Kindrich, del Departamento de Estado norteamericano, informó en 1899: "Para acceder a Colonia Juárez es necesario cruzar las estribaciones de las montañas de la Sierra Madre. El camino pasa por desfiladeros y barrancos hasta que la colonia, colocada como un verde jardín en las llanuras, se divisa de repente". Ahí, según sus palabras,

> "*los jardines tienen fragancia de flores, y los árboles de duraznos, chabacanos y ciruelas florecen al aire puro. Agua clara de la acequia que corre a lo largo de las lomas fluye hacia la cuneta de cada bocacalle. Residencias de ladrillos en red reposan entre viñedos y perales... Las verdes líneas de la alfalfa, abajo, contrastan grandemente con el café de la cima que las sombrea. De este valle, los mormones han extraído en diez años riqueza suficiente para ser independientes... La colonia principal es una hermosa villa comparable a cualquiera en Nueva Inglaterra. Existe total evidencia de frugalidad, limpieza, industriosidad, comodidad y buena administración. Hay una ausencia de*

los vicios comunes a las comunidades modernas. No hay cantinas, tabaquerías, cárceles ni casas de mala fama en la colonia... Existe un molino, una fábrica de muebles y otras industrias en Colonia Juárez. Hay una academia con cinco maestros y 400 alumnos. Es política de los mormones edificar casas de enseñanza antes que iglesias y templos".[17]

Durante los primeros veinticinco años, todas las colonias con frecuencia recibieron nuevos residentes. Hasta 1890 nuevas familias que huían de las severas persecuciones llegaron diariamente provenientes de Estados Unidos. Pero después de esa fecha, con la cuestión sobre poligamia resuelta y las colonias evidentemente prosperando, la gente continuó llegando, mas ahora por razones económicas. El agente de tierras para la Iglesia, la *Compañía Mexicana de Colonización y Agricultura,* empezó a cambiar sus acuerdos con los colonos mormones --de sus conceptos comunales y comunitarios, a empresas de capitalismo privado. La primera estaca de la Iglesia (unidad que agrupa a varios *'barrios'* o congregaciones) en territorio mexicano, fue organizada en 1895, con la Colonia Juárez como su centro; se edificaron nuevas escuelas y se construyó una academia, principalmente con medios económicos y organizativos de los propios colonos.

Esos primeros años vieron sólo dos desviaciones del patrón de desarrollo económico y aislamiento cultural que los santos angloamericanos se habían trazado en México para sí mismos. Dadas las circunstancias, quizá ambas estaban destinadas a fracasar desde el principio. Una concernía a los mormones que se encontraban cerca de la ciudad de México, quienes habían elegido permanecer ahí en espera de una oportunidad más favorable para colonizar en el norte del país, cerca del resto de los miembros de la Iglesia. La otra involucraba a *Wovoka, Toro Sentado, Shivitts* y demás nuevos profetas indios que hablaban otra vez de nuevas y espectaculares manifestaciones celestiales entre varias tribus indígenas. Para los mormones esa era una señal que significaba volcar nuevamente sus esfuerzos en favor de los lamanitas, sin importar la oposición que hubieran de enfrentar.

El esfuerzo de colonización y el renovado trabajo con los indígenas eran enteramente consecuentes con los propósitos a largo plazo que la 'Iglesia Mormona' tenía para México y Latinoamérica. Así, tan pronto como los colonizadores del norte de México tuvieron a sus familias mínimamente seguras, comenzaron una vez más a perseguir sus objetivos mayores.

COLONIZACIÓN EN EL NORTE

En 1887, viviendo aún en tiendas y otros en cuevas labradas a orillas del río *Piedras Verdes,* los miembros de la Iglesia estadounidenses comenzaron a colonizar a los mormones mexicanos. Casi todos estaban convencidos de que estos miembros necesitaban también un 'recogimiento'. Puesto que el gobierno mexicano tenía muchos deseos de que sus propios ciudadanos colonizaran el norte del país -- requiriendo que todas las compañías colonizadoras apartaran tierras para ellos, aunque sin insistir que dichas compañías les facilitaran poblarlas--, el tiempo era propicio para unir el aspecto económico y la escatología mormona. El gobierno mexicano facilitaría la adquisición de tierras adicionales por parte de la *Compañía Mexicana de Colonización y Agricultura* para los mormones norteamericanos, y pagaría algunos de los gastos de reubicación de los mormones mexicanos. Los colonos ya establecidos proporcionarían ayuda logística y de organización.

Helaman Pratt, presidente de misión en el centro de México (1884-87) lo expresó mejor: "Tierras, agua, pastos y madera suficiente han sido adquiridos para sustentar a centenares del pueblo de Dios y ser un lugar de reunión a los santos nativos, con el fin de que puedan llegar a ser libres mediante los principios del evangelio sempiterno --uno de los cuales es el del recogimiento." Pratt también pudo ver los problemas potenciales.

> "*Lo más difícil de mi labor misional se encuentra todavía en el futuro --que es cuidar y velar por los santos nativos después de que sean reunidos. Las maneras y costumbres de las dos razas son muy diferentes, y por los malentendidos que naturalmente surgirán se requerirá constante cuidado y prudencia para evitar confrontaciones. Pero espero lograr el éxito con las bendiciones de Dios y la paciente*

asistencia de nuestros hermanos y hermanas, porque esta es una misión desarrollándose sobre todos, viejos y jóvenes, hombres y mujeres; y Dios, en mi opinión, ha traído aquí a algunos de nuestros mejores santos para que puedan asistir en la redención de Su pueblo caído."[18]

Los oficiales del gobierno mexicano parecían estar complacidos sobre todo este asunto. El viceministro de Colonización, Fernández Leal, prometió visitar la nueva colonia. Comentarios favorables concerniente al establecimiento de las colonias aparecieron en la prensa de la ciudad de México en español, francés e inglés. El diario *Dos Repúblicas* publicó algo al respecto, dando un cambio radical a la posición anti-mormona que había tenido anteriormente.[19] Conforme se mandaban invitaciones a los miembros de la Iglesia locales, se hacían arreglos a pesar de otras situaciones complejas que existían. Las colonias que los mormones compraron para los miembros mexicanos cubrían un área adicional de doce mil acres cultivables, pero que también contaban con pastos, combustible y madera para acomodar a setenta y cinco familias. Concluyeron también arreglos pendientes por algunos años, para escriturar cincuenta mil acres cerca de Asunción. Al mismo tiempo, tenían otros asuntos por atender: estaban terminando de formalizar la organización de lo que sería el pueblo en Colonia Juárez; intentaban obtener una franquicia para colonizar los terrenos que habían adquirido en Corrales; buscaban permiso para abrir y construir una carretera de cuota entre Juárez y Corrales, que de ahí fuera a Sonora, y formalizaban la petición para que el servicio postal se extendiera a los poblados mormones --lo que requería que ellos mismos crearan y equiparan oficinas postales. Aparte de esas actividades, estaban esperando la llegada del primer grupo de colonos mormones mexicanos.

"El primer recogimiento de santos nativos procedentes de la ciudad de México se espera aquí a mediados de mayo", dijo el corresponsal del diario *Herald* de Salt Lake City en un reportaje publicado el 24 de abril de 1887. Llegarían por ferrocarril a la estación de San José (con el pasaje pagado por el gobierno federal mexicano). Sus hermanos de fe los recibirían y transportarían por carretas y calesas al lugar de recogimiento de los santos.

No fue un esfuerzo de colonización exitoso. Henry Eyring registró en su diario: "Una compañía de nuestros hermanos y hermanas mexicanos llegaron en mayo del interior de México. Después de permanecer un corto tiempo, la mayor parte regresaron insatisfechos."[20] El registro no indica cuántos llegaron ni qué recursos o expectativas traían consigo. ¿Nacieron hijos en el camino? ¿Viajaron familias completas? ¿Eran jóvenes o viejos, con o sin oficio? ¿Qué sacrificios o privaciones experimentaron? Todo esto se desconoce.

Varios golpes duros esperaban a los santos mexicanos en la Colonia Juárez. Por un lado, y sin importar cuál hubiera sido su situación de vivienda en el centro del país, en el norte las condiciones eran todavía más severas. En 1887 los mormones angloamericanos seguían luchando para mejorar su nueva existencia en esa tierra semi-árida. Sus poblados eran nuevos y aún no prosperaban. Los primeros miembros de la Iglesia llegados de Estados Unidos se ubicaron en tierras que --más tarde se descubrió-- formaban parte de una hacienda, y se vieron en la necesidad de volver a establecerse en un cañón angosto y rocoso. En ese sitio (hoy Colonia Juárez) los santos mexicanos podían ver a muchos de sus hermanos y hermanas estadounidenses viviendo en tiendas de campaña o cuevas excavadas en las orillas del río Piedras Verdes. Una situación similar les esperaba hasta que lograran establecerse. No era un jardín de Edén a donde los santos mexicanos llegaban.

Tampoco podían confiar en adquirir tierras. Los ideales de algunos eran comunitarios, y muchos de ellos habían practicado la costumbre ejidataria que era común entre las comunidades indígenas: tierras comunes poseídas en fideicomiso para beneficio del todo el pueblo. Pero mientras vivieran entre los mormones angloamericanos, ¿quienes tomarían las decisiones con respecto a la propiedad en común? Su *Compañía Mexicana de Colonización y Agricultura* había sido formada bajo las leyes del estado de Colorado, en Estados Unidos, pero operaba en esos días de acuerdo con la teoría de mayordomía sobre bienes raíces que practicaban los Santos de los Últimos Días --lo que involucraba la compra de tierras con fondos de la compañía. Entonces se rentaban parcelas a miembros de buena conducta, a quienes se les permitía ocuparlas y aprovecharlas mientras estuvieran de acuerdo en hacerlo apropiadamente, pero para 1887 los inmigrantes que habían llegado dos años antes ya se habían adueñado de las mejores. Los miembros mexicanos sin duda se preguntaban dónde y cuándo encontrarían seguridad y prosperidad en las nuevas tierras.

Para los santos mexicanos había otro problema de igual magnitud que el de los terrenos: la preocupación que había tenido Helaman Pratt, es decir, la diferencia étnica entre los dos grupos de mormones. Diferentes costumbres, lenguaje, aspiraciones, placeres y gozos, todas evidentes y en realidad naturales. Pero también había un elemento limitante: los estadounidenses eran algo altaneros. Por largo tiempo habían estado convencidos que tenían que hacer prosélitos entre los nativos a través de colonización. Eso por sí sólo puede no haber sido muy ofensivo --muchos miembros mexicanos sentían la misma necesidad de colonizar--, pero el asunto se hizo tan severo que se concluyó que el nativo mexicano era necesario para validar las concesiones de terrenos. Algunos de estos sentimientos ofensivos no intencionales de parte de los miembros estadounidenses han llegado a nuestro conocimiento casi intactos por medio de una nieta de Henry Eyring, quien sentía que la mayoría de los que se habían unido a la Iglesia hasta 1887 eran pobres porque estaban, "en cierta forma, viviendo no de acuerdo con la idea mormona de industria y frugalidad". Así que fueron traídos a Juárez,

> *"pero en vez de imitar las costumbres de sus hermanos blancos querían que se les diera de comer sin trabajar para obtener el alimento. La gran mayoría de esa gente se retiraron de la Iglesia y regresaron a sus casas y anteriores maneras de vivir. Esta gente contó fábulas exageradas de la aflicción, desilusión y el poco progreso que se pudo realizar entre los miembros de la* Misión Mexicana. *Casi todos ellos provenientes del centro de México, creyeron las acusaciones falsas sobre nuestra colonia, y esto resultó en un sentimiento algo amargo... Nuevos conversos no se podían considerar. La misión de mi abuelo (1887-88), cuando era presidente de Misión en la ciudad de México, no fue satisfactoria si se ve desde el punto de vista de conversiones".*[21]

Incluso Rey L. Pratt --un presidente de Misión estimado por los miembros, que sirvió de 1907 a 1931-- puede haber sido tomado como un poco altanero mientras trataba de dar más luz a los santos mexicanos.

"Puede ser que, para algunos, ellos no estaban bien convertidos, así que pronto dieron la espalda a Sión y sus caras voltearon a los viejos hogares; pero cuando uno llega a conocer todas las condiciones, no parece ser tan extraño. Eran gente que fueron sacados algunos de un clima tropical, y otros del incomparable clima primaveral del valle de México. En sus hogares nativos eran pobres, eso es verdad, pero por unos cuantos centavos podían comprar en los mercados diariamente lo que necesitaban para el día. También tenían sus hogares en los que podían vivir, en ciertos casos hechos únicamente de palos de caña u hojarascas de maíz con techos de paja, pero eran los sitios donde habían nacido y en los que sus padres habían vivido antes --y no tenían ningún concepto de cómo empezar a construir otro. Tal cosa como almacenar para el invierno nunca había cruzado sus mentes. Solo imagínense a tal gente siendo puesta en un lugar como Colonia Juárez en sus primeros días (y eso a medio invierno), donde no había casas ni zanjas ni cercos, y sobre todo sin 'plaza' ni una tienda donde poder comprar --y entonces ve si no puedes imaginarte cómo es que se desanimaron."[22]

Además del choque ambiental y las relaciones preocupantes, existía otro problema: los miembros de México no tenían que preocuparse por la persecución, como los estadounidenses. Los mexicanos podían regresar a sus hogares --tal vez a recibir una crítica social, pero sin duda a casa. Los angloamericanos sólo podían regresar a Estados Unidos con amenaza de encarcelamiento o pérdida de su vida familiar. Dado el importante sentimiento sobre este punto, su motivación para permanecer era obviamente mayor que la de los mexicanos.

En pocos meses los miembros mexicanos empezaron a regresar a sus casas, muchos de ellos haciendo la jornada de tres meses a pie. Unas cuantas familias permanecieron en Colonia Juárez por cuatro o cinco años, pero eventualmente todos, excepto dos o tres personas, regresaron al centro de México.[23]

Con todo, la idea de predicar a través de la colonización continuó. Pocos olvidarían la declaración de Brigham Young al Quórum de los Doce cuando por primera vez consideró poblar el 'lejano sur' (Arizona): "Formaremos una cadena de poblaciones que conduzcan hasta América del Sur, pero este será el primer paso."[24] Así que en 1904 los mormones intentaron colonizar Guatemala.[25] Y el presidente de la Misión Mexicana, H.S. Harris, viajó a Sudamérica en 1906 en busca de nuevas tierras para colonizar.[26]

PROSELITISMO ENTRE LOS LAMANITAS

La segunda mayor desviación del patrón de colonización de los mormones angloamericanos también sucedió en 1887. En noviembre de ese año las autoridades de la Iglesia le pidieron a Charles Edmund Richardson, residente de Colonia Díaz, y a tres miembros más --Ammon M. Tenney, Peter J. Christopherson y Gilbert D. Greer-- que hicieran otro intento entre los indios de Sonora. Parte de su llamado era también trabajar con los indígenas de Arizona si la oportunidad lo permitía. Había un gran fervor religioso entre los indios del oeste americano y el nuevo presidente de la Iglesia, Wilford Woodruff, se sintió inspirado a darle otra oportunidad a México.

La decisión de Woodruff, quien sucedió al presidente Taylor, puede ser mejor entendida en contexto. Los indígenas habían estado reportando continuamente al centro de información mormona sobre visitaciones celestiales que un indio llamado *Moroni* y otros jefes indios también habían recibido. La Iglesia no sólo mandó emisarios, sino que delegaciones de las tribus que habitaban las *Grandes Planicies* y las *Montañas Rocallosas* visitaron a los mormones.

Animados por el despertar espiritual de los lamanitas, los líderes de la Iglesia intensificaron sus esfuerzos para hacerles llegar el 'Evangelio Mormón', incrementando la cantidad de misioneros enviados entre los indios y aun asignando apóstoles para guiar y participar en la obra.[27] Los mormones les enseñaron la agricultura a los lamanitas de

Malad, Thistle, Ruby y *Grass Valley* en el estado de Idaho, y en *Deep Creek,* Nevada. Establecieron campos modelo de agricultura adjuntos a las reservas indias de *Wind River,* el *Fuerte Hall* y *Umatilla,* así como ramas de la Iglesia entre los indios, y mandaron publicaciones animando a los mormones angloamericanos a que reflexionaran sobre la importancia de las manifestaciones a los lamanitas, sus visiones y bautismos. Finalmente, los mormones trataron de preparar a sus hermanos lamanitas para su llamado profético de construir un templo en la 'Nueva Jerusalén', llevándolos y mostrándoles los templos en Utah --donde recibieron sus santas investiduras. Miles se unieron a la Iglesia.

Incrementando su labor entre los lamanitas, muchos de los mormones creyeron plenamente que estaban trabajando mano a mano con tres antiguos profetas del Libro de Mormón. La identificación y el significado se puede explicar mejor por el influyente teólogo y apóstol Orson Pratt:

> *"El Señor hizo una promesa a estos tres (nefitas) de que ellos deberían administrar como santos mensajeros en los últimos días, para y en beneficio del resto de la casa de Israel, la cual caería en una condición baja y degradada como consecuencia de la gran maldad y apostasía de sus antiguos padres; que ellos serían instrumento en Sus manos para traer a este resto al conocimiento de la verdad. Hemos escuchado que estos mensajeros han venido, no en una sola ocasión, sino en muchas. Hasta la fecha hemos escuchado que más de mil cuatrocientos indios --en el sur de Utah y el norte de Arizona, y no sé, pero aún hay más-- que han sido bautizados. Pregúntenles por qué han viajado tantos cientos de kilómetros para buscar a los élderes de la Iglesia, y ellos contestarán: 'Tal persona vino a nosotros, habló en nuestro lenguaje, nos instruyó y nos dijo qué era lo que debíamos hacer, y hemos venido para así cumplir con sus requisitos'."[28]*

Era tan evidente el intercambio, que los estadounidenses condenaron a los mormones por iniciar un 'movimiento mesiánico' entre los indios. Sólo unas semanas antes de que sucediera la infame masacre de los indios de *Wounded Knee* por el ejército americano, el general Nelson A. Miles dijo: "Es mi creencia que los mormones son la fuerza principal en todo esto (la moda de la *'Danza del Fantasma'*). Esto llegará --ojalá no-- a ser el inicio de grandes conflictos, porque cuando una raza de gente ignorante llega al fanatismo religioso, es en verdad difícil saber lo que son capaces de hacer".[29]

A pesar de los fracasos en colonizar, las persecuciones y la *Ley Edmund,* la Iglesia simplemente no estaba lista para abandonar su trabajo entre los indios. En enero de 1888 Ammon Tenney, el líder del nuevo grupo misionero, llegó con sus compañeros al valle del *Río Salado,* que había sido colonizado primeramente por el grupo de Jones en 1877. Buscaron a Encarnación Valenzuela, uno de los primeros miembros indios, y lo volvieron a bautizar con el fin de que renovara sus convenios.[30] Él, junto con su hermano de la tribu de los *cherokee,* fue comisionado para trabajar en la misión india de Sonora, actuando ambos como misioneros e intérpretes cuando menos durante el tiempo que el grupo permaneció entre los indios *pimas.*

El grupo se dirigió hacia el sur, predicando a los lamanitas y atestiguando varios acontecimientos milagrosos durante su jornada. Bautizaron a sus conversos en excavaciones hechas por ellos en el desierto y llenadas con agua de noria. Cuando llegaron a México, predicaron y bautizaron entre los indios *pápagos.* En su totalidad, hasta este punto, ellos habían agregado más de 270 lamanitas a la Iglesia.

No obstante, el presidente Woodruff estaba preocupado, pues para él no era suficiente el compromiso de predicar a los indios y bautizarlos. La Iglesia tenía que organizarse entre ellos, y esto no era posible a menos que pudieran ser recogidos en una comunidad de santos. Su carta a Tenney, escrita en la primavera de 1888, atestigua este punto. La citamos en su totalidad porque toca numerosos puntos de importancia para los mormones de entonces.

> *"Estimados hermanos:*
> *El propósito de su misión entre los lamanitas y*
> *la recomendación que han hecho concerniente*
> *al mejoramiento de las condiciones temporales*

237

de ellos ha sido considerada muy cuidadosamente por el Consejo de los Apóstoles. Estamos deseosos de hacer todo lo que esté a nuestro alcance para rescatar de su bajo estado actual a estos degradados descendientes de la Casa de Israel, e impartirles el conocimiento correcto de los principios del evangelio y las artes de una verdadera civilización, lo cual los restaurará a la gracia del Señor y cumplirá los convenios que Él ha hecho con ellos. Parece ser que rápidamente llegará el tiempo cuando el evangelio será quitado de entre los gentiles y dado a la Casa de Israel. Su éxito reciente en bautizar a esta gente nos da gran gozo y nos regocijamos al ver las perspectivas que se están abriendo. Pero como ya se les ha dicho a ustedes en otras ocasiones, esta obra tiene que ser seguida por un esfuerzo sistemático y una organización completa, además de obras continuas de hombres experimentados entre ellos. No podemos, en justicia hacia ellos y hacia las responsabilidades que tenemos sobre nosotros mismos, dejarlos en la misma condición en que los encontraron. El bautismo, en sí, es bueno y de la mayor importancia, pero en su caso se requiere más que esto para librarnos de las responsabilidades bajo las cuales responderemos ante nuestro Dios por lo que se refiere a esta gente. Ellos tienen que ser restituidos. En vista de todas estas consideraciones, el Consejo de los Apóstoles ha decidido que ustedes, quienes laboran entre los indios papagos en Arizona, sean instruidos a seleccionar un sitio adecuado para el recogimiento de los conversos lamanitas -- donde se pueda almacenar agua en canteras próximas a un sitio o sitios con tierra cultivable--, y que sean destinados 1,000 dólares de los diezmos de las estacas de Maricopa y de St. Joseph para ser distribuidos bajo la dirección de la Presidencia de la estaca de Maricopa y el hermano A.M. Tenney. Una orden de pago, indicando esta cantidad, se ha *enviado hoy junto con una carta dirigida al presidente Robson y sus consejeros. También se decidió sugerir que cuatro hombres jóvenes y capaces sean seleccionados por las presidencias de las estacas de Maricopa y St. Joseph, para que trabajen con el hermano Tenney y los hermanos asignados entre los pápagos. Estos hermanos deben prepararse aprendiendo el lenguaje de los pimas para trabajar como misioneros entre esa gente. Con el fin de que puedan lograr este objetivo, se les proporcionará ayuda financiera pero no será mayor de 250 dólares por año para cada uno -- dichos fondos serán tomados de los diezmos de estas dos estacas. Confiamos en que a estas instrucciones se les dé la atención que rinda los mejores resultados. Sentimos que es de extrema importancia que aquellos que son llamados deban aprender el idioma de aquellos a quienes van a enseñar. Ya se han dado cuenta del inconveniente de comunicar sus ideas a la gente a través de intérprete. No pueden esperarse resultados de carácter satisfactorio de hombres que están limitados por la falta de conocimiento del lenguaje de la gente a la cual han sido enviados para enseñar. Confiamos que el Espíritu del Señor descansará sobre algunos de nuestros hombres jóvenes, y que ellos lograrán dedicarse enérgicamente a familiarizarse con este importante lenguaje. En su caso, ustedes entienden el español y pensamos que no es apropiado requerirles que dediquen tiempo para aprender este idioma, ya que sin duda habrá, en corto tiempo, un campo abundante para el ejercicio de sus habilidades entre la gente de habla española. Por el momento, pensamos que es mejor que continúen sus labores entre esta gente, ya que la puerta se abrirá hasta que puedan ser cuidados por sí mismos o alguien más tome sus lugares para ustedes ir a otro. Confiando en que estas acciones que hemos tomado las encuentren aceptables a sus esperanzas y buenos deseos, y en que los resultados sean todo lo que podamos desear, y orando para que el Señor los bendiga en sus empeños y los preserve de todo mal, permanezco*

su hermano
W. Woodruff"
Gilbert D. Greer,
registrador [31]

Para poder mantener estos asuntos en perspectiva, se puede reflexionar en el hecho de que en 1888 un buen carpintero ganaba un dólar por día; así que mil dólares equivalían a la misma cantidad de días-hombre de labor especializada --o tal vez el equivalente de 80 mil ó 100 mil dólares actuales--, y todo esto de los diezmos de dos estacas (ocho a diez congregaciones mormonas),[32] aun cuando la actividad de la Iglesia vivía tiempos difíciles. En enero de 1889, en vísperas del *'Manifiesto'* por el que los mormones renunciaban a la práctica de poligamia, el presidente Woodruff relevó a Tenney de su misión y le aconsejó no regresar a su hogar en St. John, Arizona, sino que se uniera a los santos en las colonias de Chihuahua. La colonización y misión para los lamanitas se había desplomado tanto en el norte como en el sur de México, otra víctima de las frustradas relaciones Iglesia-Estado en el Territorio de Utah.

Todos los mormones en México sintieron el impacto de esos fracasos. Por ejemplo, cuando los mormones mexicanos habían hecho el intento de colonizar en el norte del país y regresaron a sus hogares en el centro de México, la mayoría se encontraron muy desilusionados --incluso resentidos-- por lo que habían experimentado allá. Poco después, el éxito misional en el centro disminuyó drásticamente. Los misioneros atribuyeron esto a los santos de Colonia Juárez. Al recordar el fracaso anterior con el grupo de Rhodakanaty, su opinión del grado de preparación de los mexicanos para recibir el mormonismo llegó a un nivel muy bajo.

Pero existían otros factores desalentadores en el centro de México. Por un lado, como consecuencia natural de las emergentes tensiones políticas y sociales ocasionadas por las controversias religiosas de la Reforma, el sentimiento católico entre los residentes de la ciudad estaba en su apogeo. Los citadinos ricos se alinearon con la Iglesia

Católica y se apegaron firmemente a las tradiciones. Cortejar otra religión era como coquetear con el ángel destructor de una oposición política derrotada. Para el ciudadano pobre el asunto era un poco más práctico: podía perder su empleo. Aun cuando los gobernantes mexicanos veían favorablemente a los mormones --no tanto por su mensaje religioso sino por sus esfuerzos de colonizar el norte--, la aprobación de estas actividades no logró que el trabajo misional en la ciudad de México se tornara más fácil.

Cuando los citadinos mostraron no estar interesados en su mensaje, los misioneros se dirigieron a poblados más pequeños. Pero allí los conversos potenciales que encontraron esperaban que la Iglesia los subvencionara, al igual que como los protestantes lo estaban haciendo en esos mismos pueblos, según se rumoraba. El clima y las enfermedades presentaron otros problemas: fiebre amarilla, tifoidea y viruela ocasionaron la muerte de Feramorz L. Young, Sylvester O. Collett y Elmer Hooks --y en 1904 la del apóstol A.O. Woodruff y su esposa Helen, quienes visitaban la Misión de la ciudad de México. También existía la apatía espiritual de muchos de los mexicanos.

En 1888 la desilusión en la obra fue suficiente para ocasionar conversaciones serias de cerrar la Misión Mexicana. Presiones financieras en Utah y la lucha final de la Iglesia con el gobierno estadounidense ocasionaron finalmente su clausura. En diciembre de 1888, el muy desanimado Henry Erying fue relevado como presidente de la Misión para que regresara a Colonia Juárez. Un mes después la *Misión India* de Sonora también se cerró. Entonces, el 3 de junio de 1889, todos los misioneros extranjeros fueron retirados y cerrada la Misión Mexicana. Los 241 mormones nativos que vivían en el centro, y los más de cuarenta indígenas mexicanos del norte,[M] fueron abandonados a su propio cuidado para velar por sí mismos en la mejor forma posible.

La Iglesia estaba ahora en bancarrota, sus líderes escondidos y su jerarquía eclesiástica amenazada de inminente destrucción. A los pocos meses del retiro de los misioneros del centro de México, el presidente Wilford Woodruff emitió el *Manifiesto*; tras lo cual la Iglesia trató de reconstruirse, encarando el problema de las familias afectadas y reacomodándose en un ambiente norteamericano hostil. Mas la fuerza para el trabajo de la Iglesia en México se había terminado.

No sabemos lo que pasó con los miembros lamanitas que habían sido convertidos en el norte. Del trabajo en el sur, algunas de las ramas en torno a la ciudad de México se desintegraron al esparcirse sus miembros; otras formaron 'sociedades religiosas independientes' y trataron de vivir de acuerdo con las enseñanzas de la Biblia. Pero muchos permanecieron fieles a la Iglesia durante este período de ausencia que duró trece años, pues los misioneros no regresaron sino hasta 1901.[33N]

No es un asunto ligero el convertir a casi trescientas personas y verse forzado a abandonarlas, como tampoco es cosa fácil unirse a una nueva fe y ser abandonado. Pero no obstante el desánimo de los misioneros y el desencanto de los nuevos conversos, en realidad fueron los problemas en Utah los que ocasionaron el fracaso del esfuerzo misional de la Iglesia de Jesucristo de los Santos de los Últimos Días en México.

Aun así, las colonias angloamericanas en el norte del país permanecieron intactas. En ellas prevalecía un patriotismo entendible: una reverencia --casi adoración-- a la bandera estadounidense. Con la posibilidad de que sus hijos pudieran ser perseguidos por el gobierno, muchos padres anglosajones se preocupaban por sus hijos que estaban en una tierra extraña, bajo otra bandera y donde la población se comunicaba en otro idioma. ¿Qué efecto tendría todo esto en ellos?, pensaban. Conforme iniciaba el siglo veinte, los mormones norteamericanos en México eran un éxito económico, pero una comunidad aislada culturalmente, e ignoraban cuál sería exactamente su misión ahora que los problemas sobre la poligamia habían disminuido y sus esfuerzos misionales se encontraban frustrados.

Pronto las colonias hallaron la respuesta: regresar a lo que ellos pudieron haber sido si no hubiera intervenido el gobierno de Estados Unidos. Así, una vez más empezaron a predicar a los indios. Alguien recordó a las ramas en la ciudad de México que habían sido abandonadas en 1889. ¿Debería la Iglesia tratar una vez más? El año de 1901 parecía ser un buen tiempo para hacerlo.

NOTAS:

1. Samuel Eliot Morison y Henry Steele Commager, *The Growth of the American Republic*, 1:624.

2. Vea Nels Anderson, *Desert Saints: The Mormon Frontier in Utah*, p. 416.

3. Gary L. Bunker, "Illustrated Periodical Images of Mormons, 1850-1860," *Dialogue: A Journal of Mormon Thought* 10 (Primavera 1977):82-94. Vea también el libro de Gary L. Bunker y Davis Bitton, *The Mormon Graphic Image*, 1834-1914.

4. U.S., *Statutes at Large*, XII, Parte 1, 501-2 (1862).

5. Edward Wheelock Tullidge, *Life of Brigham Young, or Utah and Her Founder*, pp. 420-21.

6. U.S., *Statutes at Large*, XXII, Parte 1, 30-32 (1882).

7. U.S., *Statutes at Large*, XXII, Parte 1, 635-41 (1887).

8. Benjamin F. Johnson, My Life's Review, pp. 287-96, da una descripción vívida de esta expedición.

9. Blaine Carmon Hardy, "The Mormon Colonies of Northern Mexico," pp. 49-51, 73.

10. Vea el libro de John H. Krenkel, ed., *The Life and Times of Joseph Fish, Mormon Pioneer, Autobiography*, p. 269. También, Israel Call, "Autobiography," 1854-1930.

11. Krenkel, *Life and Times of Joseph Fish*, p. 285.

12. Blaine Carmon Hardy, "Cultural 'Encystment' as a Cause of Mormon Exodus from Mexico in 1912," p. 443.

13. Como fue reportado por Lebra N. Foremaster en la comp. de Kate B. Carter, "The Mormons in Mexico," en el libro *Treasures of Pioneer History*, 3:209.

14. Eunice Stewart Harris, "Autobiography," p. 26. Vea también Harris's "Autobiographical Sketch of Eunice Stewart Harris (esposa de Denison Emer Harris) escrita por ella en 1932," para obtener una versión con uso de palabras un poco diferente.

15. La practica de "ventaja comparativa" y complementario en el sentido convencional de la integración económica fue excepcional.

16. Krenkel, *Life and Times of Joseph Fish*.

17. Charles W. Kindrich, "The Mormons in Mexico," p. 704.

18. Helaman Pratt a su hermano, Parley, citado en Journal History, 6 de Febrero de 1887.

19. Vea Journal History, 13 de Abril de 1887. p. 4.

20. El Diario de Henry Eyring, 1835-1902, p. 64.

21. Beatrice Snow Winsor, en Carter, "The Mormons in Mexico," 3:204.

22. Rey L. Pratt, "History of the Mexican Mission," pp. 491-492.

23. Ibid.

24. Sullivan Calvin Richardson, "Autobiography."

25. Gordon Irving, "Mormonism in Latin America."

26. Rey L. Pratt, "Histoy of the Mexican Mission," p. 497.

27. Lawrance G. Coates, "The Mormons, The Ghost Dance Craze, and the Massacre at Wounded Knee," pp. 11-12.

28. Journal of Discourses, vol. 26, 17:299-300; también 18:21-22.

29. Citado por Lawrence G. Coates, "The Mormons and the Ghost Dance," p. 91.

30. La practica de rebautizar por bendiciones especificas tanto espirituales como físicas era común en los primeros días de la Iglesia. (Vean el libro de D. Michael Quinn, "The Practice of Rebaptism at Navoo.") Cuando él se encontró a los Santos en California que habían navegado desde Nueva York y que habían poblado lo que hoy es el area de San Francisco, Parly P. Pratt también volvió a bautizar a un numero de ellos. Los nombres se encuentran registrados en su diario bajo la fecha del 26 de junio de 1851 y durante el mes de julio de 1851.

31. Carta de Wilford Woodruff a Elder A. M. Tenny y misioneros compañeros con fecha del 10 de Abril de 1888, citada en "Manuscript History of the Mexican Mission".

32. Una "estaca," presidida por un "presidente de estaca" usualmente se compone de tres mil a cinco mil miembros y hasta una docena de "Barrios" (congregaciones), las cuales son encabezada por un "obispo." "Ramas" son congregaciones Mormonas en distritos de las misiones donde aun no se han organizado estacas. Mormones fieles donan un diez porciento de sus ganancias a la Iglesia a través de su obispo del barrio o presidente de rama.

33. Rey L. Pratt, "History of the Mexican Mission," p. 493.

CAPITULO 3

REAPERTURA DE LA MISIÓN MEXICANA

Si las razones por la que se cerró la Misión Mexicana en 1889 eran lo suficientemente claras para todos, Anthony W. Ivins encontró que para él las consecuencias fueron desagradables. Después de años de sacrificios misionales, el resultado doloroso fue, contra cualquier justificación, un rebaño abandonado en un ambiente hostil. Sin embargo, los miembros mexicanos no fueron olvidados. Ivins, quien presidió sobre las colonias mormonas en Chihuahua, no podía descansar sabiendo que los miembros mexicanos estaban sin alguien que los animara. Le parecía que "si nosotros convertimos a la gente a la verdad del evangelio y los admitimos en la Iglesia, posteriormente deberíamos cuidarlos, es decir, darles toda la protección y el cuidado que estuviera dentro de nuestro alcance para mantenerlos en el camino de rectitud y enseñarles los principios que nosotros conocemos y les permitirían regresar a la presencia de nuestro Padre."[1]

En 1876 Ivins había viajado más de cinco mil kilómetros a caballo para hablar a los mexicanos sobre el Libro de Mormón. Seis años después había servido como misionero en el centro de México, y más tarde como presidente de misión durante los años 1883 y 1884. Tenía no sólo conocimiento directo del ambiente de México, sino también estaba familiarizado con el espíritu abierto, caluroso y gentil de la gente mexicana. Y él nunca se acobardó de sus convicciones de que la Iglesia tenía el deber de completar su misión a los lamanitas.

Mientras que casi todos los mormones angloamericanos en el país se hallaban preocupados por su supervivencia y el desarrollo de sus comunidades mormonas, Ivins continuó pensando en los mormones abandonados en el centro --algunos sus amigos personales. Si él estaba igualmente preocupado por los muchos miembros indios en el norte que también habían sido abandonados, lo desconocemos, pero pensaba y hablaba mucho sobre la misión en el centro de México. Por lo tanto, fue de sumo valor para México el que Anthony W. Ivins fuera llamado en 1895 para dejar su confortable hogar en Saint George, Utah, e ir a las colonias de Chihuahua a presidir sobre todos los mormones en México.

Seis años más tarde comenzó a enfocarse en la otra parte de su llamamiento --los santos en el centro del país. En uno de sus viajes a Utah, presentó todo el asunto a la Primera Presidencia de la Iglesia, hablando no sólo sobre las ovejas perdidas que necesitaban un pastor, sino también de los hombres y mujeres jóvenes de las colonias, quienes hablaban español y estaban familiarizados con las costumbres y cultura de los mexicanos. A pesar de fracasos anteriores, ahora las cosas se veían más prometedoras. La presión del gobierno estadounidense había disminuido; en las colonias una nueva generación se había levantado, y estaba no sólo deseosa sino también excepcionalmente calificada para llevar el mensaje mormón de nueva cuenta; además, los logros de las colonias habían generado un excedente económico y de recursos humanos para sostener un nuevo intento misional. Las quejas de los miembros mexicanos también habían disminuido, cuando menos un poco. Era un nuevo día, tiempo para un nuevo esfuerzo. La Primera Presidencia estuvo de acuerdo.

El hombre recomendado por Ivins para encabezar la labor en el sur fue Ammon M. Tenney, quien lo había acompañado en la primera expedición a México, en 1876. Tenney estuvo a la cabeza de la misión india mexicana durante los años 1887 a 1889; luego, siguiendo el consejo de Wilford Woodruff de salir de Arizona y dirigirse a México y establecerse en las colonias, construyó casas para sus familias en las de Díaz y Juárez. En las colonias y durante varias conversaciones que sostuvo con Ivins, había estimulado la idea de presentar a la Primera Presidencia el asunto de volver a abrir la misión en el sur. Así que cuando le llegó el llamamiento a Tenney, obedientemente aceptó sus nuevas responsabilidades, aunque no estaba muy feliz con la idea de dejar otra vez a sus familias.

El esfuerzo misional era de suma importancia para las autoridades de la Iglesia, tal como lo había sido la misión de Moses Thatcher en 1879. Anthony Ivins y el apóstol John Henry Smith acompañaron a Tenney a la ciudad de México para ver cuántos de los miembros originales habían permanecido fieles y cómo les había ido. Ivins conocía a muchos de ellos personalmente, pues durante sus días misionales en los principios de la década de 1880 había hecho contacto con ellos y estaba deseoso de verlos otra vez.

La primera parada fue Cuernavaca. El operador del hotel, mormón de nombre H.L. Hall, vivía ahí. Era uno de aquellos que con optimismo y evidente eficacia vestía su religión para que todos la vieran.[2] Varios de sus empleados se habían unido a la Iglesia y conocía una familia venida de Suiza que también estaba interesada. El hotel de Hall les proporcionó una base de operación, así como un lugar sereno para que el 8 de junio de 1901 el apóstol Smith apartara a Ammon M. Tenney como presidente de la Misión Mexicana. Tenney estaba bajo la supervisión directa del presidente Ivins de la estaca Juárez, pero con su nuevo título no hubo duda de que su misión debería iniciar sus labores de inmediato.

Después de hacerse cargo de los asuntos preliminares de organización y recibir consejo de Hall sobre la política en la capital mexicana, los misioneros una vez más sintieron la necesidad de hacer una visita al presidente Porfirio Díaz. Aun cuando éste se encontraba envuelto en una controversia política mayor que la que enfrentaba cuando los mormones acudieron a él por primera vez para solicitar su ayuda --y por tanto sumando enemigos--, todavía era bastante amigable y cooperador con los santos. Por lo tanto, después de escasas dos semanas en México, el 17 de junio los misioneros pidieron y recibieron una audiencia con el presidente del país.

El apóstol Smith agradeció al mandatario y al pueblo mexicano por su hospitalidad hacia los mormones, además de explicarle la nueva misión de la Iglesia. Díaz expresó su gran satisfacción --para entonces la prosperidad de los mormones del norte había sido reconocida y gozaba de reputación nacional-- y deseó toda clase de éxito a los misioneros. Le pidió al apóstol Smith que extendiera un caluroso saludo al presidente Lorenzo Snow, quien había sucedido a Wilford Woodruff; lo que Smith hizo, diciéndole al Presidente Snow: "No hay otro hombre en este mundo de Dios con mayor heroísmo que el que está a la cabeza del gobierno de México."[3]

Durante la década siguiente nubes obscuras ocultarían la relación de Porfirio Díaz con la Iglesia; pero por lo pronto los mormones lo consideraban como su benefactor, y los líderes de la Iglesia se lo declaraban en cada ocasión posible. Típica de su estima por Díaz en ese tiempo fue la visita que le hicieron los apóstoles John Henry Smith, Mathias F. Cowley y Charles W. Penrose el 24 de noviembre de 1904. Ellos, junto con Richard W. Young, un doctor Faust, John Beck, D. W. Johnson y Hyrum S. Harris, lo felicitaron por su reelección como presidente de México.

En 1901 Díaz era un héroe para los extranjeros que vivían en el país. Los defendía contra todos los disidentes que había dentro del sistema político mexicano. Ellos respondieron efusivamente, sabiendo, tal como lo explicó el historiador Lesley Byrd Simpson, que "como dijo Disraeli: si uno extiende halagos a la realeza con un rociador, sobre don Porfirio Díaz uno tiene que usar una manguera... Él había sido casi sofocado con condecoraciones extranjeras, cada una con su respectivo pergamino. Díaz escuchaba tal cantidad de discursos que le hubieran causado dolor de estómago a Santa Anna."[4] Pero ninguno de estos comentarios sobrepasó los halagos de un brindis ofrecido en 1907 por el secretario de Estado norteamericano, Elihu Root:

"Si yo fuera un poeta, escribiría elogios; si fuera músico, compondría marchas triunfales; si yo fuera mexicano, sentiría que no sería mucho el dar mi lealtad inquebrantable de por vida, a cambio de la bendición que él (Díaz) ha traído a mi país.

Pero como yo no soy poeta ni músico ni mexicano, sino sólo un americano que ama la justicia y la libertad y desea ver que entre toda la humanidad reine el progreso, se fortalezca y llegue a ser perpetuo, veo en el presidente Porfirio Díaz a uno de los grandes hombres que deben ser venerados, como héroes, por toda la humanidad".[5]

Hubert Herring, un observador conocedor del orden prusiano, caracterizó el gobierno de Díaz como "una respuesta a las oraciones de la gente fatigada por más de medio siglo de confusión. La paz pretoriana que les proporcionó fue el período más largo que la nación había gozado desde el día en que el padre Hidalgo sonara las campanas de Dolores."[6]

No todos sus contemporáneos estaban de acuerdo, particularmente aquellos que por alguna razón objetaron --o se pensaba que objetaban-- la 'mano dura' de Díaz para controlar el mayor número posible de mexicanos. Su lema fue: 'Pan y garrote'. Pan para el ejército, los burócratas, los extranjeros y aun el clero, y garrote para los que se le oponían y para el ciudadano común y corriente.[7] Cuando la marcha de Porfirio Díaz entró en la ciudad de México para declarar el fin de la Reforma de 1876, la nación sufría de anarquía, caída fiscal, vandalismo, indios altamente irrespetuosos hacia los mexicanos con dinero y propiedades, y una economía nacional primitiva y vergonzosa. Encontró amigos: políticos que podía manejar, un ejército capaz de dividir y hacer que sus generales se enfrentaran entre sí, la Iglesia Católica, el capital extranjero, los mormones, así como los tenedores de inmensas propiedades.

Bajo la dirección de Díaz, México llegó a ser un gigantesco feudo de servidumbre. Sus pistoleros --*'los rurales'*-- tenían poder para disparar sin hacer preguntas. Indios problemáticos, huelguistas, oradores y escritores indiscretos, además de gente honesta pero acusada y tratada como bandidos por el régimen, desaparecieron en los apestosos calabozos de la vieja *Penitenciaria de Belén* o fueron fusilados "mientras trataban de escapar". México prosperó, mas solamente la parte que le interesaba a Díaz. Aquellos con títulos, dinero y bienes raíces estaban altamente complacidos. Muchos otros mexicanos no lo estaban, pero sus voces no fueron escuchadas por más de diez años. Los mormones, sabedores de su vulnerabilidad a las vicisitudes de la política estatal de Chihuahua, intentaron cubrir todas las bases políticas --una de las cuales era *Don Porfirio*. El apóstol John Henry Smith se emocionó durante su visitade dos semanas al centro del país. Encontró ahí "gente amable y considerada que había sido lastimada en el pasado, y cuyo espíritu hasta cierto punto había muerto en los años vividos en servidumbre". No obstante, era obvio que Smith no consideraba a Porfirio Díaz como parte del problema. El apóstol estaba convencido de que muy pronto los mexicanos "entrarían en la puerta diseñada por su Creador, y estarían comprometidos en construir templos al Señor".[8]

Ciertamente él, como otros líderes, estaba sorprendido de encontrar a tantos mormones en el centro de México, cuya fe había sobrevivido a la prolongada falta de dirección. Habló con algunos de los viejos miembros --entre ellos varios que habían sido bautizados desde 1879, durante la misión de Moses Thatcher. Ivins mismo estaba "sorprendido del entendimiento profundo que tanto los hombres como las mujeres parecían tener sobre la doctrina y los principios del plan de redención".[9]

Sin embargo, cuando Ivins y Smith regresaron a casa, no tenían duda sobre la magnitud de la asignación de Tenney para revitalizar la obra misional y reorganizar la Iglesia en la ciudad de México. Como la mayoría de los miembros habían sido originalmente protestantes, durante la larga separación de la Iglesia introdujeron muchas costumbres de sus antiguas creencias. A causa de que el mormonismo no es dado a los ritos públicos, cualquier desviación o embellecimiento pronto es calificado como 'sectario' o apostata y puede molestar a ciertos miembros de la Iglesia. Ciertamente la gente habían mantenido actividad religiosa, en su mayor parte, pero decididamente en una forma no mormona. Además, muchos se habían vuelto sexualmente promiscuos --práctica altamente contraria a las enseñanzas de la Iglesia, independientemente de la aceptación que tuviera entre la sociedad. Así, el trabajo de Tenney era difícil a pesar de los contactos favorables que se habían vuelto a hacer. Y por encima de todo esto, algunos miembros habían establecido sus propias congregaciones y no estaban dispuestos a perderlas, algo que una religion centralizada no puede tolerar. Lucharon un poco con Tenney, aceptando cuando su nuevo presidente de Misión les prometió que el sacerdocio y los misioneros nunca más serian quitados de México. (Pasó menos de una década antes de la llegada de la Revolución Mexicana, y como consecuencia el segundo de los tres retiros misionales, hiciera romper esa promesa.)

La cronología que Tenney escribió nos da una idea de como se desarrolló el periodo de la nueva apertura. Después de dejar a los otros misioneros en la estación central del ferrocarril para que emprendieran su viaje a El Paso via la ciudad de Chihuahua, Tenney regresó a Cuernavaca para mantener otras reuniones y aprender todo lo posible. Después salió rumbo a Amecameca para visitar a Silvestre López, un viejo amigo de los mormones dispuesto a hacer cualquier cosa para la Iglesia menos unirse a ella.

De Amecameca se fue a Cuautla, en el estado de Morelos, donde visitó a Simón Zúñiga, uno de los viejos conversos que había estado con los colonos de Chihuahua en 1887, pero cuya experiencia lo hizo regresar con su familia decepcionado y a pie. Los mormones de Cuautla le dieron la bienvenida a Tenney y éste utilizó su tiempo para reorganizar las ramas aledañas, reenseñar los procedimientos organizativos de la Iglesia y sus principios fundamentales --enfatizando el ayuno, los diezmos y la oración. Aunque los santos mexicanos se habían desviado un tanto del tipo de culto y doctrina convencionales, con los que se reunía parecían todos estar dispuestos a aprender y creer. Tenney bautizó en Cuautla a seis nuevos conversos.

De Cuautla viajó al pie del volcán Popocatépetl para visitar el poblado de Ozumba. Ninguna de esas áreas ni la zona circunvecina habían cambiado mucho desde 1884, cuando el misionero Milson H. Pratt anotó una descripción de esos lugares.

"Ozumba se encuentra casi al sur de la ciudad de México, a una distancia aproximada de sesenta kilómetros, y es el centro de varios poblados protegidos por el elevado y notable Popocatépetl. Está situada en la parte más sureña del valle de México, que redondea y contiene cerros y montañas como si fuera el fondo de un gran lago --que sin duda la mayoría de la región lo fue en otros tiempos. Esta zona ha sido afectada terrible y frecuentemente por erupciones volcánicas, ya que se encuentran cráteres extintos en todas partes, y éstos dan un testimonio abundante de ello... El 'gran volcán' Popocatépetl se eleva en forma de cono a una altura de 5,500 metros sobre el nivel del mar, y todavía emite una pequeña columna de humo que puede ser vista claramente desde el poblado de Aclantla^o en cualquier mañana despejada; más tarde, sin embargo, ya no es posible verlo a causa de la atmósfera pesada."[10]

Más tarde Pratt describiría el área circunvecina, mencionando muchas de las ramas que Tenney regresó a visitar.

"La bajada desde Ozumba hasta la parte tropical, un valle ubicado al sur, llamado 'tierra caliente', es muy rápido. Desciende casi 1,000 metros en dieciséis kilómetros, y aun así el valle está a más de 1,300 metros sobre el nivel del mar. Aclantla se encuentra al este de Ozumba, al noroeste está San Juan de Guadalupe con sus plantaciones inmensas, y al noreste Tecalco... Chimal, un poblado lleno de peras y flores, se encuentra al sur. Estos poblados están alrededor de Ozumba y lo que los hace más interesantes para nosotros que cualquier otra cosa es que todos son poblados indios: sus habitantes son lamanitas, israelitas, ya que corre muy poca sangre

blanca entre ellos, con excepción de aquí en Ozumba. En los otros pueblos usualmente hablan mexicano (nahuatl) en vez del español, aunque pueden entender y hablar ambos... Nosotros también tenemos dos congregaciones en la 'tierra caliente', una en Coahuixtla y la otra en San Andrés de la Cal."[11]

En Ozumba, Tenney conoció a Lino Zárate, quien había sido misionero mormón en 1879 y 1883. En cierta ocasión, Zárate y Milson Pratt, sabiendo que todo culto religioso al aire libre estaba prohibido por las leyes mexicanas, fueron arrestados en 1883 por andar predicando en la plaza central de Ozumba.[12] Ahora, dieciocho años después, Zárate estaba gozoso de ver a Tenney, y ansioso por que éste le ayudara a sanar a su esposa, que se encontraba enferma. De acuerdo con la costumbre mormona, Zárate y Tenney pusieron sus manos sobre la cabeza de ella y le dieron una bendición. La restauración de la salud de la señora Zárate resultó incomprensible para todos, menos para Tenney y el marido.

Después de estar menos de dos semanas en Ozumba, Tenney viajó a Atlautla con Zárate y otro mormón apellidado Camacho. Ahí encontraron a Simón Páez y su familia, quienes habían vivido en Colonia Juárez por más o menos cinco años después de que la mayoría de los colonos originarios del centro de México regresaran. Páez los recibió amablemente, deseándoles éxito.

Con espíritus animosos, Tenney, Zárate y Camacho viajaron enseguida a Chimal, donde visitaron a la familia de Nicolás Rodríguez. Todos estuvieron de acuerdo en regresar a la Iglesia, con la condición de que no fueran abandonados de nuevo.

Entonces, en Tecalco, encontraron a Julián Rojas. Su iniciativa, independencia, dedicación y celo, características que lo habían hecho un exitoso misionero durante los días de Thatcher e Ivins, ahora representaban un problema para los misioneros. Rojas presidía una congregación y quería mantener absoluto control sobre ella, recordándoles que por muchos años su gente habían sido 'un rebaño sin pastor'. Hablaron por mucho tiempo, y finalmente Lino Zárate y Rojas llegaron a un acuerdo de que éste se afiliaría de nuevo a la Iglesia.

Un mes después, el 18 de agosto de 1901, Tenney regresó a Tecalco y volvió a bautizar a Rojas y a 75 de sus seguidores como miembros de la Iglesia de Jesucristo de los Santos de los Últimos Días. Una semana más tarde, Rojas demostró su sinceridad cuando fue avanzado al sacerdocio mayor de la Iglesia y aceptó el llamamiento de Febronio Pérez como presidente de la recientemente organizada rama de Tecalco --que había sido la congregación anterior de Rojas. Un año después Pérez fue relevado y llamado a servir como misionero, y Rojas fue instalado como presidente de la congregación de Tecalco, que él había mantenido junta por tanto tiempo.

Una vez reorganizada la rama de Tecalco, Tenney regresó a Amecameca, pero encontró que los miembros de la Iglesia ahí estaban resentidos y rebeldes. Viajó entonces a Ixtacalco --en las afueras de la ciudad de México--, donde encontró a otra familia Páez que sinceramente aceptó su juicio cuando les dijo que ellos habían permitido la entrada de algunas ideas extrañas en su modo religioso de pensar. Y así continuó día con día durante casi un año, trabajando solo --con excepción de cuando lo acompañaban miembros locales como Lino Zárate, Ángel Rosales o el hermano Camacho.[P]

Además de visitar y enseñar a los miembros, Tenney deseaba organizar ramas lo más pronto posible y conferir el sacerdocio a miembros dignos de la Iglesia. Empezó a hacerlo tan pronto como creía que algunos de los santos podían ser líderes de otros, bajo su dirección. Después de la rama de Tecalco se estableció otra en San Andrés de la Cal, con Francisco Miranda asignado para dirigirla. Necesitando ayuda, Tenney le pidió a Lino Zárate, Julián Rojas, Juan Méndez, Simón Zúñiga y al hermano Camacho que sirvieran misiones de corta duración con el fin de instruir a las ramas.

La mayoría de estos misioneros eran casados y tenían familias numerosas. Sus misiones fueron un ejemplo de servicio, amor y sacrificio. Pronto se unieron a ellos Ángel Rosales, Margarito Bautista, Jacobo González y Juan Mairet --uno de los hijos de la familia

Suiza que en Cuernavaca H.L. Hall interesara en la Iglesia. Durante los siguientes meses, Juan Páez fue llamado para presidir la rama de Ixtacalco; a José González se le asignó el mismo oficio en Chimal; y, cuando regresó de su misión, Ángel Rosales fue llamado para dirigir la rama de Trigales, convirtiéndose así en el primer misionero nativo que a su regreso presidió una entre su propia gente (12 de julio de 1902).

De 1902 a 1910 se establecieron varios patrones constantes de acción que emergieron consistentes en la obra misional de los mormones en el centro de México. Primero: los misioneros con un amplio dominio del idioma español llegaron regularmente de las colonias en el norte; muchos de ellos eran casados y habían dejado a sus esposas e hijos en casa para ser cuidados por otros miembros de la Iglesia mientras ellos predicaban. Segundo: especialmente durante la presidencia de Tenney --y después en la de Rey L. Pratt-- se incrementó el liderismo de hermanos indígenas en las ramas locales; otros nativos fueron llamados e instruidos para servir como presidentes de rama o consejeros. Las *Sociedades de Socorro* (organización de mujeres de la Iglesia, dedicada a promover caridad y educación) fueron conformadas y dirigidas por mujeres locales, quienes aprendieron el arte del servicio compasivo adecuado a su tiempo, así como las técnicas de salud y cuidado prenatal. Un par de ejemplos. Cuando Lino Zárate murió, en 1903, dejó a su esposa con siete hijos. Todos, excepto su esposa y una de sus hijas menores, estaban en cama contagiados de tifoidea --la causa de la muerte de Zárate--; la Sociedad de Socorro de su rama y las de poblados aledaños cuidaron a los miembros de la familia hasta que se recuperaron, ayudándoles material y espiritualmente. Y cuando el Apóstol A.O. Woodruff y su esposa contrajeron viruela mientras hacían un viaje por la ciudad de México, Juana Páez proporcionó a la señora Woodruff la atención competente y cuidadosa que su enfermera inglesa no pudo o no quiso proporcionarle, arriesgando su vida por una hermana en la fe que estaba muriendo.

Una tercera característica de los años previos a 1910 fue la atención continua que la autoridades en las colonias y en Salt Lake City daban a la nueva Misión.

Anthony W. Ivins la visitaba tan frecuentemente como podía, para llevar a cabo conferencias y animar e instruir a los miembros y misioneros locales. Cuando fue llamado como apóstol en 1907, su sucesor Junius Romney hizo lo mismo. Otros apóstoles --A.O. Woodruff, John Henry Smith, Mathias F. Cowley, Charles W. Penrose, Heber J. Grant, Anthony W. Ivins-- hicieron una o más visitas entre 1902 y 1910; incluso el apóstol Cowley permaneció un mes entero yendo a cada rama para organizar *Escuelas Dominicales* y enseñar técnicas básicas de música a los miembros locales.

Un cuarto patrón de acción fue el constante intento de recuperar a los santos que habían sido abandonados. Una búsqueda de registros que se realizó el 13 de agosto de 1902, arrojó que de los casi trescientos miembros que habían sido convertidos para 1889, cincuenta y cinco todavía eran mormones activos. Muchos misioneros revisaron los registros y contactaron a los hermanos perdidos. En algunos casos tuvieron éxito, en otros no. Por ejemplo, en julio de 1903 dos líderes viajaron a los poblados de Tula y Nopala con el propósito de buscar a hermanos que habían sido bautizados en dichos lugares. En San Sebastián, un pueblito cercano a Nopala, encontraron a José María Yáñez, quien junto con otros miembros de su familia había sido bautizado años atrás. Recibió algo fríamente a los misioneros, pero les mostró fotografías del élder James Z. Stewart, Melitón G. Trejo y otros que había conocido. Yáñez les relato la conversión de su madre, quien había soñado que unos hombres estaban publicando un periódico que le ayudaría espiritualmente. Ella mandó a su hijo --Yáñez-- a que encontrara a esos hombres y él conoció a Plotino Rhodakanaty, quien los remitió a donde Moses Thatcher publicaba los folletos. Después de leerlos, la señora pidió a los misioneros que fueran a bautizarla. Su hijo y la esposa de él también fueron bautizados, y posteriormente Yáñez fue ordenado élder. Mas durante el largo abandono perdió el espíritu y renunció a su sacerdocio. Aparte de Yáñez, los misioneros encontraron a muchos otros miembros que se gozaron al verlos de nuevo, por lo que continuaron buscando a las personas de los registros.

La última característica constante fue que muchos nuevos conversos se unieron a la Iglesia. Durante los catorce meses que Tenney había presidido la Misión, se llevaron a cabo 175 bautismos, y para 1911 la membresía superaba el millar. Se abrieron nuevas áreas, otras ramas fueron organizadas y la obra se expandió para incluir a más gente en ambientes diferentes.

Naturalmente y como era de esperarse, hubo oposición. Se presentaron enfermedades y muertes, problemas personales, transgresiones que ameritaron la excomunión, y fallas en el liderismo y desempeño. Dados los impedimentos al progreso, lo maravilloso fue que la expansión de la Iglesia siguió su marcha en gran forma. Los mormones mexicanos habían deseado que los angloamericanos contemporáneos, que en algunos casos los habían criticado, pudieran notar lo que estaba sucediendo.

Durante este periodo hubo uno o dos intentos menores para volver a los días de la colonización y el 'recogimiento'. En 1903, H.L. Hall y otros abogaron fuertemente para establecer una colonia mormona en el poblado de Trigales, donde una nueva rama se había organizado y donde el valle y clima parecían ser perfectos para recibir a los Santos de los Últimos Días como un lugar de recogimiento. Pero las autoridades de la Iglesia se inclinaban por la alternativa que Helaman Pratt había propuesto muchos años atrás, es decir, llevar una colonia de mormones al norte del país. Así que cinco meses después, el 15 de diciembre de 1903, José Zúñiga y su esposa salieron para Dublán a estudiar las posibilidades de colonizar entre los mormones angloamericanos. Esto llamó la atención en Salt Lake City cuando un reportero escribió: "Ya que son los primeros en inmigrar desde que se reabrió la Misión, muchos de los santos mexicanos esperan con interés su informe sobre el trato que recibirán, etcétera, ya que algunos otros están pensando en salir pronto a las colonias."[13]

Entonces, durante la organización de la rama de San Pedro Mártir, para lo cual viajó a la ciudad de México en 1907, Ivins dijo a la congregación que él esperaba en un tiempo no muy lejano obtener tierras apropiadas en el norte, cerca de las colonias, donde los santos mexicanos pudieran colonizar.[14] Dos años después, tras haber sido llamado como apóstol, participó en una reunión del Quórum de los Doce en la que se aportaron 5,000 dólares para comprar tierras donde los mexicanos pudieran colonizar. Los apóstoles Ivins, John Henry Smith y Francis M. Lyman habían hecho la propuesta, recomendando que la Iglesia comprara tierras cerca de una de las colonias mormonas que ya había sido establecida por 'nuestra gente', y 'que no tratáramos de colonizarlos a todos en un mismo lugar, sino que se hiciera en dos pequeñas colonias".[15] Pero esa iniciativa nunca tuvo su oportunidad.

Al paso de los años, mientras los misioneros angloamericanos festejaban cada 4 de Julio en el *Parque Tívoli* y los miembros mexicanos el 16 de Septiembre en sus poblados, nubes de guerra se divisaban en el horizonte. Sólo poca gente importante pudo ver estas señales, especialmente los residentes extranjeros en México. Así pues, en septiembre de 1910, cuando el país celebraba el centenario del 'Grito de Dolores' con el que Miguel Hidalgo iniciara la guerra de Independencia contra España, según los periodistas de los diarios todo parecía estar bien.

Desde donde se viera, el festejo de septiembre fue una ocasión magnifica. El presidente Porfirio Díaz no reparó en gastos para atender a los miles de invitados, muchos de los cuales provenían de otros países. En toda la reuniones y cenas, así como en los informes al extranjero, varias cosas eran claras: México era el vivo ejemplo de estabilidad y éxito en este continente. El país era próspero, el presupuesto nacional estaba balanceado y la moneda era tan sólida como el oro que la respaldaba; el capital extranjero, seguro, rendía generosos dividendos a quienes habían invertido sabiamente en tierras agrícolas, propiedades petroleras, minería y acciones del ferrocarril.[16]

En realidad se vivía una época de oro. Antes de un año esas ilusiones, así reconocidas por el mexicano común --cuyo nivel de vida se había desplomado mientras la economía nacional crecía--, fueron destruidas para todo el mundo. Los mormones en el centro de México y las colonias del norte pronto sintieron el filo de la espada revolucionaria.

NOTAS:

1. Anthony Woodward Ivins a el Apóstol Francis M. Lyman, registrado en la Historia Manuscrita de la Misión Mexicana el 30 de Abril de 1902.

2. John Womack, Jr., influenciado en gran forma por el revolucionario Emiliano Zapata, ve a Hall en una luz particularmente negativa. Cuando inició la revolución en el Sur, Hall se movió rápidamente por todos lados, incluyendo tratando de adquirir influencia en los Estados Unidos, con el fin de proteger sus inversiones. Después que se aplacó la revolución, intentó establecer una compañía colonizadora en el valle de Cuernavaca. Esto fue visto por Womack como otro intento capitalista, donde nuevos patrones reemplazaban a los viejos y el campesino seguía en la misma pobreza. Womack esta criticando: "Entre estos tipos (listos, ventajosos, vendedores ambulantes, y engañadores), el mas vivaz y mas persistente era un hombre de la Nueva Inglaterra quien había vivido los últimos veinte años en México, Hubert L. Hall. Un hombre de negocios, Mormon, y un soplón en su país adoptivo, el cual impresionaba favorablemente a los Americanos que conocía." (Vea Womack, *Zapata and the Mexican Revolution*, p. 236.)

3. Journal History, 30 de Junio de 1901, p. 2.

4. Lesley Byrd Simpson, *Many Mexicos*, p. 292.

5. Ibid. Aquellos Mexicanos que habían sido beneficiados por Díaz, en igual forma eran efusivos en sus halagos. En referencias directas sobre comentarios similares sobre Díaz dados por el Secretario de Estado Elihu Root en otra ocasión durante su visita a México en 1907, José F. Godoy dijo en su prefacio al libro titulado *Porfirio Díaz, presidente de México, el fundador de una gran república*: "Estas palabras, pronunciadas por el Senador Elihu Root....ampliamente justifican la publicación de cualquier obra que contenga información válida, y que de una relato imparcial y honesto de la vida del Presidente Díaz. La brillante carrera de este gran hombre, tanto por sus proezas militares como su habilidad de gobernar, no pueden fallar, y nunca fallado, en captar la atención no solo de sus paisanos pero de toda persona en el mundo civilizado" (traducido por el autor).

6. Hubert Herring, *A History of Latin America*, p. 325.

7. Por uno de los relatos indicativo de los métodos de operación del dictador estamos endeudados a Carleton Beals, uno de los primeros Americanos que estudió México, y el cual después llegó a ser un conferencista y escrito prolífico. Vea su libro "Bread or the Club," en la ed. de Carlos B. Gil, *The Age of Porfirio Díaz*, pp. 61-70. Vea también la obra de John W. Kitchens "Some Considerations of the Rurales of Porfirian Mexico," y Pedro Santoni, "La policía de la Ciudad de México durante el

Porfiriato: los primeros años (1876-1884)." Juán Gómez Quiñones en su libro *Porfirio Díaz, los intelectuales y la revolución* ofrece un punto de vista interesante de las emergentes políticas sociales durante el periodo de Díaz. John Hart("The Porfiriato in Time and Space") proporciona composiciones breves pero con considerable perspectiva. Vea también el libro de Jesús Romero Flores, *Del Porfirismo a la revolución constitucionalista* un repaso episódico. La fundación filosófica del porfiriato, es expuesta por Leopoldo Zea en su libro *Positivism in Mexico* y también en la edición editada de Abelardo Villegas *Positivismo Porfirismo*.

8. *Journal History*, 30 de Junio de 1901, p. 2.

9. *Ivins al Apóstol Francis M. Lyman*, 30 de Abril de 1902.

10. *Journal History*, 16 de Febrero de 1884, p. 3.

11. *Ibid.*

12. Rey L. Pratt, "History of the Mexican Mission," p. 489.

13. *Manuscript History of the Mexican Mission*, 15 de Diciembre de 1903.

14. *Ibid*, 19 de Mayo de 1907.

15. *Journal History*, 20 de Enero de 1909, p. 4.

16. Vea en general la obra de David M.Pletcher, *Rails, Mines, and Progress: Seven American Promoters in Mexico, 1867-1911.* Una composición sobre la penetración de capital Britanico en México durante el periodo de Díaz, vea el libro de Alfred Tischendorf, *Great Britain and Mexico in the Era of Porfirio Díaz.*

CAPITULO 4

REVOLUCIÓN, ÉXODO Y CAOS

El hablar de la 'tercera revolución en México, o de la Revolución Mexicana, como los mexicanos prefieren llamarle, es entrar en una esfera de hecho frecuentemente desmesurada. Vencedores como derrotados percibían en forma diferente tales trastornos, sus causas y consecuencias. Para la mayoría de los mexicanos, la guerra civil que empezó en 1910 y duró --con respiros periódicos-- hasta 1930, trajo tanto esperanza como sufrimiento. La esperanza se cifraba en ser liberados de una rígida sociedad dividida en clases que la mayor parte del tiempo menospreciaba y frecuentemente explotaba a la generalidad de los mexicanos. Sin embargo, como en casi todas las revoluciones, fanatismos se enfrentaban con fanatismos; la crueldad reemplazaba a otro tipo de crueldad, y el bandidaje, la anarquía y el derrame de sangre indiscriminadamente se extendían hasta los poblados más aislados del país. ¿Sería posible que la Revolución fuera una iluslón falsa?[1] Algunos mormones empezaron a dudar, especialmente los colonos angloamericanos en el norte, quienes eventualmente fueron exilados de nueva cuenta. En una sola generación fueron de exilio en exilio, primero a México y luego a Estados Unidos. No es sorpresa que estos mormones llegaran a sentir desprecio por la política y los políticos.

La Revolución, ante cuya comparación todas las demás guerra en México palidecen, explotó durante los últimos años del gobierno de Porfirio Díaz y sus asesores de confianza, los *científicos'*, cuyo reinado legitimó e impuso una tortuosa especie de 'Darwinismo Social' en el país.[2] La consecuencia fue una racha de descontento que mermó la fibra social mexicana; sin embargo, el ejército y la policía de Díaz pudieron mantener unida a la nación. Así que los *científicos* apreciaban a Porfirio Díaz como una aceptable alternativa a la anarquía --y ese sentimiento era popular entre muchos de los ciudadanos de la clase alta.

Los mormones angloamericanos ciertamente estaban de acuerdo con Díaz sobre el punto de vista de la anarquía. Pero la opinión de los científicos y los mormones sobre el lugar que los indios deberían tener en la sociedad mexicana era muy diferente. Mientras que muchos de los primeros estaban de acuerdo con Díaz en cuanto a que "el futuro de México caía sobre el hombre blanco, y que el indio era útil solamente como cargador,"[3] los mormones en todos los aspectos pensaban lo contrario. Habían tratado casi por un siglo de extender a los indígenas las promesas que se encontraban en el Libro de Mormón, y se ofendían cuando el régimen de Díaz hablaba de los indios simplemente como sirvientes o como una reserva de mano de obra barata para el régimen, los mexicanos y extranjeros adinerados, las compañías, y los gobiernos extranjeros que apoyaban tal idea. Pero también es obvio que los mormones simpatizaban con Díaz porque apoyaba su causa en el norte.

Un día apacible, en el mes de septiembre de 1910 Díaz recibía elogios de los dignatarios que se habían reunido para celebrar el día de la Independencia de México. Pero no lejos de allí, una fuerza mercenaria policiaca conocida como '*los rurales*', peleaba para calmar el levantamiento campesino en las afueras de la ciudad. La legislación que respaldaba el uso de la fuerza policiaca era de gran ventaja para los ricos hacendados, que de hecho subvencionaban sus operaciones a costillas de campesinos mal pagados o explotados. El historiador Huber Herring informa que los salarios en efectivo de los campesinos "habían permanecido prácticamente sin incremento desde los últimos días del siglo XVIII hasta los primeros del XX", pero su valor adquisitivo había disminuido en un cincuenta por ciento.[4] Con *los rurales* al frente, los abusos continuaron siendo desenfrenados.

Además, la justicia fue reemplazada casi en su totalidad por la '*ley fuga*', que permitía que un judicial disparara a quien 'parecía' huir de la 'justicia'. A aquellos que ofendían la sensibilidad de las élites, frecuentemente se les disparaba por la espalda, independientemente de si estaban huyendo o no. Como no había más ley que la de *Don Porfirio,* pocos eran los que se preocupaban aun de los casos más serios. Protestar significaba morir, sencillamente.

Es más, conforme Díaz transfería los derechos minerales a norteamericanos e ingleses, arbitrariamente desposeía a miles de indios para quienes los campos de maíz eran más deseables que los de petróleo. Y con la ley sobre propiedades de 1883, que se modificó en 1894, cinco mil pueblos indígenas fueron despojados de sus tierras ancestrales --las cuales Díaz concesionó a compañías tasadoras extranjeras-- y después, por una miseria, vendidas a hacendados. 'No compensación, no acuerdos', fue el dictado bajo amenaza de muerte. Para el fin del régimen de Díaz, menos del diez por ciento de esas comunidades contaban con tierras propias. En los 'levantamientos' subsiguientes de *mayas* y *yaquis,* el ejército y *los rurales* mataron a miles, encarcelaron a otros tantos y los vendieron como esclavos para cultivar el henequén y el tabaco en Yucatán y Oaxaca, respectivamente.

En tanto que la política del *Darwinismo Social* limitaba el acceso y control de tierras, capital y derechos de subsuelo mineral, la élite de los mexicanos y sus homólogos europeos y estadounidenses prosperaba. En la mayoría de los mexicanos, excluidos de participación económica significativa, aumentó el enojo y la desesperación. En su opinión, México había sido lacerado y destripado, presa fácil, riqueza para carroñeros extranjeros y para la aristocracia nacional que había llegado a ser 'vende-patrias'. Esto no era un punto de vista particularmente imparcial, pero sí el que prevalecía.[5]

Con toda razón, muchos mexicanos odiaban a Díaz y a las instituciones privilegiadas y poderosas que lo apoyaban, asegurando la explotación mexicana. Por lo mismo, la posición mormona era ambigua: el cometido ideológico para la liberación espiritual de la gente, y el soporte político a un régimen opresivo y económicamente ambicioso que estaba basado en capital y técnicas extranjeras.

La mayoría de los mexicanos no sólo estaban enojados con Díaz y sus 'científicos', sino también con Estados Unidos, que sesenta años atrás había adquirido casi la mitad de México como botín de la

Guerra México-Estados Unidos.[6] Un mormón de Piedras Negras agrupó el impacto que esto había tenido en México cuando dijo a sus visitas norteamericanas de la misma fe: "Yo les amo como misioneros, pero no puedo olvidar el hecho de que su país le haya quitado al mío su territorio".[7] Para 1910 mucha gente pensaba que Porfirio Díaz y sus asesores estaban regalando el país, una actitud que complicó la posición de los mormones en México.

Por muchos años el Departamento de Estado norteamericano --por no mencionar a numerosos ciudadanos de ese país interesados en petróleo, minerales y tierras-- había apoyado abiertamente a Díaz y simpatizado con los científicos. Para muchos mexicanos esto comprobaba que Estados Unidos estaba convirtiendo a México en un estado drenado y vulnerable. Tiempo atrás habían saqueado a México en la guerra, y los mexicanos los veían, así como a los de otros países, no menos destructivos ahora. La explotación extranjera de las tierras, minerales y gente mexicanos había llegado a ser más ingeniosa. Porfirio Díaz y sus científicos la permitieron. Algunos mexicanos describían a su país como "la madre de los extranjeros y la madrastra de los mexicanos".[8]

La milicia federal y estatal, apoyada por *los rurales,* rápidamente habían reprimido varias rebeliones que surgieron en contra de la arbitrariedad. En víspera de la Revolución la nación parecía estar estable y pacífica; así que en septiembre de 1910 cuando se festejaba el primer centenario de la Independencia, "delegados especiales (de embajadas foráneas) convinieron ensalzar las virtudes y el poder del régimen de Díaz".[9]

Pero él había cometido dos errores. Primero, desde comienzos del siglo (gobernaba desde 1876) y en forma progresiva había reducido la base social de su régimen. Ya que la mayoría de los mexicanos no habían llegado a ser importantes, para 1910 tuvo que depender casi en su totalidad de extranjeros o criollos --que se enorgullecían de ser 'más extranjeros que mexicanos', por su mezcla de sangre europea-indígena. Prácticamente nadie más que ellos se benefició bajo el gobierno de Díaz. Segundo: en 1908 había prometido públicamente realizar elecciones populares en 1910, permitiendo que un movimiento político contrario iniciara sus preparativos para tal fin. Sin embargo, cuando la oposición constitucionalista empezó a adquirir inmenso soporte popular, un alarmado Díaz de repente encarceló a sus líderes y aterrorizó a quienes los seguían.

En efecto, Díaz forzó a su oponente principal, Francisco I. Madero --hombre callado y sensible cuyas ideas principales habían sido: 'Gobierno constitucional y no reelección'-- a ser uno de los más inesperados revolucionarios del mundo. Educado, rico, urbano y proclamando una campaña basada en una plataforma constitucionalista de ley y orden, Madero se encontraba haciendo un desganado llamado a las armas. Muchos se unieron a él e intentaron destruir el régimen de Díaz. Desde el punto de vista de la gente, el *'porfiriato'* --la sociedad entre extranjeros y mexicanos elitistas-- había llegado a su fin. Muchos ciudadanos ahora se encontraban listos para comprometer sus vidas y honor personal en una campaña de cambio, aun cuando significara violencia y finalmente guerra civil.

Iniciaron una revolución que abarcó lo económico, social, intelectual y religioso tradicional a nivel de la sociedad mexicana. Toda la actividad del país fue interrumpida o devastada durante los siguientes diez años. Más del quince por ciento de los ciudadanos murieron víctimas de heridas, enfermedad o el hambre que acompañaron a esta guerra civil causada por las diferencias entre clases sociales.[10] En 1913, Madero fue asesinado bajo condiciones que implicaron severamente al embajador estadounidense Henry Lane Wilson.[11] Aunque hay poca evidencia que indique que el gobierno norteamericano estuviera involucrado, pocos mexicanos lo dudaban. Para ellos, Wilson *era* el gobierno de Estados Unidos, y entonces siguieron adelante con la Revolución.

El embajador Wilson simpatizaba con el porfiriato y trabajó diligentemente para su regreso. Estaba ansioso de conseguir a Victoriano Huerta como el reemplazo de Madero, pero rápidamente fue frustrado. Encontró que Huerta estaba asediado por Emiliano Zapata, Venustiano Carranza, Álvaro Obregón y Francisco 'Pancho' Villa, cada cual dirigiendo un frente revolucionario contra él. La guerra civil continuó.[12] Los revolucionarios comprendieron que el usurpador de Madero beneficiaría a los Estados Unidos y a sí mismo, reinstalando el porfiriato. No había conjetura alguna, en razón de que así lo declaraba Henry Lane Wilson; por lo que el usurpador Huerta y sus partidarios, los Estados Unidos, eran considerados como el enemigo.

La gota que derramó el vaso, en 1916, fueron dos pelotones de tropas norteamericanas que entraron a México bajo el mandato del general John Joseph 'Black Jack' Pershing, en una campaña inútil por capturar al legendario revolucionario Pancho Villa.[13] En México, tanto amigos como enemigos de Villa odiaban a los estadounidenses. Es más, Venustiano Carranza, al cual apoyaron en 1916 con el fin de eliminar a Villa, dio la espalda y peleó en tierra mexicana contra soldados norteamericanos intentaban capturar a Villa. Una gran cantidad de mexicanos estuvieron intensamente orgullosos del marginal éxito de Carranza en tales enfrentamientos. 'México es para los mexicanos, no para los españoles, franceses o americanos', pensaban. Seguro que el porfiriato no regresaría:[14] la Revolución continuaría.

Al principio, los mormones en el centro de México, Chihuahua y Sonora no estaban en su mayoría involucrados en la Revolución. Más de 4,000 mormones angloamericanos vivían en el norte, y más de 1,600 mexicanos vivían en la parte central de México. Sus líderes les instruyeron a que se mantuvieran ostensiblemente neutrales durante la Revolución. Pero eventualmente las comunidades fueron molestadas y miembros encarcelados, torturados y muertos tanto por tropas federales como revolucionarias. La Iglesia perdió tierras e inversiones en el norte, y los misioneros una vez más fueron obligados a abandonar el redil en el centro de México, que con tanto cuidado habían cultivado.

ÉXODO DE LAS COLONIAS DEL NORTE

Cuando Elizabeth Williams y Heber Farr contrajeron matrimonio en la casa del padre de la novia, dentro de la Colonia Dublán en la Navidad de 1893, sus regalos de boda no sólo eran prácticos sino típicos de la circunstancia económica mormona: dos platos de hojalata, dos cuchillos y tenedores, dos cucharas grandes, dos cucharas chicas, dos metros de encaje para funda de almohadas y un platón para pastel. Su primera casa fue una carpa y su cama, mesa y demás muebles estaban hechos con cajas de madera usadas para embarque.[15]

Para 1912 los regalos de boda eran mucho más generosos y diversos, incluyendo no sólo utensilios de cocina sino algunos artículos de lujo, muebles de casa, ropa, ganado y hasta un terreno donde construir la nueva casa. En vísperas del éxodo mormón de Chihuahua y Sonora --a pesar de rumores de levantamiento-- las colonias eran más prósperas que nunca. Eunice Harris, quien años atrás dejara su hogar en Payson, Utah, sin más esperanza de ganancia material que el seguir a su familia después de escapar de los comisarios estadounidenses, estaba comprensiblemente feliz sobre las inesperadas mejorías económicas. Ellen E. B. McLaws escribió lo siguiente en 1912 desde su granja, en Sonora:

> "Este lugar está creciendo y mejorando todo el tiempo. Nuestros campos de trigo ahora son hermosos. Pienso que las perspectivas financieras nunca estuvieron mejor en nuestras vidas." Thomas Cottam Romney dijo en los años previos a la Revolución: "Teníamos casi todo lo que deseábamos."[16]

Pero para los recién casados, así como para sus padres, ya nada importó después de julio de 1912. "Recuerdo los regalos que recibimos en la boda, algunos de lo cuales nunca se abrieron y se quedaron para ser destruidos por los mexicanos que incendiaron nuestras casas", dijo Luella R. Haws."[17] Eliza Tracy Allred agregó: "Dejamos cosas que nos habían costado 25 años de trabajo. Nuestros huertos empezaban a dar fruto. Por primera vez en nuestra vida de casados teníamos almacenado bastante pan y frutas para un año. Salimos como animales, llevando nuestras cosas en furgones, sin nada más que unos cuantos acolchados."[18] Alvin M. Larson, uno de los refugiados de Colonia Díaz, recuerda cómo los revolucionarios "quemaron la mayoría de los edificios, esparcieron el ganado y mataron todo lo que no se llevaron." Mientras 500 residentes se encontraban a salvo antes de que llegaran los revolucionarios, la ciudad fue casi totalmente destruida. Cuando finalmente llegó la familia Larson a Logan, Utah, en agosto de 1912, tenían únicamente "la ropa que vestían y 2.50 dólares."[19] Aunque esperaban regresar en corto tiempo y reclamar sus tierras y propiedades, la mayoría de los mormones eventualmente aceptaron la idea de que todo lo habían perdido. Quienes sí regresaron se encontraron con una década de experiencias desafiantes, conforme la Revolución continuaba desarrollándose.

Los santos que habían vivido en el norte tenían dos desventajas: eran relativamente prósperos, y eran anglosajones. Permanecer neutrales fue un desafío delicado, ya que primeramente los ejércitos federales y luego los revolucionarios descendieron sobre las colonias, cada cual indicando que él era la 'ley' a la que los mormones debían sujetarse y pagar impuestos.

Tanto el ejército federal como los revolucionarios tomaron la precaución de no destruir la motivación de los colonos o su capacidad de producir un exceso que pudieran confiscar; pero conforme continuó la Revolución, también la demanda de proveerles de comida, provisiones y servicios. Además de eso, los tiempos de revuelta dieron paso a robos, abuso personal, saqueos y ocasionalmente matanzas. Tampoco los revolucionarios ni los federales podían mantener una disciplina militar, pero los primeros -- especialmente Pancho Villa-- ejecutaron a varios de sus propios hombres por rebasar el límite tolerable de hurto señalado para las colonias.

Una aguda disputa continúa hoy en día entre los mormones angloamericanos que sobrevivieron la Revolución y sus descendientes, sobre si en realidad el éxodo fue algo necesario. ¿Se encontraban los santos en gran peligro? ¿Pudieron haber negociado un poco más con los revolucionarios? ¿No podrían simplemente haber rehusado entregar sus armas y de esta manera retar al rebelde ('red flagger') General Salazar, quien tenía sus cañones amenazando a Dublán? Ellos tenían su propia milicia --¿no podían haberla enlistado? Pero el peligro era claro, especialmente para las mujeres, los niños y muchos de los hombres. Junius Romney, el presidente de Estaca de las colonias, dio la orden de evacuación de Dublán mientras su vista penetraba el barril de uno de los cañones de Salazar. No entregar sus armas --que eran numerosas-- hubiera significado el bombardeo de Dublán y posteriormente de Juárez. En contraste, era demasiado arriesgado entregarlas teniendo solamente la palabra de Salazar en el sentido de que no haría más daño a los mormones.

A pocas horas de dicha instrucción, los santos de los últimos días se encontraban cargando a cientos de mujeres y niños en carros abiertos para ganado, que pertenecían al Ferrocarril Central Mexicano para su evacuación con destino a El Paso, Texas. Los hombres los siguieron a caballo y arriando el ganado que podían. El éxodo de las colonias ubicadas en las montañas también fue por carreta y caballo hacia Arizona. Ciertamente algunos tenían recelo, razón por la cual la controversia sobre el éxodo continúa. Pero una vez que las autoridades locales de la Iglesia decidieron evacuar, los colonos llevaron a cabo el plan tan pronto como les fue posible.

De todos los americanos que radicaban en el norte, los mormones sufrieron menos. Tanto los federales como los revolucionarios les trataron en una forma menos severa que a otros americanos o a la población nativa. Más aún: durante las primeras etapas de la guerra, los revolucionarios les molestaron menos que las tropas federales, lo que ocasionó una simpatía considerable hacia ellos entre los mormones. Sin dicha información, sería extraño el hecho de que varios colonos eventualmente hicieran arreglos para que se le proporcionaran las ordenanzas vicarias del templo a uno de los más famosos revolucionarios: Francisco Villa. Él había expresado su creencia en la fe mormona a algunos de los santos que había capturado y encarcelado;[20] ocasionó a los mormones mucho menos daño del que su posición o inclinación hubiera permitido, y anunció también que ejecutaría a cualquiera de sus soldados que violara a una mujer mormona --ninguna lo fue.[21]

La ciudadanía norteamericana que tenían los santos llegó a tornarse negativa cuando se hizo evidente que la política extranjera estadounidense favorecía a Carranza en lugar de a Pancho Villa, permitiendo que fuerzas *carrancistas* entraran en territorio americano y por la retaguardia le ocasionaran a éste un golpe devastador. A pesar de ser leales a los Estados Unidos, pero al mismo tiempo viviendo en México, los mormones angloamericanos fueron muy afortunados en salir de todo ello en la forma en que sucedió.

El 11 de septiembre de 1912, el general Salazar dio un discurso a sus compatriotas y a los colonos mormones que se habían reunido en contra de su voluntad y bajo sus órdenes en la saqueada Colonia Morelos. Su discurso, interpretado por Moroni Fenn, ilustra ampliamente los sentimientos xenofóbicos de esos tiempos. Según Fenn, un colono capturado y conscripto por Salazar con la finalidad de que transportara materiales para sus tropas, Salazar consideraba al presidente estadounidense Howard Taft como un "perro repugnante" que encabezaba una nación que había tomado bajo traición el territorio mexicano de Arizona y Nuevo México. Como recompensa, Salazar anunció que los revolucionarios iban a "correr de México a todos los norteamericanos."[22]

A pesar de la fanfarronería de Salazar, muchos de los mexicanos respetaban a los mormones, especialmente aquellos alrededor de Juárez. Y aunque la Revolución casi destruyó Colonia Díaz y las colonias mormonas de las montañas, la Colonia Juárez quedó relativamente ilesa --en parte por el cuidado que los mexicanos locales proporcionaron mientras los dueños estaban fuera. Por ejemplo, cuando Junius Romney ordenó la evacuación de Dublán y Juárez, el obispo de ésta, Joseph C. Bentley (quien vigorosamente se opuso a la orden de evacuación pero la obedeció) y Alonzo Taylor fueron de noche a visitar a Felipe Chávez, el oficial del gobierno en Colonia Juárez y a varios otros mexicanos. Bentley y Taylor responsabilizaron a estos hombres para que cuidaran la colonia mientras sus habitantes estuvieran ausentes. Encargaron de las propiedades a Chávez y le proporcionaron dos cartas --una dirigida a los federales y la otra a los rebeldes-- con el fin de explicar su mayordomía a cualquiera que ocupara el territorio. Asimismo, pidieron a otros mexicanos que velaran por su mercancía, huertos y ganado. Cuando algunos de los colonos regresaron a Juárez después del éxodo, encontraron que los mexicanos habían honrado su compromiso en todo sentido. Los mormones de Chuichupa hicieron arreglos similares que permanecieron por algún tiempo. Sin embargo, en Dublán "algunos estaban deseos de ver la salida de los Santos de los Últimos Días."[23] La colonia sufrió, sin duda alguna, pero el cuidado de los residentes locales mexicanos la salvó de una destrucción indiscriminada.

Cuando los santos llegaron a El Paso, una discusión acalorada surgió tratando de decidir cual sería su siguiente movimiento. Recibiendo tratamiento amable de los ciudadanos de ahí, algunas de las familias esperaron semanas para ver si podían regresar a sus hogares. Finalmente, cuando el gobierno norteamericano decidió pagar los gastos de traslado, cientos de ellos optaron por radicar allá. El presidente Joseph F. Smith, quien había tomado el lugar de Lorenzo Snow, cerró la estaca Juárez y relevó a sus miembros de la responsabilidad en México. Eran libres para reasentarse donde pudieran.

A pesar de este fin aparente, el apóstol Anthony W. Ivins y el obispo Joseph C. Bently --conectados emocional y económicamente a las colonias mormonas-- hablaban con frecuencia de la posibilidad de volver. Finalmente Bentley y otros cuantos regresaron y se reasentaron en Juárez, Dublán y Chuichupa. A veces su estancia era precaria, otras casi imposible. Durante los siguientes años, el presidente estadounidense Woodrow Wilson mandó a los *marines* a Veracruz, y muchos mexicanos temían que también ordenara la invasión de la Capital (1914).[24] Todo esto fue comprensiblemente seguido por la orden del presidente Smith para una segunda evacuación. La expedición inútil a México del general Pershing en 1916, buscando a Pancho Villa, también complicó grandemente la situación para los santos que habían regresado. Diversos episodios dramáticos en los que la vida de ellos dependía de una decisión rápida, aseguraron que el obispo Bently y su rebaño estuvieran en la mentes de todos aquellos que pensaban en las colonias anglosajonas de México.[25] Al menos de una manera todo esto era benéfico para los mormones: En los años por venir, los colonos seguirían proveyendo la habilidad de la lengua española para el esfuerzo misional en otros lugares de Latinoamérica.

LOS MORMONES DEL CENTRO PADECEN
LA REVOLUCIÓN

Mientras que los mormones en el norte tenían sus encuentros con la Revolución, también los que se encontraban en el sur la sufrieron. Para abril de 1911 el movimiento abarcaba a toda la nación, siendo el centro el menos afectado. Nadie había molestado a los misioneros o su trabajo, pero algunos miembros sí tuvieron sus sustos de vez en cuando. El 19 de abril de 1911, los misioneros escribieron al presidente de la Misión Mexicana, Rey L. Pratt, diciéndole que la gente del lugar y en las poblaciones indígenas vecinas con ramas mormonas, estaban preocupados por rumores de que pronto Zapata atacaría. Emiliano Zapata, con algunos simpatizantes en Ozumba y un número mayor en los pueblos circunvecinos, continuaba reclutando a miles para la causa revolucionaria.[26]

Para mediados de mayo la situación de Porfirio Díaz era obviamente insostenible. Villa y Orozco habían invadido Ciudad Juárez en el norte, y entre el 13 y el 17 de mayo Zapata había atacado furiosamente Cuautla, haciendo huir a muchos de sus habitantes y provocando gran daño a edificios e instalaciones del gobierno. Algunos de los santos permanecieron en la ciudad durante este episodio, y aunque nadie resultó herido, los hogares de Zúñiga y Aguilar se encontraban llenos de agujeros de bala. Conforme se extendió la Revolución a través del país, el ejército federal y aun *los rurales* empezaron a caer en forma sorprendente. José Yves Limantour, el brillante ministro de Finanzas del *Don Porfirio,* vio lo inevitable y acordó la dimisión de Díaz aun sin consultarlo.

Limantour y Madero acordaron que se estableciera un gobierno de transición dirigido por Francisco de la Barra, hasta que Madero pudiera ser elegido presidente --lo cual era un hecho. Cuando la noticia de dicha capitulación se dio a conocer en la capital el 23 de mayo de 1911, hubo aclamaciones en muchos hogares. Al día siguiente miles de personas desfilaron por las calles y en el *Zócalo* (la plaza principal de la ciudad de México), gritando: "¡Renuncie! ¡Renuncie!" --lo que no se había escuchado por más de treinta años. Chusmas con frases similares rodearon el Palacio Nacional, gritando. La respuesta del presidente fue disparar a matar a más de doscientos de ellos. Otros murieron en sus casas --algunos de inmediato, otros lentamente, ya que ningún doctor se atrevía a atender sus heridas. Los misioneros, observando desde una posición apartada, contaron ocho muertos e indicaron que el gozo de la gente "no reconocía límites" cuando Díaz por fin renunció el día 25.[27] Aparentemente pronto fue posible viajar, ya que los misioneros de varios de los pueblos se juntaron para llevar a cabo reuniones.[28]

Algunos mormones habían desarrollado sus propias ideas acerca de la Revolución. Los misioneros y ciertos miembros en Ozumba pensaban que Zapata era un 'bandido sureño'; otros, en los poblados indígenas, pensaban que era el 'salvador sureño'. Cuando el 16 de Septiembre se celebró la Independencia, los miembros y seis misioneros en Ozumba escucharon lo que Zapata había hecho en Cuautla y creyeron en los rumores de que definitivamente estaba por llegar a Ozumba --lo cual fue solamente un rumor. Empezaron a sostener menos reuniones nocturnas, pero sí llevaron a cabo la conferencia de distrito programada para el siguiente febrero, reportando que en general los trabajos misionales marchaban relativamente bien.

Mientras las autoridades centrales mexicanas se derrumbaban a la vista de espantados diplomáticos extranjeros, ansiosos hombres de negocios y alarmados hacendados, la situación de la Iglesia en el centro de México llegó a ser más confusa y desesperante. Los mormones mexicanos y otros ciudadanos fueron afligidos no tanto por balas y fuego de cañones, sino por enfermedad y falta de abrigo.[29] Por la naturaleza anti extranjera del conflicto, los misioneros angloamericanos del centro corrían el riesgo de ser asesinados.

En abril de 1912 el presidente Joseph F. Smith envió un telegrama a Rey L. Pratt, indicándole que hiciera lo que pensara fuera mejor para proteger a los misioneros: que actuara en armonía con la Embajada Americana. Al día siguiente, diez de los misioneros -- casi la mitad de las colonias en Chihuahua – se registraron con un comité que había asignado Henry Lane Wilson para proteger a los norteamericanos en la ciudad de México. Posteriormente Pratt se puso en contacto con todos los misioneros que se encontraban fuera de la capital, indicándoles que no permanecieran fuera de la oficina central que les correspondía durante la noche. Si se requería evacuación, él no quería tener demoras para comunicarse con ellos.

Después de tomar esas precauciones, Pratt y los misioneros continuaron sus actividades normales. Él y Ernesto Young --secretario de la Misión que después contribuyo significativamente al desarrollo de la Iglesia en Latinoamérica-- terminaron el trabajo de editar y publicar una nueva edición del himnario en español, que tenía composiciones y traducciones hechas por los mismos misioneros y miembros mexicanos. Expandieron los esfuerzos misionales específicamente a Cholula, en el estado de Puebla, un lugar que capturó su atención porque, como lo indicó un misionero, sus habitantes eran "una gente culta".[30] Continuaron su obra en Toluca, San Marcos, Ozumba y todos los demás lugares con excepción de Cuautla, punto estratégico de disputa entre los zapatistas y las tropas federales, que fue aislada frecuentemente para visitantes hasta por seis meses.

Viajes apropiados, menos reuniones por las noches y un poco de precaución permitieron a los misioneros efectuar sus tareas diarias. Después supieron que miles de mormones angloamericanos de Chihuahua y Sonora habían tenido que abandonar sus colonias y huir a Estados Unidos. Pratt relevó de sus deberes eclesiásticos a los misioneros cuyas familias habían sido afectadas para que pudieran ayudarlas. Poco después la Primera Presidencia de la Iglesia anunció que debido al peligro no mandaría nuevos misioneros a México,[31] lo que fue bastante deprimente para los miembros.[32]

Para el 12 de agosto de 1912 la situación había empeorado también en el centro de México, donde había más de 1,600 santos.[33] Algunos de ellos fueron echados de sus hogares en la distrito de Toluca. En otros sitios la vida rutinaria era insegura. Los federales culpaban al movimiento zapatista, que se había incrementado durante el mes con los reclutas de los pueblos, que veían una oportunidad de librarse y vengarse. Para los misioneros llegó a ser imposible visitar las inseguras ramas sureñas, donde varios trenes habían sido asaltados y quemados, con guardias asesinados. Así que los misioneros enfocaron sus actividades al "área fría o a los valles cercanos a las oficinas de conferencia (Distrito), donde pudieron trabajar sin molestias."[34]

El sube y baja entre federales y zapatistas afligió a numerosas familias mormonas. Muchas veces los miembros no podían mantener una apariencia neutral en el conflicto, y otras el conflicto se utilizó para cobrarse viejos rencores --como en el caso de Camilo y Modesto Ramos, Leonardo Linares y Regino García, de Cuautla, quienes se vieron atrapados entre los zapatistas y los federales. En una ocasión, cuando se llevó a cabo un bombardeo indiscriminado y los federales no pudieron encontrar ningún enemigo en la zona de batalla, acusaron a estos hombres de ser zapatistas y los encarcelaron. Como muchos otros, los cuatro santos desafortunadamente se encontraban en un sitio donde se sospechaba que los zapatistas se infiltrarían. Tal vez algunos fueran simpatizantes de esos grupos, pero no estaban armados.

Los federales los trasladaron al Departamento de Guerra del gobierno en la ciudad de México, que por costumbre, una vez ahí, los reclutaba al ejército. Muy pocas preguntas se hacían sobre la lealtad, ya que este tipo de hombres se consideraban como forraje para los cañones: fusilados de frente por los revolucionarios o por los federales a la espalda, en realidad no importaba. Los cuarteles de *La Canoa* recibían cientos de ellos.

Rita Ramos y Sabina Linares no se despegaron de sus esposos durante el viaje a la capital. Luego, en comprensible desesperación, contactaron la Casa de Misión y le dijeron al presidente Pratt lo que había sucedido. Todos sabían cómo los federales trataban a los 'sospechosos'. No se podía perder ni un minuto.

Pratt consiguió permiso para visitarlos y contactó al Departamento de Guerra, donde se le dijo que tenía él que 'probar' su inocencia. Sabina Linares y Rita Ramos prontamente regresaron a Cuautla con el fin de conseguir los documentos necesarios. Viajaron por tren a Ozumba y luego caminaron y lograron que se les llevara en burro unos 50 kilómetros hasta llegar a sus hogares en Cuautla --que casi estaba destruida. Se hicieron de cartas y documentos de los oficiales de la ciudad que quitarían toda duda de lo que se les acusaba. Entonces, a pie, iniciaron su regreso a Ozumba, Rita Ramos cargando a su niño de pecho y jalando a otro pequeño. De allí continuaron por tren a la ciudad de México. La terrible experiencia les había costado tres días y considerables privaciones.

Pratt presentó los documentos en la oficina del secretario de Guerra e hizo arreglos con el comandante militar de La Canoa para que los hombres no fueran trasladados de la capital hasta que el asunto de su libertad fuera resuelto. Se les aseguró que no sucedería así, pero en menos de una semana los dos mormones fueron enviados al norte sin dar aviso ni a sus esposas ni a Pratt. Éste de nuevo visitó las oficinas de Guerra. "Es un error, porque hay evidencias suficientes que prueban su inocencia", se le dijo.[35] Iban a regresarlos de inmediato, pero nunca sucedió. Los federales indicaron que Camilo Ramos murió poco después de 'una enfermedad incurable' --dejando a su esposa e hijos ante un futuro inseguro. Los miembros locales se encargaron de la familia Ramos, mas por la Revolución sufría tanta gente que era difícil prestar mucha ayuda.

Hubo otros casos. Alguien informó que un miembro de la rama de San Pablo acusó a Julia Olivares, de la misma comunidad, de ser zapatista. Antes de que Pratt pudiera tomar acción sobre su caso, los federales la mandaron como esclava a un campo de trabajo que se encontraba en Quintana Roo. Tropas federales ejecutaron a Juan Rodríguez, de la rama Chimal, así como a Jesús Rojas Enriques, de Ozumba, al ser acusados de *zapatistas.* La esposa de Rodríguez ya había muerto y el dejó a dos niños. Aunque Porfirio Díaz ya había muerto, su 'estilo' de orden público continuó en apogeo. En Ozumba muchos se estaban cobrando viejos rencores utilizando métodos similares, y cuando los zapatistas arrasaron el pueblo les tocó su turno.[36] Más tarde los zapatistas ejecutaron al presidente de la rama San Marcos, con uno de sus fieles amigos.

Durante todo esto, Pratt y sus siete misioneros continuaron viajando a las ramas accesibles y ayudando donde podían. Lo más importante era mantenerlas unidas para que así la comunidad de la Iglesia pudiera ser activada cuando se viera la necesidad de uno de ellos. La Sociedad de Socorro continuó ayudando a sus respectivos miembros durante toda la guerra civil.

Fue durante una de estas visitas misionales que la familia Monroy --Rafael, Jovita, Guadalupe y su madre, de nombre Jesús--, de San Marcos, fueron convertidos y bautizados. Los misioneros habían estado haciendo proselitismo en el estado de Hidalgo desde el comienzo de la Revolución, y los integrantes de esa familia fueron los primeros miembros de ese lugar desde su apertura, en 1901. Pratt apreciaba a Rafael, un hombre relativamente rico y culto que era dueño de una tienda de abarrotes, tierras y ganado. Los dos tuvieron largas pláticas, y Pratt lo invitó con su familia al Parque Tívoli para la celebración del *4 de Julio* de 1913 que se llevaría a cabo para la colonia estadounidense, hospedándolos en la Casa de Misión. Fue una amistad fatídica. A causa de su afiliación mormona, Monroy moriría en la Revolución.

La parte central de México estaba llegando a ser una zona de tiroteo. La tensión aumentaba cada hora en la ciudad de México. El incremento de fuerzas revolucionarias indicaba a algunos que ellos intentarían tomar la capital para septiembre de 1913. Como precaución, Pratt mudó a su familia y los misioneros que trabajaban en la capital, de México a Veracruz -- aunque regresaron para efectuar una conferencia en agosto. Sin embargo, el día 28 de ese mes los periódicos imprimieron una petición hecha por el Departamento de Estado norteamericano para que todos los estadounidenses salieran de inmediato del país. Recordando las instrucciones previas que el presidente Smith había dado, Pratt juzgó prudente considerarla como una orden para los misioneros mormones. Notificó a todos sus élderes de las áreas circunvecinas que se prepararan para partir a Veracruz.

Hubo detalles organizativos de último minuto que se tenían que hacer para asegurar la viabilidad de las ramas. Y aunque la mayoría de ellas eran dirigidas por miembros nativos, ese no era el caso de algunas de las más nuevas, como San Marcos. Rafael Monroy vino para despedir a los misioneros y Pratt lo ordenó élder y lo llamó para presidir a los mormones en San Marcos, efectuar reuniones y organizar allí la rama. Entonces partió con su familia y los misioneros.

Los mormones en el centro de México se encontraron solos una vez más. Cuando Ammon Tenney prometió a Julián Rojas y a la familia Páez en 1901 que los misioneros y los poseedores del sacerdocio de la Iglesia no los abandonarían de nuevo, no podían haber previsto lo que sucedería en septiembre de 1913. Mas no estaba del todo equivocado: los élderes anglosajones habían salido, pero permanecieron los líderes mexicanos, que asumieron la carga y continuaron haciéndolo, solos, durante más de cuatro años.

Cuando Pratt llegó a la Salt Lake City en el mismo mes, se encontró con que las autoridades de la Iglesia estaban decepcionados de México. Les preocupaban los santos que radicaban en el centro del país, y se hallaban también inquietos por los más de cuatro mil miembros que radicaban en las colonias del norte y acababan de ser expulsados de sus tierras y hogares. Se habían perdido vidas y millones de dólares en personas y propiedades que habían sido destruidas. Los líderes dudaban que se pudiera predicar de nuevo en México.

Percibiendo sus sentimientos, Pratt trato de tranquilizarlos. En la Conferencia General de la Iglesia de octubre de 1913, les dijo: "Yo tengo la sangre de esa misión en mis venas, a tal punto que me es casi imposible hablarle a la gente aquí a menos que hable sobre la Misión Mexicana."[37] Con insistencia, les recordó a los santos angloamericanos la necesidad de mantener una misión entre los lamanitas.[38] Su hija, Mary Pratt Parish, pensó que algunas de la autoridades se impacientaron un poco con su padre por su incesante recordatorio de la obra en México, pero la percepción del padre era correcta: después de que los mormones norteamericanos dejaron Chihuahua, el interés de las autoridades de la Iglesia por la obra en México disminuyó notablemente.

¿Qué hacer ahora? Si no se podía trabajar en México, razonaron los líderes, ¿por qué entonces no trabajar entre los cientos de miles que vivían en Estados Unidos? Así, la situación negativa dio pie a la creación de la Misión Hispano Americana, y Pratt fue llamado para dirigirla. Ahora los norteamericanos de ascendencia mexicana podrían escuchar el evangelio en su idioma preferido, el español.

Aunque Pratt deseaba regresar a México y la Primera Presidencia de la Iglesia no estaba ansiosa por dejar a los miembros de la Iglesia solos --debido al peligro físico--, las autoridades finalmente decidieron no mandar a nadie hasta que la guerra civil terminara. Esto se lo indicaron específicamente a Pratt. Él podía intercambiar correspondencia con ellos y velar lo mejor posible de esa manera; pero el servicio postal que se interrumpía frecuentemente hizo que se tratara de un esfuerzo limitado, pero al que Pratt imprimió energía y convicción.

La correspondencia con los miembros mexicanos era a la vez alentadora y dolorosa. Los presidentes de rama estaban haciendo lo mejor que podían para mantener a sus congregaciones unidas y al mismo tiempo ser neutrales ante las fuerzas armadas --lo que mayormente lograron, salvo cuando los santos fueron reclutados en uno u otro de los grupos armados. Efectuaron sus reuniones cuando la situación era calmada y aun mantuvieron un tanto la obra misional. Por otro lado, algunos santos mexicanos y muchos de sus conciudadanos frecuentemente sufrieron de hambre. Pratt llegó a enterarse de que fueron "obligados a buscar entre la basura para obtener alimento, y a comer quizá sólo una vez al día. Varios de los miembros fueron reclutados al servicio militar, con escasez de ropa y mala paga, dejando a sus familias para mantenerse por sí mismas."[39]

Lo más triste para Pratt fue cuando recibió una carta el 16 de diciembre de 1915, escrita por Jesús Monroy y procedente de San Marcos, en la que le indicaba que su hijo Rafael y su compañero Vicente Morales habían sido fusilados, y que Emiliano Zapata había transformado el pueblo en zona de guerra, destrozando rieles del ferrocarril, incendiando máquinas y cabuses, y semanalmente alternando el control del pueblo. Como en el resto de México, ambas partes utilizaban Ozumba para cobrarse deudas personales, políticas y religiosas. En cierta ocasión, cuando los zapatistas mantenían el control de San Marcos, Monroy fue acusado de simpatizar con Carranza y asociarse con norteamericanos. (Se había visto obligado, por causa de lo que almacenaba en su tienda, a recibir a los oficiales carrancistas cuando estaban en el pueblo.) Los zapatistas lo arrestaron. Encarcelado por un tiempo, averiguaron que era mormón y le ofrecieron perdonarle la vida si denunciaba su religión. Él y Morales no aceptaron. Años después, los niños de la escuela mormona en San Marcos, Hidalgo, ocasionalmente visitaban las tumbas de Monroy y Morales para rendirles homenaje.[40]

En su mayoría, a pesar del caos y derramamiento de sangre, los miembros que radicaban en el centro de México siguieron los consejos que Pratt les había dejado a su partida: Manténganse unidos, permanezcan neutrales lo más que se pueda, cumplan con los convenios, sigan a sus líderes. Lo hicieron bastante bien, incluso algunos de ellos guardando la décima parte de sus limitadas entradas para pagar el diezmo.[41]

En noviembre de 1917, cuando la Revolución se apagaba, Rey L. Pratt recibió permiso de regresar a México y darle seguimiento a sus esfuerzo de ayuda. Antes había persuadido a las autoridades de la Iglesia a que mandaran dinero para algunos de los miembros en México, pero nadie sabía con seguridad si dichos fondos habían llegado intactos. Ahora Pratt regresaba para ver quién y bajo qué condiciones había sobrevivido. Pronto supo que muchos de los santos, especialmente niños, habían muerto de hipotermia y hambre durante la guerra. La bienvenida que recibió le indicó también otras dos cosas: los Santos de los Últimos Días habían tratado de mantener unida a la Iglesia y estaban gozosos de ver de nuevo a su presidente de Misión.

Pratt notó que un indígena, Isaías Juárez, había llegado a ser un líder respetado e importante entre los mormones de México. En los años por venir Juárez se

convertiría en alguien todavía más importante, cuando los misioneros de la Iglesia una vez más tendrían que huir de México para permanecer fuera por más de diez años mientras el gobierno federal hacia las paces con la Iglesia Católica. De nueva cuenta, para su continuación en México, la Iglesia de Jesucristo de los Santos de los Últimos Días dependería de sus líderes locales.

NOTAS:

1. Es difícil saber qué tan extenso era este sentimiento de desesperación, pero ciertamente para 1914-15 era bastante extenso. Sin embargo como lo es en otras traumas, tanto personales como colectivas, la desesperación en México fue de poca duración, siendo finalmente seguida por la euforia de la victoria. Las canciones folklóricas que aun sobreviven sobre la Revolución en su mayoría son optimistas. No le hace que tan mala haya sido la situación, la gente de alguna manera escogió recordar lo que fue su propósito en vez de lo que les estaba sucediendo en el proceso. Así como en anécdotas de la Guerra de Revolución Americana, y de gente que ha sido victoriosa en todas partes, desesperación iluminada por la luz de la victoria es vista como valentía, fuerza y fortaleza.

Entre los extranjeros, la percepción era claramente la opuesta. Uno solo necesita estudiar los registros familiares de los Mormones Anglo-Americanos los cuales perdieron sus tierras y seres queridos en la guerra, para ver que para ellos, los vencedores eran los malos.

2. En el libro de Hubert Herring (p. 328) *A History of Latin America* ofrece la mejor descripción de los científicos.

Desde 1882 en adelante, nuevas caras aparecieron en el circulo do confianza de Díaz, la mayoría creollos, los cuales reemplazaron a los mestizos sobre los cuales había anteriormente confiado, dichos hombres llegaron a ser popularmente conocidos como los científicos. Su fe política y económica se debió en gran parte al positivismo de Auguste Comte y ellos aceptaron su conclusión ingeniosa de que la sociedad podía ser rescatada a través de las técnicas de la ciencias "sociales" que no habían sido corrompidas por metafísica y teología. Se llamaron liberales, pero no aceptaron el liberalismo de Juárez [el presidente de México, el único indígena a quien consideraban como visionario y se enorgullecían sobre una viabilidad fuerte [una de las consecuencias fue reducir grandes sectores de la sociedad Mexicana por medio de explotación de extranjeros así como nacionales]. Los científicos, nunca más de un pequeño grupo, eran por lo regular hombres de considerable idealismo y favorecían una administración honesta, cortes imparciales y una medida de libertad de prensa y expresión. La honradez, imparcialidad y libertad se les extendió a todos menos a los Indios. Y ciertamente el hecho de que México era mas Indio que otra cosa, no molestó la conciencia de los científicos.

3. Ibid. La tendencia de Herring parece ser que los errores de Díaz fueron tácticos y no estratégicos. Así que cualquier comentario negativo de Herring sobre Díaz puede considerarse con algo de confianza en cuanto a su validez.

4. Ibid., p333. Vea la nota 7 del capitulo 3 donde se da mas información bibliográfica del periodo de Díaz.

5. Los lectores estarán interesados en el pintoresco tratamiento de Anita Brener, *The Wind that Swept México: The History of the Mexican Revolution, 1910-1942*, pp.7-36. También vea el excelente estudio regional de Mark Wesserman, *Capitalists, Caciques, and Revolution* y para un estudio mas profundo a nivel nacional, José C. Valdez, *Historia General de la Revolución Mexicana*.

6. "El tratado de Guadalupe Hidalgo" formalmente dio fin a la guerra el 2 de Febrero de 1848. México recibió $15 millones y la cancelación de todas las reclamaciones pendientes. Los Estados Unidos recibió Texas (o mas bien su derecho a ella) y los territorios que ahora son los estados de California, Nuevo México, Arizona, Nevada, Utah y parte de Colorado - mas o menos la mitad del territorio nacional Mexicano. (Herring, *History of Latin America*, p.312).

Quien ocasionó la guerra? Las respuestas indica que ambos, los Americanos y los Mexicanos, con un predominio análisis singular - variable dando el fallo en forma resuelta el cual recae resonantemente sobre los expansionistas nacionalisticos de los Estados Unidos y en los izquierdistas nacionales en México. Para cada uno de estos grupos la culpa fue "todos los Mexicanos" o "todos los Americanos". El lector interesado podrá investigar el libro de Glenn W. Price, *Origins of the War with México: The Polk-Stockton Intrigue*.

7. Historia Oral de Lorenzo A. Andersen, entrevistado por Gordon Irving, p.70.

8. La frase es del libro de Martin C. Needler, ed., *Political Systems of Latin America*, p.18. Díaz daba la bienvenida al capital extranjero en una forma tan extensa que llegó a dominar la vida económica de la nación. Herring da la observación de que "los Americanos e Ingleses eran los dueños de los pozos petroleros y minas. Los Franceses controlaban el negocio creciente de textiles y muchas de las tiendas principales. Los Alemanes, el mercado de artículos de ferretería y farmacéuticos. Los Españoles)y en especial los Gallegos de Galicia) eran abarroteros y comerciantes al por menor. Los servicios públicos - tranvías, compañías de electricidad, agua - pertenecían a los Ingleses, Americanos, Canadienses y varios otros grupos foráneos. Los

Mexicanos no entrenados en las técnicas modernas, en efecto eran extranjeros en su propia tierra". (Herring, *History of Latin America*, p. 331.

9. Charles Curtis Cumberland, *Mexican Revolution Genesis under Madero*, p. 3.

10. Como referencia general vea el libro de William Weber Johnson, *Heroic México: The Violent Emergence of a Modern Nation*.

11. Marquez Sterling ha observado que (como se cita en el libro de Herring, *History of Latin America*, pp. 340-41, n. 3):

Los Mexicanos, en general, culpan al Embajador Wilson con la responsabilidad moral de la tragedia final de Madero. Que fue indiscreto, no cabe duda. El Secretario de Estado, Philander Knox le advirtió que usara "circunspección". Su colega, el Embajador Cubano, reportó que Wilson convocó a la comunidad diplomática después de la aprensión de Madero y orgullosamente declaró "México ha sido salvado". De hoy en adelante habrá paz, progreso y prosperidad. Yo he sabido de los planes de aprensión de Madero por tres días. Estaba programado para llevarse acabo esta mañana". [Herring entonces observa que Madero y su vice presidente] firmaron su renuncia basada en la promesa dada por Huerta de darles salida segura del país; La esposa do Madero y muchos otros apelaron al embajador Americano para que persuadiera a Huerta a cumplir su promesa - pero sin éxito, ya que el diplomático había llegado a ser uno de los partidarios más fervientes del nuevo régimen. El 22 de Febrero de [1913] Madero y Pino Suarez fueron asesinados por guardias que los trasladaban a la penitenciaría.

Mientras que a Wilson se le acusa de haber estado involucrado en el asesinato de Madero y por lo tanto a favor de la junta militar que elevó al General Victoriano Huerta al poder, el embajador Alemán, Paul Von Hintze, favorecía mantener vivo a Madero con el fin de que fuera un contrapeso a la influencia de los Estados Unidos en México. Pero si uno analiza la situación, hubo bastante intriga Internacional en todo este evento. Dos relatos, desconocidos y no publicados - uno de la propia mano y puño de Wilson y el otro un memorándum dirigido a Wilson de William F. Buckley - de estos eventos dan un punto de vista interesante sobre Wilson. (Vea el libro de W. Dirk Raat y el de William H. Beezley, eds., *Twenty Century México*, pp. 104-14; vea también el de Friedrich Katz, *The Secret War in México: Europe, the United States and the Mexican Revolution*.

12. La mejor obra en general, sobre Zapata aun es la de John Womack, jr., *Zapata and the Mexican Revolution*. Sobre Carranza vea el libro de Douglas Richmond, *Venustiano Carranza´s National Struggle, 1893-1920*; Linda B. Hall a escrito una obra amena e informativa sobre Obregon. (Alvaro Obregon: *Power and Revolution in México, 1911-*

1920); y Jim Tuck, a capturado al folklórico Pancho Villa en su obra *Pancho Villa* and John Reed: *Two faces of Romantic Revolution*. Esta saliendo considerable literatura "revisionista" sobre la Revolución y la parte que cada uno de los personajes mencionados arriba desempeñaron. Vea la discusión bibliográfica de Barry Carr, "*Recent Regional Studies of the Mexican Revolution*". Un buen ejemplo de estas obras nuevas regionales es la de James C. Carney, *The Mexican Revolution in Yucatán, 1915-1924*, y la de Víctor Raúl Martínez Vasquez, ed., La Revolución en Oaxaca, 1900-1930.

13. La campaña del General Pershing fue presuntamente en respuesta a una incursión de Villa a la población de Columbus, Nuevo México. El gobierno de E. U. había permitido tropas federales Mexicanas entrar en su territorio para sorprender a Villa en su "lado protegido". Villa por lo tanto consideró que los Estados Unidos habían perdido su neutralidad en la guerra; por lo tanto ya no era exento de ataque.

Muchos observadores han notado que la campaña de Pershings a México, no fue tanto para capturar a Villa, sino para probar nuevo equipo militar en condición de guerra en anticipo de el envolvimiento de los Estados Unidos en la Primera Guerra Mundial. David Johnson, un Mormón de las colonias y el cual vendía mercancía al ejercitó de los E. U. en su campamento cerca de la Colonia Dublan en Chihuahua ha indicado las ilimitadas pruebas de aviones con alas de manta y con artillería montadas, el controversial vehículo armado motorizado y artillería automática. Todo esto se estaba llevando acabo bajo condiciones ajenas a la presencia de una campaña de capturar a Villa. (Entrevista personal).

14. Según el historiador Frank Brandenburg, "Nádie que esté familiarizado con México y los Mexicanos puede negar que una corriente profunda de sentimiento contra el extranjero fluía a lo largo y ancho de la Revolución. La historia Mexicana desde 1910 esta repleta de manifestaciones de xenofobias, chauvinistas y de fuerte nacionalismo. Las leyes Mexicanas contenían provisiones marcadamente nacionalistas en contra del extranjero. (*The Making of Modern México*, p 327).

15. Se cita a Elizabeth Williams Farr en el libro de Kate B. Carter, comp., "*The Mormons in México*", *Tresure of Pioneer History*, 3:215.

16. Citado por Blaine Carmon Hardy, "*Cultural ´Encystment´, as a Cause of the Mormón Exit from México in 1912*," p. 451.

17. Se cita a Luella R. Haus en el libro de Carter, "*The Mormons in México*", 3:212.

18. "*Autobiografía de Mary Eliza Tracy Allred 1874-1920*", p. 13.

19. Citado en el libro de Carter "*The Mormons in México*" 3:212.

20. El trabajo en el templo se llevo acabo en el Templo de Mesa, Arizona el 1 de Marzo de 1966. (Vea el libro de W. Ernest Young, "*A Brief Sketch of Lives of Francisco [Pancho] Villa and Felipe Angeles*"; El archivo también contiene correspondencia con J. H. Whetten sobre el trabajo del Templo.

21. Frecuentemente se a dicho que el asunto de "violación del honor sexual" era casi en forma fanática la que Villa tenia, la cual se derivo de la violación brutal de su hermana años atrás, por un grupo de hijos de un ranchero para la cual su familia estaba obligada a rendir servicios. Esto también se dice, fue lo que lo hizo ser revolucionario.

22. Citado en el libro de Barney T. Burns y Thomas H. Naylor, "*Colonia Morelos: a Short History of a Mormón Colony in Sonora, México*", pp. 175-76.

23. Franklin Spencer González, "*The Restored Church in México*", p. 106.

24. Muchos militares, habiendo desembarcado y asegurado Veracruz después de considerable derrame de sangre debido a resistencia Mexicana no esperada, estaban ansiosos de emprender hacia la Ciudad de México. Sin embargo tal orden nunca fue dada. El Presidente Woodrow Wilson deseaba no derramar mas sangre; era obvio que estaba sorprendido y horrorizado de la matanza que había ocurrido en Veracruz. (Vea el libro de Robert E. Quirk, *An Affair of Honor*, y el de Arthur S. Link, ed., *Woodrow Wilson and a Revolutionary World, 1913-1921*.)

25. Obras relevantes que se consultan para escribir esta sección incluyen las de B. H. Roberts, *A Comprehensive History of the Church of Jesus Christ of Letter Day Saints*; Burns and Naylor, "*Colonia Morelos*"; Thomas Cuttam Romney, *A Divinity Shapes our Ends as Seen in my Life Story*; Karl E. Young, *Ordeal in México: Tales of Danger and Hardships Collected from Mormón Colonies in México*; Nelle Spilsbury Hatch, *Colonia Juárez: an intimate Account of a Mormón Village*; Annie R. Johnson, Hearthbeats of Colonia Díaz; *Diario de John Jacob Walser (1849-1933), Eunice Stewart Harris, "Autobiography"*; Joseph Charles Bentley, *Journal*; Junius Romney, "Remarks Made in the Garden Park Ward Sacrament Meeting, Salt Lake City, Utah, 31 July 1966"; Elizabeth H. Mills, "*The Mormons in Chihuahua after the 1912 Exodus*"; Raymond J. Reed, "*The Mormons in Chihuahua: Their Relation with Villa and the Pershing Punitve Expedition, 1910'1917*"; W. Ernest Young , Oral History, interview by Gordon Irving.

26. Vea, para una opinión general, el libro de Womack, *Zapata*.

27. Historia Manuscrita de la Misión Mexicana, 25 de Mayo de 1911.

28. Ibid, de Mayo de 1911.

29. Ibid., 16 de Noviembre de 1917.

30. Ibid., 19 de Julio de 1912.

31. Ibid., 21 de Octubre de 1912.

32. Dichos sentimientos fueron registrados por W. Ernest Young el cual estuvo presente, "*Diary of My Life*", p. 72-73.

33. Dale F. Beecher, "*Rey L Pratt and the Mexican Mission*", p. 300.

34. Historia Manuscrita, 5 de Agosto de 1912.

35. Ibid., 2 de Mayo de 1913.

36. Womack, Zapata, pp. 263, 281.

37. Citado en el libro de Beecher, "*Rey L. Pratt*", p. 301.

38. Vea el libro de Rey L. Pratt, "*The Mission to the Lamanites*".

39. Beecher, "*Rey L. Pratt*", p. 301. Vea también el reporte de Rey L. Pratt en la Historia Manuscrita con fecha de 18 de Octubre de 1916.

40. El simbolismo no se debe perder en los Norte americanos. Mientras misioneros mormones asistían a la celebración del Día de Independencia en el Parque Tívoli donde escucharon elogios honrando aquellos soldados americanos que habían muerto en la Guerra México - Estados Unidos de 1846-48 (Vea por ejemplo el diario de Young pp. 67-68 así como aquellos registrados anualmente durante la celebración del Cuatro de Julio en la Historia Manuscrita), los Mormones Mexicanos estaban dando el nombre a sus primeras escuelas indígenas de sus héroes de esa misma guerra. Cada niño Mexicano escolar aprende que los jóvenes cadetes de la academia militar en Chapultepec prefirieron morir por medio de un salto suicidio de las murallas del castillo que rendirse al invasor ejercito Americano que atacaba la ciudad durante la Guerra México - Estados Unidos.

41. Rey L. Pratt, "*Review of the Mission Labor among the Lamanites*".

Capitulo 5

DESARROLLO EN EL AISLAMIENTO

En 1913 la Iglesia estaba suficientemente establecida en áreas claves del centro de México para sobrevivir la guerra civil. A pesar de que ésta afectó sus actividades, incluyendo los esfuerzos misionales, no la cerró en su totalidad. Durante el período de anarquía y desangramiento del país, varios mormones --Rafael Monroy y Vicente Morales, por ejemplo-- fueron ejecutados por razones políticas y religiosas. Muchos de los miembros originales no solamente lucharon para preservar la vida de sus familias, sino también para establecerse en un mundo cruel pero prometedor.

Entre los mexicanos, el mormonismo había sido primeramente predicado a los pueblos rurales colindantes a la ciudades de México y Puebla en lugar de a ellas mismas, patrón que se repetiría en cada uno de los países latinoamericanos. En sitios la gente primeramente había apoyado las promesas de la Revolución, pero más tarde temieron sus métodos. La simpleza y pobreza de San Marcos, Ozumba, Cuautla, Tecalco, San Andrés de la Cal, San Pedro Mártir, Ixtacalco y Atlautla contrastaron dramáticamente con el centro de la ciudad de México y sus lujosas residencias alrededor de las *Lomas de Chapultepec.* Que aquellos primeros mormones sobrevivieran en estos pueblos aislados, sin misioneros del norte, es un tributo a su fe e inventiva.

Las primeras dos generaciones de miembros mexicanos eran en su mayoría pequeños comerciantes y campesinos que vivían en casas pequeñas, que como aquellos pioneros llegados a Utah aún luchaban para satisfacer las necesidades básicas de sus hijos. Tenían expectativas, naturalmente: las familias Monroy y Parra, de San Marcos, no sólo eran comerciantes sino también dueños de tierras; la familia Hernández, de Santiago, tenía los recursos necesarios para emplear obreros temporales; las familias Bautista, González, Páez, y Balderas, de Ozumba, Tierra Blanca, Puebla y el D.F., tenían parientes en Estados Unidos --algunos incluso en Salt Lake City. Pero la mayoría de los primeros santos mexicanos sobrevivían mediante trabajo duro y dependiendo de un clima inseguro. El evento social principal era la visita de algún familiar, las reuniones de la Iglesia, los bazares de la Sociedad de Socorro y ciertas fiestas del pueblo. De vez en cuando uno de los niños tenía la oportunidad de progresar hasta el quinto año en la escuela primaria.

Los primeros miembros de la Iglesia en México eran profundamente religiosos. Un inusual número había gravitado del catolicismo a las sectas protestantes, donde habían buscado infructuosamente respuesta a sus dudas religiosas y por ello cambiaron al mormonismo. Ahora sus preguntas eran sobre esta doctrina. *¿Quiénes era los lamanitas?* Desde el punto de vista del Libro de Mormón, *¿quiénes eran los mexicanos? ¿Quienes los gentiles? ¿Cual era la doctrina mormona sobre el estado después de esta vida?* A la vista de Dios, *¿qué es lo que constituye el arrepentimiento?* Como con todo grupo, hubo aquellos que se unieron y permanecieron en la Iglesia porque era más fácil seguir que resistir; pero entre los primeros miembros este no fue el caso mayoritario. El deseo de buscar respuestas hizo que los mormones mexicanos organizaran clases de estudio sobre la *Biblia*, grupos de discusión doctrinal y otras más para estimular el intelecto. No existía ningún programa de construcción financiado por la Iglesia o administrado por ella; los primeros santos de México edificaron sus propios lugares de culto. Frecuentemente una de las familias construía un cuarto lo suficiente grande para tener en él las reuniones de la Iglesia.[1]

El mormonismo en México estaba madurando. La distancia a las oficinas centrales de la Iglesia, la inestabilidad política de México y la falta de misioneros durante ciertos períodos --todos acrecentó sus responsabilidades de liderismo. El tiempo más difícil, sin duda, fueron los años de 1913 a 1917, cuando la Iglesia se encontraba sola en México con líderes sin experiencia y miembros golpeados por la guerra, el hambre y las pestilencias. Dos sucesos significativos en el período entre 1924 y 1935 aceleraron la autosuficiencia de los mormones mexicanos. Uno fue el llamamiento de Rey L. Pratt en 1925 para abrir la Misión Argentina, lo que temporalmente lo aisló de sus deberes en México. El otro fue la *Guerra Cristera* que perturbó la vida religiosa de México durante nueve años.

En 1924 Pratt supo que pronto dejaría México para viajar a la Argentina, separándose de su familia y los miembros mexicanos por más de un año. Con el deseo de prepararse mejor, promovió concienzudamente el desarrollo del liderismo mormón mexicano. Una vez más seleccionó y autorizó a miembros del país para dirigir todas las ramas del centro de México, confiando en ellos la responsabilidad completa de sus congregaciones respectivas. Aquellos que observaron el proceso informaron que los líderes mexicanos funcionaron tan bien que los misioneros norteamericanos pudieron dedicar todo su tiempo a atraer nuevos miembros.[2] En su mayoría, el liderismo mejoró, operando de tal manera que Pratt lo calificó como sumamente alentador. Si se consideran sus elevadas expectativas, este no fue un logro pequeño. Durante la ausencia de Pratt los misioneros estadounidenses y los miembros mexicanos trabajaron tiempo extra para mantener su religión activa y creciendo.[3]

El desarrollo mexicano fue preciso, ya que en 1926 el gobierno deportó a todo clero extranjero del país, incluyendo a los misioneros mormones. La partida abrupta de los norteamericanos, como la de los españoles e italianos, fue una de las consecuencias no esperadas del *movimiento cristero* --esfuerzo vigoroso apoyado por algunos clérigos y numerosos miembros católicos, quienes desafiaron al gobierno con el intento de recuperar las prerrogativas eclesiásticas perdidas en la Revolución de 1910-17.[4] Los clérigos no querían aceptar nada menos que el control gubernamental *de facto*. Percatados del complot ideado por los españoles y títeres mexicanos, el gobierno federal, en su enojo, decidió imponer por la fuerza la prohibición del clero extranjero estipulada en la nueva Constitución. Y fue así como los misioneros, observadores y practicantes de la ley, salieron rápidamente.

Este éxodo forzado necesariamente limitó las actividades de Rey L. Pratt al sur del Río Grande, pero nunca pensó en abandonar a los santos mexicanos. Antes bien, llamó a mexicanos para que dirigieran y supervisaran a los líderes de las ramas y encargarles que con eficacia presidieran sobre los distritos de la Misión Mexicana de la Iglesia. Y en efecto, hicieron entonces lo que Pratt había dicho: coordinaron, dieron consejo, mantuvieron la doctrina y aumentaron la fe y la hermandad que la encierra.

Isaías Juárez fue llamado para presidir el distrito de México, junto con Abel Páez y Bernabé Parra como consejeros o asistentes.[5] Estos tres hombres dieron estabilidad y confianza a los pequeños grupos de la Iglesia en el centro del país. Estando ya organizadas con líderes locales y ahora gozando de dirección y ánimo continuos por parte de Juárez y sus consejeros, las ramas pequeñas sobrevivieron y algunas de ellas florecieron.

Naturalmente hubo excepciones a esta positiva tendencia general. Después de 1934, cuando empezaron de nuevo a llegar los misioneros estadounidenses a México, encontraron registros incompletos de miembros, pobres informes estadísticos y algunos otros detalles. En su celo por la formalidad, algunos de estos misioneros no reconocieron que reuniones religiosas se habían llevado a cabo, que habían sido atendidas las necesidades espirituales de los miembros ni que la organización se había mantenido a pesar de los disturbios políticos, problemas de comunicación y falta de dirección de las autoridades centrales de la Iglesia. Pero lo cierto fue que la Iglesia sobrevivió y creció bajo la dirección de los líderes mexicanos: más bautismos, nuevos esfuerzos misionales y casas de oración construidas.

Narciso Sandoval estuvo al frente de una de las ramas florecientes. Tenía solamente cuatro años de ser miembro cuando inició el movimiento cristero que resultó en la expulsión de todos los misioneros extranjeros. Poco después de este acontecimiento, invitó a todos los miembros de la ciudad de Puebla a que se reunieran en su casa para tener clases de estudio religioso. Para el año 1927, a menos de un año de su inicio, el grupo había crecido tanto que se necesitó un lugar más grande para continuarlo. Con el celo misional que tenían y el entusiasmo de Sandoval, consideraron la construcción de una capilla propia. Entonces podrían atraer más gente a la Iglesia, porque en una tierra de muchas catedrales era importante el tener un lugar apropiado para reunirse.

Pero los mormones de Puebla tenían que planear en forma realista. No podían construir una capilla tan grande como las estadounidenses ni con materiales similares, pero tampoco era eso lo que deseaban. En su lugar diseñaron una casa de reunión que ellos mismos podían construir y pagar. La mayoría de los miembros contribuyeron con fondos y participaron tanto del sudor como del entusiasmo en su construcción. Construyeron paredes y divisiones con bloques de adobe hechos con tecnología nativa comprobada. No tenían fondos suficientes para el techo, así que Juárez y sus consejeros tomaron la iniciativa con sus propios fondos --al parecer con la aprobación de Pratt, quien tenía que dedicar su tiempo a Estados Unidos. En un período de dos semanas el techo se colocó.

Y aunque la asistencia que los miembros de Puebla recibieron del fondo general de la Iglesia era pequeña en comparación con casi la totalidad que ella hace ahora para la construcción de sus edificios, fue suficiente para terminar esa capilla. La experiencia los unió, fortaleció y animó, y durante los años subsecuentes la Iglesia en Puebla creció significativamente. Es un hecho comprobado que en los siguientes cuatro años se formaron cuatro ramas relativamente fuertes en ese estado; miembros de la Iglesia construían casas de oración, llevaban a cabo actividades misionales e incrementaban su membresía.[6]

Ramas en otras partes de México también crecieron y progresaron durante este período. En Tecomatlán, por ejemplo, se construyó una capilla de piedra volcánica tallada, de la cual Pratt dijo que era "un crédito a la fe de la gente".[7] A pesar de que existían pocos centros mormones, no había misioneros de tiempo completo, escaseaba la literatura en español y casi no existían programas preparados de la Iglesia procedentes de Salt Lake City. Mas la Iglesia en México generalmente continuó funcionando.[8] Sin ayuda exterior, salvo la que Pratt podía proveer en forma discreta y a distancia, los santos sacaron fuerza de sí mismos y del consejo ocasional que Pratt podía hacerles llegar no obstante las barreras políticas --pero la fuerza principal provenía de su Dios. Ya que la mayoría pertenecían a la primera generación de mormones, el evangelio de los Santos de los Últimos Días era nuevo pero vital para ellos --y a pesar de sus circunstancias problemáticas, estaban deseos de compartirlo con otros. Como los primeros pioneros, construyeron sus propias casas de oración e hicieron proselitismo mediante un programa voluntario local. Para 1930, seis misioneros mexicanos se encontraban predicando.[9] El mormonismo en México ciertamente no estaba estancado.

Franklin S. Harris, presidente de la *Universidad Brigham Young,* visitó México en 1930 e hizo el comentario de que entre todos los extensos viajes que había realizado como científico y educador, jamás había encontrado un mejor grupo de santos que los de México.[10] Naturalmente que no estaba hablando de prosperidad, edificios espaciosos de culto y recreación, ni del nivel de conocimiento o experiencia --que comparados con el estándar de 1930 en Lago Salado eran algo deficientes.[11] A lo que él se refería era al celo y la sinceridad no común de los mormones mexicanos.

Rey Pratt estaba bastante complacido con la porción mexicana de su Misión de habla española. Estaba convencido de que los mormones mexicanos estaban dedicados a su Iglesia y por lo tanto más capacitados que antes para funcionar aislados.[12] Se había percatado, por ejemplo, de que el crecimiento de la membresía en México excedía en gran forma al de la misión de habla hispana en Estados Unidos, a pesar de que el lado americano contaba con mayor número de misioneros.[13] La asistencia a la conferencia de distrito que se llevó a cabo en 1931 también fue del agrado de Pratt: 278 personas asistieron a una de las sesiones, que se realizó en la ciudad de México presidida por líderes de este país.[14]

Tal progreso debe de ser acreditado en gran forma a la constancia y fidelidad de los numerosos miembros mexicanos, tanto líderes como seguidores, y a la delegación de autoridad cuidadosamente supervisada por Pratt, quien mantuvo contacto, aconsejó y orientó pero sin usurpar la autoridad delegada --evidentemente la condición política no se lo permitió. Pero también prefería delegar cuidadosamente, y el objetivo de su plan era desarrollar liderismo local. Rey L. Pratt calificó a sus líderes locales como "sabios y elocuentes defensores de la verdad",[15] y halagó a sus seguidores como "expresiones inspiradas del evangelio".[16]

Pratt trabajó incansablemente para ser digno de la confianza de su redil mexicano, viajando frecuentemente --y por necesidad en forma no oficial-- a México para animar a los santos y asistirlos con fondos en sus modestos proyectos de construcción. En 1927 empezó a enviar un panfleto mensual a México que tituló *El Evangelio Restaurado*, redactando la mayoría del contenido él solo. Dicha publicación es evidencia de su gran habilidad[17] (Más de medio siglo después de la publicación de su último número, el panfleto aún es recordado por quienes lo recibieron.)[18]

Pratt tenía un dominio especial del lenguaje y talento literario en inglés y español. Poseía además otro talento, difícil de describir pero fácil de sentir: una habilidad especial para utilizar un lenguaje que motivara e inspirara a sus seguidores. El uso de lenguaje en forma efectiva es mucho más profundo que tener maestría técnica. Rey L. Pratt tenía profundidad, un poder carismático, persuasivo. Un miembro mexicano dijo de él: "Tenía un don, un don para convertir a la gente y fortalecerlos espiritualmente".[19]

Las numerosas visitas que hizo a México, incluyendo paradas en los pueblos donde había congregaciones mormonas, demostraron esas cualidades. A pesar de las restricciones legales, siempre trataba de contactar a todos los santos que podía e intentaba ayudarlos de la mejor manera posible. Al concluir reuniones religiosas, inmediatamente Pratt se colocaba en la puerta para despedirse de todos, expresando amor y preocupación por su bienestar. Sin embargo, después de 1926 nunca se sentó en el podio, debido a las restricciones impuestas sobre el clero extranjero. Un saludo u ojo húmedo lo fortalecían para seguir hacia adelante. La convicción de Pratt y su amor eran bastante evidentes para ser recibidos con hipocresía o argucias.[20]

No hay muchos que puedan aparentar ser sinceros en tal intercambio de amor. Esa rara sinceridad, por lo tanto, era su 'don'.[21] Los mormones mexicanos fueron recíprocos y en ocasiones los niños de la ramas rociaban su camino con flores cuando entraba para asistir a una conferencia. Ciertamente, la otra única persona honrada así fue el presidente George Albert Smith, profeta mormón de 1945 a 1951.[22]

Pero después vino el desastre. El 14 de abril de 1931, tras una operación intestinal, Rey L. Pratt falleció.

NUEVOS LAZOS CON LOS MORMONES DE UTAH

Debido a los problemas constitucionales y la muerte de Pratt, los santos mexicanos estaban ansiosos de recibir noticias de Salt Lake City. Pronto les llegó la noticia de que Antoine R. Ivins había sido nombrado para reemplazar a Pratt como presidente de la Misión Mexicana.[23] El diario *The Desert News* publicó el anuncio de la Primera Presidencia el 23 de abril de 1931, nueve días después de la muerte de Pratt.

Al igual que Pratt, Ivins fue simultáneamente llamado a ser Autoridad General de la Iglesia y presidente de la Misión Mexicana. Cuando se hizo el llamamiento, Ivins se encontraba en Hawai supervisando una de las plantaciones de la Iglesia. No llegó a Utah para familiarizarse con las responsabilidades específicas sino hasta el 1 de julio de

1931, e hizo preparativos rápidos para poder salir a Los Angeles, donde estaban las oficinas de la Misión.[24]

El padre de Antoine Ivins, Anthony W. Ivins, un hombre gregario que había dedicado la mayoría de su vida al establecimiento del mormonismo en México, ahora era miembro de la Primera Presidencia de la Iglesia; el tío de Ivins, Heber J. Grant, era el presidente de la Iglesia. Por lo tanto los mormones mexicanos probablemente esperaban que Ivins les ayudara tanto como lo habían hecho su padre y Rey. L. Pratt. Después de todo, con una herencia familiar como esa, el presidente Ivins no podía ser sino una persona extraordinaria.

En agosto de 1931, cuatro meses después de la muerte de Pratt, Antoine R. Ivins formalmente asumió los deberes de su nueva Misión.[25] Conocía México bastante bien, ya que había pasado su adolescencia en las colonias de Chihuahua. Entonces, después de graduarse de la *Universidad de Utah* y estudiar leyes en la *Universidad de Michigan*, había asistido por dos años y medio a la *Escuela Nacional de Jurisprudencia* en la ciudad de México. Después de eso había permanecido un año más en la *Escuela de Comercio* de México, concentrándose en el español. Su padre, bilingüe, estaba particularmente ansioso de que su hijo mayor también lo fuera.

Después de recibir mucho de su educación superior en México, Ivins, persona callada e introspectiva, regresó al lugar de su nacimiento en Saint George, Utah, donde dirigió algunas de las granjas de su padre. Más tarde trabajó un año en la escuela *Lund* para jóvenes, en Centerville, Utah, tras lo cual dedicó diez exitosos años a supervisar la plantación de la Iglesia en Laie, Hawai. Desde ese oficio, que su padre esperaba le diera más madurez y confianza, Ivins había sido llamado para servir a la Iglesia en México.[26] Se había empapado en el ambiente del país durante una parte de su vida, pero después había salido. Y ahora regresaba.

En 1931 los mormones mexicanos esperaban con ansiedad que Ivins se presentara a sí mismo y trajera ánimo, dirección y saludos. Pero nada sucedió. Ivins no visitó a los santos de México, no les escribió ni les mandó panfletos mensuales. Las anotaciones sobre México desaparecieron del manuscrito histórico de la Misión, y extensos viajes misionales a la parte sudoeste de Estados Unidos no incluyeron visitas a México.[27]

De seguro las leyes mexicanas todavía restringían las actividades del clero extranjero, pero esto nunca había detenido a Rey Pratt para que operara legalmente en forma no oficial --cuidándose de nunca dirigir una reunión o sentarse en el podio cuando se encontraba en México. Antoine Ivins pudo haber hecho lo mismo, pero tal vez pensaba que la parte estadounidense de la Misión requería su completa atención, ya que los santos mexicanos habían estado progresando sin la ayuda de misioneros norteamericanos.[28] O tal vez Ivins tenía sus razones personales.[29] De cualquier forma, los santos de México se sentían desatendidos.

A finales de 1931 o principios de 1932, y bajo la dirección de su presidente de distrito, Isaías Juárez, se reunieron para tratar sus problemas comunes, tales como la falta de misioneros en México y la insuficiencia de literatura de la Iglesia en español. Sin embargo, en ese momento la preocupación principal era Ivins. Su descuido había creado un vacío entre el distrito mexicano de la Iglesia y las Autoridades Generales en Salt Lake City. Algunos miembros, sintiendo una necesidad de tomar la iniciativa, deliberaron y oraron juntos en una reunión que ha llegado a conocerse como *'la primera convención'.*[30] Entonces, por carta desde la ciudad de México, solicitaron a las Autoridades Generales de la Iglesia que les dieran un presidente de Misión de su propia nacionalidad, que pudiera funcionar legalmente en México. Esto era razonable, concluyeron, ya que su necesidad de tener un presidente de tiempo completo era real. No deseaban romper relaciones con Salt Lake City, sino únicamente tener un presidente mexicano que los representara ante las autoridades para que sus necesidades específicas pudieran ser entendidas.

Parecía razonable, pero bajo la superficie corrían emociones fuertes. Las históricamente agrias relaciones con Estados Unidos hicieron que los santos mexicanos fueran sensitivos --aun delicados. La falta de atención por parte de Ivins había azuzado el fuego del nacionalismo mexicano. Tal negligencia, aun fuera por un mes, hubiera sido ofensiva para los mexicanos; pero había durado mucho más tiempo. La falta de atención por parte de Ivins fue humillante para la totalidad de los santos de este país. Los angloamericanos, por el hecho de ignorar a sus hermanos en el sur, parecían decir que éstos no les interesaban. Así que los santos mexicanos buscaban un presidente de su propia nacionalidad no solamente por necesidad práctica, sino también porque pensaban que proveería respeto propio en vez de continua dependencia.[31]

Ni Ivins ni las autoridades de Lago Salado dieron respuesta a la carta de los miembros mexicanos. Entonces se reunieron una vez más y reiteraron nuevamente su petición por escrito. Esta reunión, probablemente efectuada en la primavera de 1932, ha llegado a ser conocida en la historia como 'la segunda convención'.[32]

A Ivins no le gustaron las acciones de los mexicanos.[33] A principios de 1932, más o menos siete meses después de haberse mudado a las oficinas de la Misión en Los Angeles y casi después de un año de su llamamiento, viajó con el apóstol Melvin J. Ballard a la ciudad de México para reunirse con los Santos de los Últimos Días mexicanos que habían participado en la primera y la segunda convenciones.[34] Reprimió su agresividad, el hecho de que hubieran efectuado reuniones extraoficiales, y el haber hecho sus peticiones. Hablando con la presidencia del distrito --Isaías Juárez, Abel Páez y Bernabé Parra--, les explicó los principios fundamentales del gobierno de la Iglesia, indicándoles que un presidente de Misión era el representante de la Primera Presidencia a la Misión, y no el embajador de ésta a la Primera Presidencia. Además, informó a los miembros mexicanos que el levantamiento de peticiones del tipo que habían enviado a Lago Salado estaba fuera de orden. En contraste con el sistema político mexicano, que animaba el recogimiento de firmas en peticiones diseñadas para llamar la atención de los funcionarios públicos indiferentes, la Iglesia veía tal acción como ofensiva y no apropiada. Pero Ivins les aseguró que, con la inspiración del Señor, la Primera Presidencia llenaría sus necesidades en el tiempo oportuno. Mientras tanto los santos mexicanos estaban obligados a apoyar al presidente de la Iglesia en sus decisiones y acciones.

A pesar de la lógica del argumento, muchos de los mormones mexicanos se sintieron groseramente reprendidos. Su entendimiento del 'Evangelio Mormón' les hacía creer que tenían tanto el derecho como la obligación de buscar la voluntad de Dios en asuntos de liderismo de la Iglesia, y eso era justamente lo que habían hecho.[35] Llegaron a la conclusión de que Ivins estaba mal informado sobre el país, y por lo tanto era incapaz de entender cuáles eran sus intereses.[36] Él consideraba que los mexicanos estaban mal informados con respecto al funcionamiento de la autoridad y la forma de gobierno en la Iglesia.

A pesar de lo anterior, los santos mexicanos no estaban tan disgustados como para salir de la Iglesia. Por un tiempo pareció que el problema de liderismo había quedado aparte, y se efectuaban las actividades normales de la Iglesia durante todo el período de la administración de Ivins --de 1931 a 1934. La situación con Ivins, aunque no la deseada, era tolerable para los mexicanos. No ayudó, pero tampoco frenó los programas o interfirió con los santos del país. El arreglo implícito entre Ivins y el presidente Isaías Juárez parecía ser, al corto plazo, aceptable para ambos lados. Si los líderes de la Iglesia en Lago Salado deseaban que los santos de México se apaciguaran y respetaran su autoridad, éstos lo hicieron. Si Ivins no deseaba preocuparse por los desconcertantes problemas mexicanos, no lo hizo. Más evidente fue el hecho de que los mexicanos deseaban liderismo local --y lo tenían: Juárez, Páez y Parra.

Mientras que la sección mexicana de la Misión oficialmente permaneció bajo el liderismo de Ivins, en realidad Isaías Juárez continuó guiando a los santos mexicanos tal como lo había hecho desde antes de la muerte de Rey L. Pratt. Sin embargo, se vio más solo después de la expulsión del clero extranjero, y sus responsabilidades se tornaron todavía más pesadas, pues no contaba con un presidente de Misión que le diera apoyo y consejo. Además, no era empleado de la Iglesia ni recibía un salario, y sus recursos económicos no eran muchos. En igual forma que todos los demás líderes mormones, él tenía su propio empleo además de sus responsabilidades eclesiásticas. Sin suficiente tiempo y dinero, no le era posible visitar frecuentemente a todas las ramas de la Misión en forma regular, razón por la que el mormonismo en México empezó a sufrir una atención inadecuada.

Los mormones mexicanos sentían la falta de ayuda en dos formas. Añoraban un líder que pudiera hacer algo para aliviar su orgullo lastimado y hacerlos sentir competentes e importantes ante las autoridades de Salt Lake City, y necesitaban un líder que pudiera dedicar toda su energía al trabajo en México. Dirigir la Misión de habla española al norte de la frontera era un trabajo de tiempo completo, como lo atestiguaron las acciones de Ivins; pero también lo era el hacerse cargo de la Misión de México, como lo demostraron los problemas de Juárez. Después de la salida de Antoine R.

Ivins como presidente de Misión, en 1934, las autoridades de Lago Salado actuaron para satisfacer estas necesidades, asignando a Harold W. Pratt --medio hermano de Rey L. Pratt-- como nuevo presidente de Misión.

La dedicación y los altos principios de Harold Pratt hicieron que sus experiencias severas como presidente de Misión parecieran inoportunas e injustas. Uno de los problemas a que se enfrentó, aparentemente sin saberlo, fue el liderismo que se desarrolló durante varios años y que funcionaba sin ser del todo satisfactorio.[37] Estaba desconcertado y espantado al ver la separación profunda que parecía dividir la parte norteamericana de la mexicana en su nueva responsabilidad. Sin embargo, su buena fe e intención de erradicar esa separación destruyó --pero no reemplazó adecuadamente-- el arreglo delicado de liderismo que había preservado a la Iglesia durante la administración de Ivins.

Los santos mexicanos no tuvieron que esperar a que Harold Pratt actuara, como lo hicieron con el presidente Ivins. A las pocas semanas de haber sido asignado en 1934, Pratt visitó México. Aprovechando la ciudadanía mexicana que tenía, prontamente se registró como ministro con las autoridades gubernamentales en Chihuahua, mismo lugar donde había operado una compañía de equipo para perforar pozos de agua. Y fue posible porque la situación política había mejorado con el declinamiento de la rebelión cristera. Ya que la guerra tenía cinco años de haber terminado, las animosidades entre la Iglesia Católica y el estado habían disminuido gradualmente. De hecho, cuando Pratt inició su trabajo, sacerdotes mexicanos de nuevo operaban abiertamente, y Pratt hizo lo mismo.

Una vez registrado en Chihuahua como clérigo, cumpliendo con la ley mexicana, Pratt inició una gira por la parte mexicana de su Misión. Trabajó eficientemente, con fuerza y en forma muy visible --presidiendo conferencias, reorganizando ramas, comprando terrenos para capillas y resolviendo directamente numerosas situaciones en la Iglesia. Manejó muchos problemas pospuestos por largo tiempo y que Juárez no había resuelto por falta de tiempo o dinero para viajar.

Harold Pratt dedicó bastante tiempo a México, haciendo cambios que consideró necesarios. También asignó algunos misioneros americanos para que trabajaran en las ciudades de México y Monterrey. Y trabajó cuidadosamente, pues no deseaba problemas con las autoridades mexicanas sobre la cuestión del clero extranjero. Ya que la mayoría de sus misioneros no eran de las colonias mormonas y por lo tanto no tenían ciudadanía mexicana, la instrucción explícita que les dio fue la de no realizar proselitismo. La responsabilidad de los misioneros nuevos era de ayudar a los santos locales por medio del desarrollo de programas, reforzando y animándolos. Pratt claramente vio la necesidad que México tenía de un fuerte líder pastoral.

Las acciones de Harold Pratt eran diferentes a las de Antoine Ivins. Algunos han dicho que se debió al gran amor que tenía para esta tierra y su gente. Y ciertamente lo demostró con su tiempo y dinero.[38] Se movió rápidamente para conseguir ayuda a los santos mexicanos, trayendo información, programas auxiliares, trabajadores estadounidenses de tiempo completo y reduciendo el aislamiento entre México y Salt Lake City. Tanto Pratt como sus misioneros americanos eran buenos trabajadores.

Pratt y ellos estaban haciendo más de lo que los mormones mexicanos habían estado haciendo, llenando muchas de las necesidades misionales, de cuidado pastoral y de desarrollo organizacional que se había descuidado por casi dos décadas. Sus esfuerzos se extendieron todavía más allá: pronto los extranjeros entusiastas se encontraban realizando lo que los santos mexicanos habían estado haciendo. Manejando casi todos los problemas relacionados con la Iglesia, el mismo Pratt impidió que los hermanos mexicanos los afrontaran. Ya que él presidía y dirigía --y por su presencia permanente--, los líderes locales tenían que ceder. Esto no ayudó a los santos mexicanos a sentirse más importantes y competentes; de hecho, golpeó en el corazón de sus inquietudes sobre su lugar entre los norteamericanos, lastimando su orgullo personal y nacional.

Sin que Pratt se diera cuenta del dilema, su drástica asunción de liderismo en la Misión rápidamente limitó las actividades de los líderes locales, quienes lo empezaron a resentir. Primero Ivins no había dado suficiente ayuda a los santos mexicanos; ahora Harold Pratt llegaba y les daba demasiada. Los líderes mexicanos estaban frustrados y confusos, provocando situaciones de tensiones entre ellos y Pratt.[39]

Sin percatarse de estas frustraciones que se acumulaban, Pratt se motivaba por lo que estaba sucediendo en México. Los miembros se veían entusiasmados y fieles al evangelio, y parecían estar respondiendo rápidamente a su liderismo. Ansiosamente motivado, Pratt se lanzó al trabajo de la Iglesia y empezó a planear una nueva capilla para la ciudad de México, que reuniera los estándares de construcción de Lago Salado, y no una que se hiciera simplemente por iniciativa local. Además --igual que Ivins--, aún tenía la responsabilidad de supervisar la Misión Hispana de la Iglesia en Estados Unidos.

Pratt se dio cuenta de que el trabajo que había sido pesado para Antoine Ivins e Isaías Juárez, ahora --con su cometido al programa de construcción-- también lo era para él. Así que solicitó a las Autoridades Generales que dividieran la Misión y asignaran a alguien más para manejar los asuntos en la parte norte y así tener la libertad de dedicarse a México.

Cuando los miembros mexicanos se enteraron de la posible división de la Misión, se alegraron sobre la posibilidad de tener una propia. Pero no deseaban que Pratt la encabezara: muchos preferían abiertamente que la división trajera incremento y oportunidades de liderismo para su gente. Ciertamente, pensaban, la Iglesia llamaría a un 'verdadero' mexicano para dirigir la nueva Misión. Para ellos el tiempo era oportuno, y supusieron que debido al crecimiento de la Iglesia en México, claramente se requería que el país tuviera su propia organización misional, con su propio presidente.

Su optimismo no era sin razón. El mormonismo había empezado en forma difícil y lenta en su país, pero ahora, en 1935, los esfuerzos habían logrado un crecimiento importante a pesar de los problemas de antaño. Varias capillas se habían construido; la membresía había crecido hasta llegar a 2,800;[40] partes del libro canónico *Doctrina y Convenios* habían sido traducidas; un nuevo himnario estaba en prensa; una hermosa y moderna capilla estaba bajo proyecto y se ubicaría a sólo ocho kilómetros del centro de la ciudad de México... Al parecer todo indicaba que el tiempo había llegado para los mormones mexicanos.

MARGARITO BAUTISTA, UN NACIONALISTA MEXICANO

No todos los santos del país creían que el dividir la Misión significaba que se llamaría a un mexicano como presidente de misión. Margarito Bautista era uno de los más elocuentes en este sentido. Bautista era mormón desde hacía mucho tiempo, con experiencia en la Iglesia, y había sido ordenado al oficio de *sumo sacerdote*; conoció y admiró a Rey L. Pratt.[41] Era un hombre instruido y dotado orador que se había esforzado para educarse a sí mismo, aun estudiando inglés y viviendo en Lago Salado durante muchos años --donde enseñó la clase dominical de la rama Hispano-Americana. Bautista había tenido la oportunidad de observar de cerca el gobierno de la Iglesia por varios años, trabajó en el Templo de Lago Salado y, como muchos de quienes laboran en los templos, llegó a ser un experto en genealogía.[42] De hecho, después de 1934 regresó a México para ayudar a los santos en su investigación genealógica.[43]

Ávido estudiante de las escrituras, estaba de acuerdo con Rey L. Pratt y muchos otros líderes mormones que le habían precedido, en que los mexicanos, su historia lamanita y la promesa a ellos contenida en el Libro de Mormón eran inseparables.[44] Pratt en varias ocasiones había expresado este concepto teológico a los santos mexicanos, muchos de los cuales tenían gran orgullo de sus importantes antepasados lamanitas. Bautista, estimulado por los sentimientos de Rey Pratt, decidió escribir un libro correlacionando las enseñanzas del Libro de Mormón con el *Antiguo Testamento*. Y Pratt, quien deseaba ver más literatura disponible para los miembros mexicanos, lo animó.[45] Aun con la muerte de Pratt, Bautista persistió, completando su trabajo tres años después.[46]

Orgullosamente presentó el manuscrito a las autoridades de Lago Salado, con la esperanza de que la Iglesia lo publicara. Las Autoridades Generales aparentemente no se habían percatado de sus esfuerzos y se sorprendieron al ver obra tan extensa. Ya que el libro estaba escrito en español y la mayoría de ellos no podía leerlo, solicitaron la recomendación de varios miembros que hablaban el idioma.

Uno de ellos fue Harold Pratt, quien no tuvo que leer mucho para darse cuenta de que la Iglesia no lo podía publicar. Era un libro muy polémico y muchas de sus conclusiones eran derivadas de literatura apócrifa, como el *Libro de Jaser*. Es más, Bautista había sobrepasado en muchos puntos la doctrina oficial del mormonismo, como preparar mapas localizando supuestos puntos geográficos del Libro de Mormón en el continente americano.[47] Siguiendo la recomendación de Pratt, las autoridades de Lago Salado le comunicaron a Bautista su decisión de no publicar el manuscrito.[48]

Margarito no podía creerlo. Sus sentimientos hacia Harold Pratt al que conocía, dejaron de ser buenos. Ya que su libro, como cualquier obra de arte, era una extensión del artista, Bautista se sintió herido e incomprendido. Estos pensamientos lo presionaban al prepararse para regresar a México, donde --pensaba-- sería mejor apreciado.[49]

Llegando a México entre abril y junio de 1934, Bautista hizo arreglos para que Apolonio B. Arzate, mormón dueño de una imprenta, publicara el manuscrito. El libro de Bautista rápidamente logro amplia circulación entre los santos mexicanos y llegó a ser un pequeño éxito editorial.[50Q] Para estas alturas Harold Pratt ya era el presidente de Misión en México. Alarmado y con el fin de que los santos no confundieran la doctrina de Bautista con la de la Iglesia, Pratt circuló una carta indicando que la Iglesia no había autorizado el libro y que su contenido en ninguna manera era doctrina oficial de la Iglesia.[51] Más tarde, los misioneros bajo las órdenes de Pratt aconsejaron a todos los miembros a "no comprar el libro, ni leerlo".[52]

Muchos mormones mexicanos habían donado tiempo y dinero para publicar y distribuir dicha obra. Bernabé Parra,[R] consejero de la presidencia de Distrito mexicana, había contribuido fuertemente para la publicación --su foto estaba en el libro con su reconocimiento-- y la mayoría de los miembros de Puebla también lo habían hecho.[53] Analizando la situación, Pratt se preocupó. Su decisión de disuadir la circulación del libro de Bautista no se derivaba de una enemistad personal contra él, como Bautista suponía, sino del posible impacto del libro. Un misionero de esa época recuerda que muchos santos preferían citar la obra de Bautista que el Libro de Mormón.

Bautista se molesto cuando la venta del libro disminuyó a causa de la indicación de Pratt y sus misioneros en el sentido de no leerlo. Muchos santos vacilaron en comprar el libro que la Iglesia desaprobaba.[54] La relación entre Pratt y Bautista continuó empeorando y la mayoría de sus discusiones eran acaloradas. Bautista amenazó con demandar a Pratt por los daños que la carta estaba ocasionando. Pratt ofreció retractarse de cualquier parte de la carta que Bautista probara que era falsa; con gran frustración, Bautista no podía indicar nada en ella que fuera probadamente falso. Por otra parte, Pratt se refería a Bautista como a un "apóstata y lobo entre las ovejas".[56] Posteriormente Bautista acusó a Pratt de intentar asesinar a Abel Páez --su sobrino--, explicando más tarde que él se refería a que Pratt había tratado de 'matar el espíritu' de Páez.[57]

¿Por qué ocasionó el libro todo este furor? De todo lo que uno puede decir acerca de él, es que resultaba ciertamente fascinante en una forma especulativa. Bautista entrelazó sus anécdotas con mucha habilidad, tomando referencias del Antiguo Testamento, el Libro de Mormón, el Libro de Jaser y los escritos de Abraham y José Smith y otros más, desarrollando totalmente a sus personajes de fuentes frecuentemente secas. Revivió personajes bíblicos a los ojos de los mexicanos de mediados del siglo veinte.[58] ¡Y los mapas! La especulación sobre la ubicación de ciudades y regiones del Libro de Mormón había fascinado a generaciones de mormones. Dicha fascinación generó aún más interés en el pensamiento teológico de Bautista.

El libro de Margarito Bautista es extenso y está organizado en forma confusa. Escribió más de quinientas hojas para poder traer a vida a sus personajes y recapitular la mayoría de las porciones históricas del Libro de Mormón de varias fuentes integradas. Parte del problema del libro era su alcance. En su extenso título (*La Evolución en México. Sus verdaderos protagonistas y su origen. El destino de América y Europa.*) Bautista proponía discutir tanto la historia de México --incluyendo sus pobladores originales y después los intrusos europeos-- como el destino de Europa y América. El intentar abarcar tan gran porción de material ocasionó que el manuscrito fuera cada vez más grande y resultara abrumador en su organización.

A pesar de ser tan voluminoso, los mormones mexicanos no leyeron el libro de Bautista con la intención que la mayoría de los norteamericanos de entonces o ahora lo leerían, sino que lo hacían completamente emocionados, como si estuvieran leyendo su propia historia familiar. En su búsqueda de un patrimonio nacional del que estuvieran orgullosos, recibían bien las historias fenomenales de los nobles aztecas y mayas y de sus antepasados, los cuales habían formado naciones grandiosas, civilizadas y escogidas.[59] Y más que todo, aceptando las interpretaciones de Bautista sobre las profecías del Libro de Mormón, querían saber que México sería de nuevo un gran país.[60] Bautista enfocó su esfuerzo en la historia y el patrimonio de las razas americanas y enfatizó el impresionante futuro profetizado para los nativos descendientes de Israel.

Nadie se preguntó sobre el impacto sustancial que el libro podía tener en los mormones mexicanos, ni sobre lo alarmante que sería para los angloamericanos. ¿Pero por qué fueron tan profundos los efectos del libro? ¿Por qué se encontraban los mexicanos tan entusiasmados con el orgullo nacional y la dignidad personal, tan preocupados por su patrimonio ancestral? Desde el inicio del siglo, pocos santos norteamericanos habían tomado interés sobre estos temas. Habían olvidado el nacionalismo postrevolucionario que se inició tras el enfrentamiento y la guerra civil, nacionalismo que se encontraba en su apogeo en México, y por lo tanto no entendieron el porqué de tanta popularidad hacia el libro. Como consecuencia --tal como las historietas de los pioneros de Utah que recitan los niños en la Escuela Dominical--, los relatos de la *Revolución Mexicana* y la *Guerra Cristera*, con la parte que formaron los mormones en ellas, inspiraron a cinco generaciones de santos mexicanos, tanto niños como padres. En estas historietas ni los Estados Unidos ni España eran bien aceptados.

El enviar a un presidente de Misión y misioneros norteamericanos a México, puede ser comparado con mandar supervisores 'yanquis' al estado de Alabama para presidir sobre la educación religiosa una década después de la proclamación de emancipación de Abraham Lincoln. Sospecha, falta de confianza y prejuicios tenían que ser vencidos cada vez que un nuevo norteamericano entraba a México para representar a la Iglesia. Es sorprendente, pero a pesar de ello muchos santos mexicanos llegaron a amar a los misioneros venidos de Estados Unidos.

Margarito Bautista y su libro se acomodaban perfectamente al crecimiento nacionalista mexicano. Los santos mexicanos se llenaban de gozo al leer las promesas referente a ellos en el Libro de Mormón. Bautista tocó a esa gente al darles un pasado de orgullo y un futuro glorioso.

¿Por qué a los angloamericanos les costó tanto el aceptarlo? Sin incluir los problemas doctrinales, para algunos patrocinaba una fuerte y desagradable posición. Bautista indicaba que la 'gente escogida' no eran sino los latinoamericanos --y en particular los mexicanos. Los 'gentiles', aquellos que no pertenecían a la 'Casa de Israel' eran, en cierta forma, personas de segunda clase. El mormonismo ortodoxo enseña que una persona puede pertenecer a la Casa de Israel ya sea por sangre o por 'adopción'. El énfasis de Bautista era poco convencional. El ser un hijo o hija de Israel por descendencia (a los miembros indígenas no les importaba qué tan diluida estuviera) era, decía Bautista, decididamente mejor que ser 'adoptado' -- como la mayoría de los santos estadounidenses. Era este prestigio racial y sentido de pertenencia lo que Margarito buscaba dar a su gente: inspirarlos y motivarlos con su grandeza futura. Al mismo tiempo, incluyó un cierto estigma al linaje de los norteamericanos y de los ya despreciados españoles.[61]

Así que además de la doctrina heterodoxa, el esfuerzo de Bautista de superar a los mormones mexicanos estaba creando una separación entre ellos y las autoridades de la Iglesia. Y ya que esto sólo perjudicaría la obra en México, Harold Pratt se oponía. Su propósito era desarrollar la fe y el testimonio entre los miembros --lo que uniría a todos en un solo grupo--, y no fragmentos numerosos de 'iglesias mormonas nacionales'. Por otro lado, Bautista interpretó la oposición a su libro como una postura personal y racial dirigida no sólo en contra de él sino de toda la *raza mexicana.* Razonaba que los líderes de la Iglesia no llamaron a un nativo como presidente de Misión durante la Revolución o la rebelión *cristera*, porque temían entregar el trabajo a un mexicano. ¿Por qué? Porque no querían que el liderismo mexicano se desarrollara. ¿Por qué? Porque temían que tal liderismo israelita los desafiara para los puestos más altos dentro de la Iglesia.[62]

Perspicaz y observador, Margarito Bautista podía ver que también el liderismo mexicano se había desarrollado, y sentía que esto había sucedido *a pesar* de las autoridades de Lago Salado. Juzgó que los líderes de la Iglesia, siendo hombres inteligentes, también lo podían ver, y por lo tanto estaban mandando anglosajones para dirigir a México una vez más y detener así el crecimiento del liderismo nacional. Esta creencia lo amargó y agotó. No podía ver nada bueno que pudiera suceder con la inminente división de la Misión Mexicana; temía que solamente trajera más americanos y, por lo tanto, disminuyera el papel que los líderes mexicanos podían desempeñar.

Bautista no estaba solo en estos pensamientos. Y aunque muy pocos coincidían en que las Autoridades Generales estuvieran conspirando contra los santos mexicanos a fin de que no progresaran espiritualmente, muchos sí veían como una necesidad esencial para su progreso el tener a un connacional como presidente de Misión. En las palabras de un mormón mexicano, "sería un gran privilegio para nuestra gente tener a un hombre de nuestra propia raza gobernar los asuntos de la Iglesia en esta parte escogida del continente". Los sentimientos y las palabras se desahogaron: "Si la Iglesia no nos da los medios y abre el camino para que podamos oficiar con autoridad entre nuestra propia gente con el fin de podernos desarrollar en forma completa, nunca podremos llevar acabo esta importante obra para nosotros mismos y nuestra gente... será imposible para nosotros tener el progreso necesario sin la oportunidad de ejercer liderismo".[63] Muchos santos de México no querían ver una creciente presencia norteamericana, y confiaban en que la autoridades en Salt Lake City fueran sensitivas a sus deseos y necesidades. Otros, como Bautista, lo esperaban y también lo temían.

Una vez que la gente supo que la Misión podía ser dividida, era claro que los puntos de vista divergían grandemente sobre lo que eso significaría para los mexicanos. Bautista y aquellos como él temían la división, en tanto que la mayoría de los santos de México la ansiaban; todos esperaban para ver si un mexicano de raza y nacionalidad sería seleccionado como presidente de la Misión. Era claro que, cualquiera que fuera la decisión, las implicaciones de ésta serían considerables.

En abril de 1936, las Autoridades Generales de la Iglesia dividieron en dos partes a la Misión Mexicana: la *Mexicana* y la *Hispano-Americana,* siendo el Río Grande la frontera común. Harold Pratt presidiría sobre la nueva Misión Mexicana. Él haría los arreglos para crear una cabecera nueva en la ciudad de México.

NOTAS:

1. Mora González, entrevistado por F. LaMond Tullis.
2. Historia Oral de William Walser, entrevistado por Gordon Irving, p. 23.
3. Esto no significa, naturalmente, que los problemas usuales asociados con la obra misionera no
permanecieron o que extraordinarios fueran evidentes. Por ejemplo, Rey L. Pratt estaba consiente de que después de su salida a la Argentina los misioneros estaban siendo deportados por el gobierno y

que otros no observaban las reglas de la misión. El comunico a su familia por medio de una carta fechada el 20 de Abril de 1926 todo su conocimiento así como su preocupación.

4. La mejor y mas comprensiva presentación del periodo Cristero es el trabajo monumental de Jean Meyer compuesta de dos volúmenes: The Cristero Revelion: The Mexican People Between Church and State, 1926'1929 y La Cristiada: los cristeros. Un análisis regional importante y perspicaz es el de Jim Tuck The Holy War in Los Altos; A Regional Análisis of México Cristero Rebellion. Un estudio regional y bien enfocado es El Movimiento Cristero: sociedad y conflicto en los Altos de Jalisco por José Díaz y Ramón Rodríguez. Vea también el libro de Ramón Jrade´s "Inquires into the Cristero Insurrection against the Mexican Revolution."

5. Abel Páez y Bernabé Parra son los que generalmente se les reconoce como los primeros llamados para asistir a Isaías Juárez. En el diario de Rey L. Pratt, fechado el 9 de Marzo de 1930 indica a Pilar Páez como el segundo consejero a Juárez en los primeros días de su administración y a Bernabé Parra como presidente de la rama de San Marcos. Así que hay algo de confusión. Sin embargo, Parra era presidente de rama, de esto no hay duda; y también sin lugar a duda es un hecho de que Parra llego a ser consejero de Juárez. Pero ¿Cuando? ¿Después de Pilar Páez?[5]

6. He confiado en dos fuentes principales para obtener información sobre el desarrollo de la Iglesia en Puebla y sus alrededores. La Historia Oral de Cruz González de la Cruz, entrevistada por Gordon Irving; y la entrevista de Santiago Mora González por F. LaMond Tullis.

7. La Historia Manuscrita de la Misión Mexicana trimestre que termina el 31 de Marzo de 1930. Durante este periodo había dos registros relevantes a los cuales a las misiones de la Iglesia se les requería mantener: La Historia Manuscrita mencionada arriba y el Registro Histórico de la Misión Mexicana. En el caso de México se superponen una con la otra. Sin embargo el Registro Histórico se dedica mas a registrar la minuta de juntas oficiales mientras que la Historia Manuscrita registra los movimientos de personal y hechos adicionales de interés para el que lleva el registro. Ambos son confiables únicamente al grado que lo fueron los secretarios de la misión y su calidad es bastante variable.

8. Literatura de la Iglesia en Español en esa época, además de la Biblia, consistía de El Libro de Mormón, dos folletos y las palabras de ciertos himnos proveídos por Rey L. Pratt; así como un himnario preparado en 1904.

9. Historia Manuscrita, trimestre que termina el 31 de Marzo de 1930.

10. Diario de Rey L. Pratt, fechado el 30 de Noviembre de 1930.

11. Eran deficientes si se comparan a nivel del área de la Ciudad de Lago Salado pero no necesariamente al nivel de algunas comunidades rurales en la parte sur y este de Utah donde los problemas y el trabajo difícil iban mano a mano. En algunos lugares de Utah las casas de culto y los poblados mormones que los rodeaban ahora se encuentran deteriorados, testigo austero de la lucha comunal de una gente cuyos hijos fueron consumidos por oportunidad y afluencia en lugares urbanos mas grandes.

12. Historia Manuscrita, trimestre que termina el 31 de Marzo de 1930.

13. Deseret News (Ciudad de Lago Salado), "Church News," 19 de Marzo de 1932.

14. Historia Manuscrita, trimestre que termina el 30 de Junio de 1931. En la conferencia que se llevo acabo en San Pedro Mártir hubo seis sesiones (4-5 de Abril de 1931) con la siguiente asistencia: 71, 107, 157, 153, 172 y 133. En las seis sesiones que se llevaron acabo en la conferencia de Tecalco (11-12 de Abril de 1931) la asistencia fue de 101, 164, 232, 223, 278 y 107.

15. Diario de Rey L. Pratt fechado el 9 de Marzo de 1930.

16. Historia Manuscrita, trimestre que termina el 31 de Marzo de 1930.

17. Copias de El Evangelio Restaurado están disponibles en los Archivos de la Iglesia SUD. Otras obras de Rey L. Pratt incluyen poesías no publicadas y material de su diario, numerosos himnos traducidos al Español (mas de sesenta se encuentran en el actual himnario en Español) y dos folletos todavía en la imprenta - La Restauración y "......y la verdad os hará libres" - y cartas personales, todo ello en los archivos de la Iglesia.

18. Historia Oral de González de la Cruz.

19. Ibid., Historia Oral come se encuentra en la grabación original.

20. En esta sección tratamos de representar a Rey L. Pratt como pensamos que los Santos Mexicanos lo percibían. Ya que la realidad y la percepción de la realidad pueden coincidir en una obra como esta, se considera mas significativa la ultima. Es la percepción de los Santos mexicanos sobre la persona de Pratt que ayuda a explicar su impacto final en dichos miembros.

21. El punto técnico que reluce aquí trata con el liderismo carismático, elementos de los cuales nosotros argumentamos, Pratt gozaba. ¿Cual es la relación especial con las masas que hace que toda la operación de un líder carismático sea tan contenedora? Uno empieza notando que la relación se refiere a una cualidad extra ordinaria de una persona, no importa si esa cualidad es real, presunta o supuesta. La legitimidad de tal mando de ese líder cae sobre la creencia de sus seguidores de que posee poderes extraordinarios, revelaciones y en la

adoración de héroes. Esto es muy diferente del mundo tradicional que tiende a ser tanto autoritario y conservador y, si es respetado, también temido.

Factores culturales (por ejemplo, las identidades tradicionales personalisticas líder -seguidor en Latino América) pueden facilitar la apariencia de líderes carismáticos, pero no en el sentido mas estricto, provee las condiciones necesarias para su seguimiento. Tales líderes aparecen en sociedades donde el personalizo y su atracción "hercules" de hombre "fuerte" no son parte de una característica cultural dominante. Y mientras que Latino América por largo tiempo se le ha considerado por sus caudillos y caciques, la legitimidad de su mando tiende a derivarse de autoridad tradicional y no carismática.

Pero consideremos a Rey L. Pratt. ¿Fue él un caudillo o cacique? A sido argumentado que él llegó en un tiempo muy oportuno para llenar la necesidad que los mexicanos tenían de satisfacer el compromiso psicológico de un líder. (Vea el libro de Dale F. Beecher, "Rey L. Pratt and the Mexican Mission," p. 294.) Pero aun así, esto no explica completamente la relación que Pratt tenia hacia los Santos mexicanos o da a conocer la naturaleza de su autoridad. Donde la cultura mexicana buscaba una fortaleza dominante, Pratt era débil; donde aprobaba dureza, él respondía con bondad; donde los mexicanos estaban acostumbrados a ser tratados con mano de hiero, Pratt persuadía a través de suplicas, contacto personal, interés genuino y sobre todo una expresión de amor imperturbable. Si los mexicanos gozaban a Pratt por que era muy "personal", es también verdadero que su base de autoridad pera tanto carismática como tradicional. Para mas discusión sobre estos puntos así como un repaso de Max Weber, refiérase a mi libro Politcs and Social Change in the Third World Countries, pp. 79-85.

El entendimiento sobre este asunto que tenían los mormones mexicanos era de que Pratt estaba expresando el amor puro de Cristo el cual, viviendo de acuerdo a principios divinos y eternos, hacia posible el poder para cambiar vidas.

22. Historia Oral de González de la Cruz. John Hawkins me indicó en una conversación personal que tuvimos en Guatemala, que el esparscr flores es un simbolismo común al recibirá santos que es parte de los ritos católicos. Ya que este mismo simbolismo existía en México, los mormones, en efecto, estaban honrando a Pratt con santidad cultural.

23. Historia Manuscrita, trimestre que termina el 30 de Junio de 1931.

24. Deseret News, "Church News," 1 de Julio de 1931.

25. Historia Manuscrita, trimestre que termina el 30 de Septiembre de 1931.

26.   La información sobre Antoine R. Ivins de su carácter y perspectiva en lo que concierne a la relación con su padre fue adquirida en una entrevista con una de sus hermanas llamada Agusta Wells.

27.   Historia Manuscrita, trimestre que termina el 30 de Septiembre de 1931 y la del 30 de Junio de 1932.

28.   Desert News, "Church News," 19 de Marzo de 1932.

29.   Por razón de que no me fue posible obtener ninguno de los papeles de Antoine R. Ivins del año 1932, y no se si papeles de otros periodos están disponibles en los Archivos de la Iglesia SUD y ya que las entrevistas orales de su administración no han producido mas que poca información, no puedo mas que dar un poco de luz de el porque Ivins ignoró la parte mexicana de su misión.

Algunas posibles ideas pueden obtenerse de un discurso que Ivins dio a una congregación de mas de ocho mil que se reunieron en el tabernáculo histórico de la Ciudad de Lago Salado en la Conferencia General de la Iglesia que se llevo acabo en Octubre de 1931. En una capacidad no oficial, trajo saludos de mas de trece mil miembros de las Islas del Pacifico. Entonces en su capacidad oficial como nuevo presidente de misión convoco "saludos de no tan numeroso grupo, pero gente mas amable los cuales viven mas cerca a nosotros, la gente mexicana. Hay algún numero de ellos en la Iglesia, son sinceros y fieles y razonablemente enérgicos en la realización de sus deberes". (Ivins en el Reporte de Conferencia, Octubre 1931, p. 72).

Les recordó a la audiencia que la obra misional entre los mexicanos se inició en 1875 cuando un grupo de media docena de hombres, (incluyendo a su padre como miembro menor del grupo) a caballo salieron de San Jorge, Utah, para llegar a la Ciudad de Chihuahua, México en el sur. Este recordatorio de la apertura que dio en su discurso le permitió repasar la obra misional en México y halagó, en forma extensa, el trabajo de Rey L. Pratt, expresando esperanza de que él (Ivins) pudiera lograr el nivel que Pratt había iniciado.

Cuando Ivins dio su discurso, solo tenia seis semanas en la misión y aun no había tenido "la buena fortuna de conocer a todos (los misioneros)." Pero esperaba visitar toda la misión dentro de pocas semanas.

En este punto de su discurso, Ivins nos dio, yo pienso, una importante clave de el porque ignoro a México. "Parece ser que la gente de la Iglesia no están completamente enterados de lo que constituye la Misión Mexicana en la actualidad," dijo él. Entonces repaso el episodio de la retirada de los misioneros extranjeros de México y anuncio que en ese tiempo únicamente un misionero ordenado estaba trabajando en México - un hermano local asignado en Monterrey. "Todo el resto del trabajo misional que se esta llevando acabo (había cuarenta y un bajo su dirección) es en Estados Unidos. Nuestra misión cubre una distancia de dos mil millas, desde Los Angeles hasta Brownsville, Texas. Además de eso tenemos una rama ahorrativa y prospera [de habla Hispana] en la Ciudad [Lago Salado] y hemos organizado ramas que se encuentran funcionando bajo el lidersimo de presidentes de rama nativos en varias ciudades en y alrededor del Valle de México". (Ivins en el Reporte de la Conferencia, p. 73). Por "Nosotros", Ivins quiso decir la Iglesia y Rey L. Pratt, el cual lo había organizado en es manera. Ivins aun no había estado ahí.

Así que Ivins parecía ser que se identificaba completamente con la parte Americana de su misión, insinuando que México era mas o menos de jure pero no de tacto parte de su preocupación. Tenemos la impresión de que Ivins, en su propia mente, se consideraba a si mismo de ser un "presidente pastoral". Para él parecía ser que era mas importante concentrar sus esfuerzos donde se encontraban los misioneros, no donde no podía estar.

30.   Las fuentes de información sobre la Primera convención incluyen la Historia Oral de González de la Cruz;   Historia Oral de William Walser, pp. 26-27;   Historia Oral de Santiago Mora González, entrevistado por Gordon Irving; Historia Oral de Harold Brown, entrevistado por Gordon Irving pp. 31-32; Historia Oral de Julio García Velázquez, entrevistado por Gordon Irving, pp. 4-34; Informe General de la Tercera Convención,   Biblioteca de la Iglesia SUD, División Histórica, Ciudad de Lago Salado; y entrevista de Santiago Mora González por F LaMond Tullis.

31.   Que la raza blanca es nuestro tutor, no lo negamos, pero también es verdad que en su debido tiempo nuestro tutor, por un acto humanitario, deberá dar la libertad de desarollarnos a nosotros mismos .... los éxitos o frutos de los labores de nuestra Iglesia entre nosotros no pueden ser reconocidos sino hasta el momento que ellos (la Iglesia) tenga la fe suficiente de conferir sobre nosotros la responsabilidad de guiar nuestros propios destinos con el fin de desarrollar nuestras vidas espirituales y la redención de nuestro pueblo..."(Informe General de la Tercera Convención, p. 20;

Es ahora el pensamiento usual a través del mundo que grupos étnicos que están experimentando rápidos cambios en sus valores (tal como lo es con los mexicanos los cuales están adaptando una nueva religión de esperanza y expectación) tienden a desarrollar una comprensión limitada a su dignidad y valor propio y luchar por el día cuando otros los respetarán, tanto por lo que esperan llegar a ser como por lo que son. Estas son algunas de las nuevas condiciones que contribuyen al rechazo del paternalismo, real o implícito. Casi todas las formas culturales, sociales o dependencias económicas, y en lo general, cualquier posición que pueda implicar "los asientos traseros del camión" son repudiados. He hecho un sumario de la nueva literatura que trata este punto que se encuentra en "Ethnicity and Ethnic Conflict".

32. Al escribir y analizar la Primera y la Segunda Convención, he tenido mucho problema en colectar la información de las fuentes originales. Hay muy pocos datos concretos disponibles de ese periodo - algunos historias orales registradas mucho después de que sucedió, algún material impreso por la Tercera Convención en 1936, un registro de las visitas a México por los Apóstoles Melvin J. Ballard y Antoine R. Ivins. Por lo tanto he puesto una foto de la realidad de ese periodo con muy pocos pedazos del rompe cabezas. Los espacios en blanco han sido llenados con extrapolaciones de la información disponible.

Para que el lector pueda evaluar lo que he dicho ilustraré mi razonamiento y como lo he "amarado" con datos y colocación de las primeras dos convenciones con los datos indicados abajo.

No parece ser posible, dado lo que conocemos de la Primera Convención, que ésta se llevo acabo antes de Abril de 1931, que fue la fecha en que murió Rey L. Pratt en la Ciudad de Lago Salado. Después de todo, se convoco para tratar en gran parte los problemas ocasionados por la muerte de Pratt. Por otro lado, ambas convenciones tienen que haber ocurrido para Marzo de 1932 cuando el Apóstol Melvin J. Ballard y el Presidente Antoine R. Ivins visitaron México. Si no, con todo lo que sabemos de Isaías Juárez, no hubiera estado a la cabeza o aun participado en la Segunda Convención. Pero si sabemos que participó en ambas, la primera y segunda Convenciones. Refiriéndonos a las fuentes, parece ser que tendremos que confiar en el Informe General en ser la información mas correcta y que se escribió treinta años antes de grabar las entrevistas de las historias orales y da las fechas mas exactas. Así que yo estoy de acuerdo de el lugar donde se llevaron acabo. Pero la fecha de la Segunda Convención tiene que estar en error - tal vez sea simplemente un error de imprenta o editorial. Podremos aventurarnos y adivinar que la fecha correcta de la Segunda Convención es el 3 de Marzo de 1932. Y aunque esto es solo un mes mas temprano haría una diferencia tremenda porque dicha fecha colocaría la Segunda Convención inmediatamente antes de la visita a México de las autoridades norte americanas. Si este es el caso, entonces todos los pedazos del rompe cabezas se unen en forma fácil. Si no, entonces no tenemos una buena explicación.[T]

FUENTE	CON VEN CION	FECHA QUE OCURRIO	LUGAR DONDE SE LLEVO ACABO
Cruz González - HO	1era	Febrero 1931	San Pedro Mártir
Cruz González - HO	1era	Después de la muerte de Rey L. Pratt	?
Cruz González - HO	2da	Septiembre 1931	San Pedro Mártir
Julio García - HO	1era	Después de la muerte	?
Julio García - HO	1era	Mientras que Rey L. Pratt era presidente	Ciudad de México
Julio García - HO	2da	Mientras que A. R. Ivins era presidente	?
Narciso Sandoval - HO	1era	1932	
Informe General, p. 16	1era	5 de Enero de 1932	Nativas, Cd. De México
Informe General, p. 16	2da	3 de Abril de 1932	San Pedro Mártir

33. En cualquier línea de autoridad, quejas del grupo mas bajo que se quejan directamente con la autoridad mas alta pone a los líderes de en medio en una posición no confortable. Esta es la razón por la cual los jefes intermediados ponen tanto hincapié en seguir "la línea de autoridad". Es también una idea del porque esa línea casi siempre esta "congestionada". El hecho es, que además de prestar servicio, jefes intermediados - e.g. presidentes de misión - están obligados a protegerce a si mismos de recriminación. Así que, la forma en que Antoine Ivins reaccionó, indicó un comportamiento de buena fe con el fin de resolver el problema, pero al mismo tiempo en una forma que legalizara su posición. Y su posición era algo delicada ya que tenia que rendir cuentas directamente a su papa y a su tío.

34. El Apóstol Ballard reporta su viaje en el diario Deseret News, "Church News" del 19 de Marzo de 1932.

35. Los Santos Mexicanos podrían haber visto el ejemplo de Brigham Young el cual amonesto a los Mormones a que tomaran parte activa en confirmar que eran dirigidos por hombres inspirados. El dijo:

Tengo mas miedo que esta gente tenga tanta confianza en su líder que no preguntaran a Dios para saber por si mismos si son en realidad guiados por El. Estoy temeroso que se conforman en un estado siego de seguridad individual, confiando su destino eterno en manos de líderes con una confianza imprudente que en si misma

313

frustraba el propósito de Dios en su salvación y debilitar la influencia que podrían rendir a sus líderes, sabían por si mismos, por la revelación de Jesús, que son guiados en la forma correcta. Dejen que cada hombre y mujer sepa por si mismo que por el susurro del espíritu de Dios, si sus líderes están caminando por el camino que Dios indica o no. (Discursos de Brigham Young, comp. John A. Widtsoe, p. 135, como es citado en The Church of Jesús Christ of Latter Day Saints, A Royal Priesthood, 1975-1976: A Personal Study Guide for the Melchizedek Priesthood Quorums of the Church of Jesús Christ of Latter Day Saints, pp. 37-38.

36. Mi información sobre los sentimientos de los Santos Mexicanos sobre la visita del Presidente Ivins se derive de el Informe General, y las Historias Orales de Harold Brown, William Walserk y Santiago Mora González.

37. Historia Manuscrita, 28 de Febrero de 1934.

38. Historia Oral de E. LeRoy Hatch, entrevistado por Gordon Irving y la Historia Oral de Ana Marie Pratt, entrevistada por Gordon Irving.

En sus tratos de negocio, Harold Pratt prefería sufrir perdidas en vez de pedir (mucho menos demandar) pago sobre deudas de gente que él sabia estaban teniendo problemas financieros. (Entrevista de John Floyd Walser por F. LaMont Tullis).

39. Este análisis es basado sobre extenso material de literatura de ciencia social que trata los movimientos sociales. (Vea mi libro Politics and Social Change, pp. 61-85 y Lord and Peasant in Perú.)

40. La figura es una extrapolación. Los registros oficiales de membresia para la misión, antes de ser dividida, enseña lo siguiente: 1933, 4,045, 1934, 4,219; 1935, 4,245; 1936, 4,317. Para el año 1937, el año después de la división, la figura es 2,854 para México. Asumiendo promedios constantes entre las secciones de México y Estados Unidos de la misión antes de su división, la membresia Mexicana antes de 1935 hubiera sido aproximadamente 2,800.

41. Mi información sobre la relación entre Rey Pratt y Margarito Bautista es tomada de la Historia Oral de Julio García Velázquez, p. 15.

42. La Historia Oral de W. Ernest Young, entrevistado por Gordon Irving, p. 33. Young es una fuente de información sobre Bautista por razón que lo conocía bastante bien. Es de esta fuente que aprendemos que Margarito Bautista tenia conocimientos de asuntos de la Iglesia como fuera de la Iglesia. Es también de Young que aprendemos del interés de Bautista y su experiencia en el trabajo del templo y la genealogía. Young corrobora nuestra impresión de que Bautista era un hombre dotado, lo cual también es evidente por sus escritos.

Aceptando la sugerencias bíblica (1 Cor. 15:31-32) que todo ser humano, vivo o muerto, requiere el bautismo para recibir exaltación, los Mormones buscan los nombres de sus antepasados con el fin de llevarlos a uno de los templos para que así los vivos puedan hacer las ordenanzas por ellos.

43. Tanto Julio García Velázquez (Historia Oral p. 60) y William Walser (Historia Oral, p. 24) indican que la Primera Presidencia mando a Bautista a México para entrenar a los Mormones Mexicanos en asuntos genealógicos. Mientras que Bautista pudo haber sido animado por algunas Autoridades Generales no sabemos por seguro si se le dio la comisión directa para llevar acabo dicha misión. Es mas seguro que lo estaba haciendo por si mismo debido a su interés intenso en todo este asunto, y aunque Walser) Historia Oral, p. 24) indica que Harold Pratt se oponía a que Bautista "fuera enviado".

44. Historia Oral de Mary Pratt Parrish, entrevistada por Gordon Irving, p. 19. A través de esta entrevista aprendemos mas sobre el interés que Rey Pratt tenia, tanto en los Lamanitas como en la promesa extendida a ellos a través de El Libro de Mormón. Pratt hizo considerable trabajo con El Libro de Mormón; para 1929 había traducido al Español los encabezados de los capítulos, las referencias, el índice y otros materiales.

45. Historia Oral de García Velázquez. A de mas, al leer los escritos de Rey Pratt "El Evangelio Restaurado", sabemos que estaba fascinado por la posible conexión entre los Indios de Latino América y la gente de El Libro de Mormón. En sus escritos Pratt especula sobre esta conexión, las cuales son muy similares a las que Bautista después escribió en su libro.

46. El voluminoso libro, incluyendo las ilustraciones y mapas, se titula La evolución de México: Sus verdaderos progenitores y su origen y el destino de América y Europa. Hay copias disponibles en la sección de Colecciones Especiales de la Biblioteca Harold B. Lee de la Universidad de Brigham Young en Provo, Utah así como en la Biblioteca de la Iglesia SUD en la división Histórica.

47. Los mapas de Bautista, sea lo que sea, son fascinantes. Tienen dos insertos doblados cerca del final del libro. Uno de ellos al abrirse enseña un mapa del mundo, el cual indica las rutas que la gente del Libro de Mormón pudieron haber tomado en su viaje a América, así como varias ciudades y regiones mencionadas en la escritura. El segundo mapa, un esbozo detallado de Centro América, indica la posible ubicación de un gran numero de poblados del Libro de Mormón así como las rutas tomadas por expediciones intercontinentales indicadas en el Libro de Mormón. Hay una pequeña grabación del continente Americano impresa en la portada del libro. En ella, Norte América es titulada "Mulek", Sur América "Lehi". Mapas como estos ciertamente no son doctrina, pero si son de gran interés para gente que

por inclinación tiene una curiosidad intelectual.   Bautista tenia tal curiosidad.

48. Historia Oral de William Walser, pp. 23-24. Walser habla sobre la acción de la Iglesia en relación al libro de Bautista y dice que Harold Pratt no tuvo que leer mucho para tomar su decisión. Tan pronto como llego al argumento a favor de religión patrocinada por el estado, supo que la Iglesia no podía publicar el libro.

49. No sabemos por seguro que la única razón por la que Bautista salió de los Estados Unidos en 1934 fue por esta frustración. Es mas, pude haber sido comisionado para hacer obra genealógica en México (vea Nota 43). Sin embargo, es también instructivo saber que Bautista era uno de entre tres y cinco mil personas de descendencia Mexicana que regresaron o se inmigraron a México entre 1931 y 1934. Algunos estaban nostálgicos, muchos estaban sin trabajo y por lo tanto indigentes, muchos eran agobiados o perseguidos por agentes federales de los E.U. Estaban cruzando la frontera rumbo a México en masa. América se encontraba en medio de la peor depresión de su historia. Una combinación de desolación Mexicana en "la tierra prometida" y el proteccionismo de E. U. de las posibilidades de empleo para sus propios ciudadanos se unieron para producir, como lo describe Andrés C. González, jr., en su entrevista, "tren tras tren llenos de Mexicanos cruzando a México por El Paso". Miles también cruzaban por otros ciudades fronterizas. Algunos de los que se les estaba deportando eran Mexicanos - Americanos que tenían documentación genuina de ciudadanía de E.U. (Vea por ejemplo el libro de Rodolfo Acuña, Occupied América: The Chicano´s struggle toward Liberation, pp. 190-195.

Si Bautista era repatriado o un hombre comisionado para desempeñar trabajo genealógico, o como mas tarde se dijo, uno cuyo intento era principalmente fomentar rebelión en la Iglesia, encontramos difícil juzgar. Una combinación compleja de motivos, no todos indicados previamente, sin duda estaban trabajando en su decisión de regresar a México.

50. Historia Oral de García Velázquez. Además, la portada del libro indica el nombre de Apolonio Arzate como el impresor.

51. Diario de Harold W. Pratt, 30 de Abril de 1936.

52. Andrés C. González, jr., que sirvió como misionero en ese tiempo, hizo esta declaración en una entrevista con F. LaMont Tullis.

53. Entrevista de Santiago Mora González.

54. Entrevista de Andrés C. González jr.

55. Este fue el análisis dado por Abel Páez y se encuentra registrado en el Diario de Harold Pratt, 3 de Mayo de 1936.

56. La información del conflicto entre Harold W. Pratt y Margarito Bautista proviene de un numero de fuentes: Diario de Harold Pratt,

Abril, Mayo y Junio de 1936, passim; Historia Manuscrita, trimestre que termina el 30 de Junio de 1936; Historia Oral de García Velázquez, pp. 4-11; Historia Oral de Brown, pp. 31-42.

57. La acusación de que Harold Pratt había intentado matar a Abel Páez fue hecha en una carta que Bautista escribió a Ester Ontiveros, una misionera que en ese entonces se encontraba trabajando en Monterrey. La carta es registrada en el Registro Histórico de la Misión Mexicana con fecha del 22 de Abril de 1936.

58. Tales esfuerzos no son nuevos, en aquel entonces o ahora, como lo puede indicar una búsqueda casual de trabajos religiosos Mormones. Sin embargo estos esfuerzos no son generalmente patrocinados por la Iglesia aunque muchos han recibido animo de una o otra autoridad general. Bautista mismo no estaba trabajando en aislamiento completo sobre este punto, aun en los años 1920´s y 1930´s. Una obra anterior por Louisa L. Greene Rihcards, *Branches That Run over the Wall: A Book of Mormón Poems and Other Writings*, Había puesto al Libro de Mormón en versos sueltos y agregado romance, nombres de las esposas y embellecimiento a la historia de la narración. El esfuerzo recibió calurosas felicitaciones de Anthon H. Land y George Reynolds, dos autoridades generales. Ya que la obra obtuvo gran popularidad en el Valle de Lago Salado, es dudoso que hubieran escapado la atención de Bautista.

59. Andrés Iduarte, quien creció durante el periodo revolucionario (ca. 1910-1940) de la historia Mexicana, escribió sobre los sentimientos que los Mexicanos tenían al estudiar el pasado de su país.

Las escuelas primaria nos hacían sentir chauvinistas. Odiábamos a los Españoles como Españoles y guardábamos un rencor especial para Pedro de Alvarado, el autor del masacre cruel de los indios; adorábamos a Cuauhtemoc, quien defendió la grande Tenochitalan (Ciudad de México) y quien, cuando forzado a rendirse a Cortes, le pidió que lo matara, pero que lo hiciera con su propio puñal; y a cacamatzín, quien apedreó a sin fin de Españoles hasta matarlos. Nos avergonzábamos con repugnancia con el solo mencionar a Moctezuma, el emperador Azteca quien entrego la Ciudad de México a los Españoles; de Malinche, la concubina de Cortes; a los indios traidores quienes apoyaron a Cortes en contra de los Aztecas y por lo tanto traicionaron a su nación. Fuimos de inmediato indignados y angustiados por la inteligencia y osadía de Hernán Cortes.

Los Mexicanos sentían que " 'los malditos Españoles nunca habían tenido a alguien tan valiente y culto como (sus) héroes.' [Habían] odio hacia los despreciables Españoles como Españoles, amor para el Mexicano como Mexicano, felicidad en la matanza de Españoles, tristeza sobre la muerte de patriotas [Mexicanos]; un celo irrazonable muy similar a fanatismo religioso: pasión, derrame de sangre y lumbre para alimentar [sus] fantasías" (Niño: Child of the Mexican Revolution, pp. 66-67).

60. Vemos los mismo suceder en las nuevas naciones del Africa. Tal vez la evidencia mas notable de ese fenómeno es el dar nuevo nombre a naciones. Mali, por ejemplo, ha tomado su nombre de un antiguo reinado africano del área. Aun mas ejemplos son las repúblicas de Zaire, Zámbia y Zimbabwe.

61. Hay poco amor perdido entre los Mexicanos y Españoles. La relación colonial entre los dos fue rota a través de despiadada derramamiento de sangre y mucho resentimiento. Tan reciente como 1975 los dos países tenían relaciones muy tensas.

62. Historia Oral de Brown, p. 32.

63. Indicado por Enrique González en el Informe General, p. 18.

CAPITULO 6

LA TERCERA CONVENCIÓN

Poco después que las noticias del nombramiento de Harold W. Pratt llegaron a la ciudad de México, el primer consejero de la presidencia del distrito, Abel Páez, se encontraba en su trabajo. Impulsado por su tío, Margarito Bautista, convocó a los santos a una conferencia inesperada, ahora llamada *'la tercera convención'.* Aquellos que asistieron decidieron, de nueva cuenta, hacer una petición a la Primera Presidencia con el fin de que se llamara a un presidente de Misión mexicano. La solicitud y los subsiguientes acontecimientos ocasionaron una escisión en el distrito mexicano de la Iglesia --división que permaneció por diez años. La eventual reconciliación vio al profeta George Albert Smith viajar a México para presidir sobre la conferencia de reunificación, lo cual es un testimonio de la forma en que las barreras de idioma, tradiciones, ambiente étnico e identidad nacional pueden imbricarse en una fe singular, aun cuando los sentimientos nacionalistas hagan que la gente sea sensible, defensiva o insensible.

Las autoridades habían negado la petición mexicana dos veces. Ahora, en rebeldía y enojados, algunos de los santos mexicanos llegaron a estar más convencidos de que su líder de Misión debería poder entenderlos así como a sus necesidades --de lo cual carecían desde el liderismo del fallecido Rey L. Pratt. Leudada su sensibilidad por el orgullo étnico y viendo disminuidas sus oportunidades de liderismo, se abocaron aún más hacia sus esperanzas frustradas.

Percibiendo la disposición de la gente, el presidente Isaías Juárez se alarmó al ver los preparativos para dicha 'convención'. Podía observar sus implicaciones tal vez mejor que cualquier otro, al haber luchado durante nueve años y visto muchas situaciones difíciles dirigiendo el distrito de la Misión. Juárez había llegado a conocer perfectamente bien la forma de ser de los santos mexicanos. Sabía que esto no sería una simple petición: un buen grupo de los miembros estaban determinados a no aceptar nada menos que un líder mexicano. (Por insólito y extraño que parezca, tal era la demanda de los miembros de la Iglesia, cuyas autoridades

319

son siempre escogidas por revelación, mas nunca 'seleccionadas' por la congregación.) Juárez también había percibido correctamente la disposición de las Autoridades Generales en Salt Lake City. Sabía que no habría un presidente de Misión mexicano en un futuro próximo. Pensó que la Iglesia no se sometería a presiones políticas, y previó un inoportuno e inevitable choque. Recordaba la primera y segunda convenciones y las enseñanzas de Antoine R. Ivins de que tales cosas no eran aceptadas por la Iglesia de Jesucristo de los Santos de los Últimos Días; y aunque él estaba igualmente frustrado como muchos otros miembros mexicanos, entendía que otra convención resultaría en una ruptura dentro de la Iglesia. Por lo tanto, rehusó alinearse a la susodicha *'tercera convención'*.

Como costumbre entre los mormones, los líderes que encabezan tratan de sentir las necesidades de la gente como de su organización, haciendo asignaciones propias de acuerdo con su mejor juicio y según sean influidos por sus concienzudos esfuerzos de buscar la voluntad del Señor. Los líderes locales, se puede decir, no son 'elegidos'; por el contrario, una vez que un líder es nombrado se pide a los miembros locales que lo 'sostengan'. Isaías Juárez claramente entendía esto, y por lo tanto esperaba el inevitable encuentro. Es probable que también entendiera la posición tradicional de la Iglesia de mandar 'forasteros' cuando la fe era nueva, y gradualmente confiar en nuevos miembros conforme se iban fortaleciendo, para asegurar así las responsabilidades más significativas del liderismo.

Juárez no era un hombre pasivo al que le gustara nadar entre dos aguas. Habiendo expuesto su posición con respecto a la 'tercera convención', se dedicó a tratar de calmar y persuadir a los santos mexicanos. Finalmente hizo circular una carta explicando que la reunión no era autorizada, y que por lo tanto corrían el riesgo de ser excomulgados. Rápidamente contactó a Harold Pratt y trató de percatarlo del problema inminente y sus raíces. Repetidamente se reunió con Abel Páez para disuadirlo. Juárez desconcertó e hizo enojar a Páez. Dos veces antes, el presidente Juárez había estado de acuerdo en reuniones similares --y hasta había ayudado a redactar una petición previa--, pero ahora deseaba evitar romper relaciones con Lago Salado. Por su parte, Páez parecía estar confuso, inseguro de qué hacer, pues no veía la situación de la misma forma que Juárez. Al principio vaciló bajo la presión del presidente Juárez, recordando que la 'convención' no sólo estaba fuera de orden sino que sería en vano, y prometió suspenderla. Sin embargo, más tarde Páez cambió de opinión, indicando que el esfuerzo valía cualquier riesgo.

Por años Abel Páez había trabajado diligente y fielmente en la Iglesia. Al meditar sobre sus propias experiencias,[1] los argumentos de Margarito Bautista empezaron a tener más sentido. *¿Si los santos mexicanos no se defendían ellos mismos ahora, cuándo lo harían?*

Cansado de lo que él percibía como paternalismo, desconcertado por lo que consideraba tratamiento de segunda clase en el Reino de Dios y convencido de que los deseos de los *'convencionistas'* eran justos, Abel Páez finalmente apoyó y estuvo de acuerdo en presidir la *Tercera Convención.* Con la ayuda de Bautista comenzó a organizar el evento.

No obstante la gran discusión entre los mormones de México por la carta que Juárez hizo circular en contra de la convención, aproximadamente 120 miembros se reunieron el 26 de abril de 1936.[2] Guadalupe Zárraga asistió como observador con el fin de tomar nota para los presidentes Juárez y Pratt. Los convencionistas rápidamente decidieron que los líderes de Lago Salado habían malinterpretado sus previas peticiones. Aunque Harold Pratt era de las colonias mormonas y un ciudadano mexicano, no lo era de sangre y raza, y por supuesto tampoco culturalmente. La nueva petición de los santos era con el fin de expresar su deseo en cuanto a un presidente que fuera 'mexicano de raza y sangre'.

Razonando que tal vez las autoridades de la Iglesia, no estuvieran enteradas de la existencia de miembros mexicanos calificados, la Tercera Convención decidió nominar un candidato. Consideraron varios nombres incluyendo el de Narciso Sandoval y Margarito Bautista.[3] Pero al final propusieron a Abel Páez. Sus intenciones no eran exigir que Páez fuera llamado, sino informar en forma clara a las Autoridades Generales que existían mexicanos capaces.

Después de tomar la decisión principal, los convencionistas fortalecieron su petición de dos maneras. Primero, deseando que sus líderes reconocieran su profunda seriedad, recabaron firmas para apoyar la petición. Segundo, la Tercera Convención autorizó una comisión integrada de Abel Páez, Narciso Sandoval y Enrique González para que viajaran a Lago Salado y personalmente presentaran la petición y los documentos pertinentes a las Autoridades Generales de la Iglesia. Terminada su agenda, la Tercera Convención cerró la sesión.

Harold Pratt estaba aturdido, viajó apresuradamente a la ciudad de México dos días antes de la Tercera Convención, anticipando lo peor pero con la esperanza de algo menor. Aún no creía que Páez llevaría a cabo los planes que estaban tan fuera de carácter para los mormones ya que eran totalmente incomprensibles para la Iglesia excepto en términos de apostasía. Hubo un tiempo en que Páez había estado de acuerdo en cancelar la Convención. En vista de esto y con el fin de evitar más disensiones Juárez y Pratt habían permanecido en casa, fuera de vista. Entonces Guadalupe Zárraga trajo noticias pésimas. Isaías Juárez lloró cuando supo que su consejero de tantos años lo había traicionado.[4]

Harold Pratt se dio cuenta que los hermanos mexicanos pronto implementarían sus decisiones. Tratando de evitarlo contactó inmediatamente a Abel Páez. Llegaron al acuerdo de reunirse el jueves 30 de abril después de la convención.[5]

El día escogido, Abel Páez se reunió con Pratt, Juárez y Bernabé Parra, el segundo consejero de la presidencia del Distrito. Después de una larga discusión llegaron a un acuerdo. Primero, Páez pondría fin a todas las actividades de la Tercera Convención, incluida la recolección de firmas para apoyar la petición; es más Páez no tomaría ninguna acción unilateral sin el consentimiento de la presidencia del distrito --una práctica de liderismo respetada dentro de la fe mormona. En segundo lugar, para mostrar su unidad y armonía, viajarían juntos los cuatro para visitar todas las ramas locales. Tercero: cada uno mandaría por separado un informe de la Convención a la Primera Presidencia. Y como cuarta medida, se prepararían lo antes posible para visitar Salt Lake City y discutir los sentimientos y deseos de los mexicanos con las Autoridades Generales. Se escogió como fecha tentativa la próxima Conferencia General de octubre.[6]

Abel Páez salió satisfecho de la reunión. Después de todo la Tercera Convención había logrado algo: Harold Pratt parecía ahora, tomar más en serio los deseos de los mexicanos y ahora los mormones mexicanos tendrían la oportunidad de presentar personalmente su caso a la Autoridades Generales. De seguro dicho viaje traería de

322

inmediato una acción positiva. Páez sentía que el propósito de la Tercera Convención se llevaría a cabo dentro de los causes y estructura de la Iglesia y por lo tanto sus acciones serían apropiadas.

Pero Páez sería decepcionado. A medida que la presidencia del Distrito visitaba las ramas Pratt y Juárez parecían ambiguos con respecto a lo acordado. Pratt indicó que únicamente él llevaría la petición a Salt Lake City durante el tiempo de la conferencia. Y en vez de asegurarle a los miembros que los deseos de la Tercera Convención serían representados a través de los canales regulares de la Iglesia Juárez y Pratt indicaron claramente que tanto los procedimiento como los objetivos de la convención estaban fuera de orden. Calificaron a Páez y a sus colegas como lobos entre el rebaño del Señor y advirtieron no escucharlos.[7]

Los devotos mormones mexicanos --aproximadamente dos terceras partes de la membresía-- habían dado a conocer su opinión contraria a la Tercera Convención a Juárez y Parra. Y sin duda Pratt había recibido comunicación sobre el asunto de Lago Salado. De cualquier forma, los convencionistas estaban indignados pensando como era posible que Páez hubiera creído que Pratt presentaría el caso de la Tercera Convención de otra, que no fuera una forma negativa.[8]

Abel Páez se encontró en una delicada posición frente a sus seguidores. Había estado de acuerdo en trabajar con la presidencia del Distrito y con Harold Pratt y anunció esta decisión a todos los miembros involucrados en la Tercera Convención. Ahora los convencionistas se sentían traicionados, reprendidos y con sus objetivos menospreciados por aquellos mismos hombres con los que suponían que su líder estaba trabajando. Juzgaron a Páez como traidor a su causa e indigno de ser nominado como presidente de Misión. Pero a pesar de toda su consternación la Tercera Convención acató las decisiones anteriores.

Abel Páez naturalmente se sintió traicionado en igual forma. Después de trabajar con Juárez y Pratt para determinar sus intenciones sobre la Tercera Convención llego a una posición irreversible. Con una nota final asumió toda la responsabilidad de la Convención y de sus actividades indicando públicamente su determinación de implantar sus decisiones. Esta pensó él eran de bastante beneficio para el bienestar de la Misión como para ignorarse.[9]

Si 'los canales apropiados' estaban cerrados, entonces trabajaría fuera de ellos.

Con la misma resolución, las Autoridades Generales llevaron a cabo su plan de dividir la Misión Mexicana invistiendo a Harold Pratt con toda la mayordomía sobre las actividades de la Iglesia en México. El nuevo presidente entro al país con su esposa y cinco hijos para iniciar una experiencia no grata.

LA SEPARACIÓN DE LA IGLESIA

Así que las líneas de batalla, sin importar que tan desganadas y sin intención hayan sido, eran firmes. Páez y más de ochocientos santos mexicanos se alinearon con la Tercera Convención (para este tiempo ya una institución con su propia estructura organizada) y en forma inflexible demandaron un presidente de Misión mexicano. El presidente Pratt y más de dos mil santos que optaron por permanecer con la Iglesia (a pesar de las objeciones de algunos de ellos al sistema misional y sistema de liderismo) continuaron con la bendición de la Autoridades Generales de la Iglesia.

En noviembre de 1936 la Primera Presidencia formalmente contestó a los convencionistas. J. Ruben Clark, hijo,[10] miembro de la Primera Presidencia y antes embajador de Estados Unidos en México --y subsecretario de Estado en su país--, preparó cuidadosamente una carta que debería ser leída en todas las congregaciones.[11] En ella indicaba que quienes habían firmado la petición de la convención se encontraban completamente fuera de orden; que el presidente de Misión no era el representante de los miembros al presidente de la Iglesia, sino por el contrario él era el representante del presidente a la gente, y por lo tanto debería estar familiarizado con todos los procedimientos oficiales para así prevenir desorden e interrupciones; que ninguna otra de las misiones eran presididas sino por hombres del seno de la Iglesia; y si el presidente de la Iglesia se sintiera algún día inspirado, él asignaría a uno de entre sus miembros para presidir sobre ellos, que como quiera que fuera, los mexicanos tenían un numero no muy usual de su propia gente en posiciones de responsabilidad; que los mexicanos no eran exclusivamente --entre los mormones-- de sangre israelita, y que ambos, mexicanos y norteamericanos eran de la misma familia: la de José; que todas las promesas del Libro de Mormón aplicaban en igual forma a una gente como a la otra y así por catorce páginas escritas.[12] Como lo había previsto Isaías Juárez, en el futuro inmediato no habría un presidente de Misión mexicano.

Las autoridades que presidían la Iglesia habían tenido esperanza que la respuesta razonable de Clark le diera fin a la Tercera Convención. Pero generalmente, no fue el caso.[13] Para la mayoría de los de la Tercera Convención, la carta únicamente confirmaba lo que por largo tiempo habían sospechado : que Harold Pratt había presentado su causa en forma negativa en la *Conferencia General de la Iglesia* de octubre en Salt Lake City, y que por lo tanto los líderes todavía no entendían la naturaleza del problema. La misma Primera Presidencia pronto supo que la carta no había resuelto nada.

Sin lugar a duda y ya para este tiempo algo exasperadas, las autoridades decidieron mandar a Antoine R. Ivins a México para una vez más intentar la reconciliación. Y aunque a Ivins se le consideraba el principal experto de la Iglesia con respecto a México, sus viajes previos al país habían sido en gran medida poco exitosos, por razón como él lo percibía, de que los miembros mexicanos no respetaban su autoridad.[14] Así que el apóstol George F. Richards, uno de los miembros del Quórum de los Doce con más antigüedad, fue asignado a acompañarle.

Cuando los élderes Ivins y Richards llegaron a la ciudad de México en febrero de 1937 era claro que entendían muy mal la posición mexicana. Los americanos interpretaban las demandas de la Tercera Convención como si se redujeran a dos: un presidente de Misión mexicano y el derecho a nombrarlo.[15] La nominación de Abel Páez parece haber sido la causa de su confusión. La Tercera Convención no tenía ninguna intensión al principio de demandar el derecho de nombrar al presidente de Misión. El nombramiento de Páez fue con el único propósito de hacerle conocer a las Autoridades de la Iglesia que sí había líderes potenciales y que la membresía los prefería. Pero los convencionistas tenían toda la intensión de dejar la selección a las Autoridades Generales, prerrogativa que ellos reconocían propia y única en la fe mormona, del presidente de la Iglesia. No obstante, en lo que sí insistían era en que su presidente, fuera quien fuera, debía de ser mexicano 'por raza' para así llenar tanto el espíritu como la letra de las exigencias marcadas por las leyes mexicanas, y también para entender mejor las necesidades de los santos del país.

Bajo este espíritu, Páez, como representante de la Convención, había escrito a la Primera Presidencia, escaso un mes después de celebrar la Tercera Convención pidiendo a la Autoridades Generales que les dieran un presidente de Misión de raza pura mexicana.[16] No obstante los élderes Ivins y Richards y también David O. McKay, en ese tiempo consejero a Heber J. Grant en la presidencia de la Iglesia parecía ser que asumían que Páez estaba demandando su propia designación como presidente de la Misión Mexicana.[17] De cualquier modo toda esta ráfaga sobre llamamiento de liderismo parecía ser un golpe de presión política, o bien completa apostasía.

La Primera presidencia de la Iglesia no podía ser ni parecer como un sello de goma para nadie, ni tampoco someterse a la presión generada por cualquier grupo fuera de los canales establecidos por la Iglesia para resolver tales asuntos. Así que su mal entendimiento de los esfuerzos y motivos de la Tercera Convención para ayudar a los líderes de la Iglesia a llegar a una decisión juiciosa los puso a la defensiva. Como respuesta tomaron la ofensiva mandando a Ivins y Richards a México para poner fin a todo este asunto.

Ivins y Richards regresaron para presentar la posición de la Primera Presidencia una vez más e indicar rigurosamente que los miembros fieles de la Iglesia sostienen la palabra del profeta en los asuntos en disputa.[18] Nadie en Salt Lake City consideraba que Ivins y Richards deberían negociar o llegar a un acuerdo con los convencionistas en México. Cuando los líderes de la Tercera Convención se enteraron de la visita inminente de los apóstoles y de su propósito, se rehusaron a reunirse en privado con ellos, solicitando que Ivins y Richards hablaran con toda la gente en una reunión general. Los visitantes estuvieron de acuerdo a pesar de que eso significaba permanecer en México una semana más.

Al iniciar la reunión el 14 de febrero de 1937, dos oficiales del gobierno entraron a la reunión y se sentaron. Los convencionistas dijeron más tarde que estos hombres estaban interesados en llegar a ser mormones y que eran inofensivos, pero Harold Pratt no sabía de eso.[19] Más aún, antes de la reunión había rumores de que tal vez los convencionistas provocarían un arresto. Naturalmente Pratt empezó a ponerse nervioso, como extranjeros, según la ley ni Ivins ni Richards deberían estar oficialmente discursando en una congregación religiosa. Así que ansiedad aumentaba a cada minuto, el presidente llamó a uno de sus misioneros y a solas le dio instrucciones de que pusiera a los élderes Ivins y Richards en un tren con destino a Estados Unidos. Lo último que deseaba ver era la aprehensión de dos autoridades generales.[20]

La salida repentina de los líderes sin dar sus discursos decepcionó a los mexicanos. Después, los convencionistas de línea dura indicaron que si los apóstoles hubieran sido como los de la antigüedad no habrían temido a los oficiales del gobierno o a ninguna otra amenaza, pero habrían permanecido y presentado sus discursos sostenidos por la fe de que todo saldría bien. Después de todo, razonaban, la Tercera Convención no habría sido tan tonta como para invitar a gente que provocara la hostilidad de las Autoridades Generales.[21]

Sin lugar a dudas las autoridades se molestaron. En su debido tiempo Ivins y Richards dieron su informe a la Primera Presidencia. Comprensiblemente, las tácticas que describieron disgustaron a los hermanos que presidían. David O. McKay en particular estaba angustiado. Este intento percibido de arrestar a los representantes de la Primera Presidencia fue la gota que derramó el vaso e impulsó procedimientos de excomunión que se iniciaron de inmediato en contra de los líderes de la Tercera Convención.[22]

Harold Pratt hizo circular el texto que el apóstol Richards había planeado dar y en el cual indicaba inequívocamente que todos los santos mexicanos estaban en error y cayendo rápidamente en apostasía, demandaba que se humillaran y regresaran a la hermandad total dentro de la Iglesia apoyando a Harold Pratt y obedeciendo en todo sentido el consejo de la Autoridades Generales. Si no lo hacían, se arriesgaban a ser excomulgados. El discurso de Richards también exigía que los convencionistas suspendieran sus publicaciones no autorizadas y detener toda traducción (que incluía partes de Doctrina y Convenios todavía no publicadas en español, así como la *Perla de Gran Precio,* las *Enseñanzas de José Smith* y de otros dos escritos mormones sagrados.[23] El texto aún que correcto y apropiado fue contraproducente: poco después los de la Tercera Convención explícitamente demandaron el derecho de decidir por sí mismos quien sería el presidente de Misión.[24] El mal entendimiento previo llegó a ser una profecía cumplida.

Para mayo de 1937 era obvia la total división. La Iglesia inició los procedimientos para excomulgar a todos los líderes de la Tercera Convención. Los días 6, 7 y 8 de mayo de 1937 se convocaron tribunales en San Pedro Mártir, y las sentencias fueron dictadas. Los líderes convencionistas fueron excomulgados por rebelión --al trabajar en contra de las autoridades de Misión--, por insubordinación --al desobedecer las órdenes de las autoridades de Misión-- y por apostasía --al no reconocer la autoridad de la Iglesia.[25]

Al notar lo agresivo de la excomunión de los líderes, los mormones que simpatizaban con la Tercera Convención, ahora se daban cuenta de que cada uno de ellos tendría que definir su propia posición. Cada uno podría pertenecer a la Tercera Convención o a la Iglesia, pero nunca a ambas. Cada individuo tenía una difícil decisión que hacer. Como convencionista, ¿cómo podían participar en las ordenanzas mormonas del templo, una parte integral de la religión y sólo accesible a un mormón de buena conducta?[26] ¿Aceptaría y reconocería Dios bautismos y otras ordenanzas llevadas a cabo por los de la Tercera Convención? Viendo hacía el futuro, ¿qué es lo que los miembros de la Tercera Convenció necesitarían hacer si algún día decidían volver a entrar a la Iglesia original? Aún más importante: ¿aprobaba Dios la Tercera Convención? Participar en actividades que los líderes mormones norteamericanos no aprobaban era una cosa; pero era otra totalmente diferente el asociarse con un grupo apóstata que implicaba renunciar a su membresía en la Iglesia.[27]

La mayoría de los mormones mexicanos sentían que perder todo derecho de asociación con la Iglesia era pagar un precio muy alto por tener un presidente de Misión mexicano. La Iglesia era importante para ellos; no deseaban perderla. Deseaban seguir a la Iglesia en todo aspecto pero no bajo el liderismo de Harold Pratt.[28] Algunos miembros pensaban que la voluntad de Dios decidiría el dilema. Para muchos fue cuestión de ejercer su derecho a la revelación personal --como lo enseña la fe mormona. Si Dios sentía que su causa era justa y aprobaba su posición, optarían por la Tercera Convención. La rebeldía contra la Iglesia era aceptable razonaban, siempre y cuando no incluyera rebeldía contra Dios. Al final de cuentas casi la tercera parte de los mormones mexicanos concluyeron que Dios estaba con ellos y la Tercera Convención, y se unieron con el grupo rebelde.

Sin embargo, significativamente, dos terceras partes de los mormones mexicanos no estuvieron de acuerdo. Dios no podía, argumentaban, aprobar la Tercera Convención o cualquier otro grupo rebelde que se opusiera a la Iglesia. Sintiendo que el asunto era racial o nacionalista decidieron permanecer fieles a la Iglesia original. Para algunos, requirió asumir posiciones de liderismo con las que no estaban de acuerdo.[29] Pero era necesario según su punto de vista, mantenerse firmes en la fe de el Señor.

Naturalmente que había otras razones por las cuales uno podía unirse o no a la Tercera Convención. Familias influían unas con otras. Esposas uniéndose con su esposo e hijos con sus padres.[30] La conveniencia reinaba en otras mentes: se reunían con los convencionistas por estar cerca de su lugar de culto, o por la misma razón se reunían con congregaciones mormonas.

Pero los mormones mexicanos no enfatizaban estos motivos; miembros adultos permanecieron o se apartaban de la Iglesia original porque pensaban que era lo correcto. Los sentimientos eran intensos y a veces apasionados. Miembros fieles a la Iglesia original condenaban a los de la Tercera Convención como herejes y los veían como diablos. Si un miembro de la Tercera Convención llegaba a una capilla donde se reunían miembros de la Iglesia original y se sentaba, la banca prontamente se desocupaba. Por su parte, los de la Tercera Convención acusaban a los miembros fieles de haberse rendido y traicionado la causa de tener liderismo mexicano.[31] Pero además de gritarse de vez en cuando ambos grupos rompieron pronto sus relaciones.

CAMINOS PARALELOS

La ruptura era completa. La Tercera Convención siguió su propio camino, llevando consigo un buen numero de miembros, algunas capillas, mobiliario y registros. Pero su camino no fue fácil. Pocas semanas después, Margarito Bautista desafió al liderismo de la Tercera Convención sobre varios puntos doctrinales. Algunos pensaron que Bautista estaba usando los dichos puntos simplemente para disfrazar su deseo de colocarse en posición de asumir el liderismo de la Tercera Convención.[32] La verdad es que Margarito era en esencia serio. El abogaba el restablecimiento de la poligamia y la *Orden Unida,* doctrina de un sistema de economía cooperativa que el mormonismo había abandonado.[33]

El desacuerdo de la Tercera Convención con Salt Lake City no era doctrinal y no tenían la intención de que temas cuestionables como la poligamia y la ley de la Orden Unida ensancharan aún más la brecha que los separaba de la Iglesia original. La tensión pronto llego a ser incontrolable y la Convención expulsó a Margarito.[34] Déspota y amargado, Bautista abandonó la Tercera Convención en su 'obscuridad' y se refugio en Ozumba, México, donde estableció su propia colonia, la 'Nueva Jerusalén'.[35] Mientras que el grupo de Bautista no se aisló en su totalidad, pues mantuvo contacto con otros mormones fundamentalistas y grupos apóstatas, eran ampliamente rechazados por los convencionistas, así como los no convencionistas. Al principio Bautista había dado ímpetu a ciertos asuntos que la mayoría consideraban justificables. Ahora la memoria de su contribución fue reemplazada con una imagen de alborotados, los mormones dijeron que ya sabían esto desde hacía mucho tiempo.

Así que la Tercera Convención continuó sin Margarito, su poligamia, su visión de una utopía económica y de cualquier otra doctrina radicalmente diferente a las existentes en la Iglesia Mormona original.[36] La Tercera Convención pronto desarrolló una estructura organizativa paralela a la de la Iglesia. Después de todo su base doctrinal era la misma y sus líderes eran hombres experimentados y dedicados que anteriormente habían sido oficiales de la Iglesia. Para hacer hincapié en sus intenciones de permanecer puros doctrinalmente, los convencionistas se autodenominaron *'La Iglesia de Jesucristo de los Santos de los Últimos Días (Tercera Convención)'*, organizaron escuelas dominicales, celebraron cultos sacramentales, establecieron 'Asociaciones de Mejoramiento Mutuo' (AMM de jóvenes y señoritas de la Iglesia) y funcionaron en forma muy parecida a las congregaciones mormonas. Como la Iglesia original, bendecían bebés, bautizaban niños y ordenaban hombres al sacerdocio.[37]

Ya que la obra misional era especialmente importante para la Tercera Convención, entrenaron a sus jóvenes para hablar en público, un talento especialmente apreciado en México.[38] Jóvenes convencionistas --hombres y mujeres-- fueron enviados a 'predicar la palabra' a todo el que quisiera escucharla. Y el siempre misionero, Narciso Sandoval, también mantuvo su esfuerzo. Sin embargo el trabajo proselitista era sólo una parte de las preocupaciones de la Tercera Convención. Sabían que para poder sobrevivir tendrían que mantener una organización viable y con vida. Así que además de enfatizar la actividad misional y desarrollar todos los demás programas de la Iglesia que conocían, los convencionistas lanzaron un ambicioso programa de construcción.[39] Donando terrenos, mano de obra y capital, construyeron no menos de seis nuevas casas de oración y, de acuerdo con la costumbre mormona, las dedicaron al Señor.

La Tercera Convención también imprimió alguna literatura religiosa, una revista titulada *'Sendero Lamanita* - con artículos titulados: *'Cómo* llegó el *Evangelio a México',* *'Los gentiles bendecidos de que hablan las Escrituras'*- a informes de varias conferencias y actividades de la Convención.[40] El editor del libro de Margarito, Apolónio B. Arzate, fue quien imprimió la revista mencionada. La Tercera Convención también publicó un informe de los sucesos que ocasionaron el establecimiento del grupo: un documento prolijo preparado expresamente para las Autoridades Generales, que contenía una transcripción de las cartas y minutas correspondientes a las varias juntas oficiales, además de otros materiales.[41]

Otro de los proyectos patrocinados por la Tercera Convención fue el de aprender el idioma inglés. En principio esto parece extraño, ya que los convencionistas se consideraban abiertamente nacionalistas. Sin embargo, ansiosos de aprender más del evangelio, se impacientaban al ver el lento trabajo de traducción en Lago Salado. Deseaban ser capaces de leer más de las treinta secciones de Doctrina y Convenios que habían sido traducidas por Antoine R. Ivins, y poder leer y estudiar los libros *Artículos* de Fe y *Jesús el Cristo* del apóstol James Talmage - textos no canónicos pero fundamentales para la fe mormona.[42]

A pesar de toda su estrategia separatista poco aconsejable, es evidente que la Tercera Convención obtuvo algunos extraordinarios logros. Entre ellos fue el entrenamiento de líderes indígenas, la expansión del programa misional que incluyó a sus hijos e hijas, el desarrollo y oportunidades educativas y la circulación de literatura doctrinal traducida al idioma español.[43] Abel Páez sobresalió en su función como presidente, llegando a conocer los nombres y problemas de casi todos sus miembros. Trabajó diligentemente por su gente y ellos le respondieron con gratitud, creyendo y aceptando sus juicios con una confianza singular. En los primeros años, antes de que se dieran los pleitos internos de liderismo, el nombre de Abel Páez y la Tercera Convención llegaron a ser sinónimos. Es más, los miembros de la Iglesia original llamaban a los disidentes el grupo de Abel Páez de la Tercera Convención'.[44] La Convención continuó operando por diez años - desde abril de 1936 hasta mayo de 1946 -, creciendo y progresando paralelamente a los grupos mormones. A pesar de que los miembros originales no tenían un presidente de Misión Lamanita, recibieron sin embargo considerable cantidad de material y ayuda organizativa de Lago Salado, con Harold Pratt trabajando lo más que podía a su favor. Así que tanto los mormones como los no muy mormones crecieron en categoría y organización, paralelos en sentimientos y estructura pero apasionadamente divididos sobre quién debería ser su presidente de Misión.

Harold Pratt trabajó sin cesar para establecer una cabecera permanente de la Misión en la ciudad de México. Estableció un programa de acción para sus 25 misioneros y visitó cada una de sus congregaciones tan frecuentemente como le era posible. Pero ya se encontraba muy enfermo y su pesada agenda de trabajo lo debilitó aún más; sin embargo, los mormones mexicanos de la iglesia original pudieron haber dado más ayuda a Pratt, pero él pensaba que debería hacerlo solo. Finalmente fue relevado en 1938 por razones médicas y el presidente A. Lorenzo Anderson lo reemplazó.[45]

Anderson, también mormón de las colonias, aceptó el llamamiento aunque con mucho desgano. Entre otras cosas le preocupaba cómo respondería su esposa. Algunos pensaban que a ella no le gustaban los mexicanos y que nada bueno saldría de los mormones oriundos de ese país. A Anderson también le preocupaba cómo seria recibido en la ciudad de México.[46]

Llegaron rumores a la Capital indicando que algunos de los mormones estadounidenses de las colonias de Chihuahua estaban encantados con el llamamiento de Anderson, ya que pensaban que haría lo que Harold Pratt no había podido lograr: enderezar a esos miembros, enseñarles quién era el jefe y ponerlos en su lugar. La Tercera Convención? ¡Qué escándalo![47]

Si era verdad, exagerado o falso, conforme el inoportuno rumor se extendía, los de la Tercera Convención le dieron a Lorenzo Anderson el sobrenombre de *'El domador de salvajes mexicanos'.*[48] Por razón de la animosidad resultante y la falta de confianza, hubo poco contacto entre la Tercera Convención y la Iglesia durante la presidencia de Anderson. No importaba lo que él y su esposa hicieran: la situación estaba en su contra. El presidente llevó la dirección de la Misión por cuatro años, sosteniéndose a flote y manteniendo la raya. Finalmente en mayo de 1942, fue reemplazado por Arwell L. Pierce.[49]

DIPLOMACIA Y PERSUASIÓN: REUNIFICACIÓN

Pierce no era mexicano, ni de raza ni de nacimiento; arreglos especiales tuvieron que hacerse para que pudiera ser presidente de la Misión Mexicana, ya que él no era ni siquiera mormón de las colonias.[50] Pero era un hombre con gran experiencia eclesiástica, un diplomático y un líder políticamente sensitivo. Desarrolló un enorme sentimiento de pertenencia con la sociedad de mormones mexicanos que no se había visto desde que la Iglesia había mandado a Rey L. Pratt a México.

Pero el trabajo de Pierce en México no sería fácil. Después de evaluar a los misioneros cuya dirección se le había asignado, concluyó que sus conocimientos del evangelio eran inadecuados y que sus métodos de enseñanza sobre lo que sí sabían no eran lo suficientemente eficaces. Inmediatamente implementó un régimen de estudio y de trabajo para ellos, que eventualmente le ganaron el respeto y la admiración de todos. Pierce trabajó entusiasta y vigorosamente, cambiando procedimientos y estableciendo nuevas políticas.[51]

Arwell L. Pierce trabajó con la Tercera Convención -- es un hecho que éste era su llamamiento en particular. Al llamar a Pierce como presidente de Misión, J. Ruben Clark, hijo, le había dado un llamamiento especial de trabajar para la *reunificación* de la Iglesia.[52]

La Tercera Convención genuinamente desconcertó a Pierce. Entre más la investigaba más cuenta se daba de que sus miembros estaban siguiendo los programas de la Iglesia en una forma vital y enérgica. Los 1,200 miembros tenían 15 ramas funcionando, 6 capillas construidas y un pequeño grupo de misioneros.[53] Enseñaban la doctrina mormona con firmeza y fe. Su razón de apostatar, concluyó él, ciertamente no era doctrinal --sin embargo los convencionistas se encontraban fuera de la comunidad de la Iglesia. Al estudiar la situación, pensaba cómo era posible que la hermandad se hubiera degradado a tal extremo.

A través de los años las diferencias se habían nublado, las memorias estaban olvidadas o alteradas, y las pasiones habían cambiadas. Aun cuando al principio Pierce no podía ver los puntos involucrados, sí reconocía que la Convención traería gran fuerza a la Iglesia en México -- siempre y cuando sus integrantes pudieran ser traídos al redil. Así que lenta y minuciosamente ejerció todas sus habilidades diplomáticas en la obra. El nuevo presidente se dio cuenta de que muchos sentimientos habían sido lastimados en el pasado, por lo que se dedicó primero a sanar heridas y después a eliminar las cicatrices. Y aunque al principio se abusó de él, la actitud pronto cambió -- inicialmente a respeto, después a admiración.[54]

Pierce empezó asistiendo a las reuniones y conferencias de la Tercera Convención, dándose a conocer y desarrollando amistades con los miembros y líderes convencionistas. Incluso trató de ayudar a la Tercera Convención en sus programas, invitando a sus miembros a la *Casa de Misión* para darles información de Salt Lake City, dando consejo cuando se le solicitaba y distribuyendo literatura de la Iglesia que recientemente había sido traducida.[55] También habló con Abel Páez y su esposa, con Othón Espinoza, Apolónio Arzate, Julio García y aun Margarito Bautista. Siempre listo para escuchar, ver y extender hospitalidad y aceptación sin condiciones.

Después de valorar todo lo que había escuchado, Pierce llegó a la conclusión de que el problema de la Tercera Convención había sido mal manejado. Dadas las circunstancias, pensó que algunas de las quejas de los convencionistas estaban justificadas.[56] Ya que las preocupación principal de la Tercera Convención era tener un presidente de Misión mexicano, también deseaban un programa de construcción de capillas como lo tenían los norteamericanos, la misma clase de literatura que ellos tenían, un sistema educativo para sus hijos como el de los mormones anglosajones en el norte de México, y una oportunidad para sus jóvenes de realizar misiones como aquellos lo hacían. *¿Había algo malo en esto?* Sí y no, concluyó Pierce. No se oponía a sus metas, aunque uno legítimamente podía pensar cómo tales programas podrían llegar a ser financiados en los años treintas. Por otro lado, veía que los métodos empleados por la Tercera Convención le habían ocasionado problemas.

Pierce no aprobaba la rebelión de la Tercera Convención y su retiro de la Iglesia, pero no tenía problemas en aceptar la mayoría de sus metas. Entendía la manera en que sus miembros habían decidido abandonar la Iglesia, y por razón del entendimiento que el presidente Pierce obtuvo, por vez primera en diez años hombres con diferencias trataban los asuntos, en vez de gritarse el uno al otro.

El que ahora las diferencias se entendieran, no las nulificaba; ni tampoco las simplificaba. Pero las cosas habían cambiado en una década. La Iglesia ahora podía estar más comprometida con México. Tenía mucha literatura en proceso de traducción y había todavía más por delante. Ahora que la *Segunda Guerra Mundial* había terminado, se estaba desarrollando un fuerte programa misional y pronto más élderes serían llamados.

Al mismo tiempo, los convencionistas habían mantenido en lo general la pureza doctrinal. Habían llevado a cabo un vigoroso proselitismo y promovido bastante interés en el Libro de Mormón. Dado todos estos factores, la reunificación se veía posible. Ciertamente era deseada.

Así que Arwell Pierce escuchó, persuadió, argumentó, discursó, simpatizó y trabajó largas horas, porque sentía la necesidad de que la Convención regresara a la Iglesia. Pierce amó el 'evangelio mormón' y amó a México. Estaba seguro de que el mormonismo ahora podía tomar pasos gigantescos en México si tan solo los mormones se unían, y dedicó el tiempo de su misión a este fin.[57]

Al paso del tiempo, los esfuerzos de Pierce empezaron a dar fruto. La Convención lo reconocía como un amigo, sus líderes incluso empezaron a invitarlo para que hablara en las conferencias de la Convención. Lo hizo cuidadosamente, honrando la confianza demostrada, evitando temas delicados y hablando en cambio sobre temas 'neutrales' como la oración.[58] Habló de su propio deseo de reunificación únicamente cuando tal tema era apropiado. A su vez, los de la Tercera Convención empezaron a visitar reuniones de la Iglesia, y Pierce, cortésmente, les pedía que se sentaran en las primeras bancas.

Sin embargo no fue solamente acción calmada que ayudó a la convención a ver el punto de vista de Pierce. Después de haberlo aceptado Pierce empezó a involucrarlos en varias maneras. Usualmente lo acompañaba Harold

Brown, su asistente personal, a las asignaciones donde tenía que predicar, instruyéndolo que el 'diera la palabra'.[59] La 'palabra' era práctica y directa. Entonces Pierce continuaba con "un discurso dulce, amoroso a venir a Sión". Así que Brown, como el 'hombre duro', aguantaba el enojo de la Tercera Convención y Pierce --por ser 'un hombre que entendía'-- recibía la respuesta de aceptación.[60]

Las circunstancias internas de la misma convención ayudaron a Pierce a granjearse el apoyo de sus miembros. La salud de Abel Páez, que por largo tiempo había sufrido de un caso severo de diabetes, tal vez fue lo más importante. Ya que él era el responsable del bienestar espiritual de más de mil personas, se preocupaba por lo que sería de ellos después de que muriera. Pierce podía ver que este pensamiento era bastante preocupante para Páez y empezó a apelar a su sentido de responsabilidad. ¿Quién dirigiría a la gente después de la muerte de Páez? Si la Convención era una forma temporal de llegar a nombrar liderismo de México, ¿cómo podría la gente regresar a la Iglesia al estar ausente Páez? ¿Sería posible que generaciones futuras no gozaran de las bendiciones de la Iglesia y que Páez deseara asumir tal responsabilidad?[61] Finalmente éste comenzó a ablandar su corazón, acercarse a Pierce y el guerrero renuente empezó a pensar con precavido entusiasmo en la reunificación.

Durante este período la Iglesia de Salt Lake City estaba cambiando. El presidente Heber J. Grant había fallecido y en 1945 fue sucedido por George Albert Smith. Dicho cambio de liderismo fue significativo: el presidente Smith inició su ministerio con una conciencia sensitiva hacia los santos en todo el mundo. Predicó amor y perdón a aquellos miembros que por razón de la Segunda Guerra Mundial habían estado en lados opuestos. Y esa misma influencia de amor y bondad tuvo su efecto en México.[62]

George Albert Smith especialmente confiaba en David O. McKay, el miembro de más antigüedad en el Quórum de los Doce Apóstoles y también consejero al previo presidente Heber J. Grant. El presidente Smith le pidió a David O. McKay que continuara como consejero a la Primera Presidencia. Esto favoreció a la Misión Mexicana, ya que el apóstol McKay había recorrido extensa y felizmente las unidades de la Iglesia en México dos años antes. Entre otras cosas, deseaba iniciar un programa extenso de construcción en México y por lo tanto dedicó tiempo para examinar varios sitios para capillas.

También conoció, se hizo amigo y aconsejó a los santos en forma individual, escuchando sus deseos y aspiraciones para la Iglesia en su tierra nativa. Mientras escuchaba se contuvo de argumentar. Aceptó su hospitalidad amablemente e incluso fue a visitar el hogar del convencionista Othón Espinoza para dar una bendición a su nietecita.[63] Los santos mexicanos estaban impresionados; los convencionistas, asombrados. Salt Lake City, a través de la persona de David O. McKay, ahora mostraba más atención.[64] Si otros estaban ofreciendo la rama de olivo de la paz, ¿por qué no responder con igual espíritu? Así fue como razonaron muchos convencionistas.[65]

Conforme la Iglesia se hizo más atractiva para los santos mexicanos, la atracción de la Convención disminuía proporcionalmente. Y a pesar de la grandeza de Páez, para 1945 serias disputas sobre liderismo se desarrollaban entre los convencionistas. Algunos miembros que anteriormente habían apoyado a Páez, empezaron a modificar su lealtad. Othón Espinoza, leal convencionista y uno de los líderes excomulgados, se encontró confuso e indeciso sobre el cauce futuro que debería tomar, y el impresor Apolónio Arzate había empezado desde 1943 a decir que "estaba casi listo para abandonarla".[66] En tanto no lo hizo, sus sentimientos denotaron el cambio de apoyo, de Páez a Pierce.

Totalmente enterado de esto, el presidente mantuvo su iniciativa. Llevó literatura a Apolónio Arzate para que la imprimiera --luego aprovechó la ocasión para hablar por largo tiempo. Usó su auto para llevar a líderes de la Tercera Convención a diversos lugares, conversando con ellos durante todo el camino. Razonó, argumentó, e imploró --en todo tiempo y en todo lugar.[67]

Y Arwell Pierce era tan humilde como riguroso en ayudar a los convencionistas a contener y entender su propio orgullo. Esto, tal vez más que cualquier otra característica singular, le permitió tratar a la Tercera Convención con éxito, ya que nunca tomó crédito por los logros obtenidos. Siempre decía: "Yo sólo no, pero yo con su ayuda y con la ayuda de los de la Tercera Convención, unidos, podemos llevar a cabo una gran obra".[68] Nunca vengativo o punitivo, ni preocupado en forma apreciable por su propio orgullo, Pierce podía recibir abuso sin regresarlo.[69] Por esta razón los convencionistas lo recuerdan como "un hombre sabio, un hombre muy bueno, muy diplomático, uno que sabía cómo tratar con toda clase de gente en el mundo".[70]

Conforme la Tercera Convención empezaba a confiar en el presidente Pierce, sus argumentos se volvieron verdades. "No entiendo por qué desean un presidente de Misión de sangre mexicana," les decía.

"Un presidente de Misión es solamente un representante de la Primera Presidencia de la Iglesia. Es sólo un encargado de los misioneros y de la obra de proselitismo. El presidente de Misión y los misioneros supervisan las ramas únicamente hasta que estén suficientemente fuertes y numerosas para organizarse como estaca. Lo que ustedes necesitan aquí en México es la organización de una estaca, lo mismo que tienen los hawaianos.[71] Una estaca es una unidad independiente e indirectamente bajo la supervisión de la Primera Presidencia de la Iglesia. Pero no podemos tener una estaca en México hasta que estemos más unidos. Vamos todos a unirnos bajo el liderismo de la Primera Presidencia de la Iglesia, fortalezcamos nuestras ramas y preparémonos para llegar a ser una estaca. Nunca lograremos esto si estamos divididos y somos pocos en número".[72]

El presidente llevaba entonces el punto a su conclusión, aconsejando a los que escuchaban que la Iglesia jamás daría a la Tercera Convención un presidente de Misión mexicano mientras persistieran en su rebelión. Su causa era inútil. Y de todas maneras su meta no era deseable. Si querían liderismo mexicano, deberían buscar tener un presidente de estaca nacido en el país. Y para formar una estaca debían regresar a la Iglesia y edificar el 'Reino' en su país. Pierce incluso les dijo que México rápidamente calificaría para que se formara una estaca, una vez que la Tercera Convención regresara a la Iglesia.[73]

Dadas las circunstancias involucradas, el argumento tenía mucho sentido para los miembros de la Convención. Es más, Pierce apoyaba sus palabras con hechos, los cuales prepararían una nueva generación de líderes mexicanos. Tradujo los manuales del sacerdocio y otros sobre liderismo, mimeografiando algunos y contratando a Apolónio Arzate para imprimir los demás. Organizó nuevos distritos bajo el liderismo de hermanos mexicanos. Llevó a cabo seminarios de liderismo y dijo a los santos mexicanos que tenían que empezar a resolver problemas por sí mismos, en vez de traer hasta los más insignificantes al presidente de Misión. La gente empezó a notar que el presidente Pierce estaba logrando las metas mexicanas.[74] Sintieron que él Señor lo acompañaba.

Pierce estaba eliminando efectivamente el problema de liderismo, que ahora se veía como el único tema genuino de la Tercera Convención restante. Líder carismático, implementó un programa atractivo que hizo que las Autoridades Generales se mostraban más abiertas y favorables a México. Por otra parte, había disensión en el liderismo entre los convencionistas, y la salud de Abel Páez se estaba deteriorando. En consecuencia, para muchos integrantes de la Tercera Convención el tema central empezó a cambiar de *'¿debemos unirnos de nuevo a la Iglesia?'* a *'¿cómo podemos regresar de nuevo a la Iglesia sin perder nuestra dignidad personal?'*

Pierce entendía el dilema y el papel importante que tenía la dignidad en la cultura mexicana. La pérdida de dignidad tendría un efecto devastador, al grado de que la gente no habría podido funcionar dentro de la Iglesia. Si ello hubiera ocurrido, miembros fuertes y fieles que también eran convencionistas, así como su descendencia, se habrían perdido para siempre. Enérgicamente, Pierce trató de evitarlo --"aunque fuera necesario tomar medidas extraordinarias" por parte de la Iglesia.

Pierce trató en varias maneras que los líderes de la Convención preservaran su dignidad. Una de ellas involucró razonamientos para salvar las apariencias. Después de todo, argumentaba, la Tercera Convención no estaba haciendo a un lado la idea del liderismo mexicano, sino tomando los pasos para lograrlo. Podían razonar que la Tercera Convención había expuesto su punto de vista y ahora Salt Lake City estaba escuchando. Después de la reunificación la Iglesia se desarrollaría rápidamente en México, y se organizaría una estaca con liderismo local para presidirla.[75]

Tal vez el logro principal de Arwell Pierce fue el inicio de una revisión eclesiástica de la excomunión de los líderes convencionistas. En abril de 1946 la Primera Presidencia de la Iglesia cambió el veredicto a *'suspensión'*, una suspensión cómoda que permitiera el regreso de los convencionistas a la Iglesia más fácilmente.[76] Esta decisión fue sin duda influida por el punto de vista del presidente George Albert Smith de que los problemas de la Iglesia en México parecían ser más un pleito familiar que apostasía.[77] De cualquier forma el cambio --de excomunión a suspensión-- ayudó en gran forma en cuanto a la dignidad. Más visiblemente, sus líderes no tenían que ser rebautizados para poder regresar a la Iglesia, aunque sí hubieron de ser repetidas las ordenanzas que administraron mientras estaban fuera de la hermandad de la Iglesia. En forma menos obvia, el cambio implicaba que la Iglesia podía haber cometido algunos errores en su tratamiento durante el episodio de la Tercera Convención. Los santos mexicanos reconocían todas estas implicaciones y este cambio hizo más fácil el camino a la reunificación.[78]

Lago Salado hizo otro movimiento que ayudó a salvar la apariencia, al tratar con aquellos miembros de la Convención que habían sido bautizados sin la autoridad sancionada de la Iglesia. Se les dijo que no tenían que ser bautizados de nuevo --que comúnmente hubiera sido el caso--, pero que en su lugar una restitución o ratificación de sus previos bautismos se tendría que hacer. Rebautismo, restitución, ratificación, el efecto era el mismo: miembros fueron bautizados de nuevo por aquellos que tenían la autoridad propia del sacerdocio mormón.[79] Pero la terminología preservó la dignidad así como el hecho de que Pierce mismo administró la mayoría de los bautismos necesarios.[80]

La visita a México en 1946 de George Albert Smith fue otro suceso importante. Ambos, mormones y convencionistas se encontraban inmensamente orgullosos y honrados de recibir al hombre que todos los santos reconocían como Profeta, Vidente y Revelador (el título oficial del Presidente de la Iglesia). Para su visita a la conferencia de Tecalco, sede de la Tercera Convención, esparcieron flores a lo largo de la calle que conducía a la capilla y en ambos lados un gran número de hermanos cantaban: 'Te damos, Señor, nuestras gracias, que mandas de nuevo venir, profetas con tu Evangelio, guiándonos cómo vivir...", al tiempo que el Profeta caminaba por el pasillo cubierto de flores.[81]

A pesar de la enfermedad que sufrió mientras se encontraba en México, George Albert Smith fue un estupendo éxito. La gente empujaba por ambos lados, deseando estrechar su mano y estar al menos más cerca de él: estaban gozosos de que se sentara a su mesa y compartiera sus alimentos. Naturalmente muchos deseaban recibirlo en sus hogares. Aceptó la hospitalidad mexicana cortésmente, tal como lo había hecho David O. McKay tres años antes.[82]

La conferencia de la ciudad de México bajo la dirección de George Albert Smith vio el regreso al rebaño de aproximadamente 1,200 hermanos de la Tercera Convención. La tensión era elevada al iniciar la conferencia. Nadie estaba seguro de lo que el presidente Smith diría. Podía hablar en tono condenatorio, reprendiendo a la Tercera Convención. Podía acusar, pero no lo hizo : su amor y bondad prontamente disiparon la tensión. Harold Brown, quien tradujo para él en esa ocasión, indicó que la tensión se calmó, la gente se relajó y empezaron a sonreír y responder. Brown recuerda que esa ocasión fue algo verdaderamente extraordinario.[83]

El Presidente de la Iglesia habló en las sesiones de la mañana y de la tarde, enfatizando la necesidad de armonía y unión. El coro de la Convención, un conjunto de más de ochenta voces, proveyó la música.[84] El presidente Smith pidió que Abel Páez dirigiera la palabra a la congregación, y el líder de la Tercera Convención expresó el gozo que tenía por haber podido regresar a la Iglesia, así como su felicidad sobre la obra que ahora se podía realizar.[85] Se tomaron fotos y un extenso artículo con fotos fue publicado en el diario *Deseret News*, propiedad de la Iglesia.[86] Obviamente, el regreso a la Iglesia de la Tercera Convención fue, para la mayoría, feliz e importante.

Hubo algunos descontentos. Varios acusaron a la Iglesia de haberle pagado a Páez 25,000 dólares para que traicionara a la Tercera Convención.[87] Otros, dando eco a Margarito Bautista, acusaron a Páez de entregar las ovejas de Israel a los gentiles.[88] Margarito Bautista y su grupo permanecieron en Ozumba, dándose a ver ocasionalmente para lanzar epítetos --" !Gentiles! !Hijos de egipcios! !Padres de obscuridad!"[89] Algunos santos estadounidense también estaban molestos, diciendo que Pierce había restado importancia al grupo de la Tercera Convención y traído a sus miembros de nuevo a la Iglesia bajo falsos pretextos.[90]

Sea como sea, los convencionistas regresaron, viendo la mano del Señor en el asunto. Pierce, cumpliendo su intención declarada de desarrollar el liderismo local, puso de inmediato a trabajar a la gente. Mediante un permiso especial de la Primera Presidencia, el 19 de junio de 1946 seleccionó y organizó *el Comité de Consejo y Bienestar*. Guadalupe Zárraga, Abel Páez, Bernabé Parra, Apolónio Arzate e Isaías

Juárez --fuertes líderes con antecedentes diversos-- fueron llamados a servir en dicho comité.[91]

Zárraga --el 'espía oficial' de Harold Pratt-- había permanecido fiel a la Iglesia durante los años difíciles ; Parra lo había sido también, aunque había sido excomulgado por razones morales no relacionadas con la Tercera Convención.[92] Recientemente había regresado y sus derechos de miembro restablecidos. Páez y Arzate eran, naturalmente, los que habían sido líderes de la Convención. Y ¿qué de Isaías Juárez? El que había sido presidente del Distrito de México se había inactivado durante la presidencia de Harold Pratt.[93] Primeramente había sido exilado a Guatemala por actividades políticas; después, de acuerdo con sus principios y talentos de liderismo, había regresado a México para ayudar a fundar la *Confederación Nacional Campesina* de su país.[94] Ese esfuerzo y su trabajo con el Departamento Agrario del gobierno mexicano lo habían mantenido viajando casi todos los domingos.[95] Aunque frustrado con el liderismo angloamericano en México, buscó otros foros para sus talentos, manteniendo contacto con muchos miembros de la Iglesia.

Aunque estos hombres eran bastante diferentes, ahora se unían en un nuevo espíritu de hermandad y trabajaron en armonía en la Iglesia. Aconsejaron e informaron al presidente de Misión, ayudaron en conferencias de rama y de distrito y trabajaron en todo para preparar a México para que fuera estaca. También Narciso Sandoval, quien aun en su quinta década de vida salió para servir una misión más en la Iglesia.[96] Muchos desafíos permanecieron, naturalmente, pero todos fueron ensombrecidos por dos factores: la Iglesia estaba unida de nuevo, y había un espíritu de paz y de optimismo sobre el futuro.

Sin embargo pasarían quince años antes de que madurara la nueva viña. La primera estaca para los santos mexicanos se organizó hasta 1961 --más de seis décadas después de la primera, creada en 1895 en la Colonia Juárez. Sin embargo, una vez constituida no fue presidida por Juárez, Parra, Hernández o López, sino por Harold Brown. Santo de las colonias, como muchas de las principales autoridades anteriores en México, Brown era del mismo molde que Rey L. Pratt y Arwell Pierce, y muy pronto abrió camino para que existieran oportunidades de liderismo entre sus hermanos mexicanos. Su primer consejero no fue otro que Julio García Velázquez, quien previamente había servido como líder de los convencionistas; Gonzalo Zaragoza sirvió como su segundo consejero, y Luis Rubalcava como su secretario.[U]

Para 1986 México tenía 8 misiones y 80 estacas funcionando, y mexicanos por nacimiento y raza presidían en casi todas ellas. El liderismo en el país había comenzado en la década de los 30's, y ahora ya había madurado.

Pero regresemos a la ciudad de México en 1946, cuando había un número de angloamericanos y mexicanos -- cada cual profundamente individual-- disputando menos en cuanto a sus percepciones personales, deber, religión, etcétera, que lo que lo habían hecho diez años atrás. Por el lado estadounidense se encontraba principalmente Arwell L. Pierce, experimentado presidente de la enormemente probada pero de nuevo unida Misión Mexicana: más de 45 misioneros estadounidenses llenaban sus filas. Y entre los mexicanos estaban Isaías Juárez, un político astuto y dotado líder; Abel Páez, trabajando fielmente en la Misión; y otros más, como Julio García, Bernabé Parra, Apolónio Arzate, Guadalupe Zárraga, Narciso Sandoval y Othón Espinoza -- además de varios misioneros mexicanos--, todos ellos provocando un recogimiento a raíz de la reunificación de la Tercera Convención con la Iglesia de Jesucristo de los Santos de los Últimos Días. En ese momento casi todos estaban contentos.

NOTAS:

1. Abel Páez también sirvió como misionero en la Misión Mexicana cuando esta incluía la parte sur oeste de los Estados Unidos. Su servicio fue prácticamente en Texas, donde aprendió algo de Ingles (Historia Oral de Harold Brown, entrevistado por Gordon Irving, p. 34.

2. Diario de Harold W. Pratt 27 de Abril de 1930.

3. Historia Oral de Julio García Velázquez, entrevistado por Gordon Irving, p. 9. Esta información también menciona el nombre de Andrés González como uno de los nombres nominados aunque Andrés González jr., en una entrevista personal (1976), expreso dudas de la autenticidad de esto. Ya que llevaba el nombre de su padre y fue misionero en México durante el periodo de la Tercera Convención, esta seguro que alguien se lo hubiera indicado. Es interesante saber que el nombre Andrés González también fue sugerido como un posible candidato en el caso de que Harold Pratt fuera reemplazado (carta de Antoine R. Ivins a la Primera Presidencia fechada el 2 de Septiembre de

1936). González se había inmigrado a los Estados Unidos y hablaba Ingles, pero también mantuvo íntimos contactos con México.

Andrés González jr. Menciono en una entrevista personal que su padre había sido contactado por el Apóstol Melvin J. Ballard con respecto a un llamamiento para dirigir la misión, ambos estuvieron de acuerdo que no seria posible por razón de deudas substanciales de negocios que González estaba en proceso de pagar en ese tiempo.

4.   Diario de Pratt fechado el 27 de Abril de 1936. Los líderes de la Tercera Convención veían las lagrimas de Juárez en diferente forma. Lo acusaban de haberse vendido, creerse mejor que ellos y UN "escaqueo" para los norte americanos (Vea el Informe General p. 41.)

5.   Diario de Pratt fechado el 27 de Abril de 1936.

6.   Registro de la Historia de la Misión Mexicana fechado el 22 de Abril de 1936. (Datos de Mayo fueron registrados en esta fecha.)

7.   Informe General, passim.

8.   Historia Oral de García Velázquez, pp. 8-9, 13.

9.   Registro de la Historia de la Misión Mexicana, fechada el 22 de Abril de 1936.(Datos de Mayo fueron registrados en esta fecha).

10.   J. Ruben Clark, jr., un Mormón de E. U. A. había vivido entre los Mormones de México cuando fue embajador de los E.U.A. desde el 3 de Octubre de 1930 hasta el 3 de Marzo de 1933. Era de agrado y respeto para los Santos Mexicanos. (Vea Martin B. Hickman, "The Ambassadorial Years: Some Insights," en Ray C. Hillam, ed., J. Ruben Clark, jr., Diplomat and statement, pp. 175-84 y Frank Fox, J. Ruben Clark, jr., The Public Years.)

11.   Diario de Pratt, fechado el 11 de Noviembre de 1936.

12.   Un sumario preparado en una carta de Antoine R. Ivins a Harold W. Pratt fechada el 27 de Octubre de 1936. Una copia de la carta de la Primera Presidencia fue archivada en los Archivos de la Iglesia SUD, pero a esta fecha que se escribe este libro el personal de este archivo no la pudieron encontrar. Por lo tanto no pude repasarla.

13.   Los Convencionistas habían estado previamente de acuerdo que ellos respetarían cualquiera que fuera la decisión de la Primer Presidencia. Por lo tanto y por implicación, apoyarían a Harold Pratt si su petición no fuera aceptada. Ahora, sin embargo, consideraban que el acuerdo anterior era nulo y sin valor por razón de que sus propios líderes no habían sido permitidos presentar la petición personalmente a las autoridades en la Ciudad de Lago Salado. Los Convencionistas llegaron a la conclusión que Harold Pratt, quien la había presentado, lo había hecho con prejuicio. (Vea la Historia Oral de Santiago Mora González).

Bautista había estado de acuerdo en apoyar la decisión de la Primera Presidencia aun cuando el fallo fuera en contra de la Tercera Convención. Una decisión a favor o en contra no seria en vano, pensaban. Si la Primera Presidencia actuaba positivamente con respecto a la petición, "se satisfarían nuestro deseos. Si no, la petición, sin embargo, motivaría a Harold Pratt para poner mas hincapié en el trabajo de la misión y lo quitaría del camino que llevaba." (Según fue reportado por Santiago Mora González en una entrevista, 1975).

Cuando la indicación negativa finalmente llegó, Bautista era el mas inflexible en su cambio total. Esto ocasionó la primera fisura entre los Convencionistas. Sobre este tema los miembros de la rama de La Libertad (Puebla) renunciaron a la Tercera Convención y le indicaron a Harold Pratt que era lo que tenían que hacer para regresar a la Iglesia. Su gran preocupación fue que si permanecían con la Convención no podrían participar en la obra del templo, que se les impidiera llevar registros aceptables al Señor, no poder extender la obra misional y verse obligados de tomar custodia de fondos de diezmos que deberían ser entregados a la Iglesia.

Pratt viajo a Puebla donde se encontraba la rama La Libertad y habló con el presidente de rama, Santiago Mora González:

> "Estabamos en la Convención", dijo el presidente de la rama, "pero ahora lo hemos dejado y ya no somos miembros de ella. Ahora necesitamos saber cuales son sus condiciones, o las condiciones de la Iglesia para poder regresar como miembros y tener todos los derechos".
>
> Pratt respondió: "¿Alguno de ustedes ha recibido el Sacerdocio en la Convención?
>
> "No"
>
> "¿Alguno de ustedes ha sido bautizado en la Convención?"
>
> "No"
>
> "Entonces ustedes todavía son miembros de la iglesia. No hay condiciones para ustedes. Nada mas regresen con fidelidad." (Entrevista de Santiago Mora González)

14. Antoine R. Ivins había hecho dos viajes antes para tratar el problema con el liderismo Mexicano. En 1932 viajo con el Apóstol Melvin J. Ballard Luego en el verano de 1936 fue con el fin de ayudar a Harold Pratt (Historia Manuscrita fechada el 30 de Junio de 1936). Los Santos Mexicanos no le dieron la bien venida en ambas visitas. En una carta fechada el 11 de Diciembre de 1936 dirigida a la Primera Presidencia, el Presidente Ivins les indico que los Santos no lo consideraban competente.

15. "Mensaje del Presiente George F. Richards para ser leído en el culto de Tecalco el Domingo 17 de Febrero de 1937." P. 4.

16. Esta carta es mencionada en el "Mensaje" de George F. Richards, p. 5. Se lee así:

El verdadero objeto de dichas convenciones fue llegar a un acuerdo con los presidentes de ramas, hermanos del Sacerdocio, y miembros de la iglesia quienes estaban presentes, a pedir a la Primera Presidencia de la iglesia, a concedernos el favor de nombrar a un presidente de raza pura mexicana para dirigir los destino de la Misión primero, a causa de la necesidad existente, y segundo, a causa del verdadero espíritu de la ley existente del país, como seguramente sabrán Uds. Lo que es el requisito de la ley en asuntos de culto actualmente, por consiguiente fuimos obligados a tomar ese curso.

17. "Mensaje del Presidente George F. Richards," p. 6.

18. Ibídem, pp. 13-14.

19. Historia Oral de García Velázquez, pp. 24-25; Historia Oral de Harold Brown p. 32; y Historia Oral de E. LeRoy Hatch, entrevistado por Gordon Irving, p. 12.

20. Historia Oral de Hatch. Percepciones del Presidente Pratt justificando sus acciones precipitadas, se encuentran en el Registro de la Historia de la Misión Mexicana, fechada el 14 de Febrero de 1937. También vea el Manuscrito Histórico, trimestre que termina el 31 de Marzo de 1937.

21. Historia Oral de García Velázquez pp. 24-25; Historia Oral de Brown p. 32; Este episodio se detalla en la historia Oral de Hatch p. 12.

22. Carta de Ivins a Harold Pratt fechada el 25 de Febrero de 1937.

23. "Mensaje del Presidente George F. Richards," p. 16. Doctrina y Convenios y la Perla de Gran Precio, dos de los libros canónicos de la Iglesia, los otros siendo el Libro de Mormón y la Biblia. Unicamente parte de Doctrina y Convenios había sido traducida al Español pero la Perla de Gran Precio no se había hecho. "Las Enseñanzas de José Smith" (no se debe confundir con Las Enseñanzas del Profeta José Smith que salió de la imprenta dos años después) era una obra doctrinal clave la cual había recibido extensa circulación entre los miembros de habla Ingles, pero tampoco había sido traducida al Español. Por razón de previas malas experiencias con literatura circulada en Europa, se dio el fallo de detener traducciones autónomas. (Vea carta de Ivins a A. Lorenzo Anderson, fechada el 27 de Diciembre de 1938.)

24. Informe General, p. 36.

25. La minuta de los hechos se encuentra en el Registro Histórico de la Misión Mexicana fechado el 6, 7, y 8 de Mayo de 1937. Vea también las notas 13 y 65 de este capitulo.

26. Investiduras, sellamientos y bautismos para los muertos tenían un lugar santificado en los corazones de los miembros Mexicanos a pesar de que muchos de ellos no habían participado en el trabajo del templo. La comprensión sale a relucir en la entrevista de Santiago Mora González, es aludido en el Informe General y es un tema que se menciona repetidamente durante la Presidencia del Pierce.

27. En es sentido los temores eran infundados. Solo ocho excomuncaciones se llevaron acabo. La mayoría de los disidentes

simplemente fueron catalogados como "inactivos" en lo que concernía al registro oficial de la Iglesia.

28. Historia Oral de Mora González, entrevistado por Gordon Irving.

29. Ibid., y también la Historia Oral de González de la Cruz, entrevistado por Gordon Irving; también la Historia Oral de Cirilo Flores Flores, entrevistado por Gordon Irving.

30. Historia Oral de A. Lorenzo Anderson, pp. 83, 90.

31. Historia Oral de García Velázquez; Historia Oral de Brown, p. 35.

32. Historia Oral de Brown, pp. 33'34. Brown declara que Margarito Bautista se consideraba así mismo como la persona indicada para ser presidente de la misión antes de que la convención se separar de la Iglesia. A Bautista no le gustaba que las autoridades de la Iglesia no lo consideraran. (Era un Sumo Sacerdote; Harold Pratt un Setenta y por lo tanto a su modo de ver de mas "bajo rango".) Sus movimientos para colocarse en mejor posición de liderismo después de la cisma pude haber sido desafío insoportable para los líderes de la Tercera Convención, quienes se encontraban en un periodo difícil de organización. Este punto de vista, sin embargo, debe ser balanceado por la minuta de la reunión inicial de la Tercera Convención, en la cual indica que Margarito Bautista rechazo la nominación ofrecida para ser presidente de misión. (Informe General, pp. 18-19).

33. El termino correcto técnico, polígonas, no se usa aquí por no ser de uso común. Toda referencia a poligamia o polígamo debe de entenderse que se refiere a una relación polígona.

34. Historia Oral de Mora González; Historia Oral de Walser, p. 27; Historia Oral de Brown, pp. 27, 86; Historia Oral de García Velázquez, p. 14.

35. Historia Oral de Eran A. Call, entrevistado por Gordon Irving.

36. "Pureza Doctrinal" era una de las metas desde el principio. (Vea la Historia Oral de Mora González y la Historia Oral de García Velázquez).

37. El certificado de Virgilio Aguilar Paéz, fechado el 13 de Noviembre de 1938 y preparado por la Tercera Convención, dice lo siguiente: BENDICION DE NIÑOS, Expedido por la Tercera Convención, Rama de Atlautla México. El presente certifica que el niño Virgilio Aguilar ha sido bendecida en la Iglesia de Jesu Cristo de los Santos de los Ultimos Días de la Misión Mexicana el día 13 del mes de Noviembre de 1938 por el Anciano Felipe Barragán." Firmado por Abel Páez como presidente y Othón Espinosa como secretario. El logo tipo es de la Manzana del Templo de la ciudad de Lago Salado. Gordon Irving le dio una copia del certificado al autor.

38. Historia Oral de García Velázquez, p. 92.

39. Historia Oral de Call; Historia Oral de Hatch.

40. Historia Oral de Call.

41. Historia Oral de Brown. Unas cuantas copias de la publicación El Sendero LaMond se encuentran en el Archivo de la Iglesia SUD.

42. Historia Oral de García Velázquez. El informe titulado Informe General de la Tercera Convención se encuentra en el Archivo de la Iglesia SUD.

43. Historia Oral de García Velázquez.

44. En vista de las tendencias contemporáneas de la Iglesia, uno se ve forzado a llegar a la conclusión que la única cosa mala de las metas de la Tercera Convención, además de su estratagema para obtenerlas, fue que no se llevo acabo en el momento oportuno. (y su mal entendimiento de como funciona la autoridad). Considera que la Tercera Convención buscaba (1) liderismo indígena, (2) expandir el programa misional para poder incluir a sus propios hijos e hijas, (3) oportunidades educacionales para sus hijos, (4) una completa lista de literatura doctrinal, y (5) oportunidad de trabajo en el templo. En la actualidad en México prácticamente todas las unidades eclesiásticas (ramas, barrios, estacas y misiones) están bajo la dirección de un miembro nativo; entre las misiones mas productivas de la Iglesia, ahora con cientos de jóvenes nativos así como norte americanos, han sido las de México; el sistema educativo en México ha sido calificada por todos los círculos como un logro decisivo, no solo para la Iglesia, pero para todo el país; servicio de traducción produciendo volúmenes de literatura para los miembros Mexicanos se encuentran funcionando en México, la ciudad de Lago Salado y en la Universidad de Brigham Young; excursiones regulares fueron promovida por la Iglesia al templo de Mesa, Arizona donde miles de visitantes Mexicanos han sido atendidos por Mormones Norte Americanos; los miembros Mexicanos ahora tienen su propio templo en la Ciudad de México. Todas las metas trazadas por la Tercera Convención se han realizado en México.

45. Manuscrito Histórico de la Misión Mexicana, trimestre que termina el 30 de noviembre de 1942.

46. Diario de Pratt fechado el 6 de Agosto de 1938. Harold Pratt había sufrido de un apendicitis agudo desde Abril de 1937 fue sometido a una operación para removerla. Poco después de haberse recuperado, empezó a sufrir de lo que el llamo "cólico del riñón" y eventualmente se le saco un riñón. Fue relevado cuando regreso para esta segunda operación.

47. Diario de Pratt fechado el 6 de Agosto de 1938; Entrevista personal de Andrés González, jr. Hecha por F. LaMond Tullis.

48. Historia Oral de García Velázquez, p. 26.

49. Ibid.

50. Manuscrito Histórico de la Misión Mexicana, trimestre que termina el 31 de Mayo de 1942.

51. Desconozco los arreglos exactos, pero si se que Pierce tomó gran cuidado en resolverlos "propiamente". La Tercera Convención previamente había contratado a un abogado de la Ciudad de Lago Salado para investigar el servicio de entrenamiento militar de Harold Pratt que llevo acabo en el Colegio de Agricultura de la Universidad del Estado de Utah (Utah State University) localizada en Logan Utah. Habían intentado usar dicha información como base para expulsarlo de México, pero las autoridades Mexicanas no aceptaron su argumento ya que Pratt era un ciudadano Mexicano de buena fe - una condición que consideraba no haber cambiado por el hecho que su servicio militar fue obligatorio en una universidad Americana. Sin embargo, las autoridades en la Ciudad de Lago Salado estaban confiadas que si los Convencionistas descubrían que Pierce había nacido en los Estados Unidos, trabajarían para expulsarlo también. (Carta de A. Lorenzo Anderson a Arwell Pierce, fechada el 16 de Abril de 1942). Hubo especulación irreverente de que Pierce había pagado mordidas y el disgusto subsecuente de J. Ruben Clark concerniente a tal actividad (Historia Oral de Anderson, P. 103.)

52. Historia Manuscrita de la Misión Mexicana, trimestre que termina el 31 de Marzo de 1943.

53. Arwell Lee Pierce, "La Historia de la Tercera Convención," p. 1.

54. Vea la Historia Oral de García Velázquez.

55. Historia Oral de Brown, pp. 34-35.

56. El antecesor de Pierce, A. Lorenzo Anderson, se había rehusado a dar literatura a la Tercera Convención. Lo correcto de esta política de tratar con mano dura a los disidentes fue confirmada en una carta fechada el 3 de Julio de 1939 de Antoine R. Ivins a Anderson.

57. Historia Oral de Brown, p. 34.

58. Algunos Mormones de las colonias objetaron vigorosamente el esfuerzo de Pierce, aun acusándolo de haber engañado a David O. McKay, haciéndolo creer que los Convenciónistas no habían apostatado de la Iglesia. (Historia Oral de Walser, p. 28.)

59. Vea, por ejemplo la Historia manuscrita del 30 de Noviembre de 1942.

60. En 1946 Brown había discursado en una conferencia de distrito en Cuautla que analizaba los errores ideológicos de la Tercer Convención, el cual estaba documentado y basado en escrituras que los mismos Convenciónistas estaban utilizando. Fue un discurso clave que estableció la base de otros que Brown daría al acompañar a Pierce y después fue publicada en la Liahona bajo el titulo "Efrain esparcida entre los Gentiles".

61. Es aparente que estos hombres habían estado empleando una técnica conocida como "whip sawing". En el libro de Paul H. Hahn, titulado The Juvenile offender and the Law, p. 223, describe un método

de interrogación donde agentes de la policía, uno de buen corazón y el otro duro, interrogan en forma alternativa a un sospechoso. Con tiempo, el acusado tiende a temer y rechazar al agente duro pero responde al de buen corazón. Si Pierce estaba conscientemente utilizando este método, lo desconocemos, pero el efecto fue el mismo. Vea la Historia Oral de Brown, p. 38.

62. Ibid.

63. Los Mormones por largo tiempo han notado diferencias en el estilo de operación e hincapié sobre programas de sus líderes.

64. Historia Manuscrita, trimestre que termina el 31 de Diciembre de 1943.

65. En los primeros días de la dificultad, David O. McKay, en ese entonces consejero al presidente de la Iglesia, Heber J. Grant, había tomado actuar con mano dura, un enfoque punitivo al tratar con los líderes Convenciónistas. Sin embargo después de regresar de México, aparentemente veía las cosas en forma diferente. Le pidió a Antoine R. Ivins volver a investigar la correspondencia de la Tercera Convención para ver si había alguna cosa que impidiera a la Primera Presidencia reconsiderar o repasar, los casos de aquellos que habían sido excomulgados. (Vea la carta de Ivins a David O. McKay fechada el 9 de Marzo de 1944.

66. Historia Oral de García Velázquez.

67. Historia Manuscrita, trimestre que termina el 30 de Septiembre de 1943.

68. Historia Oral de Brown, pp. 34-36; Historia Oral de Call; Registro Histórico de la Misión Mexicana, passim para este periodo; Historia Manuscrita, passim para este periodo, con ilustraciones especificas en el trimestre que termina el 31 de Marzo de 1943.

69. Historia Oral de González de la Cruz.

70. Historia Oral de Brown, pp. 34-36.

71. Historia Oral de Flores Flores, con corroboración sacada de las Historias Orales de Mora González y González de la Cruz.

72. Harold W. Pratt anteriormente había hablado con la Tercera Convención sobre una estaca, pero cuando reportó esto a la Primera Presidencia, esas autoridades respondieron que tuviera cuidado "en prometerles organizar una estaca o aun la posibilidad que uno de ellos presidiera sobre la misión. El privilegio de que recibieran el Evangelio debería ser suficiente mérito para apreciar y apoyar a los que son enviados y apartados para presidir sobre la misión. El Señor indicará cuando hay que reasignar o cuando haya necesidad de reorganizar. Mientras tanto es el deber así como el privilegio de los miembros de corresponder a las enseñanzas y requerimientos e ideales de la Iglesia". (La carta estaba firmada por Heber J. Grant y David O McKay y

apuntada en la Historia Manuscrita del trimestre que terminó el 30 de Junio de 1936.)

73. Reconstruido de la Historia Manuscrita, trimestre que termina el 31 de Marzo de 1943. Una "estaca," presidida por un "presidente de estaca" usualmente se compone de entre tres y cinco mil miembros y hasta mas o menos doce "barrios" (congregaciones), las cuales son encabezadas por un "obispo". "Ramas" son congregaciones Mormonas en los distritos de las misiones donde aun no se han organizado estacas.

74. Historia Oral de Narciso Sandoval Jiménez, entrevistado por Gordon Irving..

75. Historia Oral, Brown, p. 36.

76. Ibid., p. 34.

77. Para fines de 1975 solo en la Ciudad de México ya había doce estacas (Aragón, Arbolillo, Camarones, Churubusco, Ermita, Zarahemla, Industrial, Villa de las Flores, Satélite, Tacubaya, Moctezuma, Netzahualcoyotl) además de catorce mas en el resto del país. Para 1983 seis mas se formaron en la Ciudad de México, (Azteca, Chapultepec, Iztapalapa, Linda Vista, Tlanepantla y Tlalpan). La mayoría presididas por hermanos Mexicanos. Esto a sido la tendencia que continuó hasta Agosto de 1986, con la formación adicional de las estacas Ciudad de México norte y Ciudad de México Sur y seis mas en la República Mexicana dando un total de ochenta. Interesante pero no sorprendente, dos de los nombres de las estacas en la Ciudad de México se derivan de famosos personajes Aztecas y una del nombre de una ciudad del Libro de Mormón.

78. En Febrero de 1937, la Primera Presidencia (Heber J. Grant, David O. McKay, J. Ruben Clark jr.) dio instrucciones a Harold W. Pratt para que convocara un tribunal eclesiástico para los líderes de la Tercera Convención. (Diario de Harold Pratt fechado el 27 de Febrero de 1937. Pero la carta de notificación de la Primera Presidencia dirigida a los líderes de la Convención fue firmada por Antoine R. Ivins y George F. Richards para así no comprometer la posición de la Primera Presidencia en el caso de un apelo. (Carta de A. R. Ivins a la Primera Presidencia fechada el 27 de Febrero de 1937; y la de Ivins a Harold W. Pratt, del 2 de Marzo de 1937). Pratt llevo acabo las cortes disciplinarias el 6, 7 y 8 de Mayo de 1937, en la cual fue votado excomulgar a Margarito Bautista, Abel Páez, Narciso Sandoval, Pilar Páez, Othón Espinosa, Apolónio Arzate, Felipe Barragán y Daniel Mejía. La minuta esta registrada en el Registro Histórico de la Misión Mexicana con fecha 6,b 7, y 8 de Mayo de 1937). La Mayoría de los que fueron excomulgados eran presidentes de rama y Abel Páez miembro de la presidencia del distrito.

Poco después, David O. McKay le pregunto a Harold Pratt si seria buena idea invitar a los líderes involucrados a El Paso, Texas para reunirse con algunos de los hermanos. Tal vez con el fin de revisar sus juicios (Diario de Harold Pratt fechado el 18 de mayo de 1937). Esto parecía sugerir que si los hermanos nada mas desarrollaran un espíritu contrito, la decisión "local" podría ser cambiada. Si se extendió la invitación, los hermanos no la aceptaron (ninguno de ellos fue a su juicio) ya que pensaban que la corte se llevo acabo bajo inrectitud. Por lo tanto concluyeron que el veredicto era nulo y sin efecto a los ojos de Dios. (Historia Manuscrita, trimestral que termina el 30 de Junio de 1943; también el que termina el 31 de Diciembre de 1943).

En "La Historia de la Tercera Convención", Arwell Lee Pierce nos indica lo siguiente:

El Presidente Jorge Alberto Smith, en una reunión especial que yo tuve con él y sus consejeros en las oficinas de la Primera Presidencia en Abril de 1946, me pidió que leyera el apelo a la Primera Presidencia de la Iglesia traduciéndolo del Español al Ingles y también la recomendación del Presidente de la Misión dirigida a la Primera Presidencia sobre lo mismo. Mi recomendación como presidente de la misión fue que aceptáramos el apelo como se había presentado y yo recomendé que la acción tomada en contra de estos hombres en el inicio, excomunicación de la Iglesia por razón de rebeldía, fuera cambiado de excomunicación a perdida de derechos porque pensaba que excomunicación era muy severo al analizar las circunstancias. El Presidente Smith entonces pregunto si uno de los consejeros apoyaba esta propuesta y el Presidente McKay indico que el apelo, como era presentado, se aprobara en forma favorable....Esto se aprobó favorablemente por la Primera Presidencia y a petición del Presidente Smith el Presidente Pierce voto con ellos.

79. Pierce, "La Historia de la Tercera Convención", p. 5.
80. Historia Oral de Brown, p. 36.
81. Historia Oral de García Velázquez.
82. Historia Manuscrita, trimestre que termina el 30 de Septiembre de 1946.
83. Historia Oral de Hatch; Historia Oral de García Velázquez.
84. Historia Oral de García Velázquez.
85. Historia Oral de Brown.
86. Deseret News, "Church News", 15 de Junio de 1946.
87. Historia Oral de González de la Cruz.
88. Deseret News, "Church News", 15 de Junio de 1946.
89. Historia Oral de García Velázquez.

90.   Daniel Mejía, come es citado en la Historia Oral de González de la Cruz.

91.   Historia Oral de Brown.

92.   Historia Oral de Walser.

93.   Historia Manuscrita, trimestre que termina el 31 de Diciembre de 1946. Pierce hizo publico el anuncio de la acción en "Anuncio de Interés a la Misión Mexicana," pp. 405, 433 y enérgicamente pido a los miembros que apoyaran a estos hombres en sus llamamientos.

94.   Historia Oral de Anderson, p. 61.

95.   Diario de Pratt fechado el 15 de Septiembre de 1937; Historia Manuscrita, 31 de Marzo de 1943.

96.   Entrevista de Agricol Lozano Herrera; Historia Oral de García Velázquez.   Ya que se había peleado la Revolución y reformas implementadas, la mayoría de los trabajadores y campesinos en realidad nunca beneficiaron al punto que ellos deseaban. La actividad de organizar sindicatos continuo mucho después que las pistolas se callaron y aveces la actividad solamente consiguió enemistad del gobierno al cual posiblemente hayan ayudado a instalar. Isaías Juárez fue uno de ellos. (Para un bosquejo mas general vea el libro de Ann L. Craig, The First Agraristas: Una Historia Oral del Movimiento Mexicano de Reforma Agraria y para ver un énfasis regional, el libro de Heather Fowler Salamini, Agrarian Radicalism in Veracruz, 1920-38 y Romana Flacón, El Agrarismo en Veracruz: La Etapa Radical [1928-1935].

97.   Historia Manuscrita, 31 de marzo de 1943.

98.   Entrevista de Lozano Hererra por F. LaMond Tullis.

Interviews*

Anderson, A. Lorenzo. Oral History. Interview by Gordon Irving, 1973. LDS Church Historical Department Oral History Program, transcription copy.

Aranda Carrazco, Mario Jaime. Provo, Utah. 31 July 1975.

Barreras, José. Mexico City, México. 30 May 1975.

Barten, Rebecca. San Marcos, Hidalgo, México. 19 May 1975.

Brown, Harold. Mexico City, México. 3 June 1975.

——————. Oral History. Interview by Gordon Irving, 1973. LDS Church Historical Department Oral History Program.

Call, Eran A. Oral History. Interview by Gordon Irving, 1973. LDS Church Historical Department Oral History Program.

Call, Waldo Pratt. Colonia Juárez, Chihuahua, México. 6 May 1975.

Clark, Bryant R. Colonia Juárez, Chihuahua, México. 5 May 1975.

Colina Malpica, Arturo. Mexico City, México. 25 May 1975.

Cornejo de Trujillo, Florencia. San Marcos, Hidalgo, México. 20 May 1975.

Crofts, John William, III. Torreón, México. 10 May 1975.

Delgado Rodríguez, Francisco. Mexico City, México. 25 May 1975.

Esparza, Pablo. San Luís Potosí, México. 13 May 1975.

Fairchild, Theodore. San Marcos, Hidalgo, México. 17 May 1975.

Flores, Marco Antonio. Mexico City, México. 26 May 1975.

Flores Flores, Cirilo. Oral History. Interview by Gordon Irving, 1974. LDS Church Historical Department Oral History Program.

García Velázquez, Julio. Oral History. Interview by Gordon Irving, 1974. LDS Church Historical Department Oral History Program.

González, Andrés C., Jr. Provo, Utah. 12 January 1976.

González, Santiago Mora. Puebla, Puebla, México. 5 May 1975.

González, Manuel. Colonia Juárez, Chihuahua, México. 6 May 1975.

González de la Cruz, Cruz. Oral History. Interview by Gordon Irving, 1974. LDS Church Historical Department Oral History Program, magnetic tape.

Hatch, Crenna O'Donnel. Colonia Juárez, Chihuahua, México. 5 May 1975.

Hatch, E. LeRoy. Oral History. Interview by Gordon Irving, 1974. LDS Church Historical Department Oral History Program.

——————. Colonia Juárez, Chihuahua, México. 5 May 1975.

Hatch, Herman. Colonia Juárez, Chihuahua, México. 5 May 1975.

---

*Interviews by the author, unless otherwise stated. Latin American interviewees are listed with their two customary surnames (the first paternal, the second maternal). Thus, for example, Julio García Velázquez is found alphabetized as García Velázquez, Julio.

Hatch, Nell S. Colonia Juárez, Chihuahua, México. 5 May 1975.

Johnson, David. Colonia Juárez, Chihuahua, México. 6 and 7 May 1975.

Lloyd, Glen Earl. Veracruz, México. 7 June 1975.

Lozano, Isaías. Mexico City, México. 2 June 1975.

Lozano Herrera, Agrícol. Mexico City, México. 31 May 1975.

Lozano Peña, Saúl. Mexico City, México. 25 May 1975.

Lyman, Deane. San Marcos, Hidalgo, México. 19 May 1975.

Macías y de la Mora, Josefina. Torreón, México. 9 May 1975.

Martínez, Arturo. Interview by Douglas Lowe, Salt Lake City, Utah. 23 May 1974.

Mejía, Esteben. Mexico City, México. 5 June 1975.

Meza Ceniceros, Edmundo. Torreón, México. 9 May 1975.

Monroy de Villalobos, María Concepción. San Marcos, Hidalgo, México. 17 and 19 May 1975.

Montoya, Ezequiel. San Marcos, Hidalgo, México. 18 May 1975.

Montoya, Jorge. San Marcos, Hidalgo, México. 17 May 1975.

Montoya Ortíz, Ezequiel. San Marcos, Hidalgo, México. 20 May 1975.

Mora González, Santiago. Oral History. Interview by Gordon Irving, 1974. LDS Church Historical Department Oral History Program.

——————. Puebla, México. 5 June 1975.

Parra de Pérez, Elena. Mexico City, México. 25 May 1975.

Parrish, Mary Pratt. Oral History. Interview by Gordon Irving, 1974. LDS Church Historical Department Oral History Program.

Pérez, José. Mexico City, México. 25 May 1975.

Pérez de Villalobos, Violeta. San Marcos, Hidalgo, México. 15, 16, 17, and 19 May 1975.

Pérez Parra, María Elena. San Marcos, Hidalgo, México. 21 May 1975.

Pratt, Ana Marie. Oral History. Interview by Gordon Irving, 1975. LDS Church Historical Department Oral History Program.

Reyes, Eulario. Mexico City, México. 30 May 1975.

Ricks, Dianne. San Marcos, Hidalgo, México. 19 May 1975.

Sánchez, Marcelino. Torreón, México. 10 May 1975.

Sandoval Jiménez, Narciso. Oral History. Interview by Gordon Irving, 1974. LDS Church Historical Department Oral History Program.

Schmidt, Howard. Colonia Juárez, Chihuahua, México. 6 May 1975.

Severino Portela, Híram. San Luís Potosí, México. 12 May 1975.

Sion, Denia. San Marcos, Hidalgo, México. 19 May 1975.

Smith, Emma, viuda de Benjamín Díaz Flores. Torreón, México. 9 May 1975.

Smith, Greg. Torreón, México. 8 May 1975.

Taylor, Daniel. Mexico City, México. 29 May and 1 June 1975.

Thomasson, Gordon. Provo, Utah. 15 February 1976.

Treviño, Daniel. Torreón, México. 8 May 1975.

Trujillo Linares, Emilio. San Marcos, Hidalgo, México. 19 May 1975.

Valadez Arvizú, José. San Luís Potosí, México. 13 May 1975.

Valdez, José. Veracruz, México. 7 June 1975.

Villalobos, Saúl, San Marcos, Hidalgo, México. 21 May 1975.

Villalobos Rodríguez, Benito. San Marcos, Hidalgo, México. 16, 17, and 19 May 1975.

Villalobos Vásquez, Efraín. Mexico City, México. 27 May 1975.

Villarreal, Sergio. Torreón, México. 8 May 1975.

Viscaíno, Rubén. Colonia Juárez, Chihuahua, México. 6 May 1975.

Wagner, A. Kenyon. Mexico City, México. 27 May 1975.

Wagner, Nona. Mexico City, México. 27 May 1975.

Wagstaff, Dorothy. San Marcos, Hidalgo, México. 17 May 1975.

Walser, John Floyd. Provo, Utah. 23 July 1975.

Walser, William. Oral History. Interview by Gordon Irving, 1973. LDS Church Historical Department Oral History Program, magnetic tape.

Wells, Augusta Ivins. Interview by Elizabeth Hernandez, Hamden, Connecticut. 10 February 1976.

Whetten, Dianne. Mexico City, México. 29 May 1975.

Whetten, Othello Jean. Mexico City, México. 29 May 1975.

Wilds, Camille. San Marcos, Hidalgo, México. 17 May 1975.

Young, W. Ernest. Oral History. Interview by Gordon Irving, 1973. LDS Church Historical Department Oral History Program.

───────────. Provo, Utah. 22 February 1977.

Bibliography

"A Threat from Mormondom," *New York Times*, 22 June 1875, p. 6.

Abbot, Graham Sumner. *Mexico and the United States: Their Mutual Relations and Common Interests.* New York: Putnam, 1869.

Acuna, Rodolfo. *Occupied America: The Chicano's Struggle toward Liberation.* San Francisco: Canfield Press, 1972.

Allred, Mary Eliza Tracy. "Autobiography," 1874–1920. Typescript. Historical Division, Library–Archives of The Church of Jesus Christ of Latter-day Saints, Salt Lake City, Utah. Hereafter cited as LDS Church Archives.

Anderson, A. Lorenzo. Letter to Arwell Pierce, 16 April 1942.

Anderson, Nels. *Desert Saints: The Mormon Frontier in Utah.* Chicago: University of Chicago Press, 1966.

Arrington, Leonard J. *Building the City of God: Community and Cooperation among the Mormons.* Salt Lake City: Deseret Book Co., 1976.

——————. *From Wilderness to Empire: The Role of Utah in Western Economic History.* Salt Lake City: University of Utah Press, 1981.

——————. *Great Basin Kingdom: An Economic History of the Latter-day Saints, 1830–1900.* Cambridge, Mass.: Harvard University Press, 1958.

Bailey, Paul. "The Church of Jesus Christ of Latter-day Saints." In *The Religious Heritage of Southern California*, edited by Msgr. Francis J. Weber, pp. 83–95. Los Angeles: Interreligious Council of Southern California, 1976.

Ballard, Melvin J. "Visit to Mexico." *Deseret News*, "Church Section," 19 March 1932.

Barrett, David B., ed. *World Christian Encyclopedia.* Oxford: Oxford University Press, 1982.

Bautista, Margarito. *La evolución de México: Sus verdaderos progenitores y su orígen y el destino de América y Europa.* México: Talleres Gráficos Apolonio B. Arzate, 1935.

Beals, Carleton. "Bread or the Club." In *The Age of Porfirio Díaz*, edited by Carlos B. Gil, pp. 61–70. Albuquerque: University of New Mexico Press, 1977.

Beecher, Dale F. "Rey L. Pratt and the Mexican Mission." *Brigham Young University Studies* 15:3 (Spring 1975):293–307.

Bentley, Joseph Charles. Journal. LDS Church Archives, Salt Lake City.

Brandenburg, Frank. *The Making of Modern Mexico.* Englewood Cliffs, N.J.: Prentice–Hall, 1964.

Brenner, Anita. *The Wind That Swept Mexico: The History of the Mexican Revolution, 1910–1942.* Austin and London: University of Texas Press, 1943. Reprint, 1971.

Brown, Dee. *Bury My Heart at Wounded Knee: An Indian History of the American West.* New York: Holt, Rinehart & Winston, 1971.

Brown, Harold. "Ephraim esparcida entre los Gentiles." *Liahona*, November 1947, pp. 446–51.

——————. "Gospel, Culture, and Leadership Development in Latin America." In *Mormonism: A Faith for All Cultures*, edited by F. LaMond Tullis, pp. 106–15. Provo, Utah: Brigham Young University Press, 1978.

Bunker, Gary L. "Illustrated Periodical Images of Mormons, 1850–1860." *Dialogue* 10:3 (Spring 1977):82–94.

Bunker, Gary L., and Davis Bitton. *The Mormon Graphic Image, 1834–1914: Cartoons, Caricatures, and Illustrations.* Salt Lake City: University of Utah Press, 1983.

Burns, Barney T., and Thomas H. Naylor. "Colonia Morelos: A Short History of a Mormon Colony in Sonora, Mexico." *Smoke Signal* 27 (Spring 1973):142–80. Tucson: The Westerners.

Bush, Lester E., Jr. "The Spalding Theory Then and Now." *Dialogue* 10:4 (Autumn 1977):40–69.

Call, Israel. "Autobiography," 1854–1930. Typescript. LDS Church Archives, Salt Lake City.

Carey, James C. *The Mexican Revolution in Yucatan, 1915–1924*. Boulder, Colo.: Westview Press, 1984.

Carr, Barry. "Recent Regional Studies of the Mexican Revolution." *Latin American Research Review* 15:1 (1980):3–14.

Carter, Kate B., comp. "The Mormons in Mexico." In *Treasures of Pioneer History*, 3:189–252. 3 vols. Salt Lake City: Daughters of the Utah Pioneers, 1954.

Church of Jesus Christ of Latter-day Saints. "Missionary Department Statistical Report," 1974–79.

——————. *Priesthood Bulletin* 8:4 (August 1972).

——————. *A Royal Priesthood, 1975–76: A Personal Study Guide for the Melchizedek Priesthood Quorums of The Church of Jesus Christ of Latter-day Saints*. LDS Church Archives, Salt Lake City.

Coates, Lawrence G. "The Mormons and the Ghost Dance." *Dialogue* 18:4 (Winter 1985):90–111.

——————. "The Mormons, the Ghost Dance Craze, and the Massacre at Wounded Knee." Paper presented at the Mormon History Association meeting, Rapid City, South Dakota, September 1974.

Costas, O. F.. *Theology of the Crossroads in Contemporary Latin America*. Amsterdam: Rodopi, 1976.

Council of Twelve Apostles. Quorum Meeting Minutes, 31 August 1841. LDS Church Archives, Salt Lake City.

Craig, Ann L. *The First Agraristas: An Oral History of a Mexican Agrarian Reform Movement*. Berkeley: University of California Press, 1983.

Cumberland, Charles Curtis. *Mexican Revolution: Genesis under Madero*. Austin: University of Texas Press, 1952.

Cunha, Euclides da. *Rebellion in the Backlands*. Translated from the Portuguese by Samuel Putnam. Chicago: University of Chicago Press, 1944.

Dawson, Glen, ed. *California: All the Way Back to 1828*. Los Angeles: Glen Dawson, 1956.

Dealy, Glen Caudill. *The Public Man: An Interpretation of Latin American and Other Catholic Countries*. Amherst: University of Massachusetts Press, 1977.

DeHoyos, Arturo, and Genevieve DeHoyos. "The Universality of the Gospel." *Ensign* 1 (August 1971):9–14

Deloria, Vine, Jr. *Custer Died for Your Sins: An Indian Manifesto*. New York: Macmillan, 1969.

Deseret News. *Church Almanac*. Salt Lake City: Deseret News Press, annually.

Deseret News, "Church News," 19 March 1932, 15 June 1946, and 1 September 1979.

Deseret Weekly, 13 September 1876.

Díaz, José, and Ramón Rodríguez. *El movimiento cristero: Sociedad y conflicto en los altos de Jalisco*. México: Editorial Nueva Imagen, 1979.

Doctrine and Covenants (LDS canonical work).

Duke, K. E. "Melitón González Trejo, Translator of the Book of Mormon into Spanish." *Improvement Era* 59 (October 1956):714-15, 753.

Evans, John Henry. *Joseph Smith: An American Prophet.* New York: Macmillan, 1933.

Eyring, Henry. Journal. Special Collections, Harold B. Lee Library, Brigham Young University, Provo, Utah.

Falcón, Romana. *El agrarismo en Veracruz: La etapa radical (1928-1935).* México: El Colegio de México, 1977.

Fox, Frank. *J. Reuben Clark, Jr.: The Public Years.* Provo, Utah: Brigham Young University Press, 1980.

Gil, Carlos B., ed. *The Age of Porfirio Díaz.* Albuquerque: University of New Mexico Press, 1977.

Godoy, José F. *Porfirio Díaz: Presidente de México, el fundador de una gran república.* México: Muller Hnos, 1910.

Gómez Quiñones, Juán. *Porfirio Díaz, los intelectuales y la revolución.* México: Ediciones el Caballito, 1981.

Gonzalez, Franklin Spencer. "The Restored Church in Mexico." MS. LDS Church Archives, Salt Lake City.

González, Justo E. *Historia de las misiones.* Buenos Aires: La Aurora, 1970.

Gruening, Ernest. *Mexico and Its Heritage.* New York: Century Company, 1928.

Hahn, Paul H. *The Juvenile Offender and the Law.* Cincinnati: W. H. Anderson, 1972.

Hall, Linda B. *Alvaro Obregón: Power and Revolution in Mexico, 1911-1920.* College Station: Texas A&M University Press, 1981.

"Handling Moral Transgressors." *Priesthood Bulletin* (LDS church), 8:4 (August 1972).

Hardy, Blaine Carmon. "Cultural 'Encystment' as a Cause of the Mormon Exodus from Mexico in 1912." *Pacific Historical Review* 34 (November 1965):439-54.

_____. "The Mormon Colonies of Northern Mexico: A History, 1885-1912." Ph.D. diss., Wayne State University, 1963.

Harris, Eunice Stewart. "Autobiography." Typescript. LDS Church Archives, Salt Lake City.

Hart, John M. *Anarchism and the Mexican Working Class, 1860-1931.* Austin: University of Texas Press, 1978. Also published as *El anarquismo y la clase obrera mexicana: 1860-1931.* Translated by María Luisa Puga. México: Siglo Veintiuno editores, 1980.

_____. "Historiographical Dynamics of the Mexican Revolution." *Latin American Research Review* 19:3 (1984):223-31.

Hartz, Louis. *The Founding of New Societies: Studies in the History of the United States, Latin America, South Africa, Canada, and Australia.* New York: Harcourt, Brace & World, 1964.

Hatch, Nelle Spilsbury. *Colonia Juárez: An Intimate Account of a Mormon Village.* Salt Lake City: Deseret Book Co., 1954.

Haven, Gilbert. "Our Nearest Neighbor." *Harper's New Monthly Magazine* 44 (June 1874):1–15; (July 1874):68–180; (August 1874):323–34.

Herald (Salt Lake City), 24 April 1887.

Herring, Hubert. *A History of Latin America.* 3d ed. New York: Alfred A. Knopf, 1972.

Hillam, Ray C., ed. *J. Reuben Clark, Jr.: Diplomat and Statesman.* Provo, Utah: Brigham Young University Press, 1973.

Hu–DeHart, Evelyn. "Sonora: Indians and Immigrants on a Developing Frontier." In *Other Mexicos: Essays on Regional Mexican History, 1876–1911*, edited by Thomas Benjamin and William McNellie, pp. 177–211. Albuquerque: University of New Mexico Press, 1984.

_____. *Yaqui Resistance and Survival: The Struggle for Land and Autonomy.* Madison: University of Wisconsin Press, 1984.

Hyde, John, Jr. *Mormonism: Its Leaders and Designs.* New York: W. P. Fetridge and Co., 1857.

Hyde, William. Journal. LDS Church Archives, Salt Lake City.

Iduarte, Andrés. *Niño: Child of the Mexican Revolution.* Translated by James F. Shearer. New York: Praeger Publishers, 1971.

Informe general de la tercera convención. LDS Church Archives, Salt Lake City.

Irving, Gordon. "Mormonism and Latin America: A Preliminary Historical Survey." Task Papers in LDS History 10, November 1976. LDS Church Historical Department, Salt Lake City.

_____. "An Opening Wedge: LDS Proselyting in Mexico, 1870–1890." Andrew Jenson Lecture, 4 June 1976. LDS Church Historical Department, Salt Lake City, Utah.

Ivins, Anthony Woodward. Journal. Anthony Woodward Ivins Papers. LDS Church Archives, Salt Lake City.

_____. Letter to Apostle Francis M. Lyman, 30 April 1902. Manuscript History of the Mexican Mission. LDS Church Archives, Salt Lake City.

_____. "Letter to James G. Bleak [18 February 1889, from Mexico City]." *Utah Historical Quarterly* 26 (April 1958):176–82.

Ivins, Antoine R. Address delivered at the October 1931 General Conference of the LDS Church. In *Conference Report*, pp. 71–74.

_____. Letters: to A. Lorenzo Anderson, 27 December 1938 and 3 July 1939; to David O. McKay, 9 March 1944; to the First Presidency, 2 September 1936, 11 December 1936, and 27 February 1937; and to Harold W. Pratt, 27 October 1936, 25 February 1937, and 2 March 1937. Antoine R. Ivins Papers. LDS Church Archives, Salt Lake City.

Jenson, Andrew, comp. *Church Chronology: A Record of Important Events Pertaining to the History of The Church of Jesus Christ of Latter-day Saints.* 2d ed., revised and enlarged with two supplements and an elaborate index. Salt Lake City: Deseret News Press, 1914.

_____. *Latter-day Saint Biographical Encyclopedia.* 4 vols. Salt Lake City: Andrew Jenson History Co., 1901.

_____. Manuscript History of the South American Mission. LDS Church Archives, Salt Lake City.

Johnson, Annie R. *Heartbeats of Colonia Díaz*. Salt Lake City: Publishers Press, 1972.

Johnson, Benjamin F. *My Life's Review*. Independence, Mo.: Zion's Printing and Publishing Co., 1947.

Johnson, Clark V. "Mormon Education in Mexico: The Rise of the Sociedad Educativa y Cultural." Ph.D. diss., Brigham Young University, 1977.

Johnson, William Weber. *Heroic Mexico: The Violent Emergence of a Modern Nation*. Garden City, N.Y.: Doubleday, 1968.

Jones, Daniel W. *Forty Years among the Indians: A True Yet Thrilling Narrative of the Author's Experience among the Natives*. Salt Lake City: Juvenile Instructor Office, 1890.

_____. Letter to R. W. Driggs, 18 November 1875. Daniel W. Jones Papers, LDS Church Archives, Salt Lake City, Utah.

Jones, Daniel W., Helaman Pratt, and James Z. Stewart. "Mission Report," 5 October 1876. Manuscript History of the Mexican Mission. LDS Church Archives, Salt Lake City.

Journal History of the Church. LDS Church Archives, Salt Lake City, Utah.

Journal of Discourses. 26 vols. Liverpool: Joseph F. Smith, 1854–66.

Jrade, Ramón. "Inquiries into the Cristero Insurrection against the Mexican Revolution." *Latin American Research Review* 20:2 (1985):53–70.

Katz, Friedrich. *The Secret War in Mexico: Europe, the United States and the Mexican Revolution*. Chicago: University of Chicago Press, 1981.

Kimball, Spencer W. "The False Gods We Worship." *Ensign* 6 (June 1976):3–6.

Kindrich, Charles W. "The Mormons in Mexico." *Review of Reviews* 19 (June 1899):702–5.

Kitchens, John W. "Some Considerations of the *Rurales* of Porfirian Mexico." *Journal of Inter-American Studies* 9 (July 1967):441–55.

Krenkel, John H., ed. *The Life and Times of Joseph Fish, Mormon Pioneer: Autobiography*. Danville, Ill.: Interstate Printers, 1970.

Lindsey, David. "The Reign of the Vigilantes." *American History Illustrated* 83 (June 1973):22–36.

Link, Arthur S., ed. *Woodrow Wilson and a Revolutionary World, 1913–1921*. Chapel Hill: University of North Carolina Press, 1982.

Los fracasos escolares. México: Fondo de Cultura Económica, 1974.

Lozano Herrera, Agrícol. *Historia del Mormonismo en México*. México: Editorial Zarahemla, 1983.

Madsen, Harold S. "The Magnificent Obsession in Nineteenth-Century Mormondom to Master and Refine the English Language." Paper presented at 1973 Conference on the Language of the Mormons, Brigham Young University, Provo, Utah.

Manuscript History of the Mexican Mission. LDS Church Archives, Salt Lake City.

Martínez Vásquez, Víctor Raúl, ed. *La revolución en Oaxaca, 1900-1930.* Oaxaca: Escuela Naval Militar y Calzada Porfirio Díaz, Instituto de Administración Pública de Oaxaca, 1985.

Meacham, J. Lloyd. *Church and State in Latin America.* Chapel Hill: University of North Carolina Press, 1934.

"Mensaje del Presidente George F. Richards para ser leída en el culto en Tecalco el Domingo 14 de Febrero de 1937." LDS Church Archives, Salt Lake City.

Mexican Mission Historical Record. LDS Church Archives, Salt Lake City.

"Mexico: Reported Intentions of Mormons to Migrate to Mexico." *New York Times,* 22 December 1974.

"Mexico's Education Push Still Falling Far Short." *Salt Lake Tribune,* 15 October 1979, A-7.

Meyer, Jean A. *The Cristero Rebellion: The Mexican People between Church and State, 1926-1929.* Translated from the French by Richard Southern. Cambridge: Cambridge University Press, 1976. Also published in Spanish as *La Cristiada: El conflicto entre la iglesia y el estado 1926-1929*; 6a edición corregida. México: Siglo Veintiuno editores, 1980.

——————. *La Cristiada: Los Cristeros.* México: Siglo Veintiuno editores, 1981.

Meyer, Jean A. et al. *Historia de la revolución mexicana.* 23 vols. México: El Colegio de México, 1977-79.

Mills, Elizabeth H. "The Mormon Colonies in Chihuahua after the 1912 Exodus." Parts one and two. *New Mexico Historical Review* 29:3 & 4 (1954):165-310.

Mooney, James. *The Ghost-Dance Religion and the Sioux Outbreak of 1890.* Part two of the fourteenth annual report of the Bureau of Ethnology to the Secretary of the Smithsonian Institution, 1892-93. Washington, D.C.: U.S. Government Printing Office, 1896.

Morison, Samuel Eliot, and Henry Steele Commager. *The Growth of the American Republic.* 4th ed. New York: Oxford University Press, 1957.

Mouritzen, Paul Thomas. "Mormon Beginnings in Mexico: The 1876 Missionary Expedition." Unpublished student paper, Brigham Young University, 1977.

Naylor, Thomas S. "Colonia Morelos and the Mexican Revolution: Consul Dye Inspects an Evacuated Mormon Colony, 1912." *Journal of Arizona History* 20 (1979):101-20.

Needler, Martin C., ed. *Political Systems of Latin America.* 2d ed. New York: Van Nostrand Reinhold, 1970.

New York City Sun, 13 August 1879.

Nibley, Hugh. "Commencement Address." Brigham Young University, 19 August 1983.

O'Dea, Thomas F. *The Mormons.* Chicago: University of Chicago Press, 1957.

Palmer, A. Delbert. "Establishing the LDS Church in Chile." Master's thesis, Brigham Young University, 1979.

Patton, Analeone Davis. *California Mormons by Sail and Trail.* Salt Lake City: Deseret Book Co., 1961.

Perissinotto, Giorgio. "Mexican Education: Echeverría's Mixed Legacy." *Current History*, March 1977, pp. 115–19.

Pierce, Arwell Lee. "Anuncio de interés a la misión mexicana." *Liahona*, October 1946, pp. 405–33.

————. "The Story of the Third Convention." Typescript. LDS Church Archives, Salt Lake City.

Pletcher, David M. *Rails, Mines, and Progress: Seven American Promoters in Mexico, 1867–1911*. Ithaca, N.Y.: Cornell University Press, 1958.

Pratt, Harold W. Journal. LDS Church Archives, Salt Lake City.

Pratt, Helaman. Letter to his brother, Parley. Cited in Journal History, 6 February 1887. LDS Church Archives, Salt Lake City.

Pratt, Lucile. "A Keyhole View of Mexican Agrarian Policy as Shown by Mormon Land Problems." Master's thesis, Columbia University, [ca. 1960].

Pratt, Parley P. "Address to the Red Man." *Millennial Star* 14 (18 September 1852):469–70.

————. *Autobiography of Parley Parker Pratt*. Edited by Parley P. Pratt, Jr. 9th ed. Salt Lake City: Deseret Book Co., 1972.

————. *Journal and First Book Commencing the Pacific Mission, 1851*. Special Collections, Harold B. Lee Library, Brigham Young University, Provo, Utah.

————. *A Key to the Science of Universal Theology*. Liverpool, England: F. D. Richards 1855.

————. Letter to Agatha Pratt sent from Chile, 9 February 1852. Courtesy of Steven Pratt.

————. Letter to his family, sent from Quillota, Chile, 31 January 1852. Courtesy of Steven Pratt.

————. Letter to his family, sent from Valparaíso, Chile, 24 November 1851. *Millennial Star* 14 (15 February 1852):54–55.

Pratt, Rey L. "History of the Mexican Mission." *Improvement Era* 15 (1911–12): 486–98.

————. Journal. LDS Church Archives, Salt Lake City.

————. "The Mission to the Lamanites." *Improvement Era* 16 (1912–13): 497–503, 577–85, 686–90, 796–801, 1021–25.

————. "Review of the Mission Labor among the Lamanites." *Liahona* 14:19 (7 November 1916):293–97.

Pratt, Steven. "Eleanor McLean and the Murder of Parley P. Pratt." *BYU Studies* 15:2 (Winter 1975):225–56.

Prescott, William H. *History of the Conquest of Peru*. 2 vols. New York: Harper and Brothers, 1847.

Price, Glenn W. *Origins of the War with Mexico: The Polk–Stockton Intrigue*. Austin and London: University of Texas Press, 1967.

Quinn, Michael. "The Practice of Rebaptism at Nauvoo." *BYU Studies* 18:2 (Winter 1978):226–32.

Bibliography

Quirk, Robert E. *An Affair of Honor: Woodrow Wilson and the Occupation of Veracruz.* New York: W. W. Norton, 1967.

Raat, W. Dirk, and William H. Beezley, eds. *Twentieth-Century Mexico.* Lincoln: University of Nebraska Press, 1986.

Reed, Raymond J. "The Mormons in Chihuahua: Their Relation with Villa and the Pershing Punitive Expedition, 1910–1917." Master's thesis, University of New Mexico, 1938.

Reynolds, George. *Dictionary of the Book of Mormon.* Salt Lake City: Joseph Hyrum Parry, 1891.

Reynolds, Noel B. "Cultural Diversity in the Universal Church." In *Mormonism: A Faith for All Cultures,* edited by F. LaMond Tullis, pp. 7–22. Provo, Utah: Brigham Young University Press, 1978.

Rhodakanaty, Plotino C. *Escritos.* Edited by Centro de Estudios Históricos del Movimiento Obrero Mexicano. México: Editorial Popular de los Trabajadores, 1976.

Richards, Louisa L. Green. *Branches That Run over the Wall: A Book of Mormon Poems and Other Writings.* Salt Lake City: Magazine Printing Company, 1904.

Richardson, Sullivan Calvin. "Autobiography." Typescript. LDS Church Archives, Salt Lake City.

Richmond, Douglas. *Venustiano Carranza's Nationalist Struggle, 1893–1920.* Lincoln and London: University of Nebraska Press, 1983.

Roberts, B. H. *Comprehensive History of The Church of Jesus Christ of Latter-day Saints.* 6 vols. Salt Lake City: Church of Jesus Christ of Latter-day Saints, 1930.

_____, ed. *History of The Church of Jesus Christ of Latter-day Saints.* 7 vols. Salt Lake City: Deseret Book Co., 1946.

Rocca–Arvay, Marie Lucille. *Assimilation and Resistance of the Yaqui Indians of Northern Mexico during the Colonial Period.* Ph.D. diss., Columbia University, 1981. Ann Arbor, Mich.: University Microfilms International, 1986.

Romero Flores, Jesús. *Del porfirismo a la revolución constitucionalista.* Volume 1 of *Anales históricos de la revolución mexicana.* México: Editores Libro Mex, 1960.

Romney, Junius. "Remarks Made in the Garden Park Ward Sacrament Meeting, Salt Lake City, Utah, 31 July 1966." LDS Church Archives, Salt Lake City.

Romney, Thomas Cottam. *A Divinity Shapes Our Ends As Seen in My Life Story.* N.p.: By the author, 1953.

_____. *The Mormon Colonies in Mexico.* Salt Lake City: Deseret Book Co., 1938.

Salamini, Heather Fowler. *Agrarian Radicalism in Veracruz, 1920–38.* Lincoln: University of Nebraska Press, 1978.

Santoni, Pedro. "La policía de la Ciudad de México durante el porfiriato: Los primeros años (1876–1884)." *Historia mexicana* 33 (July–September 1983):97–129.

Schindler, Harold. *Orrin Porter Rockwell: Man of God, Son of Thunder.* 2d ed. Salt Lake City: University of Utah Press, 1983.

Simons, Jeffery, and John Maestas. "The Lamanite: Past, Present, Future." Mimeo. N.d., n.p.

Simpson, Lesley Byrd. *Many Mexicos*. 4th ed., revised. Berkeley and Los Angeles: University of California Press, 1966.

Smith, George A. Journal History, 23 September 1855. LDS Church Archives, Salt Lake City.

Smith, Joseph Fielding. *Essentials in Church History*. 13th ed. Salt Lake City: Deseret News Press, 1953.

Spicer, Edward H. *The Yaquis: A Cultural History*. Tucson: University of Arizona Press, 1980.

Stanley, Reva Holdaway, and Charles C. Camp. "A Mormon Mission to California in 1851, from the Diary of Parley Parker Pratt." *California Historical Society Quarterly* 14:1 & 2 (March and June 1935):59–73, 175–82.

Statutes at Large of the United States of America, 1789–1872. Washington, D.C., 1862. Vol. 12, part 1, pp. 501–2.

————————. 1882. Vol. 22, part 1, pp. 30–32.

————————. 1887. Vol. 24, part 1, pp. 635–41.

Stewart, James Z. Journal. LDS Church Archives, Salt Lake City.

Stout, Wayne D. *A History of Colonia Dublán, Mexico*. N.p., 1975.

Taylor, John. "Discovery of Ruins." *Millennial Star* 13 (March–April 1851):120–21.

Thomas, Estelle Webb. *Uncertain Sanctuary: A Story of Mormon Pioneering in Mexico*. Salt Lake City: Westwater Press, 1980.

Tischendorf, Alfred. *Great Britain and Mexico in the Era of Porfirio Díaz*. Durham, N.C.: Duke University Press, 1961.

Todd, Jay M. "My Sons, My Friends." *Ensign* (June 1979):22–23.

Tuck, Jim. *The Holy War in Los Altos: A Regional Analysis of Mexico's Cristero Rebellion*. Tucson: University of Arizona Press, 1982.

————————. *Pancho Villa and John Reed: Two Faces of Romantic Revolution*. Tucson: University of Arizona Press, 1984.

Tullidge, Edward Wheelock. *Life of Brigham Young; or, Utah and Her Founder*. New York: N.p., 1876.

Tullis, F. LaMond. "California and Chile in 1851 as Experienced by the Mormon Apostle Parley P. Pratt." *Southern California Historical Quarterly* 67:3 (Fall 1985):291–307.

————————. "The Church Moves Outside the United States: Some Observations on Latin America." *Dialogue* 13 (Spring 1980):63–73. Revised version appeared in *Mormonism after One Hundred and Fifty Years*, edited by Thomas Alexander, pp. 149–69. Salt Lake City: Signature Books, 1983.

————————. "The Current View on Rural Development: Fad or Breakthrough in Latin America." In *An International Political Economy*, vol. 1 of the International Political Economy Yearbook series, edited by W. Ladd Hollist and F. LaMond Tullis, pp. 223–54. Boulder, Colo.: Westview Press, 1985.

————————. "Early Mormon Exploration and Missionary Activities in Mexico." *BYU Studies* 22:4 (Fall 1982):289–310.

_____. "Ethnicity and Ethnic Conflict." A paper presented to the faculty of the Department of Political Science and its guests from Anthropology and the School of Law, Brigham Young University, 18 March 1976. Reserve section, Harold B. Lee Library, Brigham Young University, Provo, Utah.

_____. "Food Aid and Political Instability." In *Food, the State, and International Political Economy*, edited by F. LaMond Tullis and W. Ladd Hollist, pp. 215–38. Lincoln: University of Nebraska Press, 1986.

_____. *Lord and Peasant in Peru*. Cambridge, Mass.: Harvard University Press, 1970.

_____. "Mormons and Revolution in Latin America." *BYU Studies* 16:2 (Winter 1976):235–49.

_____. *Politics and Social Change in Third World Countries*. New York: John Wiley, 1973.

_____. "Politics and Society: Anglo-American Mormons in a Revolutionary Land." *BYU Studies* 13:2 (Winter 1973):126–34.

_____. "The Reopening of the Mexican Mission in 1901." *BYU Studies* 22:1 (Winter 1982):441–53.

_____ "Three Myths about Mormons in Latin America." *Dialogue* 7:1 (Spring 1972):79–87.

_____, ed. *Mormonism: A Faith for All Cultures*. Provo, Utah: Brigham Young University Press, 1978.

Tullis, F. LaMond, and Elizabeth Hernandez. "Mormonism in Mexico: Leadership, Nationalism, and the Case of the Third Convention." MS. August 1976.

Tyler, Daniel. *A Concise History of the Mormon Battalion in the Mexican War, 1846–47*. 1881. Reprint. Glorieta, N.M.: Rio Grande Press, 1964.

Utah the Inland Empire. Salt Lake City: Deseret News Press, 1902.

Valdés José. *Historia general de la revolución mexicana*. 10 vols. México: Ediciones Germika, 1985.

Valensuela Frías, Francisco. *Manual de historia de Chile*. Santiago, Chile: Editorial Nascimento, 1969.

Villalobos Vásquez, Efraín. "Church Schools in Mexico." In *Mormonism: A Faith for All Cultures*, edited by F. LaMond Tullis, pp. 126–35. Provo, Utah: Brigham Young University Press, 1978.

Villegas, Abelardo, ed. *Positivismo porfirismo*. México: Secretaría de Educación Pública, 1972.

Viñas, David. *Anarquistas en América Latina*. México: Editorial Katún, 1983.

Voss, Stuart F. "The Porfiriato in Time and Space." *Latin American Research Review*, 18:3 (1983):246–54.

Waite, Mrs. C. V. *The Mormon Prophet and His Harem*. 5th ed., revised and enlarged. Chicago: J. S. Goodman, 1867.

Walser, John Jacob. Journal. LDS Church Archives, Salt Lake City.

Wesserman, Mark. *Capitalists, Caciques, and Revolution: The Native Elite and Foreign Enterprise in Chihuahua, Mexico, 1854–1911*. Chapel Hill: University of North Carolina Press, 1984.

Wheat, Carl I., ed. *California in 1851: The Letters of Dame Shirley.* San Francisco: Grabhorn Press, 1933.

Wilson, Henry Lane, and William F. Buckley. "Decena Trágica." In *Twentieth-Century Mexico,* edited by W. Dirk Raat and William H. Beezley, 104–14. Lincoln: University of Nebraska Press, 1986.

Womack, John, Jr. *Zapata and the Mexican Revolution.* New York: Alfred A. Knopf, 1969.

Woodruff, Wilford. Letter to "Brother Johnson" in the Salt River Valley, Arizona, 7 December 1881. LDS Church Archives, Salt Lake City.

—————. Letter to Elder A. M. Tenney and fellow missionaries, 10 April 1888. Manuscript History of the Mexican Mission. LDS Church Archives, Salt Lake City.

World Bank. *World Development Report, 1983.* New York: Oxford University Press, 1983.

Young, Brigham. *Discourses of Brigham Young.* Compiled by John A. Widtsoe. Salt Lake City: Deseret Book Company, 1954.

—————. Letter to Thomas L. Kane, 14 January 1859. Thomas L. Kane Papers, Stanford University Library.

Young, Joseph. "Remarks on Behalf of the Indians," 13 July 1855. In *Journal of Discourses,* 9:229–33. 26 vols. Liverpool, England: Joseph F. Smith, 1854–86.

Young, Karl E. *Ordeal in Mexico: Tales of Danger and Hardship Collected from Mormon Colonists.* Salt Lake City: Deseret Book Company, 1968.

Young, W. Ernest. "A Brief Sketch of the Lives of Francisco (Pancho) Villa and Felipe Angeles." MS. LDS Church Archives, Salt Lake City.

—————. "Diary of My Life." Bound typescript. Copy in author's possession.

Zea, Leopoldo. *Positivism in Mexico.* Translated by Josephine H. Schulte. Austin and London: University of Texas Press, 1974.

Author Citation Index

Womack, John, Jr., 84, n. 2; 106, n. 12; 107, n. 26; 108, n. 36
Woodruff, Wilford, 50, n. 81, 82; 72, n. 31

Young, Joseph, 9, nn. 9, 13
Young, Karl E., 107, n. 25
Young, W. Ernest, 48, n. 59; 107, nn. 20, 25, 32; 108, n. 40; 133, n. 42

Zea, Leopoldo, 85, n. 7

Subject Index

Abraham, 124
Aclantla, 79
Africa, 136, n. 60; increase of Mormon membership in, 204
Agriculture, 209; development of in Mormon colonies, 59; Mormon efforts to teach Indians, 65
Aguilar Páez, Virgilio, 163, n. 37
Aircraft, role of in Mexican revolution, 106, n. 13
Alexander the Great, 58
Alfaro, Alfredo, 193
Allen, James B., x
Allred, Eliza Tracy, 92
Altamirano, Ignacio Manuel, receptivity of to Mormon ideological position on the Indians, 34–35
Alvarado, Pedro de, 135, n. 59
Amecameca, 78; 80
Americans, 105, n. 8; economic interest of in Mexico, 16; effect of Mexican civil war on living in Mexico, 94
Anderson, A. Lorenzo, 149–50; 164, n. 56

Apaches, war of with townspeople in Casas Grandes, 30. *See also* Indians
Apostles, Quorum of Twelve, appeal to by Moses Thatcher to accept land-grant offer from Emelio Biebuyck, 38; rethink new mission to Mexico, 38
Aragón, 166, n. 77
Aranda Carrazco, Mario Jaime, 183
Arbolillo, 166, n. 77; 199, n. 31
Argentina, 16; 127, n. 3; author's research in, x; number of Mormons in, xv, n. 1; Rey L. Pratt's appointment to, 111
Arísiachic, 26
Arizona, 38; 41; 53; 64; exodus of Mormons to, 94; plans to colonize Mexican members in, 43; Salt River Valley in explored by first missionaries to Mexico, 20
Arrington, Leonard J., x
Arteaga, Silviano, 36; 42
Arzate, Apolonio, 123; 135, n. 50; 148; 151; 154; 155; 158; 159; 166, n. 78
Asia, increase of Mormon membership in, 204
Asunción, 61
Atlautla, 79, 109
Australia, 16; Mormon mission to, 11, n. 20
Authority, Mexican notions about, 181–86 passim; Spencer W. Kimball's views on exercising, 185
Aztecs, 124; 166, n. 77

Balderas family, 110
Ball, J. P., 9, n. 14; contribution by to fund for original translation of Book of Mormon, 45, n. 18
Ballard, Melvin, 131, n. 32; 160, n. 3; 161, n. 14; visit of to Mexico City, 117
Baptism, 36; 42; 66; 78; 82; first for Mormons in Mexico conducted